Sex in Tourism

ASPECTS OF TOURISM
Series Editors: **Chris Cooper** *(Leeds Beckett University, UK)*, **C. Michael Hall** *(University of Canterbury, New Zealand)* and **Dallen J. Timothy** *(Arizona State University, USA)*

Aspects of Tourism is an innovative, multifaceted series, which comprises authoritative reference handbooks on global tourism regions, research volumes, texts and monographs. It is designed to provide readers with the latest thinking on tourism worldwide and in so doing will push back the frontiers of tourism knowledge. The series also introduces a new generation of international tourism authors writing on leading edge topics.

The volumes are authoritative, readable and user-friendly, providing accessible sources for further research. Books in the series are commissioned to probe the relationship between tourism and cognate subject areas such as strategy, development, retailing, sport and environmental studies. The publisher and series editors welcome proposals from writers with projects on the above topics.

All books in this series are externally peer-reviewed.

Full details of all the books in this series and of all our other publications can be found on http://www.channelviewpublications.com, or by writing to Channel View Publications, St Nicholas House, 31-34 High Street, Bristol BS1 2AW, UK.

ASPECTS OF TOURISM: 93

Sex in Tourism

Exploring the Light and the Dark

Edited by
Neil Carr and Liza Berdychevsky

CHANNEL VIEW PUBLICATIONS
Bristol • Jackson

DOI https://doi.org/10.21832/CARR8595
Library of Congress Cataloging in Publication Data
A catalog record for this book is available from the Library of Congress.
Names: Carr, Neil, editor. | Berdychevsky, Liza, editor.
Title: Sex in Tourism: Exploring the Light and the Dark/Edited by
 Neil Carr and Liza Berdychevsky.
Description: Bristol; Blue Ridge Summit: Channel View Publications,
 [2022] | Series: Aspects of Tourism: 93 | Includes bibliographical
 references and index. | Summary: 'This book encompasses the diversity
 and complexity of sex in tourism, including the light, dark and shades
 of grey between. It studies the affects and effects of diverse sexual
 encounters in tourism; romance tourism, sex tourism and exploitation in
 tourism, including the sexual exploitation of children in travel and
 tourism and sexual harassment' – Provided by publisher.
Identifiers: LCCN 2021031705 (print) | LCCN 2021031706 (ebook) | ISBN
 9781845418588 (paperback) | ISBN 9781845418595 (hardback) | ISBN
 9781845418601 (pdf) | ISBN 9781845418618 (epub)
Subjects: LCSH: Sex tourism. | Sex tourism – Moral and ethical aspects. |
 Travelers – Sexual behavior.
Classification: LCC HQ444 .S53 2022 (print) | LCC HQ444 (ebook) | DDC
 306.7091 – dc23
LC record available at https://lccn.loc.gov/2021031705
LC ebook record available at https://lccn.loc.gov/2021031706

British Library Cataloguing in Publication Data
A catalogue entry for this book is available from the British Library.

ISBN-13: 978-1-84541-859-5 (hbk)
ISBN-13: 978-1-84541-858-8 (pbk)

Channel View Publications
UK: St Nicholas House, 31-34 High Street, Bristol, BS1 2AW, UK.
USA: Ingram, Jackson, TN, USA.

Website: www.channelviewpublications.com
Twitter: Channel_View
Facebook: https://www.facebook.com/channelviewpublications
Blog: www.channelviewpublications.wordpress.com

The policy of Multilingual Matters/Channel View Publications is to use papers that are natural, renewable and recyclable products, made from wood grown in sustainable forests. In the manufacturing process of our books, and to further support our policy, preference is given to printers that have FSC and PEFC Chain of Custody certification. The FSC and/or PEFC logos will appear on those books where full certification has been granted to the printer concerned.

Typeset by Riverside Publishing Solutions

Contents

Figures and Tables

Acknowledgements

First, thanks are due to Sarah Williams at Channel View. It is thanks to her that the idea for this book came to be. Thanks are also due to Sarah for all the patience she has shown through the process of creating this book.

It is also important to acknowledge all the authors who have contributed to the final version of the book, but also those, who for a variety of reasons, had to drop out. Regarding the latter, we certainly hope that the wonderful ideas and perspectives they have on sex in tourism are, in due course, published elsewhere.

On a more personal level, Neil, as always, is very grateful for the support of all his family, both human and non-human, who help him in his work, distract him when it is good for him (and even when it is not!) and put up with his ramblings and foibles. So thanks Sarah, most especially you, for putting up with me. To Ben, Tat and Gus, for all the distractions and fun kids offer. To Ebony for all the walks and laughs. To Catkin, I know you are a cat who must therefore show the world due disdain, but deep down you are a softy. And, finally, to the assorted ducks, your quacking demands for food are always loud enough to drag me away from the computer.

Liza would like to thank her amazing husband Michael and wonderful daughters Abigail and Arielle for their patience with Mommy's hectic schedule and endless support and inspiration that they provide.

Contributors

Vitor Ambrósio has a PhD in Geography, MA in Geography, BA in Modern Languages and Literatures from Lisbon University and BA in Tourism (Tour Guiding). He is a senior lecturer of ESHTE – Escola Superior de Hotelaria e Turismo do Estoril (Estoril Higher Institute for Tourism and Hotel Studies), Portugal, since it was founded in 1991. Over the last decades he has been publishing scientific articles, book chapters and a book on tourism.

George Ariya is a lecturer and researcher at University of Eldoret, Department of Tourism and Tour Operations Management. He obtained his doctoral degree in Tourism Management from Moi University. His research interests include sustainable tourism businesses and destinations, tourist-community interactions and livelihoods and destination attractiveness.

Liza Berdychevsky is an associate professor in the Department of Recreation, Sport and Tourism at the University of Illinois at Urbana-Champaign. Her research revolves at the nexus of sexual health and wellbeing in tourism and leisure contexts, adopting a gender-sensitive and life course-grounded approach. She investigates sexual behaviour, positive sexuality, risk taking and sexual education needs among young and older adults in various leisure and tourism contexts. Her research contributes to a deeper understanding of the issues associated with sex in tourism and leisure contexts and offers directions for health education programmes. Dr Berdychevsky co-edited a special issue on innovation and impact of sex as leisure in research and practice in *Leisure Sciences*. She serves as a consulting editor in *The Journal of Sex Research*, an associate editor in *Leisure Sciences* and an editorial board member in *Tourism Management*, *Annals of Tourism Research Empirical Insights* and *Annals of Leisure Research*.

Neil Carr is a professor in the Department of Tourism at the University of Otago. His research focuses on understanding behaviour within tourism and leisure experiences, with a particular emphasis on children and families, sex and animals. He has co/authored and co/edited numerous books, including *Tourism and Animal Welfare* (with D. Broom, CABI, 2018) *Wild Animals and Leisure: Rights and Welfare* and *Domestic Animals, Humans, and Leisure: Rights, Welfare, and Wellbeing* (both edited with J. Young, Routledge, 2018).

S. Emre Dilek has a PhD from the Department of Gastronomy & Culinary Arts, School of Tourism and Hotel Management, Batman University, Batman, Turkey. He completed his master thesis titled 'Green Marketing Applications in Tourism Businesses: A Field Research' in 2012. His PhD thesis, titled 'Evaluation of Moral Responsibility of Tourism Regarding Animals in the Context of Meta-Criticism', was completed in 2016. The topics he is interested are tourism sociology, tourism and animal ethics, philosophy and green marketing.

Phoebe Everingham is an early career researcher and sessional academic at the University of Newcastle, Australia. Her PhD thesis explored embodied intercultural encounters in volunteer tourism, drawing on fieldwork conducted with two organisations in Peru and Ecuador. Phoebe is an interdisciplinary researcher drawing on insights from Sociology, Anthropology, Human Geography and Tourism Management. She is particularly interested in working with theories that centre the body, subjectivity and affect – to expand the scope of how power and agency is conceptualised.

Amanda Jenkins has over 30 years' experience working in Travel and Tourism. She holds a BA (Hons) in Tourism Management, a Master of Research (MRes) in Human Sciences and is currently completing her PhD in Humanities at the University of Wolverhampton. Amanda has won numerous awards and recognition for her outstanding academic achievements including the prestigious Institute of Tourism (ITT) Centre of Excellence, Student of the Year Award (2017), The CABI Prize (2017) for the best dissertation in Leisure and The Ironbridge Gorge Museum Trust Prize (2017). Amanda's research interest includes issues of race, gender and sexuality, with a focus on sex tourism.

Arnoud Lagendijk is professor of Economic Geography at Radboud University, Nijmegen, The Netherlands. After graduation, he worked as a Research Fellow at the Universities of Reading and Newcastle upon Tyne, in which he coordinated UK and European projects on regional development and governance topics. Since 1998, he has been working at Radboud University Nijmegen, initially as a postdoc and lecturer, and since 2012 as a full professor. He has a long track record in the field of regional development and policy, and he has published widely on themes such as innovation, clustering, strategy making, regional identities and the diffusion of socioeconomic practices. Lagendijk is an Editor of *Regional Studies*, and active as a board member of an academic labour union.

Frans de Man currently works as a tourism advisor for GIZ's Sustainable Rural Development programme in Albania. He was managing director of the Retour Foundation from 1987 to 2019. In this capacity, he represented Civil Society tourism organisations in international governance processes and carried out consultancies varying from project management to monitoring and evaluation. Between 2002 and 2010 he owned and ran a windsurf shop and a restaurant on the beaches of southern Spain where he put sustainability principles into practice. Throughout his career he has maintained contact with his alma mater, Radboud University, on the one hand to apply the newest scientific insights into innovative and sustainable tourism development at the local level, and on the other, to contribute to the accumulation of academic knowledge.

Jose A. Mansilla López has a PhD in Social Anthropology. He is a lecturer in the Department of Social Sciences and Communication at the Ostelea School of Tourism and Hospitality-Universitat de Lleida, Barcelona, Spain. His research interests include urban conflicts, social movements, tourism impact and planning and architecture.

Amie Matthews is a senior lecturer in the School of Social Sciences at Western Sydney University, Australia, where she researches and teaches in sociology and tourism studies. Having spent over 15 years studying the backpacking culture and other facets of youth tourism, Dr Matthews' research interests include tourist discourses and behaviours, tourism media and the tourist imaginary and ethical and responsible tourism.

Naomi Moswete is a senior lecturer in the Department of Environmental Science, University of Botswana. Her research interests include tourism as a strategy for rural development, community-based tourism, transboundary conservation areas, ecotourism, protected areas – people relationships, natural resource management, cultural heritage resource management, poverty and gender-based empowerment via tourism. She is a member of the editorial board – section editor – of the Journal of Parks and Recreation Administration. She has published journal articles and book chapters at both local and international levels. Her latest publications are titled: 'Local communities' attitudes and support towards the Kgalagadi Transfrontier Park in Southwest Botswana' and a co-edited book titled *Natural Resources, Tourism and Community Livelihoods in Southern Africa: Challenges for Sustainable Development* (with M.T. Stone & M. Lenao, Routledge, 2019).

Leonardo Nava Jimenez gained his PhD at the Department of Tourism, University of Otago. His thesis was entitled 'The Evolution of the Camp'. He has also been awarded an MSc in Sustainable Tourism Management from the Universidad de Quintana Roo (Mexico). His research expertise encompasses the origin, evolution and current state of national camping/outdoors systems, the utilisation of historical GIS, biopolitics and assemblage theory and camp mobility networks.

Ruth Nyamasyo is a junior researcher and sales executive officer at Neptune Hotels. She obtained a Bachelor of Tourism Management degree from the University of Eldoret. Her research interests include sex tourism, romantic tourism and sales and marketing. She is also passionate about gender issues in tourism.

Irina Oliveira is currently finishing her Doctorate in the Business Administration programme ISCTE – Lisbon University Institute Business School. She has a master's degree in Hospitality and Tourism Management from the same University. Her main research interests focus on work and life satisfaction among employees in leisure industries. Her academic works (scientific articles and book chapters) contribute to improving an ambience where internal and external workers can feel and be safe.

Athina Papageorgiou is an assistant professor at the Department of Tourism Management of the West Attica University, Athens, Greece. Her PhD thesis was on Alternative Tourism Development through Marketing Management of Tourism Organizations, Institutions and Enterprises of the Public and the Private Sector. She is the author or co-author of six books on the topics of her interest (tourism management, alternative tourism and dark tourism). Her latest book is on events management and MICE tourism.

Roya Rahimi is a reader in Marketing and Leisure Management at the University of Wolverhampton. She teaches across tourism, hospitality and marketing subject areas and supervises undergraduate/postgraduate dissertations as well as PhD students. Her research interests are innovation, big data, CRM, organisational culture, gender equality and tourism higher education. Her work has been published in top-tier journals such as *Annals of Tourism Research*, *Journal of Tourism and Hospitality Research*, *Journal of Travel & Tourism Marketing*, *International Journal of Contemporary Hospitality Management* and *Anatolia*. Her work has also been presented at various international conferences and appears in book chapters released by Routledge, CABI, Emerald and IGI. She has been published in a variety of languages. Roya is the Associate Editor for *Journal of Tourism Management Perspectives*, book reviews editor for *Journal of Hospitality & Tourism Management* and book review editor for *Journal of Hospitality and Tourism Technology*. She sits on the editorial board of different leading journals including *Journal of Hospitality and Tourism Technology*,

European Management Review, European Journal of Tourism Research, Journal of Hospitality & Tourism Management and the *International Journal of Tourism Sciences*. She was nominated and shortlisted for her outstanding contribution to research in the University of Wolverhampton's Vice Chancellor awards for staff excellence in 2017 and 2018. In 2017, one of her papers, 'Impact of Customer Relationship Management on Customer Satisfaction: The Case of a Budget Hotel Chain', became the most read paper of the year in tourism and hospitality journals published by Taylor and Francis. In 2018, two of her papers were selected as Outstanding Papers of the year in the 2018 Emerald Literati Awards.

Peter Robinson is Head of the Centre for Tourism and Hospitality Management at Leeds Beckett University. He is a member of The Tourism Society and the Tourism Society Consultants Network, a Director and Fellow of the Institute for Travel and Tourism (ITT), a Fellow of The Tourism Management Institute and a Principal Fellow of the Higher Education Academy. Peter is Trustee and Chair of the Elvaston Castle and Gardens Trust and is also a National Council Member for the Tourism Management Institute and Regional Representative for Yorkshire and the Humber. Peter has been an external adviser for a number of public and private sector education institutions, has advised on QCF frameworks and has worked with a number of exam boards and professional bodies. He has an international publishing profile and has spoken at a number of international conferences. Peter has also taken part in television and newspaper interviews.

Octávio Sacramento has a PhD in Anthropology (ISCTE-IUL, Lisbon). He is an assistant professor at the University of Trás-os-Montes e Alto Douro (UTAD, Vila Real, Portugal), researcher at the Centre of Transdisciplinary Studies for Development (CETRAD-UTAD) and collaborator of the Centre for Research in Anthropology (CRIA). His main research experiences include ethnographic fieldwork on female prostitution in the Iberian border regions; HIV/AIDS in the Northeast of Portugal; Euro-Brazilian mobilities and transnational configurations of intimacy; and borders and migrations.

Sheila Sánchez Bergara is a lecturer in the Department of Law and Political Sciences at the Ostelea School of Tourism and Hospitality-Universitat de Lleida, Barcelona, Spain. Her research interests include tourism and law, digital leisure, health tourism and qualitative research.

Elsa Soro is a postdoc researcher in the Department of Philosophy and Educational Sciences, University of Turin and lecturer in Media and Tourism and Event Tourism at Ostelea School of Tourism and

Hospitality, Barcelona. Her research interests include semiotics of tourism, event tourism and social media.

Tamara Young is a senior lecturer in the Newcastle Business School, The University of Newcastle, Australia. Her research is in the multidisciplinary field of tourism studies, with a particular emphasis on critical tourism theory and cultural research methodologies. She has researched the social and cultural significance of tourism for over 15 years, particularly in the context of youth travel, and co-authored *Tourist Cultures: Identity, Place and the Traveller* (with S. Wearing & D. Stevenson, Sage, 2010). Tamara's research on tourism curriculum, in particular the indigenisation of curriculum, is internationally recognised. Her commitment to delivering research informed and industry engaged teaching to educate future leaders in the tourism industry has received national recognition.

1 Introducing the Light and Dark Sides of Sex in Tourism and the Fifty Shades of Grey in Between: Using the Social-Ecological Model

Liza Berdychevsky and Neil Carr

Sex is a fundamental part of life and lies at the core of the whole person (Berdychevsky & Carr, 2020a; Resnick, 2019). Hence, it is not surprising that sex and tourism have historically dovetailed each other (Littlewood, 2002). Indeed, 'tourism, romance, love, and sex have been cosy bedfellows for a long time' (Bauer & McKercher, 2003: xiii). Furthermore, it is not a coincidence that the notorious Four Ss – sun, sea, sand and sex – became hallmarks signifying the essence of various tourism experiences, both in popular culture and in academic literature. In the societal imagination, tourism is characterised by the supremacy of the senses, the primacy of enjoyment, and a coded promise of adventure, which often involves sexual escapades (Berdychevsky, 2016).

As we are writing this chapter, the world is tormented by the COVID-19 (Coronavirus) pandemic that has already taken hundreds of thousands of lives and has far-reaching consequences for all the areas of human life, including sex and tourism. Sexual behaviour, sexual and reproductive health and sexual rights are inevitably affected by the sense of powerlessness, poverty, fear, intolerance and exploitation of social divisions caused or augmented by the pandemic (Hussein, 2020; Jones, 2020). Also, due to the interruptions in the supply chain, contraception and condom shortages and stock-outs are expected in various countries (MacKinnon & Bremshey, 2020; Purdy, 2020).

The non-pharmaceutical intervention efforts, including quarantine, social distancing, border control and shelter-in-place orders, have changed many people's sex lives, with both steady and casual sexual partners. Stress and isolation have augmented the rates of intimate partner violence throughout the world, devastating some people's relationships with regular sexual partners (Bradley *et al.*, 2020; Taub, 2020). Conversely, for other couples, the lockdown seems to have brought some positive changes associated with emotional bonding through sex due to seeking intimacy and support or simply having more time (Arafat *et al.*, 2020).

The quarantine confinement and social distancing have also virtually obliterated the sex lives of people who practice casual sex, relying on a vibrant social scene and nightlife. On the bright side, however, some health experts believe that this lockdown and self-isolation offer a 'rare opportunity' to launch healthcare services and online testing to drive down certain sexually transmitted infections (e.g. HIV, syphilis) permanently (Baggs, 2020; MacKinnon & Bremshey, 2020). Nevertheless, while coronavirus is mainly transmitted through the respiratory droplets and contact, there is conflicting evidence regarding its presence (Li *et al.*, 2020; Peng *et al.*, 2020; Wang & Xu, 2020) or absence (Pan *et al.*, 2020; Song *et al.*, 2020) in semen, testes, and anal swabs, which technically might turn it into a sexually transmitted infection as well (Kelland, 2020). Although, if the partners are close enough to touch each other, then they are close enough to spread the virus with or without intercourse.

Tourism has been associated with the geographical expansion of various sexually transmitted infections (Brown *et al.*, 2014; Qvarnström & Oscarsson, 2014; Vivancos *et al.*, 2010). Likewise, tourism has contributed to the spread of COVID-19 throughout the world (Hall *et al.*, 2020; Wilson & Chen, 2020). In turn, the COVID-19 pandemic and its rapid spread have had an unprecedented obliterating impact on tourism and hospitality industries due to social distancing, quarantine requirements, curbs on crowding, and domestic and international travel restrictions (Rosen, 2020).

As of the end of March 2020, over 90% of the world's population resided in countries with some restrictions concerning international travel, and many countries also imposed restrictions on domestic travel (Gössling *et al.*, 2020). The global economic tourism-related loss might amount to US$ 2.1 trillion in 2020 and cost about 75 million jobs (World Travel & Tourism Council, 2020). The short-term prognoses for tourism revival are cautious. Steps towards this revival include various coronavirus-related surveillance and safety precautions, such as avoidance of high-risk destinations and an initial focus on domestic travel, mandatory quarantine, airport entry or exit screening, medical certificates/health passports, liability waivers, high standards of hygiene and a new etiquette for distance keeping (AIEST, 2020; Hall *et al.*, 2020; Rosen, 2020).

COVID-19 is changing our world, and it might never be the same again. However, our necessity or capacity for sexual expression and travel will not disappear. Tourism will rebound in some shape or form. Some scholars even argue that in the long term, despite the current COVID-19 devastation, people will resume travelling for leisure purposes with hardly any significant changes (AIEST, 2020). For example, despite the recent nightmare of the stranded cruise ships with the outbreaks of coronavirus on board and the fact that the global cruise operators have been grounded indefinitely, the world's largest cruise companies report that their levels of bookings for 2021 are already within historical ranges, and they even see demand for 2020 (Sampson, 2020). Hence, people are anxious to 'get back on the road' and travel for leisure purposes, and sex and the sexual will inevitably be an integral part of many tourism experiences. Indeed, sexual health experts believe that people will be anxious to get their sex lives back and will be eager to blow off some steam as soon as the lockdown restrictions are lifted (Baggs, 2020).

When this happens, we will need solid and up-to-date foundations of knowledge to inform research, practice, policy and advocacy at the nexus of sex and tourism. This is where this edited book comes in. To the best of our knowledge, the last concerted effort to assemble theory and evidence regarding various links between sex and tourism was conducted a decade ago – namely, the edited book entitled 'Sex and the sexual during people's leisure and tourism experiences' (Carr & Poria, 2010).

Around the same time, in the leisure field, a special issue named 'Sexy spaces' was published in *Leisure Studies* (Caudwell & Browne, 2011). Recently, the body of knowledge on sex as/in leisure was updated in a special issue titled 'Innovation and impact of sex as leisure in research and practice' published in *Leisure Sciences* (Berdychevsky & Carr, 2020b). With tourism and leisure being sibling fields, many advances in knowledge are relevant and translatable from one field to another. Nevertheless, it is crucial to promote the cutting edge, state-of-the-art, sex-related research in each field. This will allow us to showcase the newest ideas on the roles of sex in tourism and to incorporate the most up-to-date experiences. Thus, we strongly believe that it is time to update the body of knowledge on the nexus of sex and tourism to help study, manage and plan for the future concerning sex and the sexual in tourism.

Purpose and Focus of the Book

Sex in tourism has arguably been an understudied area of research relative to the central roles that sex plays within tourism experiences (Berdychevsky, 2018; Carr, 2016). Under the broad umbrella of sex, concepts such as sensual, sexual, love, romance, erotic and exploitation have similarly been under-researched within the tourism field (Carr & Poria, 2010). As a result, much of the complexity and nuanced nature of sex in tourism has arguably yet to be explored in detail.

It has been suggested that this situation is a consequence of social norms and values that continue to mitigate against open discussions of sex (Berdychevsky, 2018; Carr, 2016), even in a world that is increasingly saturated by public displays of sex (Attwood & Smith, 2013; Lucas & Fox, 2019). Perhaps, the sentiments of the Victorian and Puritan ethics still overshadow sex-related matters, rendering them taboo topics. These pervasive attitudes may have contributed to the situation where sex is considered to be marginal and unworthy of scholarly attention (Carr & Poria, 2010). Nevertheless, the complex and meaningful links between sex and tourism should not be trivialised as they have consequences for individuals, communities, societies and the tourism industry.

One of the primary foci of the relatively small amount of research on sex in tourism has been on the dark side of the issue; concerning the abuse of individuals and segments of society and focused on commercial sex tourism (Frohlick, 2010). While an important area of study, the focus on the dark side of sex in tourism has arguably overshadowed the light side of sex in tourism, which is not related to abuse of power and individuals but is, instead, about pleasure and fun; issues which are themselves important and worthy of investigation. The tendency to focus on the dark side of sex in tourism creates a narrow 'tunnel vision', which is oblivious to the complexity and multidimensionality of the roles of sex and the sexual in various tourism experiences (Berdychevsky et al., 2013b). Conversely, if combined, the light and dark sides of sex in tourism can speak to issues of disempowerment and empowerment, and social and individual self-identity and wellbeing.

Consequently, the aim of this edited book was to provide a forum for the discussion of all aspects of sex and the sexual within the various tourism experiences. This forum is based on practical evidence and relevant theories (including both empirical and conceptual chapters), while exploring the trends and nature of all the aspects of sex and the sexual within tourism. The chapters utilise various methodologies (qualitative, quantitative and mixed) and cover the links between sex and tourism all over the world (including Africa, Asia, Australia, Europe, the Caribbean, South America and North America). The foci of analysis throughout the chapters span the individual, interpersonal, community, societal and global levels. Such exploration is vital to help those who suffer in the dark side of sex in tourism and to allow those seeking the light(er) side to explore it without having to hide from the censorious eye of society.

This analysis fleshes out both differences and commonalities between the experiences that are stereotypically construed as belonging to either the dark or light sides of sex in tourism, showing that the either/or dichotomy oversimplifies these experiences and providing foundations for more flexible and comprehensive conceptualisations. The insights and implications of this analysis empower currently marginalised populations and shed light on some poorly understood links between sex and tourism. Such an approach also enables the tourism industry to manage and plan for the future in relation to sex and the sexual.

Complex Links between Sex and Tourism

Understanding sex in tourism requires a broad and flexible perspective. Sex definitions vary from narrow (i.e. penile-vaginal or penile-anal intercourse; Barnett *et al.*, 2018) to broad(er) approaches (i.e. sex as any activity with sexual overtones with or without penetration; Kashdan *et al.*, 2019). Narrow sex definitions have been described as inadequate because they obscure the complexity of sexual matters in general (Resnick, 2019) and in tourism in particular (Berdychevsky *et al.*, 2013). Conversely, broad(er) approaches to conceptualising sex accommodate a variety of sexual activities, perceptions, motivations and meanings in tourism (Eiser & Ford, 1995; Opperman, 1999; Ryan & Martin, 2001).

Tourism literature presents confusing and overlapping terminology concerning sexual behaviour in tourism. Namely, sex tourism (Ryan, 2000; Ryan & Hall, 2001; Ryan & Kinder, 1996), prostitution tourism (Jeffreys, 1999), romance tourism (Belliveau, 2006; Dahles & Bras, 1999; Pruitt & LaFont, 1995) and sex in tourism (Carr, 2016; Carter & Clift, 2000; McKercher & Bauer, 2003). Each term is imbued with different connotations based on the various scripts associated with sexual behaviour in tourism (e.g. sexual actors involved, motivations, power relations, gender, race and the presence or absence of commercial transaction). Nevertheless, the inevitable overlap between these scripts causes confusion.

Terminology and conceptualisations of sex tourism, prostitution tourism, child sex tourism, and romance tourism

In the tourism literature, commercial sex became the dominant focus in the 1990s, with 'sex tourism' in the early 1990s and 'romance tourism' since the mid-1990s. Since then, a plethora of studies on sex and romance tourism have been conducted in different geographical areas (e.g. Aston, 2008; Bandyopadhyay, 2013; Brennan, 2004; Brents *et al.*, 2010; Cabezas, 2009; Frohlick, 2013; Hall, 1992; Jacobs, 2010; Jeffreys, 1999; Kibicho, 2009; Piscitelli, 2007; Rivers-Moore, 2016; Ryan & Hall, 2001; Sánchez Taylor, 2001; Schifter, 2007; Williams, 2013), fleshing them out as complex and multidimensional phenomena. Some of the key destinations for sex/romance tourism include Thailand, the

Philippines and the Caribbean, while the tourists commonly come from North America, Europe, Australia, Japan and, more recently, China.

The majority of literature on commercial sex tourism creates an illusion that the rest of tourism activity is sex free. For instance, Ryan (2000) defined sex tourism as 'sexual intercourse while away from home – an all-inclusive term, but one which permits a discussion of different paradigms' (2000: 36). However, attributing any sexual intercourse occurring during the tourism experience to sex tourism may prove inadequate for understanding the complexity of this phenomenon. Therefore, an alternative, more nuanced definition of sex tourism might offer a more precise lens. However, achieving this is challenging because sex tourism is a term that eludes definitions (Sánchez Taylor, 2001).

For the sake of simplicity, it might be tempting to narrowly define sex tourism as sex for money in tourism contexts. Some scholars define sex tourists as 'individuals who plan their travel around the purposes of obtaining sex' (Blackburn et al., 2011: 122). Following on from this, the principal motivation of sex tourists for taking a holiday has been defined as the consumption of commercial sexual services (Kibicho, 2009). Nevertheless, in essence, sex tourists can be preferential (a category that encompasses sex tourists described above) and situational (namely, tourists who might take advantage of sexual services while travelling but are not necessarily motivated to travel by them; Mattar, 2007). Moreover, unidimensional definitions obscure multiple meaningful nuances.

Sex tourism is more than the illicit commercial exchange of sex for money, as it involves ambiguous elements such as different kinds of opportunities for recreation, romance, consumption, exploitation, travel, migration and marriage (Herold et al., 2001; McKercher & Bauer, 2003; Oppermann, 1999; Ryan & Hall, 2001). Furthermore, a narrow definition ignores the variety of sex workers, their self-perceptions and gendered double standards that affect the outcomes of the sexual encounter for the tourist and local sex worker (Cabezas, 2004; Frohlick, 2013; Piscitelli, 2007).

Thus, it is important to employ comprehensive and flexible conceptual models for sex tourism that can reflect the diversity of tourist-related sexual-economic exchange and the complexity of power relations that corroborate them (Sánchez Taylor, 2001). Such models might encompass multiple parameters. For instance, Ryan and Hall (2001) suggested that to define sex tourism, sexual encounters should be located along two axes: (1) a continuum between voluntary participation on behalf of the sex worker, on the one end, and a position of total exploitation, on the other end, and (2) the level of commerciality that underpins the sexual encounter. Ryan (2000) added a third axis where on the one end of the continuum, a sexual encounter enhances feelings of self-integrity while, on the other end of the continuum, a sexual experience degrades a person's sense of integrity.

In a similar vein, McKercher and Bauer (2003) suggested examining sex tourism based on the following three dimensions: (1) the role of sex as a motivation for travel, (2) the nature of the sexual encounter ranging from positive and mutually rewarding for all the participants to negative and exploitative for at least one of the partners and (3) the roles of the tourism industry in facilitating sexual encounters. Further, Oppermann (1999) offered a holistic model with six parameters to grasp the complexity of sex tourism: (1) the importance of intention to engage in sex with strangers as a purpose of travel, (2) the nature of the financial exchange, (3) amount of time spent with a sex worker, (4) prostitute-tourist relationship, (5) the nature of the sexual encounter and (6) consideration of who travels (sex seeker, sex provider or both).

Besides the debates regarding the scope and flexibility of the models for grasping sex tourism, some scholars contest the term itself. Another alternative term appearing in tourism literature is 'tourism prostitution' (Bender & Furman, 2004; Hall, 1996). Jeffreys (1999), based on her work in the Philippines, argued that 'the expression "sex tourism" is a euphemism' as it does not reflect the exploitative nature, commodification, objectification and the abuse of women and children and called to understand it as 'prostitution tourism' (1999: 180). Other scholars, however, caution that such an approach essentialises all forms of sex tourism as victimisation, which is not always the case (Herold *et al.*, 2001; Oppermann, 1999; Ryan, 2000; Ryan & Hall, 2001). Specifically, this approach presupposes that all adults working in the sex industry servicing tourists have been forced into the sex industry. Yet a highly emotive debate continues to rage concerning the accuracy of this claim, both inside and beyond the tourism context. Indeed, Ryan and Hall (2001: 151) 'deny that all sex workers are, by definition, victims', a view supported by Kempadoo and Doezema (1998).

In comparison, such a statement is completely irrelevant in the 21st century regarding the children involved in child sex tourism, who can never be considered workers but are victims of exploitation and/or trafficking. This heinous manifestation of sex tourism is a clear case of abuse of power by criminals forcing children into sexual exploitation and tourists paying for such experiences (e.g. de Vries, 2020; Koops *et al.*, 2017; Panko & George, 2012; Tepelus, 2008). The clear abuse of children by the child sex industry and consumers has contributed to the suggestion by the Interagency Working Group on Sexual Exploitation of Children (2016: 56) that everyone should cease using the term 'child sex tourism' and, instead, label it as the 'sexual exploitation of children in travel and tourism'. In making this call, they reason that the term 'child sex tourism' may inadvertently give the idea that this is a legitimate form of tourism, and may also associate the crime with the entire industry. Furthermore, by referring exclusively to tourism and tourists, it excludes many types of travelling offenders, such as business travellers and military personnel, and offenders in transit or residing out of their country more generally. Lastly, the term completely omits the fact that it refers to serious criminal conduct that a large number of countries have included in the scope of extraterritorial legislation. Consequently, the Interagency Working Group on Sexual Exploitation of Children has stated that potential 'normalisation' of the practice through the use of the term 'child sex tourism' risks being harmful to the child (2016: 56).

There is much value in the claims made in favour of the utilisation of the term 'sexual exploitation of children in travel and tourism' by the Interagency Working Group on Sexual Exploitation of Children. Certainly, there is no argument regarding the desire to recognise the abuse of children and do everything possible to bring it to an end. While it is not the intention of this book or the chapters within it to deconstruct the work of the Interagency Working Group on Sexual Exploitation of Children, it is necessary to explain why the Interagency's terminology has not been adopted, and the child sex tourism label has been used instead. In part, this speaks to the focus of this book on tourism (i.e. travelling for pleasure and recreational purposes), not the wider travel industry (which would include travelling for work, healthcare, visiting friends and relatives, long-term journeys, etc.) that the Interagency's definition incorporates. This choice recognises that there is a distinct difference between tourism and travel, with tourism requiring travel, but not all travel being tourism.

In addition, it could be argued that 'exploitation' misses the point and that child sex tourism is more accurately a case of abuse rather than the potentially milder term 'exploitation'. Perhaps of most concern, though, is the idea that using the term 'child sex tourism' 'may also associate the crime with the entire industry' (Interagency Working Group on Sexual Exploitation of Children, 2016: 56). While the entire industry is not directly involved in child sex tourism, it is clear that throughout the whole tourism value chain/network, businesses are making money from tourists that abuse children, which implies moral (and even legal) responsibilities, especially in this era of corporate social responcibility. In this way, whether the tourism industry likes it or not, child sex tourism is associated with the entire industry. The child sex tourism label is, potentially, not perfect. As the Interagency rightly notes, it does not explicitly mention child exploitation or abuse. At the same time, it recognises the roles the entire industry plays in child sex exploitation and abuse.

Furthermore, the implicit notion of abuse and exploitation within the child sex tourism term is both undeniable and clear. To say this is not the case is clearly erroneous when everything published, both inside and outside of academia, on child sex tourism has spoken clearly of the abuse and exploitation that is core to this segment of the tourism experience. Despite not conforming to the Interagency's statement that the term 'child sex tourism' 'should be avoided' (2016: 56), this body of knowledge is undeniably of significant value, particularly, in its highlighting of the exploitation involved in child sex tourism and drawing together a range of agencies and organisations around this issue. In this way, it is hoped that differences in definition utilisation do not impinge on attempts to work together to end child sex tourism or the 'sexual exploitation of children in travel and tourism'.

There is also no consensus in the literature as to whether the term 'sex tourism' should be applied to female tourists who engage in sexual activity with local men. In other words, should these women be framed as sex tourists or do they constitute a separate category of romance tourists? Pruitt and LaFont (1995), based on their study of sexual relations between western female travellers and local males in Jamaica, coined the term 'romance tourism' to emphasise that the relationships between female tourists and local men are 'constructed through a discourse of romance and long-term relationship, an emotional involvement usually not present in sex tourism' (1995: 423). Moreover, they argued that neither female tourists nor local men perceive their relationships as prostitution. In turn, Dahles and Bras (1999), based on their fieldwork in Indonesia, conceptualised local men engaging in sexual relations with female tourists as romantic entrepreneurs (rather than sex workers) because they do not perceive the money they get from female tourists as payment for sex.

The concept of romance tourism is imbued with controversies that spurred debates regarding the similarities and differences between the gendered notions of male sex tourism and female romance tourism. For instance, Jeffreys (2003) explained that the main similarities proposed by the researchers who seek to include women among the ranks of sex tourists are the economic, class and racial privileges of western tourists compared to their local sexual partners. She argued, however, that 'careful attention to the power relations, context, meanings and effects of the behaviours of male and female tourists who engage in sexual relations with local people, makes it clear that the differences are profound' (Jeffreys, 2003: 223), while an ungendered approach fails to demonstrate these differences and obscures gendered power relations.

Conversely, Sánchez Taylor (2001), based on her research in the Dominican Republic and Jamaica, problematised the gendered distinction between male sex tourism and female romance tourism using four arguments. First, sexual-economic exchanges are not always straightforward, and tourists and sex providers might not necessarily perceive themselves as prostitute users and prostitutes. Second, both female and male tourists can be sexually predatory and hostile, and it is not always clear who is exploiting whom (if at all). Third, this distinction reproduces the essentialist understandings of female and male sexuality, according to which men benefit from sexual access to women's bodies. Finally, the idea that female tourists having sex with local men are not sex tourists tends to downplay the significance of racialised and economic power.

While some feminist scholars tend to advocate for the distinction between male sex tourism and female romance tourism, this categorisation might inadvertently reproduce detrimental traditional gender stereotypes and cause gross oversimplifications (Carr, 2016). Indeed, the presumption that all women necessarily seek romance in their sexual encounters in tourism while all men are uninterested in it is erroneous. Following this logic, Herold *et al.* (2001), based on their study in the Dominican Republic, conceptualised sex tourism and romance tourism as two ends of a continuum of motivations rather than distinct categories. Their findings, however, revealed that more female tourists were located toward the romance end and more male tourists toward the sex end of the continuum.

Nevertheless, even this continuum-based approach might be questionable as it is based on the assumption that sex and romance are two distinct (perhaps even dichotomous) constructs, which might not always be the case (Carr, 2016). Furthermore, Weichselbaumer (2012), based on her study of sexual relations between female travellers and local males in Trinidad and Tobago, called on researchers to transgress the dichotomy of sex tourism and romance tourism. She employed the concept of carnivalesque to conceptualise a temporary liberation from the established social order and the celebration of bodily excess, with both ideas being broader and more complex than only sex or romance.

This section illustrates the debate around the terms proposed in the literature to address the roles and meanings of sex in tourism contexts, with a focus on relations involving at least some degree of commerciality. However, a variety of sexual encounters in tourism that do not involve commercial transactions do not fit conceptually under any of these terms. Sexual behaviour is related to identity formation, building relationships and conforming to or resisting social stereotypes and double standards. Using the idea of commercial sex tourism as a vantage point to approaching all sexual behaviours in tourism or juxtaposing all sexual activities *vis-à-vis* the aforementioned parameters for defining sex/prostitution/romance tourism does not do justice to the complexity and heterogeneity of sexual behaviour in tourism. Moreover, analytically, such a focus serves only a limited range of research questions and does not apply to some populations.

For instance, couples constitute a dominant tourist unit in most hotels and tourist attractions, and it would make sense to suggest that most sexual activity in tourism occurs among those couples (Pritchard & Morgan, 2006). Nevertheless, the research focus on sex/prostitution/romance tourism, while contributing important insights, has downplayed the incidence and importance of sexual behaviour among consenting adults engaged in sexual activity devoid of any commercial transaction (Berdychevsky *et al.*, 2013). This can be explained by the tendency of the field to focus on the socially defined righteous topics (e.g. fixing the wrongs of sex tourism, preventing the spread of sexually transmitted infections through tourism), to the point that sexual pleasure and expression have been virtually ignored (Berdychevsky & Carr, 2020a; Frohlick, 2010). Failing to comprehend the roles of pleasure in the links between sex and tourism is problematic because 'to ignore this reality is to fail to understand the position of sex in tourism' (Carr, 2016: 194).

A flexible umbrella approach to sex in tourism

The relationship between tourism and sex cannot be narrowly confined to the scope of commercial trade (McKercher & Bauer, 2003). It is important to distinguish between 'sex tourism' and 'sex in tourism', with the latter being a broader term including sexual behaviour without commercial transaction (Carr, 2016; Carter & Clift, 2000). Understanding non-commercial sexual activity among the tourists themselves offers a different perspective on the interpersonal sexual dynamic in tourism compared to commercial sex/prostitution/ romance tourism (Berdychevsky *et al.*, 2013), which is often grounded in economic, social, cultural, and racial power differentials between tourists and locals (Cabezas, 2004; Sánchez Taylor, 2001, 2006). Also, as a term, 'sex in tourism' (as opposed to sex tourism) seems to be less imbued with negative connotations, leaving more room for (1) consideration of the unique social atmosphere in tourism contexts and (2) complex interpretations of sexual behaviours, perceptions, motivations and meanings.

Scholars argue that tourism offers a special social reality affecting people's sexual behaviour (Berdychevsky, 2016; Eiser & Ford, 1995; McKercher & Bauer, 2003; Milhausen *et al.*, 2020; Qvarnström & Oscarsson, 2014; Thomas, 2005). To highlight the links between sex and tourism, the latter has been conceptualised as a liminoid phenomenon – a state of being between and betwixt the social worlds where ordinary rules do not seem to apply (Turner, 1974). Selänniemi (2003) offered an understanding of liminoid sun lust tourism as a fourfold transition/ transgression in terms of time, space, mind and senses, arguing that liminality explains why tourism and sex are so closely linked. Indeed, it is often assumed that travel per se is liminal and liberatory (Black, 2000).

By entering a liminoid state, or in simple terms, by travelling, people are provided with an opportunity to fulfil sexual fantasies that they have to repress at home (Ryan & Kinder, 1996). Due to the anonymity and perceived tolerance offered by the liminoid tourism atmosphere, people may experiment with their sexual behaviour in terms of the choice of partners, frequency, accelerated progression and nature of the sexual experience (Bauer & McKercher, 2003; Thomas, 2005). Indeed, the concept of a liminal 'dirty weekend' was proposed to describe the transgression of everyday norms in tourism due to the sense of being 'out-of-time', 'out-of-place' and 'out-of-mind' (Pritchard & Morgan, 2006: 764).

Tourism has also been conceptualised as heterotopia – a counter-site for transgression, inversion and contestation of everyday social order (Foucault, 1986) – to understand sexual behaviour in tourism. For instance, Andriotis (2010) conceptualised a gay nude beach as a heterotopia, suggesting that in this setting people can experiment with inversions of morals and practices, as well as with their bodies, sexualities and pleasure. Similarly, Apostolopoulos et al. (2002) defined various types of tourist experiences as 'contra-normative settings', with a mixture of sex, alcohol and drugs encouraging the suspension and rejection of personal inhibitions and everyday social norms (2002: 733). Likewise, Eiser and Ford (1995), while exploring the sexual activity of young tourists, suggested the concept of 'situational disinhibition' – the sense of being a different person and feeling less responsible for one's sexual escapades in tourism (1995: 323).

To further elucidate the links between sex and social atmosphere in the tourism experience, certain sun lust destinations (e.g. Ibiza, Rhodes) have been labelled as the 'Gomorrah of the Med', supplying a 'hedonistic cocktail of sun, sea, music, cheap alcohol and drugs, sex, and expectation for excess' (Diken & Laustsen, 2004: 99). Concerning some tourism experiences (e.g. Spring Break, Schoolies Week), opportunities for casual sex (combined with binge drinking and taking drugs) were found to be the major motivating factors for embarking on such vacations (Apostolopoulos et al., 2002; Sönmez et al., 2006). The general attitudes of sexual permissiveness and tolerance of transgressions in tourism are reflected in social myths and marketing slogans like, 'What happens in Vegas, stays in Vegas' (Yeoman, 2008: 119), or 'What happens in Tenerife, stays in Tenerife' (Thomas, 2005: 571).

Another link between sex and tourism that cannot be captured by terms like sex tourism, prostitution tourism and romance tourism, is the capacity of sex in tourism to be an arena for sexual self-exploration, self-discovery and transformation (Ragsdale et al., 2006; Thomas, 2005). For instance, studies of women's sexual behaviour in tourism found that some women innovate and experiment with their sex lives and sexual repertoires (with steady and casual sexual partners) to have fun, achieve new self-understandings and negotiate or resist oppressive sexual double standards (Berdychevsky, 2016). In turn, for some women, sexual experimentation in tourism leads to rewarding inversions of sexual roles and a sense of empowerment and self-transformation, sometimes temporary and sometimes permanent (Berdychevsky et al., 2013a, 2015).

The diversity and complexity of sexual risk-taking perceptions and motivations in tourism, as well as the multiple types of sexual risk takers, can also not be grasped through the narrow lens of sex/ prostitution/romance tourism. Sexual risk perceptions in tourism, for instance, are far more complex and multidimensional than the fear of sexually transmitted infections. These risk perceptions have been found to include physical, sexual health, social, emotional, mental, and cultural considerations (Berdychevsky & Gibson, 2015a). Likewise, a study of sexual motivations in tourism revealed a far more complex understanding than any of the sex tourism models described above suggests. Such motivations include anonymous experimentation, safe thrills, sense of empowerment, fun-oriented state of mind, and less inhibition in tourism (Berdychevsky & Gibson, 2015b). This complex constellation of sexual risk-taking perceptions and motivations suggests different types and profiles of sexual risk-takers in tourism (Berdychevsky, 2017), which cannot be grasped through the lens of sex, prostitution or romance tourism.

To conclude, considering the degree of overlap and confusion between the stereotypical conceptualisations of sex/prostitution/ romance tourism, as well as their inability to grasp tourism as a social atmosphere and the complexity of interpretations of sexual behaviours and meanings, the field might need a more flexible and comprehensive alternative definition. It is against this backdrop that it was suggested for the tourism field to 'divest itself entirely of the label "sex tourism" and instead fully embrace the idea of "sex and tourism"' (Carr, 2016: 196). In this edited book, we would like to take this proposition even further and complicate the continuum of the light and dark aspects of sex in tourism by analysing them throughout the levels of the integrative social-ecological model (Bronfenbrenner, 1979, 1989).

The Light and Dark Sides of Sex in Tourism Based on the Social-Ecological Model

Sexual expression in tourism is diverse and complex and has multilevel impacts and ripple effects at the individual, interpersonal, community, societal and global levels. Understanding these processes requires a multidimensional approach that considers psychological and socio-cultural influences. Such a perspective is offered by the social-ecological model grounded in the ecological systems developmental theory (Bronfenbrenner, 1979, 1989). According to this theory, people encounter different interconnected environments throughout their life course that influence their behaviour. These environments include the microsystem (e.g. family and peer relationships), the mesosystem (e.g. work, school, healthcare institutions), the exosystem (e.g. community contexts, distal social networks), the macrosystem (e.g. sociocultural, economic and political contexts) and the chronosystem (i.e. individual's transitions across the lifespan contextualised in the socio-historical circumstances) (Bronfenbrenner, 1979, 1989).

Consequently, the social-ecological model grasps a complex interplay between individual, relational, community and societal factors affecting human behaviour, attitudes and values. The social-ecological model was adopted extensively to conceptualise and inform praxis on various health-related issues, including sexual health and violence prevention (e.g. Centers for Disease Control and Prevention, 2020; DiClemente *et al.*, 2013; Larios *et al.*, 2009; Raffaelli *et al.*, 2012; Tolman *et al.*, 2003). We propose to recruit the social-ecological model for conceptualising the light and dark aspects of sexual expression in tourism, as illustrated in Figure 1.1.

According to the proposed model, on the light side of the continuum of sex in tourism, we can find mutually rewarding and safe sexual expression between consenting adults (between tourists or between tourists and locals) that is also respectful to local sexual norms and values. Conversely, on the dark side of the continuum, we can find the most heinous manifestations of sexual exploitation in tourism, such as

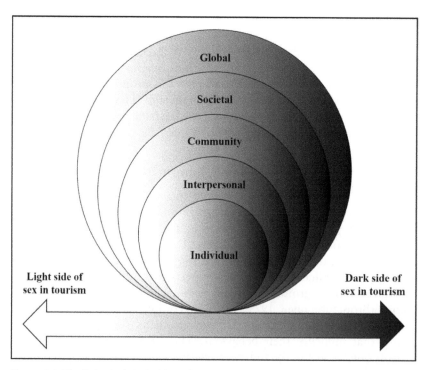

Figure 1.1 The light and dark sides of sex in tourism and the fifty shades of grey in between across the levels of the social-ecological model

child sex tourism and human trafficking. We will use these examples from the two ends of the continuum to illustrate the social-ecological levels below. Various other kinds of sexual encounters in tourism (e.g. sexual risk taking, non-forced/chosen prostitution, semi-commercial liaisons and sexual harassment) can be located along this continuum with multifaceted light and dark aspects as well as various shades of grey in between. In each scenario, the multidimensional influences can be analysed at and throughout the social-ecological levels, including individual, interpersonal, community, societal and global tiers. The factors at these levels may overlap and cross-pollinate each other, but this multilayered heuristic is useful for analytical purposes.

The individual level includes knowledge, attitudes, values, skills, biological factors and personal history affecting sexual behaviour. At the individual level, on the light side of the continuum of sex in tourism, we can find expression, pleasure, increased knowledge through exploration, wish fulfilment, empowerment, positive transformation, increased skills and an improved sense of wellbeing for all the parties (tourists and locals) involved in a sexual encounter. Due to societal sexual taboos, inhibitions and double standards, some of these benefits might be unavailable to people at home, but not in anonymous and permissive tourism environments. Conversely, on the dark side of the continuum, we might find a sense of fear, humiliation, denigration, powerlessness and mental and physical health issues for at least one of the sexual partners (e.g. if they are forced to sell their bodies).

The interpersonal level includes the relationship between the sexual or romantic partners (either between tourists or between tourists and local people) and their immediate social networks (e.g. travelling companions, family and friends). At this level, on the light side of the continuum of sex in tourism, we can find safe and fulfilling sexual relationships (regardless of their duration or degree of commerciality) between consenting adults that do not jeopardise their social status at home or within their travel party. On the dark side of the continuum, we might find sexual encounters between tourists and locals that are characterised by severe power imbalances, exploitation, coercion, victimisation and violence that may also stigmatise at least one of the involved parties in their social circles.

The community level refers to the resources and characteristics of the community receiving tourists that might affect or be affected by sex in tourism. At the community level, on the light side of the continuum, sex in tourism can raise awareness of sexual health matters in the community and contribute to improved local sexual healthcare and education policies, services and programmes for both locals and tourists. Moreover, it can offer recreation, economic and employment opportunities. However, on the dark side of the continuum, we can find illegal prostitution, violence, crime, degradation of the community and locals' increased hostility toward tourists who are perceived as sexual exploiters. In the context of this analysis, the community can also be broadly construed as a subculture with collective identity (e.g. backpackers, voluntourists or online community users).

The societal/country level includes sexual liberal vs. conservative attitudes, sexual double standards, women's and sexual minorities' rights and the ways they are reflected in laws, policies and healthcare services. Concerning tourism, it is important to consider destination image and the roles of sex in it, as well as the resultant economic implications. At the societal level, on the light side of the continuum of sex in tourism, we might find contributions to equal sexual rights, attenuated sexual double standards, improved policies and services and cosmopolitan destination images. However, on the dark side of the continuum, we may find an exacerbation of cultural norms that condone the violation of human rights, reproduction of power imbalances between genders and social classes, corruption, deteriorating policies and services and the 'world's brothel' destination image. At the societal level, it is important to consider both countries that receive and send tourists.

Tourism is a global industry that permeates societies and communities. The proposed model would be incomplete without the global tier. Hence, we are adding the global level, even though it was not originally envisioned in the social-ecological model. At this level, on the light side of the continuum of sex in tourism, we might find a global transfer of sexual knowledge through transnational sexual encounters, increased awareness of the differences in sexual rights and liberties throughout the world, and establishment of international sexual health and rights advocacy organisations with local chapters whose purpose is to improve global sexual health and wellbeing. On the dark side of the continuum, the global proliferation of the child sex economy and transnational human trafficking linked to the sex trade are amongst the ugliest modern-day incarnations of colonialist and neo-colonialist exploitation. Furthermore, sex tourism contributes to the global spread of sexually transmitted infections and reinforces existing power imbalances between the countries of the developed and developing worlds.

To conclude, it is important to reiterate that only a few kinds of sexual encounters in tourism would qualify as exclusively light or dark, with the majority of sexual expressions moving through the grey shades of the proposed continuum. Furthermore, the impacts of most sexual encounters cut across the social-ecological levels of the proposed model. Namely, individual and interpersonal dynamics of sexual encounters cannot be divorced from each other. Moreover, these micro-level impacts accrue at the aggregated levels and produce ripple effects at the community, society/country and global levels. In turn, social norms, laws, policies, destination images and supply and demand factors from the macro-levels produce conditions that facilitate or inhibit different kinds of sexual expression at the micro-levels. We believe that this complex constellation offers a useful prism for analysing sex in tourism. Thus, it is through the combination of the social-ecological lens and the continuum between the light and the dark aspects of sex in tourism that we have organised and presented the chapters in this book.

Book Structure

The combination of the light through the dark continuum of sex in tourism and the social-ecological lens offers a structure for this book that is designed to take the reader on a journey through the tourism experience and the position and acceptance (or a lack of it) of sex and the sexual within it. In this way, the book can be read holistically or people may dip into it according to their specific interests. Although some chapters are conceptually similar, they are situated in different locales. Having these multiple perspectives in the book highlights the influence of the community, societal/country and global social-ecological levels and the fact that space matters in relation to sex and the sexual, in terms of practices, social values, the law and behaviour.

The conceptual chapter following this Introduction spans the light-dark continuum by focusing on the ethical debates around sex in tourism. Dilek and Carr offer a critical discussion of ethics as it applies to various sexual encounters, involving, among others, women, children, robots and animals. Although most of the arguments in the chapter revolve around commercial sex tourism, the meta-issues discussed apply to sex in tourism in a broader sense as well. The chapter analyses multiple facets of sex tourism through five ethical frameworks: utilitarianism, rights-based ethics, distributive justice ethics, virtue ethics and the ethic of care. This critical analysis highlights the complexities and positionalities of ethics. While the insights provided in the chapter cut across the social-ecological levels (since ethics are both [inter] personal and social constructions), most of the chapter's discussion is situated at the societal level.

Moving along the light-dark continuum of sex in tourism, all the subsequent chapters in this book have been clustered into appropriate themes that are central to debates about sex in tourism. These themes are reflected in three sections of (1) The Light Side of Sex in Tourism: Affects and Effects of the Diverse Sexual Encounters in Tourism; (2) Fifty Shades of Grey of Sex in Tourism: Romance Tourism, Sex Tourism or Exploitation Tourism?; and (3) The Dark Side of Sex and Tourism: Child Sex Tourism and Sexual Harassment. It is the main focus of the individual chapters that has resulted in their positioning in a particular theme, and as such, the sections of the book can be read individually. However, it should be noted that many of the individual chapters have several foci that cut across different themes. This is important as it highlights the point that these themes are not isolated issues. Instead, they are integrated issues that all need to be understood to fully understand the complexities and nuances of the continuum of sex in tourism.

The first section in this book, focusing on the light aspects of sex in tourism, opens with Berdychevsky's empirical chapter on gender differences and similarities in the perceptions of and experiences with sex and sexual risk taking in tourism. Utilising a quantitative survey methodology with young adults from the United States, the chapter explores the perceptions of activities that constitute sex in tourism and examines intra- and inter-gender differences in the perceptions of and experiences with various kinds of sexual risk taking in tourism. This chapter examines how sexual double standards mutate but do not necessarily disappear in tourism, as gender-specific inhibitions regarding some perceptual and behavioural sexual patterns are relaxed but not regarding others. This analysis of the impacts of gender and sexual double standards (both being sociocultural constructions) on people's sexual perceptions and behaviour in tourism offers analytical insights into the (inter)personal and societal social-ecological levels of the light side of sex in tourism.

The next chapter in this section, by Carr and Nava, explores sex within the context of the summer camp experience in North America that generates expectations of love and sexual encounters in a highly sexually charged environment. Using a retrospective auto-ethnography, the chapter analyses sex and the sexual in camps in relation to three main actors involved in the camp experience: (1) the child as a tourist, (2) the young adult as a camp counsellor and (3) the adult as a camp superintendent. The analysis includes examples of sexual expression involving only the campers, between campers and staff members and among staff. The chapter concludes that while camps can be a space of sexual self-expression, enlightenment and empowerment, the potential for sexual abuse is also high. This chapter contributes insights at the (inter)personal, community (i.e. camp construed as a community) and societal social-ecological levels of the light side of sex in tourism.

The following chapter, by Everingham *et al.*, brings together findings from two ethnographic studies on youth tourists to examine sexual interactions in backpacker tourism (Australian backpackers throughout the world) and volunteer tourism (in South America). The analysis focuses on the embodied liminality of sexual dynamics in these contexts that emerge corporeally, affectively and discursively between tourists, and between tourists and locals. The chapter shows that sexual licentiousness is perceived as normative in backpacking culture and is reflective of backpackers' lived experiences. However, the discursive constructions of volunteer tourism (revolving around altruism and responsibility) suppress sexual possibilities. Nevertheless, the study shows that the latter representations do not necessarily reflect volunteer tourists' lived experiences. This juxtaposition between norms and lived experiences of transnational intimacy places the analysis of the light side of sex in tourism at the (inter)personal, community (i.e. backpackers' and voluntourists' communities), societal and global social-ecological levels.

The next chapter, by Sacramento, analyses the relevance of the internet in the constitution of transnational configurations of adult heterosexual intimacy (including sexual, romantic and conjugal aspects) between Brazilian women and European men. This ethnography focuses on the understanding of the cyberspace processes, contents and practices amplifying and diffusing gendered representations of sensuality, exoticism and hedonism in Ponta Negra, Brazil, that inform male tourists' expectations of intimacy. It also analyses the internet as a device for initiating and maintaining Euro-Brazilian relationships before and after the tourism experience. By focusing on the internet, tourism destination representations/images, gendered expectations and transnational intimate relationships, this chapter contributes insights into the (inter)personal, community, societal and global social-ecological tiers of analysis of the light side of sex in tourism.

The last chapter in this section dovetails the intersection between the internet, sexuality and tourism. Using netnography and individual interviews in Barcelona, Spain, Soro *et al.* examine relationships between the use of the popular dating app (Tinder), self-representation and tourism. The findings show that the app, mainly used for hooking up in everyday life, serves additional purposes while travelling and transforms into a broader phenomenon that the authors call Tinder tourism. Namely, beyond finding sex and intimacy on the move, Tinder facilitates tourists' quest for and access to authentic local experiences and connections. In turn, many people project their travel narratives in dating profile images and descriptions to boost the attractiveness/rating of their profiles/self-representation on Tinder. As such, this chapter contributes to the (inter)personal, community (i.e. Tinder community) and global social-ecological levels of analysis of the light side of sex in tourism.

The second section in this book, focusing on the fifty shades of grey of sex in tourism, opens with Dilek's conceptual chapter, which aims to develop an understanding of the sex tourism phenomenon beyond the human. The chapter analyses the complexity of animal sex tourism as a form of exploitation in the proliferation and diversification of sex tourism. In addition to human and non-human animals comprising sex tourism, the technological tools and cyberspace are increasingly becoming integral components of sex tourism, including the phenomena of remote sex, virtual sex, sex robots, immersive sexual entertainment and human augmentation. The author concludes that some of these technological advancements may offer (at least partial) solutions for the problems plaguing sex tourism, such as human trafficking, child sex tourism, human and non-human animal abuse, harassment and the spread of sexually transmitted infections. This discussion contributes to the (inter)personal (broadly construed to include non-human animals, robots and artificial intelligence) and global social-ecological tiers of analysis of the grey shades of sex in tourism.

The next chapter in this section, by Jenkins *et al.*, uses micro-ethnography in Negril to critically assess the impacts of female sex tourism on Jamaica and its development through the lens of neo-colonialism and power relations. The analysis offers stories of mutual abuse and manipulation, but also sexual wish fulfilment, upward mobility and occasional long-term relationships. The authors portray Jamaican masculinities as social constructions rooted in animalism, exoticism, sexual prowess, slavery and colonialism, whereas observed female sex tourists showed overt ownership of their Jamaican partners. They conclude that while female sex tourism may have a positive effect on Jamaica's economic development, it also involves abuse of racial and economic power differentials that facilitate the construction and consumption of Otherness. This chapter offers insights into the (inter) personal, societal and global social-ecological levels of analysis of the grey shades of sex in tourism.

The following ethnographic chapter, by Ariya and Nyamasyo, examines the influence of sex tourism on girls' and young women's education in Mtwapa, Kenya, by reflecting the lived experiences of the women involved in the sex trade. Despite the stories of assault by the clients and harassment by the authorities, the interviewees reported valuing their involvement in commercial sex work more than education because sex tourism pays more than the pursuit of education. Some felt that education would be a waste of time and resources, while sex tourism was viewed as a way to financial prosperity. The authors conclude that under the circumstances of unemployment (including among college graduates), acute poverty, gender inequalities and general social-economic malaise, an upsurge in sex tourism might ensue in the future. These foci contribute to the individual, community and societal social-ecological tiers of analysis of the grey shades of sex in tourism.

The last chapter in this section, by Moswete, utilises a mixed methods design to examine residents' awareness, knowledge and perceptions of tourism and its links to the spread of HIV/AIDS in Maun, Botswana. Based on a survey of the residents, the chapter demonstrates how people believe that tourism is very important and beneficial to the local economy. However, there is an alarming lack of awareness of the relationship between tourism and the spread of HIV/AIDS. Conversely, interviews with government personnel revealed that they are aware of this relationship, particularly, through commercial sex between tourists and locals. This spurred the suggestion to rethink the current illegal status of sex work in Botswana that drives the industry underground and increases the risks. The author concludes by advocating for local, national and international educational campaigns enlightening people about the links between tourism and the transmission of HIV/AIDS. This analysis contributes insights throughout the social-ecological tiers of the grey shades of sex in tourism, with a particular focus on community and societal levels.

The final section in this book, revolving around the dark aspects of sex in tourism, opens with the mixed-methods empirical chapter by Oliveira and Ambrósio that examines the extent and personal experiences of sexual harassment of housekeeping employees in Portuguese hotels. The survey results reveal that the majority of the participants have been sexually harassed (incorporating physical and verbal harassment) at work. There is also a severe issue of underreporting of sexual harassment, with most harassed housekeepers not complaining to their supervisors. Based on the interviews with the housekeepers, it is clear that the experiences of sexual harassment in this sector are prompted and exacerbated by the lack of security and isolation while working, as well as abusive guests and fear of confrontation. This chapter shows that sexual harassment is an acute and widespread problem in the housekeeping department of the hotel industry and contributes insights to the (inter)personal, community (in this case, organisational community) and global (i.e. tourism industry) social-ecological tiers of analysis of the dark side of sex in tourism.

The next two chapters focus on the darkest and most heinous manifestation of sex in tourism – namely, child sex tourism. The chapter by de Man and Lagendijk focuses on the distorted reach of local stakeholders in the global fight against child sex tourism. The Tourism Child Protection Code is analysed in this chapter as a vehicle to bring stakeholders together and acquire reach. The authors conceptualise *reach* as a mix of 'effect' (i.e. formal scripts and commitments) and 'affect' (i.e. informal persuasion and motivation), with both being essential to encourage and empower local businesses and non-governmental organisations to prevent tourists from sexually exploiting minors. The chapter presents three case studies about the challenges associated with developing such reach through the business sector and corporate social responsibility in Thailand, through the non-governmental organisations in the Dominican Republic and through the state/government in the Gambia. The social-ecological analysis in this chapter revolves at the community, societal/country and global levels of the darkest side of sex in tourism.

The last conceptual chapter in this section, by Papageorgiou, continues the focus on the essential roles of local communities in intervening with child sex tourism. The authors argue that the enactment of protective and supportive roles by local communities, combined with severe punishment of offenders, are the most effective measures for combating child sex tourism. They discuss the best practices of knowledge dissemination, effective policing and legal shielding and offer recommendations for involving local communities. Specifically, communities are urged to provide appropriate education, offer anti-poverty programmes, monitor tourist paedophiles, develop safety programmes for children, as well as avoid criminalisation of victims and facilitate the reintegration of those who have suffered through child sex tourism into the community. To achieve these goals, communities must be empowered and funded by governments. The foci of this chapter also provide insights into the community, societal and global social-ecological levels of analysis of the darkest side of sex in tourism.

The final chapter in the book focuses on how we can build on what we now know, from the works presented in this book and elsewhere, about sex in tourism. This requires us to look carefully at what we think we already know and to creatively speculate on what we still do not know. It is also important to consider, as this chapter does, how we can gather and analyse the data necessary to fill the gaps in our current knowledge and critically question existing knowledge. The myriad array of methods employed and methodological positions adopted by the authors of this book provide a useful starting point to this discussion. The chapter, and indeed the whole book, argues that charting a future research agenda for work in the field of sex in tourism is necessary not just, or even primarily, to facilitate the expansion of academic knowledge but to help those, both human and non-human, involved, either voluntarily or through coercion, in sex in tourism. It also seeks to help facilitate those who may wish to be involved in sex in tourism but are currently inhibited from doing so. In other words, the chapter talks to the need for academics to engage with society to help individuals and communities. In doing so, it explores the issue of whether academics should be activists or dispassionate adjudicators.

Conclusion

This edited book offers a collection of conceptual and empirical chapters, which utilise both qualitative and quantitative methodologies and offer diverse international coverage. While the existing body of knowledge on the links between sex and tourism tends to focus on the dark aspects, this book offers a more balanced and holistic view of sex in tourism by covering its light and dark sides as well as the variety of grey and ambiguous shades in between. Hence, this book contributes to the understanding of manifold pressing issues on the continuum between the light and dark sides of sex in tourism throughout the individual, interpersonal, community, society and global levels. Although the chapters in this book examine a wide array of issues, they all share a common core of seeking to understand a complex web of relationships between tourism, sexuality, wellbeing and social change in the contemporary world.

To conclude, this book advances the research agenda on sex in tourism and contributes translational recommendations for advocacy, practice and policy formulation. Nevertheless, much remains to be explored to fully understand the links between sex and tourism. The time is long overdue to set aside the social taboos and personal inhibitions and discomfort with exploring the roles of sex in tourism and *vice versa*. Thus, we hope that this edited book will serve as an invitation for increased research efforts devoted to investigating the kaleidoscopic complexity of sex in tourism.

References

AIEST (2020) (Immediate) future of tourism in the wake of relaxing SARS-CoV-2 shutdowns: Small steps to a temporary new 'normal'. See https://www.aiest.org/fileadmin/ablage/dokumente/Covid-Reports/Report_20200510_Tourism_Future.pdf (accessed July 2020).

Andriotis, K. (2010) Heterotopic erotic oases: The public nude beach experience. *Annals of Tourism Research* 37 (4), 1076–1096.

Apostolopoulos, Y., Sönmez, S. and Yu, C. (2002) HIV-risk behaviours of American spring break vacationers: A case of situational disinhibition? *International Journal of STD & AIDS* 13 (11), 733–743.

Arafat, Y., Mohamed, A., Kar, S., Sharma, P. and Kabir, R. (2020) Does COVID-19 pandemic affect sexual behaviour? A cross-sectional, cross-national online survey. *Psychiatry Research* doi:10.1016/j.psychres.2020.113050.

Aston, E. (2008) A fair trade?: Staging female sex tourism in 'Sugar mummies' and 'Trade'. *Contemporary Theatre Review* 18 (2), 180–192.

Attwood, F. and Smith, C. (2013) Leisure sex: More sex! Better sex! Sex is fucking brilliant! Sex, sex, sex, SEX. In T. Blackshaw (ed.) *Routledge Handbook of Leisure Studies* (pp. 325–342). London: Routledge.

Baggs, M. (2020) STIs: Lockdown 'once in a lifetime opportunity' for sexual health. *BBC News*. See https://www.bbc.com/news/newsbeat-52488892 (accessed July 2020).

Bandyopadhyay, R. (2013) A paradigm shift in sex tourism research. *Tourism Management Perspectives* 6, 1–2.

Barnett, M., Fleck, L., Marsden, A. and Martin, K. (2018) Sexual semantics: The meanings of sex, virginity, and abstinence for university students. *Personality and Individual Differences* 106, 203–208.

Bauer, T.G. and McKercher, B. (eds) (2003) *Sex and Tourism: Journeys of Romance, Love, and Lust*. New York: The Haworth Hospitality Press.

Belliveau, J. (2006) *Romance on the Road: Traveling Women who Love Foreign Men*. Baltimore: Beau Monde Press.

Bender, K. and Furman, R. (2004) The implications of sex tourism on men's social, psychological, and physical health. *The Qualitative Report* 9 (2), 176–191.

Berdychevsky, L. (2016) Antecedents of young women's sexual risk taking in tourist experiences. *Journal of Sex Research* 53 (8), 927–941.

Berdychevsky, L. (2017) Toward the tailoring of sexual health education messages for young women: A focus on tourist experiences. *Journal of Sex Research* 54 (9), 1171–1187.

Berdychevsky, L. (2018) 'Risky' leisure research on sex and violence: Innovation, impact, and impediments. *Leisure Sciences* 40 (1–2), 9–18.

Berdychevsky, L. and Carr, N. (2020a) Innovation and impact of sex as leisure in research and practice: Introduction to the special issue. *Leisure Sciences* 42 (3–4), 255–274.

Berdychevsky, L. and Carr, N. (eds) (2020b) Special issue: Innovation and impact of sex as leisure in research and practice. *Leisure Sciences* 42 (3–4), 255–410.

Berdychevsky, L. and Gibson, H. (2015a) Phenomenology of young women's sexual risk-taking in tourism. *Tourism Management* 46, 299–310.

Berdychevsky, L. and Gibson, H. (2015b) Sex and risk in young women's tourist experiences: Context, likelihood, and consequences. *Tourism Management* 51, 78–90.

Berdychevsky, L., Gibson, H. and Poria, Y. (2013a) Women's sexual behavior in tourism: Loosening the bridle. *Annals of Tourism Research* 42, 65–85.

Berdychevsky, L., Gibson, H. and Poria, Y. (2015) Inversions of sexual roles in women's tourist experiences: Mind, body, and language in sexual behaviour. *Leisure Studies* 34 (5), 513–528.

Berdychevsky, L., Poria, Y. and Uriely, N. (2013b) Sexual behavior in women's tourist experiences: Motivations, behaviors, and meanings. *Tourism Management* 35, 144–155.

Black, P. (2000) Sex and travel: Making the links. In S. Clift and S. Carter (eds) *Tourism and Sex: Culture, Commerce and Coercion* (pp. 250–264). London: Pinter.

Blackburn, A., Taylor, R. and Davis, J. (2011) Understanding the complexities of human trafficking and child sexual exploitation: The case of Southeast Asia. In F. Bernat (ed.) *Human sex Trafficking* (pp. 104–125). London: Routledge.

Bradley, N., DiPasquale, A., Dillabough, K. and Schneider, P. (2020) Health care practitioners' responsibility to address intimate partner violence related to the COVID-19 pandemic. *Canadian Medical Association Journal* doi:10.1503/cmaj.200634.

Brennan, D. (2004) *What's Love got to do with it?: Transnational Desires and Sex Tourism in the Dominican Republic.* Durham: Duke University Press.

Brents, B., Jackson, C. and Hausbeck, K. (2010) *The State of Sex: Tourism, Sex and Sin in the new American Heartland.* London: Routledge.

Bronfenbrenner, U. (1979) *The Ecology of Human Development: Experiments by Nature and Design.* Cambridge: Harvard University Press.

Bronfenbrenner, U. (1989) Ecological systems theory. In R. Vasta (ed.) *Annals of Child Development* (Vol. 6, pp. 187–249). London: Jessica Kingsley Publishers.

Brown, G., Ellard, J., Mooney-Somers, J., Prestage, G., Crawford, G. and Langdon, T. (2014) 'Living a life less ordinary': Exploring the experiences of Australian men who have acquired HIV overseas. *Sexual Health* 11 (6), 547–555.

Cabezas, A. (2004) Between love and money: Sex, tourism, and citizenship in Cuba and the Dominican Republic. *Journal of Women in Culture and Society* 29 (4), 987–1015.

Cabezas, A. (2009) *Economics of Desire: Sex Tourism in Cuba and the Dominican Republic.* Philadelphia: Temple University Press.

Carr, N. (2016) Sex in tourism: Reflections and potential future research directions. *Tourism Recreation Research* 41 (2), 188–198.

Carr, N. and Poria, Y. (eds) (2010) *Sex and the Sexual During People's Leisure and Tourism Experiences.* Newcastle: Cambridge Scholars Publishing.

Carter, S. and Clift, S. (2000) Tourism, international travel and sex: Themes and research. In S. Clift and S. Carter (eds) *Tourism and Sex: Culture, Commerce and Coercion* (pp. 1–22). London: Pinter.

Caudwell, J. and Browne, K. (2011) Special issue: Sexy spaces. *Leisure Studies* 30 (2), 117–265.

Centers for Disease Control and Prevention (2020) The social-ecological model: A framework for prevention. See https://www.cdc.gov/violenceprevention/publichealthissue/social-ecologicalmodel.html (accessed July 2020).

Dahles, H. and Bras, K. (1999) Entrepreneurs in romance: Tourism in Indonesia. *Annals of Tourism Research* 26 (2), 267–293.

de Vries, S. (2020) An analysis of law enforcement cooperation in child sex tourism cases involving Thailand and Canada, *Police Practice and Research*, DOI: 10.1080/15614263.2020.1724789.

DiClemente, R., Brown, J. and Davis, T. (2013) Determinants of health-related behaviors in adolescence. In W. O'Donohue, L. Benuto and L. Woodward Tolle (eds) *Handbook of Adolescent Health Psychology* (pp. 107–127). New York: Springer.

Diken, B. and Laustsen, C. (2004) Sea, sun, sex and the discontents of pleasure. *Tourist Studies* 4 (2), 99–114.

Eiser, J. and Ford, N. (1995) Sexual relationships on holiday: A case of situational disinhibition? *Journal of Social and Personal Relationships* 12 (3), 323–339.

Foucault, M. (1986) Of other spaces. *Diacritics* 16 (1), 22–27.

Frohlick, S. (2010) The sex of tourism? Bodies under suspicion in paradise. In J. Scott and T. Selwyn (eds) *Thinking Through Tourism* (pp. 51–70). Oxford: Berg.

Frohlick, S. (2013) *Sexuality, Women, and Tourism: Cross-border Desires Through Contemporary Travel*. London: Routledge.

Gössling, S., Scott, D. and Hall, C. (2020) Pandemics, tourism and global change: A rapid assessment of COVID-19. *Journal of Sustainable Tourism* doi:10.1080/09669582.2020.1758708.

Hall, C.M. (1992) Sex tourism in South-east Asia. In D. Harrison (ed.) *Tourism & the Less Developed Countries*. Belhaven Press. London, pp. 64–74.

Hall, C. (1996) Gender and economic interests in tourism prostitution: The nature, development and implications of sex tourism in South-east Asia. In Y. Apostolopoulos, S. Leivadi and A. Yiannakis (eds) *The Sociology of Tourism: Theoretical and Empirical Investigations* (pp. 265–280). London: Routledge.

Hall, C., Scott, D. and Gössling, S. (2020) Pandemics, transformations and tourism: Be careful what you wish for. *Tourism Geographies* doi:10.1080/14616688.2020.1759131.

Herold, E., Garcia, R. and DeMoya, T. (2001) Female tourists and beach boys: Romance or sex tourism? *Annals of Tourism Research* 28 (4), 978–997.

Hussein, J. (2020) COVID-19: What implications for sexual and reproductive health and rights globally? *Sexual and Reproductive Health Matters* 28 (1), 1–3.

Interagency Working Group on Sexual Exploitation of Children (2016) *Terminology Guidelines for the Protection of Children from Sexual Exploitation and Sexual Abuse*. ECPAT International. Thailand.

Jacobs, J. (2010) *Sex, Tourism and the Postcolonial Encounter: Landscapes of Longing in Egypt*. London: Routledge.

Jeffreys, S. (1999) Globalizing sexual exploitation: Sex tourism and the traffic in women. *Leisure Studies* 18 (3), 179–196.

Jeffreys, S. (2003) Sex tourism: do women do it too? *Leisure Studies* 22 (3), 223–238.

Jones, D. (2020) History in a crisis – lessons for COVID-19. *The New England Journal of Medicine* 382, 1681–1683.

Kashdan, T., Goodman, F., Stiksma, M., Milius, C. and McKnight (2019) Sexuality leads to boosts in mood and meaning in life with no evidence for the reverse direction: A daily diary investigation. *Emotion* 18 (4), 563–576.

Kelland, K. (2020) Sperm containing virus raises small risk of COVID-19 spread via sex: study. *Reuters Health News*. See https://www.reuters.com/article/us-health-coronavirus-semen-idUSKBN22J2E9?utm_camp (accessed July 2020).

Kempadoo, K. and Doezema, J. (eds) (1998) *Global Sex Workers: Rights, Resistance, and Redefinition*. London: Routledge.

Kibicho, W. (2009) *Sex Tourism in Africa: Kenya's Booming Industry*. London: Routledge.

Koops, T., Turner, D., Neutze, J. Briken, P. (2017) Child sex tourism – prevalence of and risk factors for its use in a German community sample. *BMC Public Health*, DOI 10.1186/s12889-017-4270-3.

Larios, S., Lozada, R., Strathdee, S., Semple, S., Roesch, S., Staines, H., Orozovich, P., Fraga, M., Amaro, H., de la Torre, A., Magis-Rodriguez, C. and Patterson, T. (2009) An exploration of contextual factors that influence HIV risk in female sex workers in Mexico: The social ecological model applied to HIV risk behaviors. *AIDS Care* 21 (10), 1335–1342.

Li, D., Jin, M., Bao, P., Zhao, W. and Zhang, S. (2020) Clinical characteristics and results of semen tests among men with coronavirus disease 2019. *Journal of the American Medical Association (JAMA) Network Open* 3 (5), e208–e292.

Littlewood, I. (2002) *Sultry Climates: Travel and Sex*. Cambridge: Da Capo Press.

Lucas, D. and Fox, J. (2019) The psychology of human sexuality. In R. Biswas-Diener and E. Diener (eds) *Noba Textbook Series: Psychology*. Champaign,IL: DEF publishers. See http://noba.to/9gsqhd6v (accessed July 2020).

MacKinnon, J. and Bremshey, A. (2020) Perspectives from a webinar: COVID-19 and sexual and reproductive health and rights. *Sexual and Reproductive Health Matters* doi:10.1080/26410397.2020.1763578.

Mattar, M. (2007) International child sex tourism: Scope of the problem and comparative case studies. The Protection Project. See http://www.protectionproject.org/wp-content/uploads/2010/09/JHU_Report.pdf (accessed July 2020).

McKercher, B. and Bauer, T. (2003) Conceptual framework of the nexus between tourism, romance, and sex. In T. Bauer and B. Mckercher (eds) *Sex and Tourism: Journeys of Romance, Love, and Lust* (pp. 3–18). New York: Haworth Hospitality Press.

Milhausen, R., Graham, C., Crosby, R., Ingram, H., Tetro, M., Bransfield, N., Sanders, S. and Yarber, W. (2020) 'What happens in Banff, stays in Banff': Contextual and interpersonal factors contributing to sexual risk taking among tourism workers. *Tourism Recreation Research* doi:10.1080/02508281.2019.1697549.

Oppermann, M. (1999) Sex tourism. *Annals of Tourism Research* 26 (2), 251–266.

Pan, F., Xiao, X., Guo, J., Song, Y., Li, H., Patel, D.P., Spivak, A., Alukal, J., Zhang, X., Xiong, C., Li, P. and Hotaling, J.M. (2020) No evidence of SARS-CoV-2 in semen of males recovering from COVID-19. *Fertility and Sterility* doi:10.1016/j.fertnstert.2020.04.024.

Panko, T. and George, B. (2012) Child sex tourism: Exploring the issues. *Criminal Justice Studies* 25 (1), 67–81.

Peng, L., Liu, J., Xu, W., Luo, Q., Deng, K., Lin, B. and Gao, Z. (2020) 2019 Novel Coronavirus can be detected in urine, blood, anal swabs and oropharyngeal swabs samples. *medRxiv, BMJ* doi:10.1101/2020.02.21.20026179.

Piscitelli, A. (2007) Shifting boundaries: Sex and money in the North-East of Brazil. *Sexualities* 10 (4), 489–500.

Pritchard, A. and Morgan, N. (2006) Hotel Babylon? Exploring hotels as liminal sites of transition and transgression. *Tourism Management* 27 (5), 762–772.

Pruitt, D. and LaFont, S. (1995) For love and money: Romance tourism in Jamaica. *Annals of Tourism Research* 22 (2), 422–440.

Purdy, C. (2020) How will COVID-19 affect global access to contraceptives – and what can we do about it? *DevEx*. See https://www.devex.com/news/opinion-how-will-covid-19-affect-global-access-to-contraceptives-and-what-can-we-do-about-it-96745 (accessed July 2020).

Qvarnström, A. and Oscarsson, M. (2014) Perceptions of HIV/STI prevention among young adults in Sweden who travel abroad: A qualitative study with focus group and individual interviews. *BMC Public Health* 14 (897), 891–898.

Raffaelli, M., Kang, H. and Guarini, T. (2012) Exploring the immigrant paradox in adolescent sexuality: An ecological perspective. In C. García Coll and A. Kerivan Marks (eds) *The Immigrant Paradox in Children and Adolescents: Is Becoming American a Developmental Risk?* (pp. 109–134). Washington, DC: American Psychological Association.

Ragsdale, K., Difranceisco, W. and Pinkerton, S. (2006) Where the boys are: Sexual expectations and behaviour among young women on holiday. *Culture, Health & Sexuality* 8 (2), 85–98.

Resnick, S. (2019) *Body-to-Body Intimacy: Transformation Through Love, Sex, and Neurobiology.* New York: Routledge.

Rivers-Moore, M. (2016) *Gringo Gulch: Sex, Tourism, and Social Mobility in Costa Rica.* Chicago: The University of Chicago Press.

Rosen, E. (2020) Will travel change after coronavirus? Here's what experts have to say. See https://www.travelandleisure.com/travel-tips/travel-trends/traveling-after-coronavirus (accessed July 2020).

Ryan, C. (2000) Sex tourism: Paradigms of confusion? In S. Clift and S. Carter (eds) *Tourism and Sex: Culture, Commerce and Coercion* (pp. 23–40). London: Pinter.

Ryan, C. and Hall, C. (2001) *Sex Tourism: Marginal People and Liminalities.* London: Routledge.

Ryan, C. and Kinder, R. (1996) Sex, tourism and sex tourism: Fulfilling similar needs? *Tourism Management* 17 (7), 507–518.

Ryan, C. and Martin, A. (2001) Tourists and strippers: Liminal theater. *Annals of Tourism Research* 28 (1), 140–163.

Sampson, H. (2020) The pandemic grounded cruise ships indefinitely. But bookings are still rolling in. *The Washington Post.* See https://www.washingtonpost.com/travel/2020/05/15/pandemic-grounded-cruise-ships-indefinitely-bookings-are-still-rolling/ (accessed July 2020).

Sánchez Taylor, J. (2001) Dollars are a girl's best friend? Female tourists' sexual behaviour in the Caribbean. *Sociology* 35 (3), 749–764.

Sánchez Taylor, J. (2006) Female sex tourism: A contradiction in terms? *Feminist Review* 83 (1), 42–59.

Schifter, J. (2007) *Mongers in Heaven: Sexual Tourism and HIV Risk in Costa Rica and in the United States.* Lanham, MD: University Press of America.

Selänniemi, T. (2003) On holiday in the liminoid playground: Place, time, and self in tourism. In T. Bauer and B. McKercher (eds) *Sex and Tourism: Journeys of Romance, Love, and Lust* (pp. 19–31). New York: The Haworth Hospitality Press.

Song, C., Wang, Y., Li, W., Bicheng Hu, B., Chen, G., Xia, P., Wang, W., Li, C., Diao, F., Hu, Z., Yang, X., Yao, B. and Liu, Y. (2020) Absence of 2019 novel coronavirus in semen and testes of COVID-19 patients. *Biology of Reproduction* doi:10.1093/biolre/ioaa050.

Sönmez, S., Apostolopoulos, Y., Yu, C.H., Yang, S., Mattilla, A. and Yu, L.C. (2006) Binge drinking and casual sex on spring break. *Annals of Tourism Research* 33 (4), 895–917.

Taub, A. (2020) A new Covid-19 crisis: Domestic abuse rises worldwide. *The Interpreter, New York Times.* See https://www.nytimes.com/2020/04/06/world/coronavirus-domestic-violence.html (accessed July 2020).

Tepelus, C. (2008) Social responsibility and innovation on trafficking and child sex tourism: Morphing of practice into sustainable tourism policies? *Tourism and Hospitality Research* 8 (2), 98–115.

Thomas, M. (2005) 'What happens in Tenerife stays in Tenerife': Understanding women's sexual behaviour on holiday. *Culture, Health & Sexuality* 7 (6), 571–584.

Tolman, D.L., Striepe, M. and Harmon, T. (2003) Gender matters: Constructing a model of adolescent sexual health. *Journal of Sex Research* 40 (1), 4–12.

Turner, V. (1974) Liminal to liminoid, in play, flow, and ritual: An essay in comparative symbology. *Rice University Studies* 60 (3), 53–92.

Vivancos, R., Abubakar, I. and Hunter, P.R. (2010) Foreign travel, casual sex, and sexually transmitted infections: Systematic review and meta-analysis. *International Journal of Infectious Diseases* 14, e842–e851.

Wang, Z. and Xu, X. (2020) scRNA-seq profiling of human testes reveals the presence of ACE2 receptor, a target for SARS-CoV-2 infection, in spermatogonia, Leydig and Sertoli Cells. *Cells* 9 (4), 920.

Weichselbaumer, D. (2012) Sex, romance and the carnivalesque between female tourists and Caribbean men. *Tourism Management* 33, 1220–1229.

Williams, E. (2013) *Sex Tourism in Bahia: Ambiguous Entanglements*. Urbana, IL: University of Illinois Press.

Wilson, M. and Chen, L. (2020) Travellers give wings to novel coronavirus (2019-nCoV). *Journal of Travel Medicine* doi:10.1093/jtm/taaa015.

World Travel and Tourism Council (WTTC) (2020) Latest research from WTTC shows a 50% increase in jobs at risk in travel and tourism. See https://www.wttc.org/about/media-centre/press-releases/press-releases/2020/latestresearch-from-wttc-shows-an-increase-in-jobs-at-risk-in-travel-and-tourism (accessed July 2020).

Yeoman, I. (2008) *Tomorrow's Tourist: Scenarios and Trends*. Amsterdam: Elsevier.

2 Ethical Debates on Sex Tourism, and Sex and Tourism

S. Emre Dilek and Neil Carr

Introduction

Ethics, or moral philosophy, seeks to address questions of morality using concepts such as good and bad, right and wrong, justice and virtue. Ethical enquiry aims to describe morality, criticise behaviour deemed to be immoral and, where necessary, provide reasons for making changes in behaviour. Accordingly, ethics normally relates to the morality of human or non-human animals, of individuals and groups, and even the morality of organisations, for example, business or corporate ethics (Bendel, 2015; Fennell, 2012; Singer, 1985), not only as subjects but also often as objects.

This chapter provides a critical discussion of the ethics of sex tourism as it applies to a variety of types of sex, involving, amongst others, women, children, animals and robots. In doing so, the chapter provides readers with the opportunity to reflect on not just society's ethical positions regarding sex tourism but also their own. Such reflection is important in its own right and also to help enable a fuller reading of the rest of the chapters in this book. While the chapter is focused on sex tourism, the meta-issues discussed equally apply to sex and tourism. The divide between sex tourism, and sex and tourism, as noted elsewhere (Carr, 2016; Poria & Carr, 2010) and as demonstrated in this chapter is blurred, reinforcing the idea that the points made in this chapter apply to sex and tourism and not just sex tourism.

Thoughts on the ethics of sex tourism

There are numerous ethical issues related to sex tourism because of its health, social and cultural implications. The trafficking of women and children for work in an increasingly globalised sex tourism industry is a significant issue for public health professionals, international law enforcement and human rights agencies, international labour monitors and groups concerned with women's and children's welfare (Cwikel & Hoban, 2005). Scholars state that the factors responsible for the worldwide increase in the abuse of human and non-human animals through sex tourism are as follows (Bender & Furman, 2004; Hale, 2015; Raymond, 2001; Taylor, 2010):

- The economic policies of globalisation.
- A more globalised sex tourism industry.
- Ever-increasing demand for sex tourism services.
- Gender inequality and women's economic dependence.
- The commodification of women's bodies as sexual objects.
- Child sexual abuse.
- Non-human animal sexual abuse.
- The stereotype that 'the exotic is erotic'.
- Restrictive immigration policies.

Sex tourism is an activity as it essentially refers to travel for the purpose of engaging in sexual activity with prostitutes, sex workers or those involved in servicing the desires of those participating in sex tourism, recognising the important distinctions between these three. The sex tourism industry provides a form of organised prostitution. In other words, sex tourism is not prostitution whereas prostitution is sex tourism, though, of course, prostitution is not restricted just to sex tourism. Two questions must be considered: 'Are there any conditions under which prostitution is ethically and morally acceptable?' and 'Can prostitution be seen as an ordinary job?' Kant describes prostitution as profiting from using one's person for another's sexual gratification. A person, Kant holds, cannot allow others to use his or her body sexually in exchange for money without losing his or her humanity and becoming an object (Kant, 1963: 165). This 'object' specifically relates to Kant's notion of an 'object of appetite'.

According to Herman's reading of Kant, sexual desire is initially directed towards an individual's body. She stated that 'insofar as one is moved by sexual appetite, it is the sex of the other that is the object of interest' (Herman, 2018: 55). Korsgaard agrees with Herman that what Kant finds problematic about sexual desire is the fact that it is directed towards an individual's body and self (Korsgaard, 1996). However, Korsgaard, unlike Herman, disagrees with what is involved in sexual objectification and sexual desire. She writes that 'Regarding someone as a sexual object is not like regarding him as an instrument or a tool, but more like regarding him as an aesthetic object. Viewed through the eyes of sexual desires another person is seen as something desirable and, therefore, inevitably possessable. To yield to that desire, to the extent it is really that desire to yield to, is to allow yourself to be possessed' (Korsgaard, 1996: 194–195). So, Herman and Korsgaard differ in their understanding of what is, for Kant, involved in the reduction from person (moral use) to object (immoral use) within a sexual context. While Herman argues that sexual desire is directed towards an individual's body and self in a way that reduces him/her to a mere tool for sexual purposes, Korsgaard, on the other hand, says sexual desire is directed towards an individual's body and self in a way that reduces him/her to an aesthetic object with affective price (Papadaki, 2019).

When it comes to ethical debates, there are five ethical frameworks that explain why sex tourism is immoral; utilitarianism, rights-based ethics, distributive justice ethics, virtue ethics and the ethic of care (Fennell, 2006). Utilitarianism, also known as 'the greatest happiness principle', emphasises the consequences of our actions. The term utility, the good to be maximised, was defined by John Stuart Mill as happiness or pleasure versus suffering or pain (Mill, 1863). When analysing the issues raised by sex tourism using the utilitarian approach, it is clear that sex tourism should be seen as morally wrong because the consequences of sex tourism bring suffering and pain to human and/or non-human animal sex slaves/workers. Another approach to the ethical debate surrounding sex tourism is the rights-based ethics. Theories of this kind are, by their nature, fundamentally deontological (focused on duties or rules) and are understood in contrast to consequentialist theories such as Utilitarianism (Alexander & Moore, 2007). The rights-based ethics perspective acknowledges the existence of moral rights, including rights to liberty and welfare. Rights are variously construed as legal, social or moral freedoms to act or refrain from acting, or entitlements to be acted upon or not acted upon. In this principle, sex tourism is morally wrong because of the violated rights of those people involved as providers because they have no other choice and because of the immorality of the industry. In addition, due to this industry many crimes arise which are against the principles of rights. These include crimes against humanity such as trafficking in women by syndicates that practice active, deceptive recruitment; economic abuse; rape; domestic violence; abusive, discriminatory conduct of raids by authorities, including arrests, maltreatment during raids or while in custody, and extortion for release; and anti-vagrancy laws which are unconstitutional.

Distributive justice ethics focuses on just outcomes and consequences and is concerned with what some would consider to be social issues, such as the allocation of goods in society (Blake, 2001). Since sex tourism violates those who advocate for distributive justice (whether female, male, child or non-human animal). It is also a violation of human rights, animal rights, human and non-human animal dignity and the common good. For this reason, sex tourism is immoral from the distributive justice perspective.

Virtue ethics was originally developed as an approach within normative ethics that emphasised virtues or moral character. This is in contrast to approaches that emphasised duties or rules (deontology) or the consequences of actions (utilitarianism) (Hursthouse, 1999). From the perspective of this paradigm, sex tourism is immoral because of the emphasis the paradigm places on good character and habits. The ethics of care, meanwhile, is a normative ethical theory developed by feminists in the second half of the twentieth century and is concerned with what determines whether actions are considered right or wrong (Larrabee, 2016). In this principle, people must be protected and express care in terms of special relations with each other with due protection. In this context, sex tourism providers are victimised by immoral actions where relationships are only used for the sake of sex activity and are devoid of intrinsic value. As a result, these people are treated without respect and dignity, which is immoral (Lovelock & Lovelock, 2013). An example of this is a child being engaged in child sex tourism where in care ethics, children are dependent upon parents, the elderly are dependent on their children or other caretakers, and people with disabilities have to rely on others. This points to the notion that every human being is essentially dependent on others. Each human being goes through a process of dependency according to their age, physical and/or mental condition. This stands in opposition to child sex tourism because here the children need to provide money for adults, sometimes including their family and parents who may be depended on them. In addition, most women are abused in sex tourism, a reality that is against the theory of ethic of care, where women must be treated fairly and reasonably (Larrabee, 2016; Truong, 1990). Sex tourism is morally wrong based on the ethics of care because prostitution itself involves immoral acts, such as the sexual abuse of children and non-human animals and sex trafficking.

On the other hand, most of the theoretical frameworks regarding violence against women are derived from feminist theories. Feminist theory is a broad, trans-disciplinary perspective that strives to understand roles, experiences and values of individuals on the basis of gender (Miriam, 2005). With regard to sexual exploitation, the feminist frame questions whether prostitution or any exchange of sex for something of financial value is or can be voluntary (Wilson & Butler, 2014). In this context, with regard to sexual exploitation or sex work, scholars and advocates are generally divided into two opposing theoretical camps (Gerassi, 2015). One group, usually referred to as neo-abolitionists, condemns all forms of voluntary and involuntary prostitution as a form of oppression against women. Neo-abolitionists, including radical and Marxist feminists, postulate that prostitution is never entirely consensual and cannot be regarded as such (Dobash & Dobash, 1979; Tiefenbrum, 2002). The other group, including many sex positivists (pro-sex work perspective), argues that a woman has a right to choose prostitution and other forms of sex work as a form of employment or even as a career (Ferguson et al., 1984; Russell & Garcia, 2014).

There is a need to link more clearly to the focus on ethical debates towards human-nonhuman animal sex tourism. Speciesism is the basis of the animal ethics debate regarding sex tourism. Defenders of animal rights see animal liberation as being directly linked to human liberation, and so use the concept of speciesism to refer to humans. The term speciesism is generally used to criticise a modern human-centred society. The concept was first used by Richard D. Ryder in 1970 to mirror the concept of racism (Ryder, 2010). In Singer's *Animal Liberation* (2002: 77), which is seen as an important milestone by animal rights advocates, the philosophical approach of 'animal experiments may be considered legitimate only if the intended benefits exceed the damages caused' can also be described as speciesist. Indeed, Francione criticises Singer at this point and expresses a different opinion that is opposed to the moral and ontological hierarchy (Francione & Charlton, 2015). Although the discussion that followed between animal welfare and animal rights theorists is worthy of note, it is the concept of speciesism alone that is addressed here. The legal protection provided to human beings but not to cats or dogs is described by some animal rights theorists as speciesism (Francione, 2007; Regan, 2004). From another point of view, the only reason for the societal preservation of a living being or the acceptance of its moral existence is that the society and the individuals (humans) living in that society take a speciesist attitude. In such a society, no other entity, save human beings, is considered equal in moral or legal terms. Although the views of Singer, Regan and Francione differ at certain points, they all agree on improving the existing moral conditions of animals, which is the important point where animal rights and animal welfare perspectives overlap. The outcome of these theoretical views is that animals are commoditised in almost every sector, including sex tourism, as their only value is the use and exchange value (i.e. economic value) ascribed to them by humans. This suggests that the solution against commodification of animals may be found not only in the general sense of animal rights or animal welfare debates but also in an ethical discussion within the scope of meta-production areas. In other words, continuing the discussion of the moral status, rights and welfare of animals with a philosophical understanding of inductive rather than deductive reasoning can ensure that more concrete steps can be taken on behalf of animals. On this topic, Carr (2014) looks at our relationship with dogs in the leisure experience from a historical, social and psychological perspective and discusses the sexual relations between people and dogs under the headings of bestiality and zoophilia. He stated that in the case of bestiality the rights of the animal are totally ignored and has some harsh words for those engaged in such practices: 'demeaning the dignity of the dog, even if the dog gives no thought to this, is an act of cruelty' (Carr, 2014: 77). At least in the minds of its participants, zoophilia is differentiated from bestiality. It is supposed to indicate an animal-human relationship that is more than just sexual, including an emotional component as well (Beetz, 2005; Miletski, 2002). This attempted differentiation between zoophilia and bestiality is rejected by Carr (2014). Carr (2014) emphasises that there do not need to be specific separate laws against bestiality or zoophilia because the focus needs to be on the welfare and rights of the animal, including dogs, and any prohibition against sexual acts by humans with animal needs to be grounded in animal welfare laws. This places the emphasis on animal-centric thinking rather than human-centric disgust at the thought of sexual contact between humans and animals.

Do any people engage in sex tourism seeking sexual contact with and/or gratification from animals? Evidence about the scale of human-animal sex demand and provisioning is currently very limited. Whether a lack of more detailed data is a consequence of a lack of demand/participation or a lack of willingness among people to study this field is currently unkown. However, there are certainly significant barriers facing anyone looking to find data on this topic (Carr, 2014). Despite this, there is clear evidence of the existence of bestiality and zoophilia practices. Given the geographical diversity regarding the legality of these practices, it can be argued that a portion, albeit of currently unknown scale, of the sex tourism industry is associated with the provision of sex with animals for human tourists. To assume otherwise is to potentially condemn animals to suffering, to leave them in the dark. This, of course, is an ethically dubious stance in its own right.

As well as these ethical discussions concerning human-human and human-non-human sex tourism, attention has recently been drawn to the variety of ethical and philosophical issues raised by the relationships between humans and new technological sex tools, such as robots, dolls and toys. As with other aspects of sex, the links between sex and technological sex tools is not restricted to tourism, but they are an increasing part of the sex tourism experience and associated industry. In particular, Yeoman and Mars (2012) have talked about the position of sex robots in sex tourism. The growth of interactive sexual experiences on the internet, something that may have been boosted by the COVID-19 pandemic, sits at a fluid boundary between the world of the *real* and hyper-real, and between tourism and the non-tourism experience. The internet, like tourism, offers a liminal space to escape to (Waskul, 2005).

Sex robots are different from sex toys and sex dolls. While sex toys do not take a humanoid form, sex dolls and robots do. However, sex dolls are inanimate, passive and unintelligent. They are also low-level anthropomorphic (at least just of a low class by today's standards) while sex robots, on the other hand, are high-level anthropomorphic and humanlike in behaviour (Danaher & McArthur, 2017). This is where the most interesting and pressing philosophical and ethical issues have arisen. Philosophers of technology, technologists and Silicon Valley entrepreneurs are now proposing that anthropomorphic robots should have rights (Richardson, 2016a). This suggests that we may be on the threshold of a new dawn of human-machine equivalence (Gunkel, 2012; Lin *et al.*, 2011).

In his book, entitled '*Love + Sex with Robots*', David Levy proposes a future of human-robot relations based on the kinds of exchanges that take place in the sex industry (Levy, 2007: 194). While Levy (2007) states that there is nothing wrong with using electronic devices, and therefore hiring or buying a sex robot to create sexual satisfaction, Richardson (2016a) argues that people's experiences of sex with robots contribute to a disconnect between sex and humanity and exacerbate the existing issues of objectification and abuse. In this context, Sharkey *et al.* (2017) warn that there are a number of ethical implications surrounding the use of sex robots. One of the most controversial areas in which people are proposing the use of sex robots is in the prevention of sex crimes such as rape (Sharkey *et al.*, 2017). 'The idea is robots would resist your sexual advances so that you could rape them', said Sharkey *et al.* (2017). 'Some people say it's better they rape robots than rape real people. There are other people saying this would just encourage rapists more' (Shead, 2017: 1).

Jelili and Tijani (2012), two Muslim scholars, present an Islamic perspective on sex robots, indicating that sex with robots is unethical, immoral and uncultured. Sullins (2012) and Whitby (2011) state that sex with robots is fictive, may decrease our ability to interact with other humans, and that individuals who consort with robots may become increasingly socially isolated. The reason for isolation, Richardson (2016b: 291) argues, is that 'intimate relations with robots will lead to more isolation for the human race, because robots are not able to meet the species specific sociality of human beings, only other humans can do that'. Building on this, Turkle (2011) suggests that real sexual relationships could become overwhelming because relations with robots are easier. For similar reasons, Snell (1997) thinks that sex with robots could become addictive. If these authors are right, the possibly addictive focus on human-robot relationships could isolate users from human society.

When it comes to sex in cyberspace, that is a social interaction of at least two people engaging in real time digital messages or live camera feed conversations to become sexually aroused and satisfied, the moral implications involved are numerous. Hamelink (2000) and Ronquillo (2008: 3) discussed ethics in their studies and stated that sex in cyberspace 'a) demarginalises the sexual self, b) alters the essence of sexuality from being a gift to being a commodity, c) debases the human person as an embodied spirit, d) corrupts the way one sees the body phenomenon, e) prevents the person from seeing deeper the spirituality entailed in the body and in sex, and f) degenerates values'. It is clear that there are different opinions concerning the moral issues surrounding the use of robots for intimate relations. It is the responsibility of governments and the wider international community to determine what is publicly and morally acceptable before stepping into regulatory territory (Sharkey *et al.*, 2017).

Conclusions

This chapter has provided a discussion of ethics in relation to multiple facets of sex tourism, highlighting the complexities and positionalities of ethics. While the chapter has focused primarily on sex tourism it is clear that the meta-issues discussed are also applicable to sex and tourism. What becomes clear through this chapter is that there are multiple ethical concerns related to virtually all types of sex tourism. These concerns feed into discussions of human and non-human welfare and rights, and humans obligations to those impacted and potentially impacted by sex and tourism, and sex tourism. Yet it is also clearly important to step back from these discussions of ethics to critically assess the issue of deviance (see, for example, work by Rojek (2000, 1999) and Franklin-Reible (2006) for a critique of the conceptualisation of deviance). This is necessary when we recognise that ethics are inherently linked, especially in relation to sex, to the concept of deviance. In this context, deviance is associated with ethically unacceptable desires and behaviour, and vice versa. However, it is recognised that as a socio-cultural construct, deviance is defined by those in 'power' and is also, therefore, liable to change both temporally and spatially. On the surface, it may seem irresponsible to question definitions of deviance and, in doing so, to potentially undermine what we define as ethical and therefore how we construct the rights and welfare of individuals and our obligations towards them. However, if we utilise the example of homosexuality then we can begin to show why critically reflecting on, rather than simply uncritically accepting, definitions of deviance and ethics is crucial. We do not have to go that far back in history to find a time when homosexuality was illegal in virtually all parts of the world. Indeed, it still is illegal in many countries, with the death penalty associated with it in 70 nations (e.g. Brunei, Iran, Saudi Arabia, Sudan and Yemen). When and where homosexuality is/was illegal it was constructed as a deviant behaviour where the ethical duty of society was/is to prevent it for the wellbeing of society and the individuals living within it. Today, in those countries that have enshrined the rights of homosexuals in law it is no longer portrayed as deviant, even where some segments of society continue to resist this change. In the process, ethics towards homosexuals have totally changed. What this example shows is that definitions of ethics and deviance are mutable and pliable rather than fixed and unchanging. Furthermore, it is clear that change only occurs through significant effort and contestation. Another example of this is linked directly to the sex industry. In New Zealand, prostitution was decriminalised in 2003. Prior to this, as an illegal activity, prostitution was socially and culturally constructed as being deviant and prostitutes as being deviant individuals. This coloured the ethics applied to prostitutes in New Zealand where they were treated as criminals. Today, an ethics of care position dominants New Zealand's handling of prostitutes, where the law and its enforcement agencies work hand in hand with the New Zealand Prostitutes Collective to ensure the welfare and wellbeing of prostitutes.

What does this all mean for how we think about ethics in relation to sex and tourism, and sex tourism? As noted earlier, we need to be reflexively critical rather than simply unthinkingly assign ethical positions and perspectives. In other words, it is important to consider ethical issues and then how we deal with ensuring the rights and welfare of those impacted by sex and tourism, and sex tourism with our eyes wide open. To do so requires us to reflect upon our own positionality and how that influences our own ethical perspectives. Doing so allows us to be aware of how this positionality can colour our reading of those involved, voluntarily or otherwise, in sex tourism, and sex and tourism. Opening our eyes and being critical of all we see is the best way to move on from this chapter to engage with all of the varied material presented in the rest of this book.

It is also important to remember that just as sex tourism, and sex in tourism, are part of a wider sex industry and sexual reality, the ethical discussions within this chapter apply beyond the boundaries of tourism. In this way, as in much work within the tourism studies field, tourism can be utilised as a lens to look at broad social issues, sex in this case. Yet, at the same time, it is important to remember that the specific lens (i.e. tourism) matters because of the important nuanced realities that it imposes. In particular, this speaks to the liminal/liminoid nature of the tourism experience (Berdychevsky et al., 2015).

References

Alexander, L. and Moore, M. (2007) Deontological ethics. In E.N. Zalta (ed.) *The Stanford Encyclopedia of Philosophy*. Stanford, CA: Metaphysics Research Lab, Center for the Study of Language and Information, Stanford University. See https://plato.stanford.edu/archives/fall2008/entries/ethics-deontological/ (accessed July 2020).

Beetz, A. (2005) New insights into bestiality and zoophilia. Beetz, A. and Podberscek, A. (eds) *Bestiality and Zoophilia: Sexual Relations with Animals* (pp. 98–119). West Lafayette, Indiana. Purdue University Press.

Bendel, O. (2015) Surgical, therapeutic, nursing and sex robots in machine and information ethics. In S.P. van Rysewyk and M. Pontier (eds) *Machine Medical Ethics Intelligent Systems, Control and Automation: Science and Engineering* (pp. 17–32). Cham: Springer International Publishing.

Bender, K. and Furman, R. (2004) The implications of sex tourism on mens' social, psychological, and physical health. *The Qualitative Report* 9 (2), 176–191.

Berdychevsky, L., Gibson, H.J. and Poria, Y. (2015) Inversions of sexual roles in women's tourist experiences: Mind, body, and language in sexual behaviour. *Leisure Studies* 34 (5), 513–528.

Blake, M. (2001) Distributive justice, state coercion, and autonomy. *Philosophy & Public Affairs* 30 (3), 257–296.

Carr, N. (2014) *Dogs in the Leisure Experience*. Wallingford: CABI.

Carr, N. (2016) Sex in tourism: Reflections from a dark corner of tourism studies. *Tourism Recreation Research* 41 (2), 188–198.

Cwikel, J. and Hoban, E. (2005) Contentious issues in research on trafficked women working in the sex industry: Study design, ethics, and methodology. *Journal of Sex Research* 42 (4), 306–316.

Danaher, J. and McArthur, N. (eds) (2017) *Robot Sex: Social and Ethical Implications*. London: MIT Press.

Dobash, R.E. and Dobash, R. (1979) *Violence against Wives: A Case against the Patriarchy*. New York, NY: Free Press.

Fennell, D.A. (2006) *Tourism Ethics*. Clevedon: Channel View Publications.

Fennell, D.A. (2012) *Tourism and Animal Ethics*. London: Routledge.

Ferguson, A., Philipson, I., Diamond, I., Quinby, L., Vance, C.S. and Snitow, A.B. (1984) Forum: The feminist sexuality debates. *Signs* 10 (1), 106–135.

Francione, G.L. (2007) *Introduction to Animal Rights: Your Child or the Dog?* Philadelphia: Temple University Press.

Francione, G.L. and Charlton, A. (2015) *Animal Rights: The Abolitionist Approach*. Newark: Exempla Press.

Franklin-Reible, H. (2006) Deviant leisure: Uncovering the 'goods' in transgressive behaviour. *Leisure/Loisir* 30 (1), 55–71.

Gerassi, L. (2015) A heated debate: Theoretical perspectives of sexual exploitation and sex work. *Journal of Sociology and Social Welfare* 42 (4), 79–100.

Gunkel, D.J. (2012) 'A vindication of rights of machines' in the machine question: AI, ethics and moral responsibility. In D.J. Gunkel, J.J. Bryson and S. Torrance (eds) *Proceedings of AISB/IACAP World Congress 2012 Birmingham* (pp. 46–53). Bath: The Society for the Study of Artificial Intelligence and Simulation of Behaviour.

Hale, T. (2015) The horrifying story of a sex slave orangutan. *IFL Science*. See http://www.iflscience.com/plants-and-animals/shocking-story-sex-slave-orangutan-and-her-rescue/ (accessed July 2020).

Hamelink, C.J. (2000) *The Ethics of Cyberspace*. Thousand Oaks, CA: Sage Publications.

Herman, B. (2018) Could it be worth thinking about Kant on sex and marriage? In L. Anthony (ed.) *A Mind of One's Own* (pp. 53–72). London: Routledge.

Hursthouse, R. (1999) *On Virtue Ethics*. Oxford: Oxford University Press.

Jelili, A.Y. and Tijani, I.B. (2012) Ethical and legal implications of sex robot: An Islamic perspective. *OIDA International Journal of Sustainable Development* 3, 19–28.

Kant, I. (1963) *Lectures on Ethics* (L. Infield, trans.). New York, NY: Harper & Row Publishers (original work published 1920).

Korsgaard, C.M. (1996) *Creating the Kingdom of Ends*. Cambridge: Cambridge University Press.

Larrabee, M.J. (2016) *An Ethic of Care: Feminist and Interdisciplinary Perspectives*. London and New York: Routledge.

Levy, D. (2007) *Love + Sex with Robots: The Evolution of Human-Robot Relationships*. New York, NY: Harper.

Lin, P., Abney, K. and Bekey, G.A. (2011). *Robot Ethics: The Ethical and Social Implications of Robotics*. Cambridge, MA: MIT Press.

Lovelock, J. and Lovelock, K. (2013) *The Ethics of Tourism: Critical and Applied Perspectives*. New York, NY: Routledge.

Miletski, H. (2002) *Understanding Bestiality & Zoophilia*. Bethesda, MD: East-West Publishing.

Mill, J.S. (1863) *Utilitarianism*. London: Parker, Son and Bourn.

Miriam, K. (2005) Stopping the traffic in women: Power, agency and abolition in feminist debates over sex-trafficking. *Journal of Social Philosophy* 36 (1), 1–17.

Papadaki, L. (2019) *Kantian Perspectives on Issues in Ethics and Bioethics*. Newcastle: Cambridge Scholars Publishing.

Poria, Y. and Carr, N. (2010) Conclusion: What have we done – where should we go? In N. Carr and Y. Poria (eds) *Sex and the Sexual during People's Leisure and Tourism Experiences* (pp. 181–196). Newcastle: Cambridge Scholars Publishing.

Raymond, J.G. (2001) A comparative study of women trafficked in the migration process: Patterns, profiles and health consequences of sexual exploitation in five countries (Indonesia, the Philippines, Thailand, Venezuela and the United States). *MINCAVA*. See www.mincava.umn.edu/traffick.asp (accessed July 2020).

Regan, T. (2004) *Empty Cages: Facing the Challenge of Animal Rights*. Oxford: Rowman and Littlefield Publishing.

Richardson, K. (2016a) Slavery, the prostituted, and the rights of machines: Sex robot matter. *IEEE Technology and Society* 35 (2), 46–53

Richardson, K. (2016b) The asymmetrical 'relationship': Parallels between prostitution and the development of sex robots. *SIGCAS Computers and Society* 45 (3), 290–293.

Rojek, C. (1999) Deviant leisure: The dark side of free-time activity. In E.L. Jackson and T.L. Burton (eds) *Leisure Studies: Prospects for the Twenty-First Century* (pp. 81–96). State College, PA: Venture.

Rojek, C. (2000) *Leisure and Culture*. Basingstoke: Palgrave.

Ronquillo, C.G. (2008) The challenge of cybersex to ethics. *East Asian Pastoral Review* 45 (3). See http://www.eapi.org.ph/resources/eapr/east-asian-pastoral-review-2008/volume-45-2008-number-3/the-challenge-of-cybersex-to-ethics (accessed June 2019).

Russell, T. and Garcia, A. (2014) Former sex worker & activist Maggie McNeill on why we should decriminalize prostitution: 'This is not what feminism was supposed to be'. See http://reason.com/reasontv/2014/07/14/former-sex-worker-activist-maggie-mcneil (accessed October 2019).

Ryder, R.D. (2010) Speciesism again: The original leaflet. *Critical Society* 2, 1–2.

Sharkey, N., van Wynsberghe, A., Robbins, S. and Hancock, E. (2017) Our sexual future with robots. *Foundation for responsible robotics*. See http://responsible-robotics-myxf6pn3xr.netdna-ssl.com/wp-content/uploads/2017/11/FRR-Consultation-Report-Our-Sexual-Future-with-robots-1-1.pdf (accessed July 2018).

Shead, S. (2017) A new report showed all the different ways that sex robots could be used in society, *Businessinsider*. See https://www.businessinsider.com/our-future-with-sex-robots-noel-sharkey-report-2017-7 (accessed June 2019).

Singer, P. (1985) Ethics and the new animal liberation movement. In P. Singer (ed.) *Defense of Animals* (pp. 1–10). New York, NY: Basil Blackwell.

Singer, P. (2002) *Animal Liberation* (3rd edn). New York, NY: HaperCollins Publisher.

Snell, J.C. (1997) Impacts of robotic sex. *The Futurist* 31 (4), 32.

Sullins J.P. (2012) Robots, love, and sex: The ethics of building a love machine. *IEEE Transactions on Affective Computing* 3 (4), 398–409.

Taylor, J.S. (2010) Sex tourism and inequalities. In S. Cole and N. Morgan (eds) *Tourism and Inequality: Problems and Prospects* (pp. 49–66). Wallingford: CABI.

Tiefenbrum, S. (2002) The Saga of Susannah – A US remedy for sex trafficking in women: The Victims of trafficking and violence protection act of 2000. *Utah Law Review* 107 (1), 107–175.

Truong, T.D. (1990) *Sex, Money and Morality: Prostitution and Tourism in South East Asia*. London: ZED Books.

Turkle, S. (2011) *Alone Together: Why we Expect More from Technology and Less from Each Other*. New York: Basic Books.

Waskul, D. (2005) Ekstasis and the internet: Liminality and computermediated communication. *New Media & Society* 7 (1), 47–63.

Whitby, B. (2011) Do you want a robot lover? The ethics of caring technologies. In P. Lin, K. Abney and G.A. Bekey (eds) *Robot Ethics: The Ethical and Social Implications of Robotics* (pp. 233–248). Cambridge, MA: MIT Press.

Wilson, B. and Butler, L.D. (2014) Running a gauntlet: A review of victimization and violence in the pre-entry, post-entry, and peri-/post-exit periods of commercial sexual exploitation. *Psychological Trauma: Theory, Research, Practice, and Policy* 6 (5), 494–504.

Yeoman, I. and Mars, M. (2012) Robots, men and sex tourism. *Futures* 44 (4), 365–371.

Part 1: The Light Side of Sex in Tourism: Affects and Effects of the Diverse Sexual Encounters in Tourism

3 Gender Differences and Similarities in the Perceptions of and Experiences with Sex and Sexual Risk Taking in Tourism

Liza Berdychevsky

Introduction

It is being increasingly recognised that attention to gender considerations contributes to better science, improves the effectiveness of policies and planning and helps address various gender and health inequities, yet there is still a limited uptake of gender-specific reporting of research findings (Gahagan *et al.*, 2015). Sexual behaviour and health comprise one of the areas where gender-specific research attention is particularly urgent due to the influence of sexual double standards that set divergent expectations and norms of sexual behaviour for men and women (Bordini & Sperb, 2013; Hensman Kettrey, 2016; Maas *et al.*, 2015). Sexual double standards have been found to have detrimental influences on people's health and wellbeing (Higgins & Browne, 2008; Impett & Peplau, 2003; Tolman *et al.*, 2003). However, sexual double standards are context-specific, meaning that their capacity to shape sexual behaviour varies across sociocultural contexts based on cultural and racial/ethnic differences, social class, types of relationship, levels of religiosity and specific subcultures/environments, such as college campuses (Bradshaw *et al.*, 2010; Crawford & Popp, 2003; Guo, 2019; Muehlenhard *et al.*, 2015).

Tourism literature offers evidence that sexual double standards are more relaxed in some tourism contexts, offering relative freedom from everyday sexual scripts (Berdychevsky, 2016; Thomas, 2005). Thus, exploring gender differences and similarities in sexual experiences and perceptions, with a particular focus on tourist experiences, might offer meaningful insights into the context-specific influences of sexual double standards and the uniqueness of various tourism contexts as arenas for sexual exploration and risk taking (Berdychevsky *et al.*, 2013b). Moreover, gender-specific understanding of sexual behaviour and risk taking in tourism should offer valuable recommendations for targeted sexual health education programmes and policies in general and tourists in particular (Berdychevsky, 2017a; Gahagan *et al.*, 2015; Maas *et al.*, 2015).

Despite this important potential, non-commercial sex and sexual risk taking in tourism and other leisure contexts remain relatively ignored, poorly understood and heavily stereotyped (Berdychevsky, 2018; Carr, 2016), while gender differences in these areas have been particularly neglected. Some research of women's sexual behaviour and risk taking in tourism has been conducted (cf. Berdychevsky, 2017b; Berdychevsky *et al.*, 2013a; Ragsdale *et al.*, 2006), but a systematic and nuanced gender comparison of sexual perceptions and experiences in tourism is still lacking. Given that in heterosexual relationships, women's and men's sexual behaviours are interdependent, studies investigating both genders' sexual attitudes and comportment are better positioned to clarify these phenomena (Maas *et al.*, 2015). Thus, the purpose of this study was to investigate gender differences and similarities in the perceptions of and experiences with sex and sexual risk taking in tourism.

Literature Review

This study is positioned at the nexus of sexual behaviour, gender and tourism. Hence, it is important to provide an overview of gendered sexual double standards and their influences on sexual behaviour and wellbeing in general, and then to zoom into what is currently known about non-commercial sex and sexual risk taking in tourism.

Gender and sexual double standards

Gender has been defined as socially constructed roles associated with biological sex, as cultural and historical expectations regarding performing femininity and masculinity and as a system of power where men have more power compared to women (Muehlenhard *et al.*, 2003). Gender roles are culturally and discursively constructed where the socially expected roles concerning sexuality and sexual behaviour are perpetuated via repetitive performative acts (Butler, 1990). Gender shapes sexual behaviour because men and women often adopt different socially sanctioned patterns of sexual comportment and may also experience and understand the same sexual activity differently (Maas *et al.*, 2015; McCabe *et al.*, 2010).

Sexual double standards are gendered social constructions that present women with more restrictive sexual scripts compared to men and set gender-specific standards of admissible sexual permissiveness (Eaton & Rose, 2011; Jonason & Fisher, 2009; McCabe *et al.*, 2010; Muehlenhard *et al.*, 2015). Accordingly, men are often praised for sexual achievements (or even castigated for a lack thereof), while single, sexually active women run the risk of compromising their reputations and being labelled 'sluts' – a widespread derogatory epithet used to control women's sexual behaviour uncompliant with the double standards (Attwood, 2007). Furthermore, women are stereotypically faced with conflicting ideals reflected in the Madonna-whore dichotomy, whereby they are paradoxically encouraged to be simultaneously sexually innocent, pure and inactive beyond committed relationships, on the one hand, as well as sexy, seductive and available, on the other hand (Crawford & Popp, 2003; Tolman, 2012).

The notions of gender inequality and power asymmetry associated with sexual double standards have also gained some research attention (Hensman Kettrey, 2016; Petersen & Hyde, 2011). This asymmetry grants men more opportunities for autonomy, pleasure and sexual self-determination compared to women (Blanc, 2001). Conversely, sexual double standards put women in a position of greater compliance, rendering them vulnerable to sexual risk taking (e.g. unprotected sex due a lack of confidence in negotiating safer sex), sexual violence, social disapproval and traumatic emotional experiences (Hensman Kettrey, 2016; Higgins & Browne, 2008; Impett & Peplau, 2003; Lefkowitz *et al.*, 2014). This power asymmetry negatively affects women's mental health, as well as their sexual wellbeing, agency and subjectivity (Crawford & Popp, 2003; Grello *et al.*, 2006; Tolman, 2012; Tolman *et al.*, 2003). Adolescents and young adults are particularly vulnerable to the detrimental impacts of sexual double standards because these life stages are associated with the ambivalence and messiness of developing a self-understanding concerning their changing bodies, an array of sexual feelings and relationships, as well as sexual confidence and agency (Maas *et al.*, 2015; Tolman, 2012).

While sexual double standards are fluid and constantly evolving (Muehlenhard *et al.*, 2015), gender-typed dating and sexual practices continue to be perpetuated and institutionalised both at the level of cultural scripts (e.g. general expectations and beliefs) and interpersonal scripts (e.g. actual interpersonal behaviours and emotions) (Eaton & Rose, 2011; Hensman Kettrey, 2016). Nevertheless, while people's general perceptions of sexuality at the cultural level are frequently aligned with traditional gender stereotypes and sexual scripts, their personal experiences often elicit multiple contradictions and complexities, resulting in a wide range of experiences and interpretations (McCabe *et al.*, 2010). Moreover, sexual double standards are local constructions, and their potency to affect sexual behaviour varies from one context to another (Bradshaw *et al.*, 2010; Crawford & Popp, 2003; Guo, 2019; Muehlenhard *et al.*, 2015), leaving more room for sexual freedom and experimentation in certain contexts (e.g. in tourist experiences) regardless of gender (Berdychevsky, 2016; Thomas, 2005). Investigating gender similarities and differences in sexual perceptions and behaviour in such contexts, with potentially diminished power of sexual double standards, is important because it has been found that egalitarian sexual attitudes and scripts are associated with increased sexual satisfaction for both genders and with the development of a sense of agency and empowerment for women (Hensman Kettrey, 2016; Muehlenhard *et al.*, 2003; Tolman, 2012).

Sex and sexual risk taking in tourism

Tourism has been associated with the spread of sexually transmitted infections (STIs) throughout the world (Brown *et al.*, 2014; Qvarnström & Oscarsson, 2014; Rogstad, 2019; Vivancos *et al.*, 2010). This association is attributed to the fact that many tourist experiences offer opportunities for sexual mixing (including unprotected, casual sex), which is a potential cause of morbidity (Briggs & Tutenges, 2014; Matteelli *et al.*, 2013; McNulty *et al.*, 2010). Young tourists are considered to be a high-risk group in this respect because many of them have unprotected sex with new partner(s) while travelling (Davies *et al.*, 2011; Lewis & de Wildt, 2016).

Sexual risk taking in tourism is facilitated by the perceived anonymity in the holiday space, a feeling of situational disinhibition, suspension of ordinary rules, subdued influence of sexual double standards, fun-seeking vacation/party mentality, availability of alcohol and drugs, perception of the tourism atmosphere as transient/temporary and permissive and a sense that time is being compressed into a present moment (Apostolopoulos *et al.*, 2002; Berdychevsky, 2016; Berdychevsky & Gibson, 2015b; Eiser & Ford, 1995; Milhausen *et al.*, 2020; Rogstad, 2019; Sönmez *et al.*, 2013). Hence, tourism contexts have been conceptualised as contra-normative settings, heterotopias (i.e. counter-sites for inversion and transgression of ordinary rules) and liminal/liminoid environments (i.e. places/times associated with ambiguity and a sense of detachment from everyday social order) allowing and encouraging various sexual transgressions, resistance to everyday sexual norms and rules and reversals of sexual double standards (Andriotis, 2010; Apostolopoulos *et al.*, 2002; Berdychevsky *et al.*, 2015).

Some tourist experiences have been conceptualised as liminoid fourfold transitions from (1) the sense of time/everyday schedule to the timelessness of non-regimented tourist experiences, (2) place/home to placelessness of unfamiliar tourist destinations, (3) mind to mindlessness encouraging individuals to act out of character and (4) suppressed senses to increased awareness of embodiment, sensuality and sexuality (Berdychevsky et al., 2013a; Selänniemi, 2003). These changes contribute to a temporary liminoid sense of being where a person feels out of time, out of place and out of mind, which facilitates sexual transgressions and wish fulfilment (Pritchard & Morgan, 2006). Consequently, these transitions, combined with perceived anonymity, tolerance and increased alcohol consumption and drug use, turn some tourist experiences and destinations into ultimate playgrounds for sexual exploration and risk taking in terms of the choice of sexual partners, nature of the sexual experiences, sexual protection-related decisions and the amount of time it takes to progress from initial acquaintance to sexual encounter (Berdychevsky et al., 2013a; Briggs & Tutenges, 2014; Briggs et al., 2011; Guilamo-Ramos et al., 2015; McKercher & Bauer, 2003; Milhausen et al., 2020; Ragsdale et al., 2006; Thomas, 2005; Sönmez et al., 2006, 2013).

Sexual risk taking in tourism offers both benefits and negative consequences. On the one hand, sexual exploration in anonymous and permissive tourism contexts may offer an opportunity to experiment with restrictive sexual scripts (especially for women) without necessarily jeopardising reputation. This may be a source of empowerment, excitement, maturity, conquest, freedom, confidence and meaningful reappraisals of self and society (Berdychevsky et al., 2015; Berdychevsky et al., 2013b; Falconer, 2011; Maticka-Tyndale & Herold, 1997; Mewhinney et al., 1995; Thomas, 2005). On the other hand, the potential ramifications of sexual risk taking for health and wellbeing are manifold, including sexual, physical, mental, emotional and social consequences (Berdychevsky & Gibson, 2015a, 2015c; Qvarnström & Oscarsson, 2014; Vivancos et al., 2010).

The understanding of sex and sexual risk taking in tourism is further complicated by the fact that there are different kinds of sexual risk taking activities and various types of sexual risk-takers that vary by socio-demographic and psychological characteristics (Berdychevsky, 2017b). Some research on non-commercial sexual behaviour and risk taking in tourism has been conducted with women (cf. Berdychevsky, 2016, 2017b; Berdychevsky et al., 2013a; Ragsdale et al., 2006; Thomas, 2005). However, a similar focus on men and a systematic gender comparison of sexual risk perceptions and experiences in tourism are missing. Consequently, we have a very limited understanding of sexual risk taking in tourism, as well as of the gender differences and similarities in this respect. This is problematic because a gender-sensitive approach is key to sex and health research in general, and in tourism in particular (Berdychevsky, 2017a; Maas et al., 2015). This gap is further exacerbated by the pressing need to further clarify sexual risk taking in tourism to benefit both research and practice (Berdychevsky, 2018; Milhausen *et al.*, 2020; Rogstad, 2019).

To address this gap, this study investigated gender differences and similarities in the perceptions of and experiences with sex and sexual risk taking in tourism, while addressing the following research questions (RQs):

RQ1:   Are there gender differences in the perceptions of activities that constitute sex in tourism?

RQ2:   Are there intra-gender differences in the risk perceptions of and experiences with unprotected vs. protected casual vaginal, oral and anal sex in tourism?

RQ3:   Are there gender differences in the perceptions of and experiences with sexual risk taking in tourism?

Methods

Design and measures

A sequential mixed methods qualitative-to-quantitative design was implemented for this study. The qualitative phase involved 15 in-depth individual interviews (length: 1.5–2.5 hours each) and three focus groups with 6–7 young adults each (length: 2.5–3 hours each). These qualitative findings were reported in Berdychevsky (2016, 2017a) and distilled into a set of items for the survey questionnaire that was pre-tested via cognitive think-aloud interviews, expert reviews and a pilot test. Additional information on instrumentation and validation is available in Berdychevsky and Gibson (2015c).

To address RQ1, the participants were asked to what extent they agree or disagree that various penetrative (e.g. vaginal or anal sex) and non-penetrative (e.g. fondling or making out) sexual activities in tourism should be considered as sex (7 items using a 5-point Likert scale, where 1 = 'strongly disagree' and 5 = 'strongly agree'). To address RQ2 and RQ3, the participants were asked to what extent they agree or disagree that various unprotected, protected and partner and context-specific sexual activities in tourism should be considered as sexual risk taking (25 items (for examples, see Table 3.3) using a 5-point Likert scale, where 1 = 'strongly disagree' and 5 = 'strongly agree'). Regarding the experience component in RQ3, the participants were asked whether they had experienced each of these sexual activities in tourism (25 nominal, dichotomous 'yes'/'no' items).

Data Collection and Analysis

The student body of a large public American university (enrolment of about 50,000 students) comprised the target population of this study.

Implementing a combination of systematic random sampling (with a constant sampling interval and a random entry point) and stratified random sampling (with a proportional representation by gender and class standing), every sixth student from the sampling frame (provided by the Office of the University Registrar) was invited to participate in this study (resulting in a total of 8319 invitations).

The data collection procedure and the survey questionnaire were approved by the Institutional Review Board. The data were collected using an online survey programmed in Qualtrics software. No internet protocol addresses or other personal identifiers were collected, providing participants with anonymity. First, all the invitees received a pre-notice email with brief explanations about this research project and an invitation to consider participating in it. Two days later, an invitation with the link to the survey was emailed to the potential participants. After four days, reminder notes were emailed. A week and a half later, the second round of the reminder emails was sent. The data collection was concluded a month after the invitation email.

Participation incentives were not provided in this study, but the participants were offered a summary of the study's results. After reviewing the data for missing values, the cases with the data missing not at random (e.g. partially completed surveys) were removed (i.e. listwise deletion) while the cases with some data missing at random (e.g. occasionally skipped items with no identifiable pattern) were preserved for data analysis (these missing values were treated with a full information maximum likelihood estimation method in M*plus* 7 software). This procedure resulted in a final database for the data analysis with 1278 cases. Namely, the total effective response rate was 15.36% (19.92% for women and 10.53% for men).

Data analysis was conducted using IBM SPSS Statistics 24. The independent samples t-test was used to test inter-gender (independent variable) differences in perceptions of sex (dependent variable in RQ1) and sexual risk taking (dependent variable in RQ3) in tourism. The paired samples t-test was used to test intra-gender perceptual differences relevant for RQ1, RQ2 and RQ3. The Chi-square (χ^2) test was used to test inter-gender (RQ3) and intra-gender (RQ2) differences in the experiences with sexual risk taking in tourism.

Participants

The total sample (N = 1278) was comprised of 853 women and 425 men. Reflecting the target population, the sample was relatively young (women: M = 23.50 years old, SD = 6.669, predominant age groups: 18–20 years – 40.4%, 21–23 years – 29.2%; men: M = 26.07 years old, SD = 7.854, predominant age groups: 18–20 years – 23.0%, 21–23 years – 28.7%). Among women, 63.8% were undergraduate and

34.2% were graduate students. Among men, 49.5% were undergraduate and 48.8% were graduate students. Also, 81.9% of women were born and 89.1% grew up in the United States. Similarly, 80.7% of men were born and 86.3% grew up in the United States. As for racial/ethnic background, among women, 66.6% self-identified as White/Caucasian, 13.7% as Hispanic, 8.3% as Asian and 6.4% as Black. Among men, 67.8% identified themselves as White/Caucasian, 12.8% as Hispanic, 9.9% as Asian and 3.8% as Black.

Regarding sexual orientation, 92.8% of women self-identified as heterosexual, 4.8% as bisexual and 1.4% as lesbian. As for men, 91.1% identified themselves as heterosexual, 4.5% as gay and 2.1% as bisexual. In terms of marital status, 84.4% of women were never married, 12.8% were married and 2.2% divorced/separated. Likewise, 76.6% of men were never married, 20.8% were married and 2.6% divorced/separated. Concerning dating status, 51.8% of women were in an exclusive relationship, 35.3% were not in a relationship and not dating and 10.7% were casually dating. Among men, 48.9% were in an exclusive relationship, 35.4% were not in a relationship and not dating and 13.3% were casually dating.

On average, women (M = 4.29, SD = 6.088) reported having had fewer sexual partners than men (M = 7.74, SD = 12.850). Among women, 8.3% have experienced an unplanned pregnancy, while 9.0% of the men have accidentally impregnated their partner. Also, 49.2% of women were tested for and 8.2% were diagnosed with sexually transmitted infections in the past. As for men, 46.9% were tested for and 5.9% were diagnosed with sexually transmitted infections. Furthermore, 18.4% of women and 25.7% of men reported that some of their sexual practices were putting them at risk of contracting HIV/AIDS. Finally, 10.7% of women and 4.5% of men reported having had sex without giving their consent.

To contextualise results in tourism, the participants were asked to describe the optimal tourism experiences for casual sex as well as the tourism experiences providing maximum opportunity for sex with a steady partner. They viewed group tours (women – 50.9%; men – 43.9%), rest and relaxation vacations (women – 44.0%; men – 58.6%), sightseeing trips (women – 44.4%; men – 44.8%) and backpacking journeys (women – 32.2%; men – 30.4%) as offering maximum opportunity for casual sex. For casual sex, they also preferred travelling with single, same-gender companions (women – 54.0%; men – 30.3%), single opposite-gender companions (women – 31.3%; men – 46.7%) or solo (women – 29.6%; men – 38.0%) for an average length of 8–9 days (women: M = 8.09, SD = 5.782; men: M = 9.25, SD = 6.784). As for the tourism experiences most conducive to sex with a steady partner, the participants indicated rest and relaxation vacations (women – 90.9%; men – 89.2%), sightseeing trips (women – 64.2%; men –56.4%) and backpacking journeys (women – 30.8%; men – 31.1%). For this purpose, they also preferred travelling with no other companions besides the steady partner (women – 86.6%; men –81.8%) or with other couples (women – 22.9%; men – 17.8%) for an average duration of nine days (women: $M = 9.05$, $SD = 5.416$; men: $M = 8.95$, $SD = 5.459$).

Results

Gender differences in the perceptions of sex in tourism

The first research question revolved around gender differences in viewing various penetrative and non-penetrative sexual activities as sex in tourism. As reflected in Table 3.1, both women and men ranked vaginal, anal and oral sex as highly qualifying as sex in tourism (all the rankings above 4 on a 5-point Likert scale). However, fondling and making out/kissing were not regarded highly as sex (all the rankings below 2.5 on a 5-point Likert scale). Based on the independent samples t-tests, the only significant differences by gender were found in the rankings of receiving oral sex and having anal sex (see Table 3.1). Women ($M = 4.04$, $SD = 1.024$) reported significantly lower levels of agreement than men ($M = 4.14$, $SD = 1.037$) with viewing receptive oral sex as sex in tourism ($t(1,268) = -1.671$, $p < 0.10$). Likewise, women ($M = 4.42$, $SD = 0.956$) reported significantly lower levels of agreement than men ($M = 4.53$, $SD = 0.848$) with viewing anal sex as sex in tourism ($t(935.987) = -2.216$, $p < 0.05$).

Intra-gender paired samples t-tests also revealed intriguing results for oral and anal sex. While women perceived receiving oral sex ($M = 4.04$, $SD = 1.024$) and performing oral sex ($M = 4.02$, $SD = 1.043$) as equally qualifying as sex in tourism ($t(848) = 1.652$, $p = $ n.s.), men ranked receiving oral sex ($M = 4.14$, $SD = 1.037$) significantly higher as

Table 3.1 Gender differences in the perceptions of sex in tourism

Sexual activities in tourism[1]	Women (n = 853)		Men (n = 425)		Independent samples t-test		
	M (1)	SD	M (2)	SD	M (1)–(2)	t	df
Vaginal sex	4.72	0.558	4.77	.589	−0.049	−1.444	1270
Receiving oral sex	4.04	1.024	4.14	1.037	−0.102	−1.671*	1268
Performing oral sex	4.02	1.042	4.07	1.088	−0.053	−0.849	1270
Anal sex	4.42	0.956	4.53	0.848	−0.117	−2.216**	935.987[2]
Fondling	2.35	1.135	2.46	1.262	−0.107	−1.478	766.191[2]
Making out/kissing	1.91	1.032	1.97	1.122	−0.061	−0.935	778.454[2]

Note: *, **, *** indicates significance at the 90%, 95% and 99% level, respectively.
[1]Measured on a 5-point Likert scale, where 1 = 'strongly disagree' and 5 = 'strongly agree'.
[2]Based on the Levene's test for equality of variances, equal variances cannot be assumed, which affects the degrees of freedom (df).

sex compared to performing oral sex ($M = 4.07$, $SD = 1.089$, $t(420) = 3.801$, $p < 0.001$). Men's version of the survey also distinguished between insertive and receptive anal sex. Men ranked insertive anal sex ($M = 4.53$, $SD = 0.851$) significantly higher as sex in tourism compared to receptive anal sex ($M = 4.28$, $SD = 1.191$, $t(417) = 6.251$, $p < 0.001$).

Intra-gender differences with respect to protected vs. unprotected casual sex in tourism

The second research question investigated intra-gender differences in the perceptions of and experiences with protected vs. unprotected casual vaginal, oral and anal sex in tourism. As expected, both genders have consistently rated all kinds of unprotected casual sex in tourism as significantly riskier than their equivalent protected versions (see Table 3.2). However, these risk perceptions were not necessarily predictive of women's and men's experiences with various unprotected and protected casual sex activities.

For instance, risk perceptions and experiences with respect to casual, vaginal sex in tourism were congruent. Namely, unprotected, casual, vaginal sex was perceived as significantly risker than its protected equivalent (women: *Mdifference* = 0.892, $t(848) = 23.842$, $p < 0.001$; men: *Mdifference* = 1.221, $t(420) = 1.221$, $p < 0.001$) and significantly higher numbers of both women and men have experienced protected rather than unprotected, casual, vaginal sex in tourism (women: 17.2% vs. 10.3%, $\chi^2 = 208.937$, $p < 0.001$; men: 30.9% vs. 22.3%, $\chi^2 = 135.630$, $p < 0.001$).

However, the results were the opposite for casual, oral sex. Namely, although receiving unprotected, casual, oral sex was perceived as significantly riskier than receiving its protected version (women; *Mdifference* = 0.974, $t(850) = 25.406$, $p < 0.001$; men: *Mdifference* = 1.107, $t(421) = 19.233$, $p < 0.001$), significantly higher numbers of women and men have received unprotected rather than protected, casual, oral sex in tourism (women: 15.0% vs. 2.9%, $\chi^2 = 75.219$, $p < 0.001$; men: 32.8% vs. 16.4%, $\chi^2 = 52.615$, $p < 0.001$). Likewise, although performing/giving unprotected, casual, oral sex was viewed as significantly riskier than performing its protected equivalent (women: *Mdifference* = 1.009, $t(845) = 26.191$, $p < 0.001$; men: *Mdifference* = 1.133, $t(420) = 18.795$, $p < 0.001$), significantly higher numbers of women and men have performed unprotected rather than protected, casual, oral sex in tourism (women: 17.2% vs. 5.4%, $\chi^2 = 86.206$, $p < 0.001$; men: 27.3% vs. 9.0%, $\chi^2 = 27.027$, $p < 0.001$).

Lastly, despite perceiving unprotected, casual anal sex as significantly riskier than its protected version (women: *Mdifference* = 0.873, $t(847) = 24.899$, $p < 0.001$; men: *Mdifference* = 1.033, $t(419) = 17.616$, $p < 0.001$), more or less equal numbers of the participants have

Table 3.2 Intra-gender differences in the perceptions of and experiences with protected vs. unprotected casual vaginal, oral and anal sex in tourism

	Women (n = 853)			Men (n = 425)		
	Sexual risk perceptions			*Sexual risk perceptions*		
	Paired samples *t*-test			Paired samples *t*-test		
Sexual activities in tourism[1]	*M* (1)–(2)	*t*	*df*	*M* (1)–(2)	*t*	*df*
Having unprotected (1) vs. protected[2] (2) vaginal casual sex	0.892	23.842***	848	1.221	19.947***	420
Receiving unprotected vs. protected oral casual sex	0.974	25.406***	850	1.107	19.233***	421
Performing unprotected vs. protected oral casual sex	1.009	26.191***	845	1.133	18.795***	420
Having unprotected vs. protected anal[3] casual sex	0.873	24.899***	847	1.033	17.616***	419

	Experience with sexual risk taking					
	Unprotected %	Protected %	χ^2	Unprotected %	Protected %	χ^2
Having vaginal casual sex	10.3	17.2	208.973***	22.3	30.9	135.630***
Receiving oral casual sex	15.0	2.9	75.219***	32.8	16.4	52.615***
Performing oral casual sex	17.2	5.4	86.206***	27.3	9.0	27.027***
Having anal[3] casual sex	2.0	1.8	2.146	3.8	4.1	3.231

Note: *, **, *** indicates significance at the 90%, 95% and 99% level, respectively.
[1] Measured on a 5-point Likert scale, where 1 = 'strongly disagree' and 5 = 'strongly agree'.
[2] Gender-specific versions of the survey clarified which kind of latex barrier was meant (e.g. condom, dental dam, plastic wrap).
[3] In men's cases, the data for comparison were drawn from the question on insertive (rather than receptive) anal sex.

experienced unprotected vs. protected, casual, anal sex in tourism among both women and men (women: 2.0% vs. 1.8%, $\chi^2 = 2.146$, p = n.s.; men: 3.8% vs. 4.1%, $\chi^2 = 3.231$, p = n.s.). However, it is worth noting that the frequencies for the experience of casual, anal sex in tourism were relatively low for both genders.

Gender differences in the perceptions of and experiences with sexual risk taking in tourism

The third research question examined gender differences in the perceptions of and experiences with sexual risk taking in tourism. The participants were presented with 25 sexual activities (that were construed as risky in tourism based on the preceding qualitative studies) and asked to rate the levels of risk associated with these activities (on a 5-point Likert scale). Table 3.3 presents 18 activities that were ranked as sufficiently risky (i.e. above 3) by at least one of the genders. Both women and men perceived casual, unprotected, penetrative sex in tourism as the riskiest, followed by commercial sex and sex with multiple partners. Casual, unprotected, oral sex continued the list, followed by sex under the influence of drugs. Within the list of the top sexually risky activities in tourism, the participants included only one item referring explicitly to sex with a steady partner (i.e. vaginal sex without protection from pregnancy). The rest of the items referred to protected casual sex, various settings for having sex (e.g. semi-public spaces, unfamiliar surroundings) and sexual attractions (e.g. live sex shows, strip clubs).

Table 3.3 illustrates that women have consistently rated all of the activities as significantly riskier than men. Also, significantly higher numbers of men have experienced all the risky activities in tourism compared to women. The most frequently reported experiences in tourism included having sex under the influence of alcohol (men – 52.1%; women – 46.7%), sex in unfamiliar surroundings (men – 50.6%; women – 38.3%), casual, protected, vaginal sex (men – 30.9%; women – 17.2%), sex in semi-public spaces (men – 34.9%; women – 26.7%), unprotected sex with a steady partner (men – 36.8%; women – 23.3%), attending strip clubs (men – 34.7%; women – 15.7%), receiving casual, unprotected, oral sex (men – 32.8%; women – 15.0%) and performing casual, unprotected, oral sex (men – 27.3%; women – 17.2%).

Paired samples t-test revealed some intriguing intra-gender differences in the risk perceptions regarding receiving vs. performing/giving casual, oral sex in tourism. Women perceived receiving (protected: $M = 3.48$, $SD = 1.445$; unprotected: $M = 4.45$; $SD = 0.863$) and performing (protected: $M = 3.51$, $SD = 1.124$; unprotected: $M = 4.52$, $SD = 0.817$) casual, oral sex in tourism as equally risky. This perception held for both protected ($t(848) = -1.403$, p = n.s.) and unprotected ($t(844) = -2.312$, p = n.s.) casual, oral sex in tourism. Conversely, men viewed

Table 3.3 Gender differences in risk perceptions and experiences with sexual risk taking in tourism

Sexual activities in tourism[1]	Sexual risk perceptions						Sexual risk-taking experiences		
	Women (n = 853)		Men (n = 425)		Independent samples t-test			Women (n = 853)	Men (n = 425)	χ^2
	M (1)	SD	M (2)	SD	M (1)–(2)	t	df	%	%	
Having vaginal sex with an unsteady partner without a condom	4.79	0.640	4.65	0.753	0.146	3.406***	728.380³	10.3	22.3	33.404***
Having anal sex with an unsteady partner without a condom	4.74	0.692	4.58	0.877	0.160	3.261***	685.409³	2.0	5.7	12.385***
Having sex with a sex worker (e.g., prostitute)	4.74	0.710	4.56	0.921	0.178	3.489***	673.139³	0.1	7.6	62.424***
Having sex with multiple partners (e.g., orgy)	4.62	0.712	4.34	0.868	0.283	5.797***	708.369³	5.2	14.3	30.797***
Performing oral sex on an unsteady partner without a latex barrier[2]	4.52	0.817	4.18	1.035	0.340	5.895***	689.795³	17.2	27.3	17.672***
Receiving oral sex from an unsteady partner without a latex barrier[2]	4.45	0.863	4.03	1.052	0.423	7.151***	709.737³	15.0	32.8	53.808***
Having sex under the influence of drugs	4.42	0.886	4.10	0.993	0.323	5.866***	1265	11.6	17.8	9.307**
Having vaginal sex with a steady partner without protection from	4.40	0.947	4.13	1.090	0.271	4.353***	742.034³	23.3	36.8	25.414***
Attending a swinger club	4.22	0.939	4.09	1.048	0.125	2.147**	1267	1.4	3.8	7.438**
Having sex in semi-public spaces (e.g., a restroom, elevator)	4.05	0.912	3.86	1.059	0.193	3.200***	735.826³	26.7	34.9	9.262***
Having vaginal sex with an unsteady partner with a condom	3.90	1.029	3.42	1.195	0.477	7.012***	738.647³	17.2	30.9	30.975***
Having anal sex with an unsteady partner with a condom	3.87	1.055	3.55	1.195	0.320	4.658***	751.533³	1.8	7.1	23.650***
Having sex in unfamiliar surroundings	3.84	1.094	3.35	1.160	0.494	7.278***	793.381³	38.3	50.6	17.477***
Having sex under the influence of alcohol	3.79	1.037	3.61	1.087	0.178	2.791**	803.457³	46.7	52.1	6.548**
Performing oral sex on an unsteady partner with a latex barrier[2]	3.51	1.124	3.04	1.266	0.465	6.388***	755.568³	5.4	9.0	5.931**
Receiving oral sex from an unsteady partner with a latex barrier[2]	3.48	1.145	2.92	1.275	0.555	7.561***	764.471³	2.9	16.4	73.971***
Going to live sex shows	3.38	1.246	2.91	1.356	0.463	5.871***	772.854³	3.7	8.6	13.364***
Going to a strip club	3.01	1.182	2.69	1.249	0.312	4.357***	794.578³	15.7	34.7	59.183***

Note: *, **, *** indicates significance at the 90%, 95% and 99% level, respectively.
[1] Measured on a 5-point Likert scale, where 1 = 'strongly disagree' and 5 = 'strongly agree'. A total of 25 activities were presented in the survey, but the table presents only 18 activities that were ranked as sufficiently risky (i.e. above 3; presented in descending order) by at least one of the genders.
[2] Gender-specific versions of the survey clarified as appropriate which kind of latex barrier was meant (e.g., condom, dental dam, plastic wrap).
[3] Based on the Levene's test for equality of variances, equal variances cannot be assumed, which affects the degrees of freedom (df).

performing/giving (protected: $M = 3.04$; $SD = 1.266$; unprotected: $M = 4.18$, $SD = 1.035$) casual, oral sex as significantly riskier than receiving it (protected: $M = 2.92$, $SD = 1.277$; unprotected: $M = 4.03$, $SD = 1.052$). This perception also held for both protected ($t(420) = 3.897$, $p < 0.001$) and unprotected ($t(421) = 4.737$, $p < 0.001$) casual, oral sex in tourism.

These risk perceptions were not congruent with the reported experiences of casual, oral sex in tourism among women but were aligned with men's experiences. Significantly higher numbers of women have performed (protected − 5.4%; unprotected − 17.2%) casual, oral sex rather than received it (protected − 2.9%; unprotected − 15.0%). This held for both protected ($\chi^2 = 149.747$, $p < 0.001$) and unprotected kinds ($\chi^2 = 503.463$, $p < 0.001$). Conversely, significantly higher numbers of men have received (protected − 16.4%; unprotected − 32.8%) casual, oral sex rather than performed it (protected − 9.0%; unprotected − 27%). This held for both protected ($\chi^2 = 154.122$, $p < 0.001$) and unprotected ($\chi^2 = 231.548$, $p < 0.001$) casual, oral sex in tourism.

Discussion

The contribution of this study stems from offering insights into gender differences and similarities in sex definitions as well as the perceptions and levels of experience with an array of activities comprising sexual risk taking in tourism.

Narrow(er) vs. broad(er) definitions of sex in tourism

The results reflect that in this study both women and men viewed penetrative and oral sexual activities as sex in tourism, while other sexual activities (e.g. fondling, kissing/making out) were typically not perceived as sex in tourism. This points to the distinction between traditional, narrow(er) definitions of sex (e.g. as penile-vaginal or penile-anal intercourse; Barnett et al., 2018) vs. broad(er) definitions of sex (e.g. where sex is not confined to genital contact and can include any activity with sexual overtones with or without penetration; Bredychevsky, 2018; Kashdan et al., 2019). In this context, sex definitions are important because they underlie people's perceptions of sexual risk taking in tourism (e.g. activities not viewed as sex per se are construed as less risky) and frame their psychological impacts on a sense of self (Berdychevsky, 2016; Berdychevsky et al., 2013a).

Most of the participants in this study subscribed to a narrow(er), intercourse-focused definition of sex, with the caveat that oral sex was also commonly viewed as sex, which broadens the definition. In a sense, however, oral sex might also involve penetration, at least when a woman is performing it on a man (i.e. fellatio). This focus on penetration is incongruent with the typical approach adopted by tourism scholars focusing on sex. Tourism literature reflects that researchers found broader sex definitions (including non-penetrative sex and even activities like voyeurism and exhibitionism) as more adequate and flexible heuristic tools for understanding sexual behaviour in tourism and leisure contexts (Berdychevsky, 2018; Berdychevsky et al., 2013b; Eiser & Ford, 1995; Maticka-Tyndale & Herold, 1997; Oppermann, 1999; Ryan & Martin, 2001).

Examining gender differences in sex definitions in tourism revealed that, for the most part, women and men in this study were consistent in their definitions. However, women rated receiving oral sex (i.e. cunnilingus) and having anal sex lower than men in terms of these activities qualifying as sex. These findings suggest that men tended to have a somewhat broader definition of sex than women, which contradicts a previous study arguing that more women than men hold a broad(er) definition of sex (McCabe et al., 2010). One possible explanation for women's narrow(er) definition is the possibility of alleviating some of the psycho-social weight/responsibility from the activities excluded from their sex definition (Berdychevsky, 2016). Based on the sexual double standards holding women (but not necessarily men) responsible for sexual behaviour (Attwood, 2007; Eaton & Rose, 2011), this cognitive strategy of alleviating the meaning/weight of sex from certain sexual activities might indeed be in higher demand among women compared to men.

Inspection of the intra-gender differences also highlighted intriguing tendencies. While for women, performing and receiving oral sex (i.e. fellatio and cunnilingus, respectively) equally qualified as sex, men rated receiving fellatio higher than performing cunnilingus in terms of qualifying as sex. This perceptual difference might be reflective of the power asymmetry imposed on sexual behaviour by the sexual double standards (Blanc, 2001; Hensman Kettrey, 2016; Petersen & Hyde, 2010). Specifically, this difference might suggest a belief among men in this study that when a woman attends to a man's sexual needs/desires, then it qualifies as sex more so than when a man attends to a woman's sexual needs/desires.

Perceptions of and experiences with protected vs. unprotected casual sex in tourism

Although unsurprisingly, all kinds of unprotected, casual sex were rated as significantly riskier than their protected equivalents, such risk perceptions were only predictive of the behavioural patterns in the case of vaginal sex, and not oral or anal sex. These tendencies were consistent across gender. Namely, unprotected, vaginal sex was perceived as riskier than protected, vaginal sex, and more people had protected rather than unprotected, casual, vaginal sex in tourism.

Conversely, unprotected, oral sex was perceived as riskier than protected, oral sex, but significantly more people had unprotected rather than protected, casual, oral sex in tourism. This finding might be explained by people's tendency to underestimate the risk of STIs associated with unprotected, oral sex and reluctance to use protection, despite oral sex involving the exchange of fluids salient to STI acquisition (Centers for Disease Control and Prevention, 2004; Saini *et al.*, 2010; Stone *et al.*, 2006). Likewise, while unprotected, anal sex was perceived as riskier than protected, anal sex, equal numbers of people have experienced unprotected and protected, casual, anal sex in tourism. This finding seems counterintuitive since penile-to-anal contact carries higher risks of torn tissues (due to a lack of natural lubrication) and transmission of STIs and HIV/AIDS (Schwandt *et al.*, 2006; Wilton, 2014; Workowski & Bolan, 2015).

These inconsistencies between sexual risk perceptions and actual engagement in unprotected, casual, oral and anal sex are problematic because they potentially expose tourists to STIs and HIV/AIDS. The health literature presented above does not fully explain these results. Tourism literature also offers a rather ambivalent input on condom use. In one study, people described condom use as essential in tourism, and even women felt empowered to carry condoms and negotiate condom use in tourism, but not necessarily at home (e.g. Berdychevsky *et al.*, 2015). In other studies, however, sociocultural differences, a permissive tourism atmosphere, increased alcohol consumption and a fun-seeking party mentality complicated and even prevented condom use among tourists (Berdychevsky, 2016; Milhausen *et al.*, 2020; Sönmez *et al.*, 2006). Therefore, additional research is needed to clarify risk perceptions and practices associated with unprotected, casual sex in tourism.

Perceptions of and experiences with sexual risk taking in tourism

On average, women perceived all the sexual activities presented in this study as significantly riskier than men. Also, men reported significantly higher levels of experience with all these activities in tourism than women. To some extent, this might be a result of women's higher biological vulnerability to the transmission of STIs and HIV/AIDS through sexual intercourse (Dellar *et al.*, 2015; Ostrach & Singer, 2012). However, this is unlikely to be the sole reason because, first, it does not explain women's higher risk perceptions and fewer experiences regarding non-penetrative sex and, second, biology is insufficient by itself to make sense of the complexity of various socially constructed sexual encounters and associated risks, which are shaped by biopolitical, structural and sociocultural factors (Carpenter & Delamater, 2012; DeLamater & Koepsel, 2015; Dellar *et al.*, 2015; Ostrach & Singer, 2012). Therefore, women's tendency to have consistently higher sexual risk perceptions and fewer experiences than men is also likely to be a projection/result of the sexual double standards equating sex with danger for women, particularly casual sex (Eaton & Rose, 2011; Muehlenhard *et al.*, 2015; Tolman, 2012). This supports the conclusion that even though sexual double standards might lose some of their potency in tourism, they certainly do not vanish entirely (Berdychevsky, 2016; Berdychevsky *et al.*, 2013a).

Consistent with the narrow(er) definitions of sex in tourism discussed earlier, participants also viewed casual, unprotected, penetrative sex in tourism as the riskiest. These findings highlight an emphasis on casual sex in people's collective imagination of sexual risk in tourism. Only one item explicitly addressing sex with a steady partner was highly ranked as risky. This is consistent with the literature that often focuses on casual sex when studying sexually risky behaviours in tourism (Berdychevsky *et al.*, 2013b). Nevertheless, some specific idiosyncrasies in women's and men's sexual risk perceptions and experiences in tourism raise various dilemmas, as presented below.

For instance, risk perceptions regarding casual, oral sex in tourism presented a conundrum. Women perceived performing and receiving oral sex in tourism as equally risky, while men viewed performing oral sex as significantly riskier than receiving it. These risk perceptions were consistent when women and men were rating both protected and unprotected oral sex. This raises the question of why men perceive performing oral sex/cunnilingus as riskier than receiving oral sex/fellatio. The literature search did not reveal any evidence that performing cunnilingus is riskier regarding STIs transmission than receiving fellatio. Hence, some other factors are likely responsible for this perception. Perhaps, fellatio allows men to preserve a sense of power and power asymmetry in inter-gender sexual encounters (as dictated by sexual double standards; Hensman Kettrey, 2016; Muehlenhard *et al.*, 2003, 2015; Petersen & Hyde, 2010) while cunnilingus potentially reverses this power differential and is, hence, perceived as riskier. Namely, the socio-psychological factors might explain this difference in men's risk perceptions of cunnilingus vs. fellatio rather than physical or sexual health-related reasons. Additional research is needed to explain men's tendency to associate higher levels of risk with performing casual, oral sex compared to receiving it.

To complicate things further, despite women perceiving casual fellatio and cunnilingus as equally risky, significantly higher numbers of women performed rather than received oral sex in tourism. However, this was not the case for men. They viewed receiving oral sex as less risky than performing it and significantly higher numbers of them received fellatio rather than performed cunnilingus. These differences were stable in the scenarios of both protected and unprotected oral sex. These differences could also be explained with the power asymmetry imposed on sexual behaviour by the sexual double standards (Hensman Kettrey, 2016; Petersen & Hyde, 2010). Accordingly, men have higher power to command/obtain sexual experiences that they perceive as less risky or more pleasurable and catering to their needs, while women often find themselves in a more compliant and vulnerable position (Higgins & Browne, 2008; Impett & Peplau, 2003; Lefkowitz *et al.*, 2014), which potentially negatively affects their sexual health and wellbeing (Crawford & Popp, 2003; Grello *et al.*, 2006; Tolman, 2012).

Focusing further on the cross-pollination between sex and tourism, some of the most frequently experienced sexually risky activities by both women and men while travelling were having sex under the influence of alcohol, in unfamiliar surroundings, and in semi-public spaces. Several other risky sexual activities from Table 3.3 were rather common as well. These experiences resonate with tourism contexts and characteristics, as described in the existing literature. Existing tourism literature has extensively documented the positive relationship between sexual risk taking and consumption of substances, both alcohol and drugs, in tourism (Briggs & Tutenges, 2011, 2014; Guilamo-Ramos *et al.*, 2015; Milhausen *et al.*, 2020; Sönmez *et al.*, 2006, 2013). Sex in unfamiliar and/ or semi-public tourism spaces with casual or steady sexual partners was also described as risky and titillating in previous studies (Berdychevsky *et al.*, 2015; Berdychevsky *et al.*, 2013b). Attending swinger parties, strip clubs and live sex shows was described as more available and appropriate in leisure and travel contexts as well as being conducive to risk taking, experimentation, transgression and negotiation or even reversal of sexual roles (Pilcher, 2011; Ryan & Martin, 2001; Worthington, 2005). This study contributes additional insights into the understanding of these sexual activities in tourism by providing information on activity-specific risk assessments, frequency of occurrence and perceptual and behavioural gender differences.

Conclusions and Implications for Practice

To conclude, this study sheds light on the severely under-researched topic of gender differences and similarities in the perceptions of and experiences with sex and sexual risk taking in tourism. The findings should be interpreted in light of the study's methodological limitations and delimitations. First, this study is based on a self-report instrument assessing sexual perceptions experiences. This method is vulnerable to social and cognitive biases, such as socially desirable self-presentation, underreporting of sensitive issues and memory decay. Thus, sexual perceptions and experiences reported in this study might be the lower-bound estimates of their levels and occurrence in reality, especially for women. However, the anonymity provided by the online data collection method should have mitigated the issue of social desirability and underreporting. Second, this research was cross-sectional and not experimental. Therefore, it is impossible to make any causal inferences.

As for delimitations, reported results are delimited to young, college-educated adults who felt sufficiently comfortable to participate in a sensitive, sex-related study. Furthermore, this study's sample was predominantly white and heterosexual, which was not a goal in this project but a result of self-selection by the participants. Thus, future studies should investigate this topic using different methodologies and focusing on heterogeneous populations varying by gender, age, race/ethnicity, sexual identity, social class, etc. Despite these (de)limitations, this research offers an original and important contribution to the understanding of sex and sexual risk taking in tourism.

Overall, clarifying gender differences and similarities in sexual risk perceptions and experiences in tourism benefits the literature and provides valuable and manifold input for practice. Specifically, having a clear and gender-sensitive definition of sex and sexual risk taking as perceived by young tourists can help focus and streamline sexual health education efforts for this demographic (Berdychevsky & Gibson, 2015b). Also, identifying inter- and intra-gender differences in the perceptions of and experiences with sex and sexual risk taking in tourism can help develop sexual health education programmes targeted by gender and accounting for gender differences and sexual double standards affecting sexual behaviour, which should boost their efficacy (Berdychevsky, 2017a). Also, clarifying misconceptions in sexual risk perceptions provides input for sexual health educators regarding the gaps in sexual knowledge of young tourists that should be addressed.

Finally, identifying incongruences between risk perceptions and behavioural patterns (e.g. when sexual activity is perceived as risky but is still frequently practiced in tourism, such as the unprotected, casual, oral sex) offers insights regarding the areas/scenarios in which young tourists should be empowered to take charge of their health by developing resilience and adopting various harm reduction strategies. This could be achieved by implementing an information-motivation-behavioural skills model for health behaviour change, which has been successfully applied to sexual risk taking and health (Fisher & Fisher, 1992; Fisher et al., 2006; John et al., 2017). Accordingly, young tourists would be motivated to use the information underlying their risk perceptions to inform their decision-making processes and improve their behavioural skills to achieve healthier sexual choices and behavioural practices in tourism. Achieving these goals is particularly important in tourism contexts because they were linked to the geographical expansion of STIs (Brown et al., 2014; Rogstad, 2019; Vivancos et al., 2010) and are frequently perceived as hedonistic zones of exception characterised by a fun-seeking and party-oriented state of mind, suspension of ordinary norms and inhibitions and reduced influence of sexual double standards (Berdychevsky, 2016; Briggs & Tutenges, 2014; Milhausen *et al.*, 2020).

References

Andriotis, K. (2010) Heterotopic erotic oases: The public nude beach experience. *Annals of Tourism Research* 37 (4), 1076–1096.

Apostolopoulos, Y., Sönmez, S. and Yu, C.H. (2002) HIV-risk behaviours of American spring break vacationers: A case of situational disinhibition? *International Journal of STD & AIDS* 13 (11), 733–743.

Attwood, F. (2007) Sluts and Riot Grrrls: Female identity and sexual agency. *Journal of Gender Studies* 16 (3), 233–247.

Barnett, M.D., Fleck, L.K., Marsden, A.D. and Martin, K.J. (2018) Sexual semantics: The meanings of sex, virginity, and abstinence for university students. *Personality and Individual Differences* 106, 203–208.

Berdychevsky, L. (2016) Antecedents of young women's sexual risk taking in tourist experiences. *Journal of Sex Research* 53 (8), 927–941.

Berdychevsky, L. (2017a) Sexual health education for young tourists. *Tourism Management* 62, 189–195.

Berdychevsky, L. (2017b) Toward the tailoring of sexual health education messages for young women: A focus on tourist experiences. *Journal of Sex Research* 54 (9), 1171–1187.

Berdychevsky, L. (2018) 'Risky' leisure research on sex and violence: Innovation, impact, and impediments. *Leisure Sciences* 40 (1–2), 9–18.

Berdychevsky, L. and Gibson, H.J. (2015a) Phenomenology of young women's sexual risk-taking in tourism. *Tourism Management* 46, 299–310.

Berdychevsky, L. and Gibson, H.J. (2015b) Sex and risk in young women's tourist experiences: Context, likelihood, and consequences. *Tourism Management* 51, 78–90.

Berdychevsky, L. and Gibson, H.J. (2015c) Women's sexual sensation seeking and risk taking in leisure travel. *Journal of Leisure Research* 47 (5), 621–646.

Berdychevsky, L., Gibson, H.J. and Poria, Y. (2013a) Women's sexual behavior in tourism: Loosening the bridle. *Annals of Tourism Research* 42, 65–85.

Berdychevsky, L., Gibson, H.J. and Poria, Y. (2015) Inversions of sexual roles in women's tourist experiences: Mind, body, and language in sexual behaviour. *Leisure Studies* 34 (5), 513–528.

Berdychevsky, L., Poria, Y. and Uriely, N. (2013b) Sexual behavior in women's tourist experiences: Motivations, behaviors, and meanings. *Tourism Management* 35, 144–155.

Blanc, A. (2001) The effect of power in sexual relationships on sexual and reproductive health: An examination of the evidence. *Studies in Family Planning* 32 (3), 189–213.

Bordini, G.S. and Sperb, T.M. (2013) Sexual double standard: A review of the literature between 2001 and 2010. *Sexuality and Culture* 17, 686–704.

Bradshaw, C., Kahn, A.S. and Saville, B.K. (2010) To hook up or date: Which gender benefits? *Sex Roles* 62, 661–669.

Briggs, D. and Tutenges, S. (2014) Risk and transgression on holiday: 'New experiences' and the pied piper of excessive consumption. *International Journal of Tourism Anthropology* 3 (3), 275–298.

Briggs, D., Tutenges, S., Armitage, S. and Panchev, D. (2011) Sexy substances and the substance of sex: Findings from an ethnographic study in Ibiza, Spain. *Drugs and Alcohol Today* 11 (4), 173–187.

Brown, G., Ellard, J., Mooney-Somers, J., Prestage, G., Crawford, G. and Langdon, T. (2014) 'Living a life less ordinary': Exploring the experiences of Australian men who have acuired HIV overseas. *Sexual Health* 11 (6), 547–555.

Butler, J. (1990) *Gender Trouble: Feminism and the Subversion of Identity*. New York: Routledge.

Carpenter, L.M. and DeLamater, J. (2012) *Sex for Life: From Virginity to Viagra, how Sexuality Changes Throughout our Lives.* New York/London: New York University Press.

Carr, N. (2016) Sex in tourism: Reflections and potential future research directions. *Tourism Recreation Research* 41 (2), 188–198.

Centers for Disease Control and Prevention (2004) Transmission of primary and secondary syphilis by oral sex – Chicago, Illinois, 1998–2002. *MMWR* 53 (41), 966–968.

Crawford, M. and Popp, D. (2003) Sexual double standards: A review and methodological critique of two decades of research. *Journal of Sex Research* 40 (1), 13–26.

Davies, S.C., Karagiannis, T., Headon, V., Wiig, R. and Duffy, J. (2011) Prevalence of genital chlamydial infection among a community sample of young international backpackers in Sydney, Australia. *International Journal of STD & AIDS* 22, 160–164.

DeLamater, J. and Koepsel, E. (2015) Relationships and sexual expression in later life: A biopsychosocial perspective. *Sexual and Relationship Therapy* 30 (1), 37–59.

Dellar, R.C., Dlamini, S. and Karim, Q.A. (2015) Adolescent girls and young women: Key populations for HIV epidemic control. *Journal of the International AIDS Society* 18 (1), 64–70.

Eaton, A.A. and Rose, S. (2011) Has dating become more egalitarian? A 35 year review using *Sex Roles. Sex Roles* 64 (11–12), 843–862.

Eiser, J.R. and Ford, N. (1995) Sexual relationships on holiday: A case of situational disinhibition? *Journal of Social and Personal Relationships* 12 (3), 323–339.

Falconer, E. (2011) Risk, excitement and emotional conflict in women's travel narratives. *Recreation and Society in Africa, Asia & Latin America* 1 (2), 65–89.

Fisher, J.D. and Fisher, W.A. (1992) Changing AIDS-risk behavior. *Psychological Bulletin* 111 (3), 455–474.

Fisher, J.D., Fisher, W.A., Amico, K.R. and Harman, J.J. (2006) An information-motivation-behavioral skills model of adherence to antiretroviral therapy. *Health Psychology* 25 (4), 462–473.

Gahagan, J., Gray, K. and Whynacht, A. (2015) Sex and gender matter in health research: Addressing health inequities in health research reporting. *International Journal for Equity in Health* 14 (12), 1–4.

Grello, C.M., Welsh, D.P. and Harper, M.S. (2006) No strings attached: The nature of casual sex in college students. *Journal of Sex Research* 43 (3), 255–267.

Guilamo-Ramos, V., Leea, J.J., Ruizb, Y., Haganc, H., Marlyn Delvad, M., Quiñonese, Z., Kamler, A. and Robles, G. (2015) Illicit drug use and HIV risk in the Dominican Republic: Tourism areas create drug use opportunities. *Global Public Health* 10 (3), 318–330.

Guo, Y. (2019) Sexual double standards in White and Asian Americans: Ethnicity, gender, and acculturation. *Sexuality & Culture* 23, 57–95.

Hensman Kettrey, H. (2016) What's gender got to do with it? Sexual double standards and power in heterosexual college hookups. *Journal of Sex Research* 53 (7), 754–765.

Higgins, J.A. and Browne, I. (2008) Sexual needs, control, and refusal: How 'doing' class and gender influences sexual risk taking. *Journal of Sex Research* 45 (3), 233–245.

Impett, E.A. and Peplau, L.A. (2003) Sexual compliance: Gender, motivational, and relationship perspectives. *Journal of Sex Research* 40 (1), 87–100.

John, S.A., Walsh, J.L. and Weinhardt, L.S. (2017) The information-motivation-behavioral skills model revisited: A network-perspective structural equation model within a public sexually transmitted infection clinic sample of hazardous alcohol users. *AIDS and Behavior* 21 (4), 1208–1218.

Jonason, K. and Fisher, T.D. (2009) The power of prestige: Why young men report having more sex partners than young women. *Sex Roles* 60 (3), 151–159.

Kashdan, T.B., Goodman, F.R., Stiksma, M., Milius, C.R. and McKnight, E. (2019) Sexuality leads to boosts in mood and meaning in life with no evidence for the reverse direction: A daily diary investigation. *Emotion* 18 (4), 563–576.

Lefkowitz, E.S., Shearer, C.L., Gillen, M.M. and Espinosa-Hernandez, G. (2014) How gendered attitudes relate to women's and men's sexual behaviors and beliefs. *Sexuality & Culture* 18, 833–846.

Lewis, C.T. and de Wildt, G. (2016) Sexual behaviour of backpackers who visit Koh Tao and Koh Phangan, Thailand: A cross-sectional study. *Sexually Transmitted Infections* 92, 410–414.

Maas, M.K., Shearer, C.L., Gillen, M.M. and Lefkowitz, E.S. (2015) Sex Rules: Emerging adults' perceptions of gender's impact on sexuality. *Sexuality & Culture* 19, 617–636.

Maticka-Tyndale, E. and Herold, E.S. (1997) The scripting of sexual behaviour: Canadian university students on spring break in Florida. *The Canadian Journal of Human Sexuality* 6 (4), 317–328.

Matteelli, A., Schlagenhauf, P., Carvalho, A.C.C., Weld, L., Davis, X.M., Wilder-Smith, A., Barnett, E.D., Parole, P., Pandey, P., Han, P. and Castelli, F. (2013) Travel-associated sexually transmitted infections: An observational cross-sectional study of the GeoSentinel surveillance database. *The Lancet Infectious Diseases* 13, 205–213.

McCabe, J., Tanner, A.E. and Heiman, J.R. (2010) The impact of gender expectations on meanings of sex and sexuality: Results from a cognitive interview study. *Sex Roles* 62 (3–4), 252–263.

McKercher, B. and Bauer, T.G. (2003) Conceptual framework of the nexus between tourism, romance, and sex. In T.G. Bauer and B. McKercher (eds) *Sex and Tourism: Journeys of Romance, Love, and Lust* (pp. 3–17). New York: Haworth Hospitality Press.

McNulty, A.M., Egan, C., Wand, H. and Donovan, B. (2010) The behaviour and sexual health of young international travellers (backpackers) in Australia. *Sexually Transmitted Infections* 86, 247–250.

Mewhinney, D.M., Herold, E.S. and Maticka-Tyndale, E. (1995) Sexual scripts and risk-taking of Canadian university students on spring break in Daytona Beach, Florida. *The Canadian Journal of Human Sexuality* 4 (4), 273–288.

Milhausen, R.R., Graham, C.A., Crosby, R.A., Ingram, H., Tetro, M., Bransfield, N., Sanders, S. and Yarber, W.L. (2020) 'What happens in Banff, stays in Banff': Contextual and interpersonal factors contributing to sexual risk taking among tourism workers. *Tourism Recreation Research* doi:10.1080/02508281.2019.1697549.

Muehlenhard, C.L., Peterson, Z.D., Karwoski, L., Bryan, T.S. and Lee, R.S. (2003) Gender and sexuality: An introduction to the special issue. *Journal of Sex Research* 40 (1), 1–3.

Muehlenhard, C.L., Sakaluk, J.K. and Esterline, K.M. (2015) Double standard. In P. Whelehan and A. Bolin (eds) *The International Encyclopedia of Human Sexuality* (Vol. 1, pp. 309–311) Hoboken, NY: Wiley-Blackwell|.

Oppermann, M. (1999) Sex tourism. *Annals of Tourism Research* 26 (2), 251–266.

Ostrach, B. and Singer, M. (2012) At special risk: Biopolitical vulnerability and HIV/STI syndemics among women. *Health Sociology Review* 21 (3), 258–271.

Petersen, J.L. and Hyde, J.S. (2011) Gender differences in sexual attitudes and behaviors: A review of meta-analytic results and large datasets. *Journal of Sex Research* 48, 149–165.

Pilcher, K.E.M. (2011) A 'sexy space' for women? Heterosexual women's experiences of a male strip show venue. *Leisure Studies* 30 (2), 217–235.

Pritchard, A. and Morgan, N.J. (2006) Hotel Babylon? Exploring hotels as liminal sites of transition and transgression. *Tourism Management* 27 (5), 762–772.

Qvarnström, A. and Oscarsson, M.G. (2014) Perceptions of HIV/STI prevention among young adults in Sweden who travel abroad: A qualitative study with focus group and individual interviews. *BMC Public Health* 14, 891–898.

Ragsdale, K., Difranceisco, W. and Pinkerton, S.D. (2006) Where the boys are: Sexual expectations and behaviour among young women on holiday. *Culture, Health & Sexuality* 8 (2), 85–98.

Rogstad, K.E. (2019) Sexually transmitted infections and travel. *Current Opinion in Infectious Diseases* 32 (1), 56–62.

Ryan, C. and Martin, A. (2001) Tourists and strippers: Liminal theater. *Annals of Tourism Research* 28 (1), 140−163.

Saini, R., Saini, S. and Sharma, S. (2010) Oral sex, oral health and orogenital infections. *Journal of Global Infectious Diseases* 2 (1), 57−62.

Schwandt, M., Morris, C., Ferguson, A., Ngugi, E. and Moses, S. (2006) Anal and dry sex in commercial sex work, and relation to risk for sexually transmitted infections and HIV in Meru, Kenya. *Sexually Transmitted Infections* 82, 392−396.

Selänniemi, T. (2003) On holiday in the liminoid playground: Place, time, and self in tourism. In T.G. Bauer and B. McKercher (eds) *Sex and Tourism: Journeys of Romance, Love, and Lust* (pp. 19−31). New York: The Haworth Hospitality Press.

Sönmez, S., Apostolopoulos, Y., Theocharous, A. and Massengale, K. (2013) Bar crawls, foam parties, and clubbing networks: Mapping the risk environment of a Mediterranean nightlife resort. *Tourism Management Perspectives* 8, 49−59.

Sönmez, S., Apostolopoulos, Y., Yu, C.H., Yang, S., Mattilla, A. and Yu, L.C. (2006) Binge drinking and casual sex on spring break. *Annals of Tourism Research* 33 (4), 895−917.

Stone, N., Hatherall, B., Ingham, R. and McEachran, J. (2006) Oral sex and condom use among young people in the United Kingdom. *Perspectives on Sexual and Reproductive Health* 38 (1), 6−12.

Thomas, M. (2005) 'What happens in Tenerife stays in Tenerife': Understanding women's sexual behaviour on holiday. *Culture, Health & Sexuality* 7 (6), 571−584.

Tolman, D.L. (2012) Female adolescents, sexual empowerment and desire: A missing discourse of gender inequity. *Sex Roles* 66 (11−12), 746−757.

Tolman, D.L., Striepe, M.I. and Harmon, T. (2003) Gender matters: Constructing a model of adolescent sexual health. *Journal of Sex Research* 40 (1), 4−12.

Vivancos, R., Abubakar, I. and Hunter, R. (2010) Foreign travel, casual sex, and sexually transmitted infections: Systematic review and meta-analysis. *International Journal of Infectious Diseases* 14, e842−e851.

Wilton, J. (2014) Getting to the bottom of it: Anal sex, rectal fluid, and HIV transmission. Canadian Aids Treatment Information Exchange (CATIE). See https://www.catie.ca/en/pif/fall-2014/getting-bottom-it-anal-sex-rectal-fluid-and-hiv-transmission (accessed July 2020).

Workowski, K.A. and Bolan, G.A. (2015) Sexually transmitted diseases treatment guidelines, 2015. *MMWR Recomm Rep* 64(RR-03), 1−137. See https://www.ncbi.nlm.nih.gov/pmc/articles/PMC5885289/pdf/nihms777542.pdf (accessed July 2020).

Worthington, B. (2005) Sex and shunting: Contrasting aspects of serious leisure within the tourism industry. *Tourist Studies* 5 (3), 225−246.

4 Sex and Summer Camps

Neil Carr and Leonardo Nava Jimenez

Introduction

Today, summer camps are an integral part of the tourism experience. They are focused on offering children and adolescents parent-free holiday experiences during the school summer vacation period. They originated in North America (Paris, 2008), but are now an increasingly global institution (Carr, 2011). Through their evolution they have become a 'rite of passage' and a sociocultural construct that, among other things, defines good parenting and a positive childhood. When they initially began to emerge in North America, they were designed around hegemonic masculine ideals of mastery over untamed nature and the creation of strong and healthy young males. This was set alongside concerns surrounding the urban male youth, who were perceived to be living unhealthy lives in urban centres, under the dominant guidance of their mothers. As such, they were perceived to be isolated from the rugged, outdoors, explorer ethos of their forefathers who had tamed the American (and Canadian) wilderness. At least this was the perception among the creators of the first summer camps (Paris, 2001; Van Slyck, 2006; Weyl, 1925). Indeed, writing in 1949, Goldsmith noted that 'for children of today who live in cramped and congested large cities, in small apartments with remote and limited outdoor play space, and who attend crowded schools, a summer camp in the country is of increasing importance and popularity' (Goldsmith, 1949: 510). Furthermore, in speaking about the origin of the summer camp, Van Slyck (2006: xxii) stated that, prior to the first ones being created, there was a fear 'that the sons of such households [urban, middle class] were becoming "sissies," many worried that this erosion of manliness would undermine the military might required to pursue the imperial aspirations of the United States'. From this foundation, summer camps have evolved to include a much wider segment of, first, the North American youth population and, more recently, the global population. Today, it is no longer the sole preserve of males, with camps being offered that cater to a wide array of people, either delineated according to particular personal traits and/or desires, or open to all (Carr, 2011).

Despite the evolution and diversification of camps, they still possess strong roots to the original dominant ethos of camps. In particular, there is still a strong emphasis on their wholesomeness. As such, Baker (2020: 13) has stated that summer camps are focused on 'enrich[ing] the lives of campers through educational, recreational, social, and spiritual development opportunities'. There is a strongly cherished notion that the camp is an experience that offers children time away from their parents in an environment that challenges them and enables them to undertake powerful journeys of self-discovery and development (Baker, 2020; Henderson *et al.*, 2007; McAuliffe-Fogarty & Carlson, 2007). At the same time, the wholesomeness of the camp is linked to how it the summer camp experience is viewed as a profoundly innocent time, reflecting and reinforcing the dominant modern and western social ideal of childhood as a distinct and innocent period of life. Even while it is undertaken by many people whose bodies and minds are busily making the transition from childhood to adulthood, the summer camp is not, in marketing or the minds of (adult) society, openly associated with such 'adult' holiday experiences as alcohol and drug use, and/or sex. Recognising this, it is not surprising that even when, by the 1930s, there were as many girls as boys going to camps in New York State, separation between the sexes was strictly enforced. Camps were mainly single sex and any mixing between male and female camps was carefully controlled and policed. Where mixed-sex camps existed, these tended to be for pre-adolescent children only (Paris, 2001).

Against this background, it is not surprising to see that the varied research on summer camps to date has tended to avoid questions of sex in relation to the camp experience. This arguably fits within a wider avoidance by academics of issues of sex within a tourism, leisure, and outdoor recreation context (see Carr, 2016). Likewise, the tourism experiences of children as active social agents, despite receiving increased attention in recent years, is still a relatively neglected area of academic research. The avoidance of discussions of such adult-themed issues such as sex within the context of summer camps arguably serves to reinforce the notion of the camp experience as a time of innocent discovery. It also plays to the rhythm of a global adult society that still prefers to see childhood, as broadly defined to include teenagers, as a time of innocence, which by its very definition cannot encapsulate thoughts of sex. This is despite the fact that adult members of society have gone through puberty (which occurs during the socially prescribed period of our lives known as childhood) and should easily be able to remember the sexually super-charged reality of that time of their lives. If we, as adults, cannot trust our own memories, we only need to look at the research that continually identifies that significant numbers of people are having sex during their adolescence, with many losing their virginity before they are 16 years old (Johnson & Tyler, 2007; O'Reilly & Aral, 1985;

Zimmer-Gembeck & Helfand, 2008). If that is not enough to recognise that teenagers are sexually charged individuals then more proof can be provided by analysing the research that has explored the links between this population and the sexualisation of the internet and social media services (e.g. Bale, 2010; Van Ouytsel *et al.*, 2017). Furthermore, there is plenty of evidence pointing to the sexualised experiences of adolescents in the holiday environment outside of summer camps (Maticka-Tyndale *et al.*, 2003; Smith & Rosenthal, 1997). Yet such young people are defined by a society determined to preserve the idea of innocent childhood as deviant. In this way, the sexual experiences of adolescents are defined as something that should be avoided, which can be achieved through appropriate education.

Consequently, one of the central roles of the good parent and adult is to protect children from adult (and sexualised) society. Adults are charged by society, and charge themselves, resulting in a continual feedback loop, with enacting this protection, with preparing children for the realities (including the sexual) of adult life while protecting them for as long as possible. In this way, the summer camp, with its socially constructed innocence may act as a rose-tinted version of childhood, of innocence forgotten for parents. As such, the summer camp may be utilised to help children (or their parents) avoid the sexual nature of adulthood.

However, we must consider whether, given its nature, the summer camp can be an escape root for parents seeking to instil social values into their children and hide them from the realities of a sexualised society. Alternatively, the summer camp might actually be a setting perfectly designed to enable children and youth to explore all things sexual. Within this context, we can consider both those on holiday in the summer camp and those youth/young adults working in the summer camp as a gap between high school and university.

The summer camp for children is a time away from parental supervision. As such, in line with the whole tourism phenomenon, it is a place and time of escape, both from the everyday mundane and the social bonds and gatekeepers that govern behaviour in the home environment (Carr, 2011). In other words, it is a liminal place (McKercher & Bauer, 2003). The notion of the camp as a place of escape applies to both the child as tourist and the child as camp counsellor. The latter is officially employed and therefore at work, but the roll has long been marketed and socially constructed as a holiday, which just happens to be paid, however badly. As such, the idea of the camp as a liminal space clearly also applies to them. Yet the counsellors are clearly more than just tourists. Indeed, they fill a difficult niche, acting as older siblings or adult authority figures for the child guests while themselves barely out of childhood, with many utilising the job as part of their own search for self. For many such counsellors it may be their first international travel experience and even their first time travelling without their parents. The inexperience of the counsellors is heightened by the recognition that virtually all of them have no professional or tertiary education qualifications or experience that can arm them with the tools to cope with the varied demands of working with children and adolescents in a professional sense. If the counsellors are not classified as adult workers then the number of 'adults' 'working' in summer camps is relatively small. Nevertheless, these people fill an important role, they are in charge of the camp, the 'responsible' adult for both the children and the counsellors. Such a position comes with significant responsibility for the welfare of these people and power over them (Baker, 2020).

It is against this background that the chapter seeks to explore sex within the context of the camp experience. It explores this issue in relation to all three of the main actors in the camp experience: the child as tourist, the young adult (who is making the transition from childhood to adulthood) as camp counsellor and the adult as camp superintendent. It is important to recognise that the chapter is not designed to analyse sex in summer camps but is, instead, structured to provide a window into this world. In this way, it provides an initial exploration of sex in summer camps. As such, it provides a foundation upon which more detailed and structured studies can emerge.

Where Did the Data Come From?

Hopefully as you read this section it will become apparent why it is entitled 'Where Did the Data Come From?' rather than 'Methods' or 'Methodology', despite the fact that the chapter does contain a large component of what may be termed 'primary data'. The data presented in the chapter do not stem from a study based on predetermined aims or objectives. Instead, the second author has significant experience as a camp counsellor, and it is this experience which has been drawn on to begin to recognise the position of sex, in all its variety, in the summer camp space and experience for campers, counsellors, and superintendents. The lived experiences of the second author speak of an ethnographic or auto-ethnographic study and yet these experiences were truly organic rather than constructed in any ethnographic sense. In this way, they have all the richness of an ethnographic study with none of the preconceptions that both bound any study and give it structure (both being potentially negative and positive constructs, depending on your perspective as a researcher).

Given that no data were collected specifically for this study and that everything presented is from the memory of the second author instead, it is valid to question the recall accuracy of this information. Concern regarding memory decay and the accuracy of recall is a common theme in research that relies on the memories of respondents (Aaker *et al.*,

2008; Jenkins *et al.*, 2002). Given both the significant role summer camps have played in the life of the second author and the important nature of the topic being discussed, it is possible to argue that his recall is accurate. This is supported by Larsen's (2007: 14) claim that 'It is a well established finding in memory studies that events that stand out, events that are distinctive, such as for example vacations, are among the events that people actually can recall'. The issue of recall accuracy is also negated somewhat by the point that we are focusing on issues rather than specific facts. While specific memories may help to inform the discussion they are not the focus of the chapter.

As the summer camp experiences of the second author were never undertaken with the idea of conducting research, no ethical clearance was ever gained to do so. It is not feasible to think of gaining such approval retrospectively. Does this mean that we should not report on these experiences? To suggest that is to say we should never insert our lived experiences into social science research. That would remove one of the richest sources of ideas from the field. Consequently, we deal with ethics in the sense of 'doing no harm' rather than the paperwork exercise to expunge researchers of blame should something go wrong in a manner that is akin to buying an insurance policy. In this context, the names, dates (other than to say they are 21st century experiences) and locations of the camps experienced by the second author are never mentioned and the names of anyone involved in the camps are not mentioned. In this way the identity of all those that the second author crossed paths with during his camp counsellor experiences should be protected. Where names are used, they are all pseudonyms.

It is clear that the data presented in this chapter are from one person who was not actually deliberately conducting research on the topic of sex in summer camps while a camp counsellor. As such, the data can be said to lack the rigor that we would expect as an outcome of a structured research process. As a result, caution must be applied to the use of these data. In this way, the data are not employed to make sweeping claims and/or generalisations about summer camps. At the same time, such data have an organic richness that is similar to the archival materials discussed by Saadat *et al.* (forthcoming). Indeed, these personal recollections can be viewed as archival material in many ways. Alternatively, we could define them as retrospective auto-ethnography.

Rather than proclaim the data have been analysed in a specific, standard style, it is more honest to simply say that the recollections of the second author have been utilised to raise awareness of the sexual nature of the summer camp. This reflects the fact that the chapter does not aim to provide an analysis of sex in the summer camp. Instead, it is intended as a window into this world, an initial exploration of it from which more detailed and structured studies can emerge. This is an important first step before traditional academic research is undertaken in that it opens up a new world of possibilities and leaves others to conduct the research on those possibilities. Yet without this first step the issue of sex in summer camps risks being left in the dark, bereft of the academic research needed to fully explore, and where necessary/appropriate, address it. Consequently, in the next section a series of reflections on sex in the summer camp are presented. These reflect the experiences of the second author and are consequently often written about in the first person.

Tales From the Frontline

It is 6:30 in the morning, time for the camp counsellors at Happy Camp to get ready for another day of activities with the children. Before jumping into the showers, the senior counsellors indoctrinate the newbies about the local customs, starting with the 'traditional' morning jerkoff. This was one of my first instructions when I entered the world of camping counselling, a world designed as a hermetic bubble to protect the campers, but which entails a different story for those in the backstage.

The model of organised camps works well. That is why these places have become so popular. However, the modern camp industry is a product of a long process of trial and error. It is not because of magic that a resort that hosts hundreds of minors for several days can remain orderly and avoid undesirable events. There is a myriad of situations that could easily destroy the reputation of a well-renowned camp. To avoid this cataclysm, the camps set up a series of strategies to control, or ideally prevent, events that could lead to legal actions and/or social reprisal. This chapter narrates some of the sex-related scenarios that summer camps face, and the strategies used to deal with them. The chapter is divided in three sections: sex involving the campers only, sex between campers and staff members and sex among staff.

Before continuing with the sections, it must be noted that all events occurring within a camp are the responsibility of the staff, irrespective of whether they are directly involved in an event or not. The staff is responsible for planning the appropriate strategies to prevent the occurrence of sexual acts within the camp, since most of the time the campers are minors.

I worked for more than 10 years as a camp counsellor. Most of the time, my camps were with the same two companies, but I was often invited to act as a seasonal worker in other camps across the country. The anecdotes and reflections in this chapter are a compilation of situations that I or my team had to face in relation to sex within summer camps.

Sex involving only the campers

Perhaps the first scenario that comes to mind when thinking about sex in summer camps is the sex escapades of a couple or group of teenagers sneaking out of their cabins at night. As it has been portrayed as an *uncountable* time by Hollywood, the camp generates expectations of summer love and sex encounters. The camp is an isolated, liminal space where children and teenagers are free form the daily observation of their parents. It is a space where they are trusted to behave in a responsible way. Nevertheless, teenage hormones do not necessarily obey responsibilities or social rules. From day one at the camp, groups of friends are formed, and the giggling starts surrounding discussing of attractions and potential matches. Any counsellor with a bit of experience will be expecting groups of girls to be checking out the boy and *vice versa*. It is the responsibility of the counsellor to ensure that things do not escalate into unwanted outcomes that could affect any campers, physically and/or emotionally. These counsellors are regular young adults who conserve within themselves' a spark of enthusiasm for games but who are, at the same time, expected to behave in a professional way. We will speak more about this in the next section.

In my experience, I could say that while the expectations of the campers are more focused on emotional experiences than sexual encounters, sexual acts still occur with frequency in the form of exhibitionism and sexual jokes (especially, but not exclusively, these emerge from the boys). I cannot remember a single camp with teenagers without someone swinging his penis in front of the other guys in the showers, or without someone simulating orgasms at bedtime. To stop the campers staying awake all night, saying as much garbage as crosses their mind or even bullying other boys, a couple of counsellors always sleep in the same dorms as them. In the dorms, separating the campers by gender and the constant presence of a staff member are fundamental steps taken to guarantee the safety and appropriate conduct of the campers. However, the counsellors are human too, and after a long day of activities their sleep can be really deep. Some of the situations that can be expected if a counsellor does not take the appropriate care are communal masturbation or even sexual assault among children while sleeping. As a counsellor, it just takes 10 minutes faking of being asleep to start hearing the giggling about the sexual fantasies and intentions of the most energetic campers. It just takes ten minutes before you start hearing faked orgasms, fantasies of having sex with other campers, attempts to humiliate specific campers with sexual offers and even contests to find who gets a faster erection and who comes first jerking off. These are every night talks, at least in the boys' dorms. A good counsellor must know how to establish boundaries and redirect this energy.

Every professional camp has protocols related to instances where two or more campers have any sort of sexual encounter. It is not a secret that dealing with teenagers implies having to deal with their hormones. Things get more complicated when events go beyond the 'usual expectations'. Beyond a multitude of voyeuristic/paedophilic stories about teenagers having sex during summer camps, there are other serious sex issues that can occur during a camp. The following three scenarios were situations that I faced during my time as a counsellor.

Scenario one: a camper confesses to their friends, the counsellor or in public to being homosexual. It is not uncommon that during a camp experience there will be one or two campers who act in specific manners that will be perceived as 'homosexual' by other campers. There will be gossip around (among campers and among staff) surrounding the sexual preferences of these individuals. In some cases, other campers may react aggressively (bullying) against the children that they perceive as homosexuals. A good team of counsellors maintains an environment where everybody feels safe and equal, but the risk of verbal or even physical attacks is always there. This is why someone confessing homosexual preferences in public becomes an important aspect to be monitored by the counsellors. We are clearly living in the 21st century, a supposed age of freedom and tolerance, but not everybody has realised this yet.

Scenario two: a camper confesses that they have been sexually abused. Unfortunately, child sex abuse is very common, but victims often stay silent or are unaware that the abuse is not normal (Horowitz, 2007; Hunter, 2010). Summer camps create safe spaces of freedom, where the campers are far from their usual social circle. The campers will be invited to reflect about their daily life, their role within society, and the environment (this soft indoctrination occurs in every camp). Additionally, it is common that the campers will feel attached to their camp counsellors, as if they were older siblings. It is not uncommon that girls and boys will share with the staff (and sometimes in public) that they have been abused, and indirectly imply that it was sexual. During my time as a counsellor, these confessions were especially frequent when we were working with children from the slums. Not because sexual abuse is more common in lower classes (which I do not think is the case), but because our work was to implement 'crime-prevention' camp programmes that involve deeper emotional reflections. The confessions can also be involuntary. I remember the case of a girl who had a slight level of autism. A novice male counsellor committed the terrible mistake of hugging her while she was distracted. Although the counsellor did not have the intention to harm the girl, his action triggered memories of abuse. Immediately, the girl got scared and anxious. It took a few hours and a lot of work from the female staff to calm her down. It was then that she indirectly confessed the abuses. Overall, the work of the staff is not to look for histories of abuse or to offer psychiatric treatment (although some specialised camps may have programmes for that). However, there is an ethical responsibility to seek to ensure the wellbeing of the children after the camp. In these cases, usually the camp will send a report to the institution or the person responsible for the camper, commenting on the situation.

Third scenario: a good summer camp is inclusive. Children with physical and mental disabilities are included in the activities and treated just like any other camper. Usually, there are no major issues related to these campers. In my experience, campers with high autism spectrum disorder (ASD) could on rare occasions start touching their genitals in public or even inappropriately touching other campers. The first situation does not cause a big problem because the person is only touching themselves and the other campers usually understand that the person has a particular mental condition. However, the staff must control the situation immediately and safeguard the dignity of the camper with ASD. On the other hand, a person with ASD touching another camper without their consent is a very delicate issue. These cases are rare, but they must be taken very seriously. The most complicated case that I witnessed in relation to this was during a camp with people between the ages 8 and 16. Every night at the camp there was usually a campfire where the campers and the staff took part in energetic singing and dancing. Some of the dances included physical contact with other campers. During one of these dances, a male with ASD (Tom), who was holding another boy (Max) by the waist, in a sort of conga line, got excited by the euphoria of the event and started banging his crotch against Max while holding him very hard. The staff stopped him as soon as it was possible (it was not easy because Tom was a big person), but Max was in shock because of the sexual assault and the public attention. The issue was especially delicate because Tom was 18 years old, but had been accepted into the camp because he was part of the same class as Max (who was 16 years old). Tom was warned about his behaviour but a couple of days later he again invaded the personal space of other boys and he had to go back home.

Sexual behaviour between campers and staff members

Alongside the prototypical summer camp there is also an important number of camps oriented towards young adults (e.g. university students) and middle-aged adults (e.g. team building camps for companies). These experiences are offered by the same camps that run summer camp experiences for children, diversifying their product offerings to ensure their economic sustainability. Organised camps are extremely careful when it comes to hiring their staff. However, staff turnover is high in this business. On top of that, there are strict protocols to prevent any situations that could result in a health hazard and/or legal problem. For instance, most camps have the policy that under no circumstances may a female minor camper stay alone in any closed area with a male counsellor, no matter how respectful and trustable he is.

Therefore, it is very unlikely that a sexual encounter will occur between minors (campers) and the staff, within the camp. A single instance of such behaviour will devastate the image of the camp and send guilty members of the staff to jail. However, it is very common within camps for teenage campers (both male and female) to flirt with the counsellors. Some of these campers try to attract the attention of the counsellors by showing some skin, either soaking their shirts, removing them or tearing their leggings. This often results in campers and staff exchanging contacts (WhatsApp number, Instagram, etc.), despite the fact that such behaviour is strictly prohibited by most camps. This is especially common between young staff members and teenage campers because the age difference is just between two and five years. It is an open secret that some of these contacts result in intimate conversations, social meetings and romantic dates after the camp. If the administration finds out about these encounters, it is likely that the counsellor will be fired. This warning and the fact that dating or keeping images of a minor could lead to legal prosecution does not discourage many new staff, who will see their first camps with high school students as a buffet of potential bed buddies and/or a factory of nude or semi-nude pictures (which classifies as child pornography). A responsible counsellor must avoid any type of private contact with former campers.

The situation is different when the campers are young adults. This is a tricky group because most of the campers will be adults but there may also be a few minors in the groups (we are talking of 17−19 years olds in the case of undergraduate students at tertiary education institutes). Many of these campers will be sexually active but still living under the supervision of their parents/guardians. Usually, the camp company will maintain the same policy as in the case of children of no exchange of personal contacts between campers and counsellors. However, the temptations felt by the counsellors are heightened now that there is a lesser risk of going to jail as a paedophile. It is with these groups of campers, which involve most of the after-camp sexual encounters, either among them or with the staff. This group is also more likely to have sex within the camp, but still it is not a very common thing.

During a camp, everybody is fashion-less, alcohol is usually banned and the campers, irrespective of their age, are separated by sex. However, because the counsellors are dealing with 'adults', the level of monitoring is less than in the case of camps involving children. Although sexual intercourse is still not common within the camp, in my experience, I would say that homosexual sex is more common in these groups. Why is this the case? Simply because it is easier to bump into your friend's bed in the same dorm than sneaking into the cold to have sex under a tree with another fugitive. Aside from sex between adult campers, sex also occurs between adult campers and staff within the camp. This is a major open secret but is also rare. This is a good moment for another anecdote.

Every camp company has its own way of working. Although the basic security and legal policies are similar, the philosophies and ethics vary a lot. In my experience, the larger the work team is, the easier it is for counsellors to have a sex escapade. This is simply because there are more people to cover for you while you are getting laid (i.e. there will be always a colleague willing to back you up). There is another important condition that increases the chances of sex between staff and campers. This is the recurrence of visitors by people (campers and staff) to camps. Many campers go to the same summer camp year after year. The camp is the annual opportunity to meet their friends from other schools but also the counsellors from previous years. The bond created between a child and its counsellor during one camp is strong. After several years working in/visiting the same camp such bounds may become more intimate, until a point where the counsellors can cross their professional boundaries. In some camp companies, it is an open secret that some counsellors (over 18 years old) have summer sexual relationships with their campers (around 15–17 years old) going on for two or three years.

School camps can utilise the same physical resources as summer camps. The attendees of summer camps come from different schools, they stay for one or two weeks and the communication is directly between the camp administration and the parents. In the case of school camps, the attendees already know each other, the camps usually last less than a week, and any contact between the camp and the parents is undertaken through the teachers at the school. Unlike the summer camps, every school camp comes with a small team of teachers (usually women) who in the context of this discussion are viewed as guests of the camp rather than employees of their school. Since the programme the camp provides is completely focused on the children, the teachers have plenty of time to wander around, have coffee and have sex (they are conveniently isolated from their children). If the teachers are happy with the service, it is likely that they will bring the school next year. Each camp addresses the issue of sex related to teachers in a different way. I remember a camp where the director and his friends (or sometimes a lucky counsellor) used to take the teachers in the camp's yacht and then invited them for dinner at his luxurious cabin, while the counsellors were working with the kids. On the other hand, I remember the case of a good-looking male counsellor who used to be chased by the teachers, and he was asked more than once by the administration to *take one* for the team.

Sex among staff

As in many other professions, love and sex occur between colleagues in a camp. Since many of the counsellors are young adults (18–20 years) and many of them still live with their parents, the camp becomes an opportunity to spend the night with someone else without the vigilance of their family. First and foremost, a camp is a business, and the counsellors are employees. The working day for a counsellor starts when the first camper arrives and it finishes when the last camper is gone a few days later. That means there is very little free time, and what is available is mainly used to recover energy levels. However, there will be always a couple of counsellors willing to sacrifice their sleep time for some sexual activities. The administration of the camp does not work at nights, and the people in charge at night are senior counsellors who may also be having sex. As long as there is someone monitoring the campers in each of the dorms, the rest of the staff are free to do whatever they want if they still have the energy.

The culture in every camp is different, and each team of counsellors has its unique codes and ethics. Within this context, it is not unheard of for new counsellors to be pressured to have sex. The teams of counsellors are a mix between an incestuous family and a cult. Some of them have initiations ceremonies. At night, when the other members of the staff are gone (except for a couple of watchmen and the nurse), the counsellors are free to do as much as they can with the little energy that they have. If non-consensual sex occurred in a camp, this may be the time when it occurs.

Sexual pressure can also come from the directors of the camp. It is quite common for camp directors to try techniques to take counsellors out of their comfort zone. For instance, one of my first bosses was explaining to me the working of the camp and he held my hand firmly while he was farting really loud. I have no idea what he was trying to prove. I just stayed silent throughout the incident. Another senior male director, very respected in the industry, used to say 'hi' to the counsellors by spanking them, and he used to ask the new male counsellors to give him a quick kiss on the mouth to show how brave they were.

Discussion and Conclusions

The recollections of the second author are, of course, specific to him and therefore we should not attempt to make generalisations from them. However, that was never the intention of the authors. Rather, the aim of this chapter has been to shine a light on the sexual nature of summer camps. The recollections presented in this chapter have clearly done this, identifying a wide array of issues that need to be recognised and examined in detail. These stand in opposition to the research published on summer camps to date, which has eschewed discussion of sex and the sexual. Yet it stands in opposition to popular depictions of the summer camp as a liminal and sexual space. Writing about summer camps before the Second World War, Paris (2008) recognised the sexualised nature of these spaces, where, as noted above, communal masturbation was an issue. Yet contemporary recognition of the sexual reality of summer camps continues to be missing from academic discourse. Instead, research has focused on the socially defined nature of the camp as a place of learning and development (Baker, 2020; Henderson *et al.*, 2007; McAuliffe-Fogarty & Carlson, 2007). In doing so, the work has implicitly reinforced the notion of childhood as a time of innocence.

The recollections have shown how the summer camp can be a highly sexually charged environment, involving consensual and non-consensual sexual experiences. These have the potential to involve all the actors in the summer camp space, including children/adolescents, camp counsellors barely out of childhood, managers of camps, and teachers. As recognised in the recollections of the second author, camps can be a space of sexual self-expression and enlightenment. In this way, camps have the potential to be self-empowering in very positive ways. This supports the work of Davis-Delano and Gillard (2015), who identified summer camps as a space where women could explore their sexuality and engage in same-sex relationships as part of their development. It is important, however, to note that Davis-Delano and Gillard's work was focused on adult summer camp attendees and staff.

While offering the potential for self-development and enlightenment, the potential for sexual abuse during the camp experience is high. This can be seen to conform to a pattern of potential sexual abuse of minors in situations where parents/guardians are absent, such as in the sporting environment (Dixon, 2020) the Boy Scouts (Kline, 2009; Rowan, 2006), and the Catholic Church (Dale & Alpert, 2007), for example. This abuse cuts across and exists within all the stakeholder groups. As noted in the recollections of the second author, there is the potential for abuse of minors by adults, among minors, of employees by minors, of employees by employers, and among employees. The nature of the abuse also clearly takes many forms. The abuse of sexual minorities is not restricted to the camp environment, but has been noted in this space (Oakleaf, 2013). The abuse of employees by employers may speak to the disadvantaged nature of the latter's employment position, on temporary contracts. The power differential between these two groups that can contribute to the sexual abuse of camp counsellors is similar to that reported between hotel guests and service staff by Oliveira and Ambrósio in this book.

The multiple potential sources of sexual abuse in summer camps, when set alongside the recognition of the space as a hyper-sexualised one, suggests there is a need for detailed research to fully expose and understand the sexualised nature of summer camps and the impacts of this on all the people touched by summer camps. Without this, the culture of silence (Horowitz, 2007; Hunter, 2010) in which sexual abuse victims suffer will continue unabated. Breaking this silence is required to enable the development of appropriate safeguards that do not just seek to prevent any sexual activities in summer camps but facilitate sexual self-exploration and enlightenment while at the same time guarding against all types of sexual abuse.

The starting point to such research and the development of policies that are fit for purpose is to cease attempting to ignore and/or hide from the sexualised nature of summer camps. Recognising them as hyper-sexualised sites allows research, society and camp operators to begin to openly discuss the issue in a positive and constructive manner.

References

Aaker, J., Drolet, A. and Griffin, D. (2008) Recalling mixed emotions. *Journal of Consumer Research* 35, 268–278.

Baker, M. (2020) *Becoming and Being a Camp Counsellor: A Study of Discourse, Power Relations and Emotions*. Cham, Switzerland: Palgrave Macmillan Publishing.

Bale, C. (2010) Sexualised culture and young people's sexual health: A cause for concern? *Sociology Compass* 4 (10), 824–840.

Carr, N. (2011) *Children's and Families' Holiday Experiences*. Abingdon: Routledge.

Carr, N. (2016) Sex in tourism: Reflections from a dark corner of tourism studies. *Tourism Recreation Research* 41 (2), 188–198.

Dale, K. and Alpert, J. (2007) Hiding behind the cloth: Child sexual abuse and the Catholic Church. *Journal of Child Sexual Abuse* 16 (3), 59–74.

Davis-Delano, L. and Gillard, A. (2015) Summer camp as context for girls' and women's same-sex attractions and relationships. Leisure/Loisir 39 (1), 1–36.

Dixon, K. (2020) Sexual abuse and masculine cultures: Reflections on the British football scandal of 2016. In R. Magrath, J. Cleland and E. Anderson (eds) *The Palgrave Handbook of Masculinity and Sport* (pp. 73–93). Cham, Switzerland: Palgrave Macmillan.

Goldsmith, C. (1949) The summer camp. *The Journal of Pediatrics* 34 (4), 510–515.

Henderson, K., Scheuler Whitaker, L., Bialeschki, M.D., Scanlin, M. and Thurber, C. (2007) Summer camp experiences: Parental perceptions of youth development outcomes. *Journal of Family Issues* 28 (8), 987–1007.

Horowitz, D. (2007) The silence of abused children: Policy implications. In M-E. Pipe, M. Lamb, Y. Orbach and A-C. Cederborg (eds) *Child Sexual Abuse: Disclosure, Delay, and Denial* (pp. 281–290). London: Routledge.

Hunter, S. (2010) Evolving narratives about childhood sexual abuse: Challenging the dominance of the victim and survivor paradigm. *The Australian and New Zealand Journal of Family Therapy* 31 (2), 176–190.

Jenkins, P., Earle-Richardson, G., Slingerland, D.T. and May, J. (2002) Time dependent memory decay. *American Journal of Industrial Medicine* 41, 98–101.

Johnson, K. and Tyler, K. (2007) Adolescent sexual onset: An intergenerational analysis. *Journal of Youth and Adolescence* 36 (7), 939–949.

Kline, J. (2009) Child sexual abuse in the Boy Scouts of America, 1970 – 1984. Unpublished Master's Thesis. University of New Hampshire.

Larsen, S. (2007) Aspects of a psychology of the tourist experience. *Scandinavian Journal of Hospitality and Tourism* 7 (1), 7–18.

Maticka-Tyndale, E., Herold, E. and Oppermann, M. (2003) Casual sex among Australian Schoolies. *The Journal of Sex Research* 40 (2), 158–169.

McAuliffe-Fogarty, A. and Carlson, K. (2007) Preface. *Child and Adolescent Psychiatric Clinics of North America* 16 (4), xv–xvii.

McKercher, B. and Bauer, T. (2003) Conceptual framework of the nexus between tourism, romance, and sex. In T. Bauer and B. McKercher (eds) *Sex and Tourism: Journeys of Romance, Love and Lust* (pp. 3–17). New York: The Haworth Hospitality Press.

Oakleaf, L. (2013) 'Having to think about it all the time': Factors affecting the identity management strategies of residential summer camp staff who self-identify as lesbian, gay, bisexual or transgender. *Leisure/Loisir* 37 (3), 251–266.

O'Reilly, K. and Aral, S. (1985) Adolescence and sexual behavior: Trends and implications for STD. *Journal of Adolescent Health Care* 6 (4), 262–270.

Paris, L. (2001) The adventures of Peanut and Bo: Summer camps and early-twentieth-century American girlhood. *Journal of Women's History* 12 (4), 47–76.

Paris, L. (2008) *Children's Nature: The Rise of the American Summer Camp*. New York: New York University Press.

Rowan, E. (2006) *Understanding Child Sexual Abuse*. Jackson, USA: University Press of Mississippi.

Saadat, P. Carr, N. and Walters, T. (forthcoming) Using archival material in leisure studies: beauty and the beast. In F. Okumus, S.M. Rasoolimanesh and S. Jahani (eds) *Contemporary Research Methodology for Hospitality and Tourism*. Bingley: Emerald Publishing Group.

Smith, A. and Rosenthal, D. (1997) Sex, alcohol and drugs? Young people's experience of Schoolies Week. *Australian and New Zealand Journal of Public Health* 21 (2), 175– 180.

Van Ouytsel, J., Van Gool, E., Walrave, M., Ponnet, K. and Peeters, E. (2017) Sexting: Adolescents' perceptions of the applications used for, motives for, and consequences of sexting. *Journal of Youth Studies* 20 (4), 446–470.

Van Slyck, A. (2006) *A Manufactured Wilderness: Summer Camps and the Shaping of American Youth, 1890 – 1960*. Minneapolis: University of Minnesota Press.

Weyl, C. (1925) An historical account of the summer camp movement. *Religious Education* 20 (3), 180–184.

Zimmer-Gembeck, M. and Helfand, M. (2008) Ten years of longitudinal research on U.S. adolescent sexual behavior: Developmental correlates of sexual intercourse, and the importance of age, gender and ethnic background. *Developmental Review* 28, 153–224.

5 Embodying Liminality: Exploring the 'Affects' of Sexual Encounters in Backpacker and Volunteer Tourism

Phoebe Everingham, Amie Matthews
and Tamara Young

Introduction

The topic of 'sex *and* tourism', as opposed to 'sex tourism' (which has exploitative associations), is an understudied phenomena in tourism research (Carr, 2016). This is surprising given that there is a well established association between holidays and sex (Inglis, 2000; Pritchard & Morgan, 2006), particularly the association between international mass tourism and sexual imagery in tourism marketing (Crick, 1989). As Carr (2016) argues, despite the fact that both sex *and* tourism are central facets of social life, there remains academic hesitance to look more broadly at sexual encounters in tourism, for instance, encounters that are consensual, enjoyable, fun, fleeting, intense and spontaneous. This is most likely because scholarly interest in tourism *and* sex (at least when sex is studied outside of medicalised settings) share common histories of being lampooned as frivolous areas of social inquiry (on this issue in tourism studies, see Franklin & Crang, 2001). However, as Carr (2016) points out, expanding the scope of how we understand 'sex *and* tourism' experiences can lead to more nuanced understandings of the complexities of the various sexual encounters that occur in the travel space.

With this in mind, this chapter brings together findings from two ethnographic studies on youth tourists/travellers to examine the sexual interactions that can emerge in volunteer tourism and backpacker tourism. By drawing on two studies, we make connections between volunteers and backpackers as, in both cases, the tourists at the centre of the research were young (on average between the ages of 18 and 30), travelling for longer periods of time than 'mass tourists', and on trips that might typically be positioned as being 'transformative' (see, for example, Wearing *et al.*, 2010). Further, despite growing academic interest in volunteer tourism and backpacker tourism and the connections frequently made between youth identities and these tourism forms, few studies have examined the sexual activities and encounters of these youth travellers (an exception being Berdychevsky *et al.*, 2010). This is despite the plethora of youth studies outside of the tourism literature examining sexual identity and behaviours. In this chapter we make a contribution to this gap in tourism research and, by drawing comparisons from two separate projects on youth tourism experiences, we obtain a more detailed picture of the complex and contradictory sexual dynamics that can emerge corporeally, affectively and discursively between tourists and tourists, and tourists and locals.

We approach analysis of these sexual dynamics through the theoretical lenses of liminality, affect and embodiment. Following Turner (1986, 1987), we argue firstly that the liminal or 'liminoid'[1] tourist space, and the marketing of tourism more generally as seductive and sexy, lends itself to a particular affective atmosphere of malleability, permissibility and playfulness. However, we also suggest that where the discourses of backpacker tourism make it more conducive to this permissibility, the marketing and framing of volunteer tourism experiences is governed by a particular discursive morality that silences the hedonistic and sexual 'tourism' component of the travel experience. The prevalence of development aid discourses and the resultant stereotypes of volunteer tourists is, as Everingham (2015, 2016, 2018a, 2018b) argues, at the expense of more nuanced analyses of the multifaceted aspects of volunteer experiences in these tourism spaces. Touristic representation (and, by extension academic research) focused only on this component of volunteer tourism as development aid leaves sexual licentiousness and sexual revelry absent from volunteer tourism discourses (despite similarities in the demographics of volunteer tourists with other forms of youth travel, such as backpacking). Moreover, volunteer tourists often add a backpacking component to their long-term travels, and vice versa (Everingham, 2016; Matthews, 2008b; Young, 2009). Therefore, distinctions between these two types of travel are blurry and volunteering experiences often occur in the same destinations and liminoid tourism spaces as backpacking.

By foregrounding the liminal and embodied, affective nature of sexual encounters in tourism spaces, we highlight the complex relationalities that can emerge between bodies and the sensuous dimensions of travel spaces. We argue that the sexual encounters emerging in volunteer tourism and backpacker tourism contexts are like *all* sexual encounters:

relational and intersubjective. It is these multifaceted aspects of sex *and* tourism that get lost if we isolate sexual activity from other aspects of the tourism experience. Both backpackers and volunteer tourists – as contemporary examples of youth tourists – are embedded within particular narratives that frame their expectations and experiences differently, yet they are situated in the same tourism destinations and have overlapping experiences. While the construction of tourism spaces that emphasise sexiness and licentiousness can be experienced as liberating, the ways in which tourists become embodied objects within these sexualised spaces can be discomforting and even frightening, especially for some women (Pritchard & Morgan, 2006). In recognising then that travel spaces are gendered, sexualised (Jordan & Aitchison, 2008) and racialised, attention is given to the embodiment and effects of the many different sexual experiences and encounters that emerge within, and from, these liminoid spaces. It is the liminoid and carnivalesque elements of travel spaces, and the particular affective and embodied responses these generate, that this chapter now turns to.

Liminality and the Carnivalesque

Tourism is commonly understood as generating emotionally heightened experiences that are outside the spatial, temporal and social bounds of an individual's everyday life. When we depart on a holiday of some kind we leave behind (or we expect to leave behind) our known physical environments, and the everyday rhythms, patterns and social rules that govern them. These are instead exchanged for foreign and sometimes marginal spaces, where new rules or structures, and social orders exist, which tourists are, to varying degrees, disassociated from. It is for this reason that tourism and travel are often viewed as being liminal or, more aptly, 'liminoid' (Turner, 1982). Holidays are conceived as being situated 'betwixt and between' (Turner, 1986: 41) the certainties and routines of home, and those associated with the tourism destination by the local population, and this ambiguous positioning is understood as giving rise to feelings of immense freedom and possibility. Even when the everyday persists in tourism, expectations for difference endure, and transgressions and social inversions are conceived of as being commonplace, as the 'new norm' (Larsen, 2008). The liminoid nature of tourism is also seen as being generative. It allows for greater experimentation and transformation, offering tourists a means of self-discovery or a new way of being in the world (see, for example, Desforges, 2000; Lean, 2012; Matthews, 2014; Noy, 2004; Picard, 2012; Wearing *et al.*, 2010). Indeed, the enduring discourse (both popular and academic) is that travel opens up opportunities for play, for transgressive behaviour, and for people to engage in activities extraordinary to their everyday lives.

Whether conceived temporally, socially or spatially, the 'mood of maybe' (Turner, 1986: 42) that pervades tourism spaces is deeply potent, and gives rise to embodied possibilities. In tourism spaces we see some of the playfulness that is inherent to the liminal move towards, what Shields (1991) terms, the 'carnivalesque'. In his study of the socio-cultural meanings ascribed to space and place, Shields (1991) suggests that certain tourism sites, such as seaside resorts, exist on the geographic and social peripheries of everyday life. These tourist sites provide a release from the mundane by overtly embracing pleasure and revelling in permissiveness, as well as grotesque or exaggerated corporeality (Shields, 1991). This notion of exaggerated corporeality closely relates to, what Allon and Anderson (2010: 18) identify as 'excess' in their study of the embodied experiences of backpackers and working holidaymakers residing in coastal areas of Sydney, Australia. Interrogating the tensions that emerge between some travellers and locals in these areas, Allon and Anderson (2010: 18) argue that, within the backpacker enclaves of Bondi and Coogee, there is a 'suspension of the standard controls, constraints, and regulations that define "settled" community'. The resultant lifestyle becomes one of '"too much" sex, with "too many" partners', as well as excessive drinking, partying and noise (Allon & Anderson, 2010: 18).

These contextualisations of liminality and the carnivalesque illustrate that the affective atmospheres that arise within liminal/liminoid tourism spaces are often conducive to sexual permissiveness. Whether sex is between tourists and local residents, or among tourists themselves, these encounters are also relational, and often more spontaneous than much of the research on sex in tourism suggests. Yet, while the liminal/liminoid spaces of tourism encourage transgressive behaviour that is conducive to radical openness towards sexual experiences, these experiences may not always be pleasant or even welcomed. The marketing of tourism spaces as being 'sexy', and the affective atmosphere of the sensual that liminoid tourism spaces generate, can work to rationalise and condone certain forms of sexual harassment in these spaces. For instance, Jordan and Aitchison (2008) discuss the sexualisation of local men's gaze on women tourists in their research of the solo travelling experiences of English women. While they acknowledge that the sexualised and gendered gaze is certainly not homogenous or fixed, they also observe that female tourists are often inevitably positioned as objects (Jordan & Aitchison, 2008). Consequently, it is the normalisation of the sensual in tourism spaces that can become problematic for those women who do not want to be perceived in a sexual way (Jordan & Aitchison, 2008).

The ambiguity of sexually affective atmospheres – generated in and by the liminoid – and the ways in which these atmospheres 'affect' embodied encounters in tourism (between tourists, and between tourists and locals) is the focus of this chapter. The sensuous and sexy dimensions of the liminoid are often absent in theorisations of tourism spaces, despite the fact that such dimensions mediate the experiences of tourists (and in some cases locals). We now turn our attention to affect and embodiment as theoretical framings that provide insight into the ambiguities of lived experiences and sexual encounters in liminal and liminoid travel spaces.

Affect, Embodiment and Liminality

Even in everyday life, sexualities are negotiated through encounters that are both real and imagined, involving dynamic relations between 'self' and 'others' (Hubbard 2002). These relations are 'encoded in representations of space', where representation and experiences 'entwine in specific places to create sexual identities that are fractured, contested and always becoming' (Hubbard, 2002: 365). Sexuality is constituted and practiced within particular social, cultural and historical contexts, and manifested relationally in these contexts. In liminal tourism spaces, sex can be seen as a form of liberation presenting individuals an escape from mundane everyday life (Lanca *et al.*, 2017). However, the 'sexualisation of the travel gaze' (Jordan & Aitchison, 2008) can also leave female travellers, particularly those travelling alone, feeling vulnerable. Thus, while some individuals may relish transient encounters, others may struggle with this dimension. In short, just because the *possibility* for transgression is offered, this does not mean that it is always the outcome of all tourist experiences, or that these transgressions are always desired. As Pritchard and Morgan (2006) observe, while liminal spaces are associated with freedom, tourists are still embodied within their gender, race and sexuality. These positionalities can either constrain or empower their experiences and perception of places and local people.

These notions of embodiment, affect and intersubjectivity are significant to how we understand sexual encounters in tourism, particularly as they occur within liminal/liminoid spaces. We are cognisant that sexual encounters are not necessarily planned in an *a priori* manner, and that these encounters are also somewhat outside of and beyond the rational. Sexual encounters, therefore, happen in ways that depend upon the relationalities of those involved, and how each person is 'affected' within the encounter. For instance, in theorising geographies of engagement and encounter, Hubbard (2002: 366) notes that sexual identities emerge from interaction 'between Self and Other, with feelings of attraction and repulsion entering the unconscious only to be projected back on to Others'. Theorising sexual encounters in tourism should therefore also bring the unconscious into social theory. In doing so, we can more deeply explore the dynamics between the self and the external world in 'transitional space', where 'boundaries between Self and Other are created through the entwining of fantasy and reality' (Hubbard, 2002: 336).

To this end, Everingham (2018a) acknowledges the ambiguity and complexity of the sexual encounters of volunteer tourists. Sexual desire operates in the 'in-between' spaces: in between nature, the psyche, culture and society (Dimen, 1989). At times, sexual attraction between volunteers and local residents can be fun and playful yet, as Everingham (2018a, 2018b) notes, they can also be uncomfortable and scary. As her study of lived experiences of volunteer tourism in South America reveals, sexual encounters between volunteers from the Global North and locals from the Global South can provide opportunities to break down boundaries between 'Self' and 'Other'. However, at other times, these sexual encounters can create stronger boundaries and larger divisions, highlighting the 'intersectional spaces of power determined by age, gender, class and colour' (Everingham, 2018a: 73).

By taking an approach that emphasises affect and relationality, we emphasise the non-binary nature of power relations within the sexually laden liminoid and carnivalesque spaces of tourism. Tan (2014: 26), for example, uses the term 'paradoxical affects' to describe the ways by which 'impulses, agencies, and sensations manifest themselves in ambiguous ways that cannot be predetermined in advance'. What this means is that a focus on 'affect' orients analysis towards relationality, particularly as we respond to particular affective states generated between people and geographic spaces that, in turn, generate particular atmospheres. Tan (2014) finds that notions of liminal and paradoxical spaces allow us to think beyond binaries and analyse social relations that occur in the 'interstices'. For Tan (2014), such paradoxical enactments of power can also move away from reductionist analyses by taking into account the junctions between the 'representable and non-representable' aspects of social life. In other words, the liminoid nature of touristic sexual encounters in tourism spaces generates particular affective atmospheres of sex and sexuality, which are at once connected to the unconscious and non-representational aspects of bodily desire, as well as broader representations of tourism and the exotic. While these representations undoubtedly simplify what occurs in tourism spaces, they are extremely potent. We now turn to the marketing of backpacking and volunteer tourism to consider the ways in which these representations may affect the embodied aspects of these experiences, in particular how sexuality and desire is mediated within these tourism spaces.

Representations of Sex and Sexuality in Backpacking and Volunteer Tourism

Despite the burgeoning literature on both backpacker and volunteer tourism over the past two decades, and the frequency with which this literature examines the ways these particular tourist groups are changed by their travel experiences, few studies examine their lived experiences in detail, not least their sexual encounters. Where the topic of sex in youth tourism is discussed, it is most often mentioned in passing, or the focus is on the risks that sexual experiences pose, either to the tourists themselves or to exploited others (see, for example, Egan, 2001; Hughes *et al.*, 2009). Indeed, the affective and corporeal dimensions of youth tourism are often overlooked (with exceptions, such as, Berdychevsky *et al.*, 2010; Elsrud, 2001; Maoz, 2007) and references to matters of sexuality, desire or intimacy remain scant. While some studies have looked at the connections between specific types of youth tourism, like the infamous 'Spring Break' celebrations of North American college students (Josiam *et al.*, 1998; Sönmez *et al.*, 2006), and the Australian 'Schoolies Week' celebrations designed to mark the end of secondary education (Winchester *et al.*, 1999), many of these studies tend to focus on risk and sexual health and, by extension, position sexual encounters as either responsible or irresponsible. There is little research regarding the sexual activities of youth tourists (such as, backpackers, education tourists, volunteer tourists) more generally and this omission is particularly striking given that youth tourism is often depicted as a ritual transgression or suspension of everyday life (Matthews, 2008a, 2014).

This absence is particularly remiss when sex and sexuality feature heavily in the discourses of tourism popular with young travellers, such as backpackers. Brochures and websites of backpacker tour operators are laden with images of attractive, young, seemingly single men and women 'partying' together. Industry events targeting would-be backpacker travellers, or backpacker tour-bus activities and 'ice-breakers' are often sexually charged (Matthews, forthcoming 2021). For instance, Matthews (forthcoming 2021) observes industry-sponsored events at backpacker bars in the United Kingdom finding it common practice for young travellers to be invited to 'strip' to win free travel products. Those young men and women who gave the 'best performances' could win free trips to various destinations in the United Kingdom or mainland Europe. Similarly, passengers on tour buses might be introduced through various ice-breaking (and often, drinking) games with sexual undertones. Variations on a 'traffic-light party', where introductions are made on the basis of whether one is 'red' (i.e. not available or not interested in a relationship), 'orange' (i.e. possibly open to advances) or 'green' (i.e. open to sexual advances and/or encounters) were common. So too were rounds of 'suck and blow'[2] around the bus, or strip pool or poker at one's accommodation for the night (Matthews, forthcoming 2021). Similarly, the now ubiquitous *Lonely Planet* guidebooks have a section entitled 'sex' (or, more euphemistically, 'romance' or 'social') to assist travellers negotiate their way through inter-cultural flirtations and, if successful, 'hook-ups' (Young, 2009). It is also well established that even when individuals travel independently, certain destinations and local people are actively portrayed in sexualised ways by destination marketing companies and tour operators. This latter point is not lost on the young women interviewed by Berdychevsky *et al.* (2010, 2013a, 2013b) who make clear associations between sex and, more specifically, sexual freedom within specific tourist environments (such as, hotel rooms) and specific tourist destinations (for example, Thailand and South America).

By comparison, while volunteer tourists may consume similar media to similarly aged backpackers, and there are clear overlaps between the demographics and tourism experiences (Everingham, 2017; Matthews, 2008b) there is rarely cross-over in the ways by which the two groups are marketed, represented or how their experiences are constructed. For instance, the marketing of volunteer tourism as alternative, altruistic and development-focused tends to quash any imagery associated with hedonistic or romantic pursuits. The common discourse of volunteer tourism campaigns is not of suntanned, semi-clad bodies relaxing on the beach, but of 'white women caring for black children', the 'helping imperative' personified (Tiessen, 2018: 110–111; see also Wearing *et al.*, 2018). Perhaps the increased scrutiny of volunteer tourism in recent years, the subsequent critiques of 'voluntourism' in the media and academia, and the desire for volunteer tourists and volunteer organisations to be taken seriously, has exacerbated promotion of these 'helping' images. The marketing of volunteer tourism as 'responsible' perhaps relegates sex as irresponsible and as a taboo topic in volunteer tourism research. Therefore, academic analysis of sexual encounters in volunteer tourism are largely absent (for exceptions, see Everingham, 2018a, 2018b; Godfrey & Wearing, 2018). Yet, while romance and sex are sidelined or even silenced in representations of volunteer tourism, it is possible that sexual encounters and romantic relationships can enhance emotional attachment to place for individual volunteers. Attachments to place may also increase the likelihood of return visits, and the passing of positive word-of-mouth to family and friends (Lanca *et al.*, 2017). At the same time, constructing volunteer tourism as 'altruistic' adds layers of complexity to the lived experience and embodied sexual encounters that can occur in these spaces.

While this particular moral economy within which volunteer tourism is situated has been criticised within academic studies (see for example Mostafanezhad, 2013; Vrasti, 2013; Wearing *et al.*, 2017), the marketing of volunteer tourism frames the experience as 'altruistic', 'affecting' volunteers perceptions of themselves and how they should be interacting with host communities. As Picard (2012) argues, personal experiences and public imaginaries of particular tourist sites become articulated in a hermeneutic cycle which leads to a reproduction of particular moral orders. The public semantics that shape these anticipated experiences in tourism 'has a normalising effect in that it prescribes where to go and what to do in order to have a particular experience' (Picard, 2012: 13). Subsequently, in both volunteer tourism and backpacker tourism, there are often conflicting and contradictory motivations, behaviours and desires at play.

Conflicting motivations, behaviours and desires within volunteer tourism is particularly evident in volunteer tourism, as volunteers navigate their positionalities as 'tourists', 'volunteers' and 'backpackers'. Just as our classed, racialised, and gendered embodiments affect our experiences as tourists, so too these embodiments affect the experiences of volunteers. Godfrey and Wearing (2018) discuss the experiences of mediating these sexualised tourism spaces in fieldwork on volunteer tourism in Cusco, Peru. They discuss the sexual harassment that local men directed towards the female researcher and other female volunteers who, as foreign women, were perceived to have looser sexual morals than Peruvian women, regardless of the fact they were volunteers (Godfrey & Wearing, 2018). However, while sexual harassment in the street was unwanted, they found that many of the volunteers behaved in ways deemed morally inappropriate by local standards when in the bars and discotheques and under the influence of alcohol (Godfrey & Wearing, 2018). Local men also reported being 'hunted down' by foreign women who objectified their 'exoticness' and were seeking sexual encounters (Godfrey & Wearing, 2018).

Locals and volunteers thus navigate complex interstices between different framings of tourism experiences, and constructions of masculinities and femininities in different cultural contexts at the same time as embodying these within the liminoid space of youth tourism and its associated sexual permissiveness. While the remainder of the chapter is dedicated to discussing these nuanced and layered interactions from empirical data, we firstly introduce the broader studies on backpacking and volunteer tourism to contextualise our findings.

Methodology

This chapter draws on two separate studies focused on youth tourism in the forms of backpacking and volunteer tourism. Both studies engaged autoethnographic methods and semi-structured in-depth interviews. The topic of sex *and* tourism was not a specific aim of either study and there were no research questions addressed at unearthing these kinds of experiences. However, sexual encounters emerged as a very important theme in the recounting of backpacking and volunteering experiences within both studies. At the time, the researchers were also young and female, in a position of negotiating sexual encounters as an inherent aspect of the fieldwork experience. As Malam (2004: 177, 178) notes, 'sexuality and gender impact on the way we do fieldwork' and '[p]articular bodies come to be aligned with and signify particular subjectivities'. The positionality of ourselves as young female cisgender researchers 'affected' our relationships with research participants. Thus, the researchers were perceived in particular ways in the field – as young solo female travellers – by tourist men and local men and, consequently, the women we spoke to during fieldwork were more likely to confide in us about their sexual experiences.

The research on backpackers involved multi-sited or mobile ethnography in 'glocal' (Robertson, 1995) backpacking communities in various locations, including Guatemala, Costa Rica, Panama, Cuba, the United States of America, Canada, the United Kingdom, France, Spain, India and Thailand. Adopting mobile and autoethnographic approaches (Matthews, 2018), from 2005 to 2006 a total of 34 semi-structured interviews were held with young Australian travellers in these countries. The ratio of gender was 62% female to 38% male. These travellers had been abroad for a period of three months or more, with many opting to undertake working holidays and, therefore, backpacking for what amounted to years. Media analysis and participant observation was also carried out and the results were subject to discourse analysis. This core period of research has since been supplemented by shorter autoethnographic studies carried out with backpackers in Peru and Ecuador (2007 to 2008), Cambodia (2011), Thailand (2013) and Mexico (2008 and 2013), and ongoing media analyses. The research on volunteer tourism involved two separate periods of fieldwork (2011 to 2012, and 2012 to 2013) carried out in two volunteer organisations in South America, a non-government organisation in Huanchaco (Peru) and a not-for-profit organisation in Banos (Ecuador). This research also involved autoethnographic approaches and participant observation coupled with semi-structured interviews with volunteers, local residents, and staff at both organisations. A total of 46 semi-structured interviews were conducted in the two periods of fieldwork and the ratio of gender was 63% female to 37% male (Everingham, 2018b). We draw on data from both studies in the following presentation of case studies of sex *and* backpacker and volunteer tourism.

Making sense of sex as the 'new norm' in backpacker tourism

The temporal and social disjunctures made manifest in tourism can encourage a sense of freedom and opportunism among young tourists who are commonly concerned with making the most of one's time abroad (Matthews, 2008a, 2009, 2014; Young, 2005, 2009). Such sentiments are encouraged by concerns about authenticity – particularly of an existential nature (Wang, 2000) – and the contractions of regular life-patterns (Thomas, 2005). In a sense, the extraordinariness of shared travel experiences and the compression of space and time (with many backpackers living with one another, in close confines, for 24 hours a day, 7 days a week) results not just in liminoid experiences, but liminoid experiences that are inherently corporeal and highly affective. Many backpackers discussed fast bonds and strong relationships, both sexual and platonic, that they developed with other travellers as a result of these conditions. For instance, Claudia,[3] a 19 year old Australian traveller who had recently taken a break from her university studies to complete a month-long backpacker tour of Europe (and who was intending to travel abroad for a 12-month period) observed that:

> It's quite funny how you can get *so* attached to someone when you're travelling ... Like it's a really different friendship. It's like someone's pushed a fast-forward button ... Because you have so many shared experiences crammed into a small amount of time. Plus contact time is 'sky-high'...

Noting the tendency for backpackers to be more receptive and open to new experiences when travelling than they might be at home, Christina, a young professional who had been living and working in the United Kingdom for 18 months at the time of interview, observed that a key part of travelling is 'the way you strike up quick and intense friendships with people'. She suggested this is because 'when you're travelling on your own you do need people and you're much more receptive to new experiences and new people'. This sentiment was echoed by Mel, an Australian backpacker living in London, who in reflecting on travel and life in backpacker hostels also identified a sense of vulnerability, openness and mutual reliance between backpackers:

> The friendships you form while travelling are stronger in part because you are so lonely ... and everyone is very lonely ... I think that's why a lot of people also tend to 'hook up' in hostels as well ... I think it's because it's an affection thing that a lot of people want ... And also because you are away from home and you're doing the same thing as the people here, like you're all in the same boat and I don't know, I think it's just sort of a lot stronger ... I mean you've got your friends at home and they'll always be your friends and everything ... but I think you make friends a lot more quickly here as well ... It's sort of instantaneous. Whereas at home that's not really the case.

The experiences described by these backpackers and examples for the fieldwork observations highlight that the physically close and sometimes intense living conditions – whether travelling on a cramped tour bus or living short- or long-term in a dormitory room with up to 20 other travellers – can foster a heightened sense of intimacy, vulnerability and sometimes dependency. In such environments strangers can quickly become friends, especially when expectations for sociability – and sometimes hedonism – abound.

For instance, two backpackers describe their experiences of the 'party atmosphere' and transience inherent to snow resorts where each had lived as working holidaymakers in Canada and the United States.

Their comments, below, highlight the urgency that can accompany romantic or sexual relationships when travelling:

> If you meet a guy you like when travelling and you know you only have a week together, you do what you can in that week (Julia).

> Yes! At home when you make a new friend you'll sort of see them once a week. When you're away you make a new friend and you see them like 'whoah', every day! It's the same with relationships, like if I was in a new relationship at home, maybe I'd see the guy once a week, and then twice a week ... And then when you're away it's like y'know, you're in a relationship and you're seeing each other every night, everyday (Natalie).

Similarly, another backpacker hints at the social liminality he experienced in the travel space:

> The way people relate to one another in their own country and in their own community is very defined ... But when you're travelling you have this open conversation ... and it's almost like for some reason it is okay to have sex with someone who you've only just met ... There are different social rules when you are backpacking. And it's not the same for everyone but I think people are more open to a lot of things when they're travelling (Scott).

Comments (such as those quoted above) illustrate that while the liminoid travel space may be embraced for the fun, pleasure and sexual liberation that it offers, such behaviour was still made sense of with reference to rules and norms — whether personal or social — from home. In this sense, the backpackers interviewed often expressed surprise and sometimes delight at the hedonistic encounters they had while travelling. However, they often still navigated these behaviours, and what they came to represent with respect to their sexual identities, through an 'individualised lens'. Such narratives often emerged on the basis of the specific intersubjective, corporeal and affective dimensions of participants' highly individualised sexual histories and sexual encounters within, and beyond, the spaces of travel.

Not all the backpackers interviewed had engaged in sexual behaviours, and many indicated that they chose not to engage in sexual hook-ups while travelling or that they had found unwanted sexual attention troubling at times. Further, while many backpackers demonstrated that the sexual freedom common to the backpacking culture was embraced, not all backpackers interviewed were happy about the transient nature of these experiences. Some talked, for instance, about the difficulties they faced when saying goodbye to a 'one-night stand' or 'travel fling' in order to continue their journeys. For these backpackers, some of those departures were described as being as difficult, if not more so, than the ones they had made before embarking on their extended overseas travels in the first place. Also serving to problematise the sexual licentiousness and transience of the backpacking culture were those whose stories broke the mould in so far that their 'travel flings' did not in fact end. A number of the backpackers interviewed indicated that they had become involved in longer-term relationships as a result of travel. In some cases, these relationships were with locals at the destination, resulting in the participants staying overseas for much longer than was originally planned. For others, these relationships emerged between travellers and endured the return home, resulting, in some cases, in marriage and eventually children.

The encounters explored in the narratives of these backpackers in recounting their experiences abroad indicate that the liminoid space of travel *may* encourage sexual licentiousness, but the outcomes of the corporeal and affective experiences that emerge within this space are far from foregone conclusions. Tourists still frequently have to navigate the 'new norms' that emerge in the tourism space, and negotiate what these mean for them personally. A similar pattern emerges in the study of volunteer tourists when the theme of sexual encounters emerged in the interview data, as examined below.

Negotiating desire while 'behaving morally' in volunteer tourism

The liminoid volunteer travel space generates conflicting and contradictory affective atmospheres that are tied to the broader moral economies of 'altruism', 'compassion' and 'empathy'. Such narratives are embedded not only within the broader framing and marketing of the volunteer tourism industry, but also the embodied and affective encounters between volunteers and locals. A further component that complicates the embodied navigation of these encounters is the broader constructions of tourism spaces as sexually permissive, which 'affects' the ways that locals gaze upon female volunteers. Everingham (2018a, 2018b) describes the ambivalences of her positionality as *gringa*, tourist, volunteer, and researcher, and the resulting confusion when it came to navigating the unwelcome sexual gaze of locals who may have perceived her as being sexually permissive by the mere fact that tourism spaces are so often seen as unproblematically sexualised.

The following excerpt is drawn from the field notes written by the researcher (Everingham, 2018b) during her fieldwork in South America. This excerpt illustrates the conflicting emotions of wanting to be polite and a good ambassador for one's country by being open and friendly, yet also the need to protect one's personal boundaries when it comes to unwelcome sexual encounters:

> I had an awkward interaction on the beach today. A Peruvian guy came up and asked me if I could watch his stuff while he went into the water.

He had a very battered looking surfboard and he looked very unfit and a little bit overweight – so there was no attraction there on my behalf and I became wary that he was looking for a chance to make conversation and perhaps hit on me. I wanted to be polite but I didn't really want to talk to him and he was very awkward in the way that he was interacting with me. I'm not sure if he's ever spoken to a tourist before. When I couldn't understand something that he said in Spanish he would act really embarrassed and the conversation was really draining as I felt his awkwardness and felt like I had to make him comfortable – even though I wasn't attracted to him. But I also didn't want to give him the impression that I was interested in him sexually so after a while I stopped talking to him and started reading my book. He got up and left after leaning over me to give me a kiss and getting a good look through the top of my swimmers. These encounters are really difficult to manage when you want to be a good ambassador for your country and encourage intercultural interaction but that doesn't mean that you want to invite guys to share your space either. (Field notes 15 January 2012)

Another example of unwanted sexual attention directed towards Everingham as young, female researcher is recorded below:

I was sitting on the bus coming home from one of the classes that I was teaching and a man started talking to me. I often take these opportunities to practice my Spanish and it is always a nice opportunity when someone takes time out to be patient. This guy seemed to be genuinely interested in what I was doing there in the volunteer organisation and we continued the conversation as we stepped off the bus. I had let my guard down and when he invited me to go to a party with him I hadn't thought about an excuse fast enough that wouldn't hurt his feelings. I told him I was busy and he followed me to the hostel and was quite persistent in asking me when else he could catch up. At this point I realised that he was interested in me sexually and I got a bit worried that he knew where I was staying and I wondered how I could get rid of him while still being nice, so I said to him perhaps another time. A few days later he came round to the hostel looking for me and my host family told me that he was looking for me and seemed quite confused as to why I would be hanging out with somebody like this. I didn't know how to tell them the nuances of this encounter: that in the beginning I was just practicing my Spanish and consequently probably encouraged his flirtatous behaviour. However in the end I didn't want to hurt his feelings, yet wanted to be rid of him. I ended up feeling a bit sickened and embarrassed by the whole thing blaming myself for the situation and wondering how I was going to get out of it if he turned up again. I hoped that he would just forget about it and give up but he kept coming around to the hostel. In the end I had to be quite rude to him and this made me feel terrible and I wondered whether it would have been kinder just to not have talked to him at all in the first place. It is also complicated by the power relationships – that I feel guilty about my privilege and I don't want to be rude. But when this happens in a different language it is so much harder to know how to cut off the interaction politely. I'm not attuned to the nuances of the encounter in a way I would be if it was happening in my own culture. I felt like I should have been more aware that this guy was attracted to me in the beginning but I got distracted by the fact that I was getting an opportunity to practice Spanish. I also feel like I am also an ambassador of Australia and I didn't want to give him a bad impression of foreigners. These intercultural encounters are so confusing because you just don't know what you can and can't take for granted as obvious cultural knowledge. (Field notes 25 January 2012)

Examples of encounters with unwanted sexual attention were raised in interviews with some of the young women volunteers, as well as the interviews with young women backpackers. In drawing attention to such unwelcome encounters, we wish to emphasise that there are exceptions to the seemingly unwritten rule that the licentious liminoid atmosphere generated in tourism spaces results in sex. At the same time, we do not want to negate the many times in the field where sexual desire was mutual: in both backpacking and, contrary to popular discourse, in volunteer tourism. In fact, it was quite common for the women interviewees volunteering at the organisations studied in South America to talk about their positive sexual encounters with local men. For example, many of the local men (especially local surfers) had quite close relationships with the staff at the organisation in Peru because they had been in many relationships on and off with different volunteers over the years. Volunteers and locals engaged in leisure activities outside of the formalised volunteering spaces, such as surfing, swimming, and drinking and dancing at the local bars. There were many stories of who had slept with whom within the volunteer/ local space, and many of the volunteer women grew to know which local men were known to be 'womanisers' and to be avoided, and which ones were 'the nice guys'. Equally, it became apparent that the local men talked about the volunteer women. For example, who they had kissed or slept with and whom they wanted to be with. Yet these relationships were kept separate and sometimes even secret from the more formalised volunteering setting.

A story was recounted by one of the volunteers interviewed about an Australian volunteer who had met and married a Peruvian woman and that, while they now live in Australia, they frequently return to the organisation to volunteer. Another volunteer interviewed, discussed that she had met a local man a few days after she arrived. She explained that she had only intended to volunteer at the organisation for a month but ended up staying six months because of this relationship. These longer-term relationships appeared to be quite common at this organisation where it was discussed that some of the local men were invited to go back to the volunteers' home countries, to visit, or to live. In fact, relationships and sexual encounters between locals and volunteers were so common in a nearby volunteer organisation that women volunteers were warned to be very careful if engaging in sex with local men as word gets around the town and could give the organisation a bad name. The women volunteers who discussed this issue found this warning paternalistic and even patriarchal. While they understood the position of the organisation, they all felt that women volunteers were given the moral burden of gatekeeping these encounters, and that local men (as well as volunteer men) escaped judgement when it came to sex with locals or with other volunteers.

The encounters that the volunteer *gringas* had with local men were viewed by some of the women interviewed as awkward, playful, fun, serious, annoying, uncomfortable, and sometimes even scary. The relationships that emerged from these encounters may have done so within a liminoid atmosphere of permissiveness and radical openness to desire, chemistry and seduction. However, these encounters are also relational, and the nature of sexual desire means that the volunteer tourists interviewed in the study did not always welcome the sexual gaze when the desire was not mutual. It became clear in this study that sexual encounters for the volunteer tourists interviewed were ambiguous, and the relationality of these encounters meant that many sexual experiences were not planned prior to or during travel, as is commonly the case of 'sex tourism' (Carr, 2016). Attention to these sexualised embodied encounters in volunteer tourism highlights the relationalities and ambiguities of tourism spaces and moves analysis away from dualistic evaluative generalisations and simplistic analyses of power relationships.

Conclusion

In this chapter we have explored how the sexual experiences of the backpackers and volunteers interviewed in two separate studies were, similarly, influenced by the 'radical openness' of tourism spaces. Following Ford and Eiser's (1995: 323) description of 'situational disinhibition' as the feeling of being a different person on holiday, we found that liminal travel spaces encourage 'situational sex'. However, these constructions of liminoid travel spaces are encouraged by broader cultural narratives and the expectations and the framing of their experiences by tourists themselves. Importantly, such narratives demonstrate *how* tourist spaces come to be sexualised (or not), and the layers of sexualisation within these spaces.

By positioning research on the experiences of backpackers alongside research on the experiences of volunteer tourists, our findings reveal that some tourism spaces − or forms of tourism − are more open to sexualisation than others. Whilst sexual licentiousness might be perceived as normative in backpacking culture (that is, an expected and sometimes highly sought part of the travel experience), discursive constructions of volunteer tourism (emphasising authenticity, altruism, responsibility, etc.) deny, at least officially, this same possibility. In short, sex and sexual encounters are positioned as taboo in volunteer tourism. However, what becomes evident in our research is that these representations prove problematic when it comes to tourists lived experiences as volunteers and backpackers.

First, there are intersections between backpacker and volunteer tourism, with some young travellers engaging in both activities within the same journey. Second, both forms of tourism are often carried out in the same destinations. This means that volunteer tourists often find themselves immersed in the same tourism spaces of backpacking and hedonistic excess. Volunteers may also be just as open to sexual encounters as backpackers, even if official discourses deny this. Indeed, the opposite is also true for backpackers. The highly sexualised backpacking tourism space does not mean that sexual licentiousness will result, nor that backpackers are not equally concerned with authenticity and responsibility in their travels. Finally though, and perhaps most importantly, our research suggests that even when backpackers or volunteer tourists are not open to the increased possibility for sexual permissiveness offered by the travel space, they may still be sexualised by others simply because they are co-inhabiting these shared 'play-zones' of liminality in tourism.

What we have drawn attention to then is that the sexualised spaces of tourism are constructed and experienced discursively. We have also highlighted that these sexualised spaces are experienced corporeally, emotionally and affectively. In this sense, unconscious thoughts and desires are played out in these liminoid spaces and interact with these discourses in unique and complex ways. Desires and expectations for travel may be socioculturally scripted, but sexual encounters in tourism are far from precoded. Individual beliefs and affective responses, and the relationality inherent to sexual interaction, play a significant role in the sexual experiences of backpackers and volunteer tourists. Subsequently, where some youth travellers may embrace the sense of liberation and possibility that the liminoid space of travel engenders, others may struggle with the same possibilities. Being sexualised in ways that are not welcomed, for instance, can leave both backpackers and volunteer tourists feeling vulnerable, uncomfortable and unsafe. Also, while some youth tourists may relish in transient sexual relationships, others may struggle with this dimension of their tourism experience. Indeed, the embodied, affective and relational nature of these interactions means that they are experienced differently by individual travellers, and by individual locals. While this seems an obvious point, such nuance is often lost in studies of sex and tourism which tend to isolate sexual interaction from the broader touristic and everyday life contexts in which they occur.

This chapter, therefore, draws attention to the complexities of lived experience and sexual encounters in travel spaces.

While much of the existing research on sex *and* tourism discusses the permissive atmospheres that are created in tourism environments, we have introduced embodiment and affect to add further theoretical insight into what occurs within the liminoid travel space. In this way, this chapter highlights 'the undisclosed and sometimes undisclosable nature of everyday practice' (Cadman, 2009: 456) in backpacker and volunteer tourism. In so doing, this chapter also brings to the surface the hidden layers of meaning: the 'public secrets' (Frohlick, 2008) and complexities that are often embedded, not just in tourist narratives about sex but also in the academic studies of sex *and* tourism (or tourism and sex), that they inform. By turning attention to the embodied and affective aspects of the liminal or liminoid, we have highlighted here that sexual encounters in tourism are inherently ambiguous, nuanced and complex: just as they are in everyday life.

Notes

(1) We acknowledge Turner's (1982) distinction between liminal and liminoid, the latter term being used to identify optional as opposed to obligatory rituals originating in 'complex 'societies, which tend to be leisure and consumption based and more individualised. However, in keeping with the broader tourism literature where liminality is the commonly employed term, and bearing in mind that it is the liminal *space* rather than ritual space that we are concerned with here, we use both liminal and liminoid throughout this chapter depending largely on whether we are referring to our own research or to observations on liminality made by Turner and others.

(2) A game where one person positions a piece of paper or a playing card over their mouth by sucking air in and then passes it (mouth to mouth) to someone else by blowing air out.

(3) All interview participants have been given psudonyms to ensure anonymity.

References

Allon, F. and Anderson, K. (2010) Intimate encounters: The embodied transnationalism of backpackers and independent travellers. *Population, Space and Place* 16, 11–22.

Berdychevsky, L., Poria, Y. and Uriely, N. (2010) Casual sex and the backpacking experience: The case of Israeli women. In N. Carr and Y. Poria (eds) *Sex and the Sexual during People's Leisure and Tourism Experiences* (pp. 105–118). Newcastle: Cambridge Scholars Publishing.

Berdychevsky, L., Poria, Y. and Uriely, N. (2013a) Sexual behavior in women's tourist experiences: Motivations, behaviors, and meanings. *Tourism Management* 35, 144–155.

Berdychevsky, L., Gibson, H. and Poria, Y. (2013b) Women's sexual behaviour in tourism: Loosening the bridle. *Annals of Tourism Research* 42, 65–85.

Cadman, L. (2009) Nonrepresentational theory/nonrepresentational geographies. In R. Kitchen and N. Thrift (eds) *International Encyclopedia of Human Geography* (pp. 456–463). Oxford, Elsevier.

Carr, N. (2016) Sex in tourism: Reflections and potential future research directions. *Tourism Recreation Research* 41, 188–198.

Crick, M. (1989) Representations of international tourism in the social sciences: Sun, sex, sights, savings, and servility. *Annual Review of Anthropology* 18, 307–344.

Desforges, L. (2000) Traveling the world: Identity and travel biography. *Annals of Tourism Research* 27, 926–945.

Dimen, M. (1989) Power, sexuality, and intimacy. In A. Jagger and S. Bordo (eds) *Gender/body/knowledge: Feminist Reconstructions of Being and Knowing* (pp. 35–45). New Brunswick and London: Rutgers University Press.

Egan, C.E. (2001) Sexual behaviours, condom use and factors influencing casual sex among backpackers and other young international travellers. *Canadian Journal of Human Sexuality* 10, 41–58.

Elsrud, T. (2001) Risk creation in traveling: Backpacker adventure narration. *Annals of Tourism Research* 28 (3), 597–617.

Everingham, P. (2015) Intercultural exchange and mutuality in volunteer tourism: The case of intercambio in Ecuador. *Tourist Studies* 15, 175–190.

Everingham, P. (2016) Hopeful possibilities in spaces of 'the-not-yet-become': Relational encounters in volunteer tourism. *Tourism Geographies* 18 (5), 520–538.

Everingham, P. (2017) 'I'm not looking for a manufactured experience': Calling for decommodified volunteer tourism. In S. Filep, J. Albrecht and W. Coetzee (eds) *CAUTHE 2017: Time for Big Ideas – Rethinking the field for tomorrow* (pp. 409–418).

Everingham, P. (2018a) Speaking Spanglish: Embodying linguistic (b)orderlands in volunteer tourism. *Emotion Space and Society* 27, 68–75.

Everingham, P. (2018b) Embodying hope: Intercultural encounters in the (b)orderlands of volunteer tourism. Unpublished PhD Thesis. University of Newcastle, Australia.

Ford, N. and Eiser, R. (1995) Sexual relationships on holiday: A case of situational disinhibition? *Journal of Social and Personal Relationships* 12, 323–339.

Franklin, A. and Crang, M. (2001) The trouble with tourism and travel theory? *Tourist Studies* 1 (1), 5–22.

Frohlick, S. (2008) Negotiating the public secrecy of sex in a transnational tourist town in Caribbean Costa Rica. *Tourist Studies* 8 (1), 19–39.

Godfrey, J. and Wearing, S. (2018) Negotiating machismo as a female researcher and volunteer tourist in Cusco, Peru. In B.A. Porter and H.A. Schänzel (eds) *Femininities in the Field: Tourism and Transdisciplinary Research* (pp. 23–36). Bristol: Channel View Publications.

Hubbard, P. (2002) Sexing the self: Geographies of engagement and encounter. *Social and Cultural Geography* 3, 365–381.

Hughes, K., Downing, J., Bellis, M.A., Dillon, P. and Copeland, J. (2009) The sexual behaviour of British backpackers in Australia. *Sexually Transmitted Infections* 85 (6), 477–482.

Inglis, F. (2000) *The Delicious History of the Holiday*. London: Routledge.

Jordan, F. and Aitchison, C. (2008) Tourism and the sexualisation of the gaze: Solo female tourists' experiences of gendered power, surveillance and embodiment. *Leisure Studies* 27 (3), 329–349.

Josiam, B.M., Perry Hobson, J.S., Dietrich, U.C. and Smeaton, G. (1998) An analysis of the sexual, alcohol and drug related behavioural patterns of students on spring break. *Tourism Management* 19 (6), 501–513.

Lanca, M., Marques J.P. and Pinto, P. (2017) Liminality and the possibilities for sex and romance an international bike meeting: The structural modelling approach. *Tourism and Management Studies* 13, 18–36.

Lean, G. (2012) Transformative travel: A mobilities perspective. *Tourist Studies* 12 (2), 151–172.

Larsen, J. (2008) De-exoticizing tourist travel: Everyday life and sociality on the move. *Leisure Studies* 27 (1), 21–34.

Maoz, D. (2007) Backpackers' motivations the role of culture and nationality. *Annals of Tourism Research* 34, 122–140.

Malam, L. (2004) Embodiment and sexuality in cross-cultural research. *Australian Geographer* 35 (2), 177–183.

Matthews, A. (2008a) Backpacking as a contemporary rite of passage: Victor Turner and youth travel practices. In G. St John (ed.) *Victor Turner and Contemporary Cultural Performance* (pp. 174–189). Oxford: Berghahn Books.

Matthews, A. (2008b) Negotiated selves: Exploring the impact of local-global interactions on young volunteer travelers. In K. Lyons and S. Wearing (eds) *Journeys of Discovery in Volunteer Tourism: International Case Study Perspectives* (pp. 101–117). Wallingford: CABI.

Matthews, A. (2009) Living paradoxically: Understanding the discourse of authentic freedom as it emerges in the travel space. *Tourism Analysis* 14 (2), 165–174.

Matthews, A. (2014) Young backpackers and the rite of passage of travel: Examining the transformative effects of liminality. In G. Lean, R. Staiff and E. Waterton (eds) *Travel and Transformation* (pp. 157–171). Burlington: Ashgate.

Matthews, A. (2018) Ethnographic approaches to tourism research. In W. Hillman and K. Radel (eds) *Qualitative Methods in Tourism Research: Theory and Practice* (pp. 50–71). Bristol: Channel View Publications.

Matthews, A. (forthcoming, 2021) *An Ethnography of the Backpacking Culture: Life on the Road*. Abingdon: Routledge.

Mostafanezhad, M. (2013) The geography of compassion in volunteer tourism. *Tourism Geographies: An International Journal of Space, Place and Environment* 15 (2), 318–337.

Noy, C. (2004) This trip really changed me: Backpackers' narratives of self-change. *Annals of Tourism Research* 31 (1), 78–102.

Picard, D. (2012) Tourism, awe and inner journeys. In D. Picard and M. Robinson (eds) *Emotion in Motion: Tourism, Affect and Transformation* (pp. 1–21). Oxford: Ashgate.

Pritchard, A. and Morgan, N. (2006) Hotel Babylon? Exploring hotels as liminal sites of transition and transgression. *Tourism Management* 27 (5), 762–772.

Robertson, R. (1995) Glocalization: Time-space and homogeneity-heterogeneity. In M. Featherstone, S. Lash and R. Robertson (eds) *Global Modernities* (pp. 25–44). London: Sage.

Shields, R. (1991) *Places on the Margin: Alternative Geographies of Modernity*. London: Routledge.

Sönmez, S., Apostolopoulos, Y., Ho Yu, C., Yang, S., Mattila, A. and Yu, L.C. (2006) Binge drinking and casual sex on spring break. *Annals of Tourism Research* 33 (4), 895–917.

Thomas, M. (2005) 'What happens in Tenerife stays in Tenerife': Understanding women's sexual behaviour on holiday. *Culture, Health & Sexuality* 7 (6), 571–584.

Tan. Q.T. (2014) Postfeminist possibilities: Unpacking the paradoxical performances of heterosexualized femininity in club spaces. *Social & Cultural Geography* 15 (1), 23–48

Tiessen, R. (2018) *Learning and Volunteering Abroad for Development: Unpacking Host Organization and Volunteer Rationales*. Abingdon: Routledge.

Turner, V. (1982) *From Ritual to Theatre: The Human Seriousness of Play*. New York: PAJ Publications.

Turner, V.W. (1986) Dewey, Dilthey, and drama: An essay in the anthropology of experience. In V.W. Turner and E. M. Bruner (eds) *The Anthropology of Experience*. Urbana and Chicago: University of Illinois Press.

Turner, V. (1987) *The Anthropology of Performance*. New York: PAJ Publications.

Vrasti, W. (2013) *Volunteer Tourism in the Global South: Giving Back in Neoliberal Times*. London: Routledge.

Wang, N. (2000) *Tourism and Modernity: A Sociological Analysis*. Amsterdam: Pergamon.

Wearing, S., Stevenson, D. and Young, T. (2010) *Tourist Cultures: Identity, Place and the Traveller*. London: Sage.

Wearing, S., Young, T. and Everingham, P. (2017) Evaluating volunteer tourism: Has it made a difference? *Tourism Recreation Research* 42 (4), 512–521.

Wearing, S., Mostafanezhad, M., Nguyen, T. and McDonald, M. (2018) 'Poor children on Tinder' and their Barbie saviours: Towards a feminist political economy of volunteer tourism. *Leisure Studies* 37 (5), 500–514.

Winchester, H.P.M., McGuirk, M. and Everett, K. (1999) Schoolies Week as a rite of passage: A study of celebration and control. In E. Kenworthy Teather (ed.) *Embodied Geographies: Spaces, Bodies and Rites of Passage* (pp. 59–76). London & New York: Routledge.

Young T. (2005) Between a rock and a hard place: Backpackers at Uluru. In B. West (ed.) *Down the Road: Exploring Backpacker and Independent Travel* (pp. 33–53). Perth, Australia: API Network.

Young, T. (2009) Framing experiences of Aboriginal Australia: Guidebooks as mediators in backpacker travel. *Tourism Analysis* 14, 155–164.

6 Tourism, the Internet and Euro-Brazilian Intimacies[1]

Octávio Sacramento

Introduction

The internet has gradually become the paradigm of global connections, configuring a prominent space for exposure and access to the world, although its use is still marked by significant asymmetries resulting from the unequal 'power geometry' of globalisation (Massey, 1994; Warf, 2013). From multiple signification systems, the information and communication flows in the digital space provide symbolic resources that constitute subjectivities and mental maps, allowing the formulation of assumptions about much of what is culturally and geographically distant. It is within these processes of global imagination (Appadurai, 1996) that more reflexive postures emerge in the face of tradition and lifestyles – 'reflexive cosmopolitization' (Beck, 2000: 79) – and, at the same time, the desire-possibility of accessing other geographies, widening the scale of relational landscapes and drawing up alternative biographies. One of the most immediate results of these conditions is the increase of individual elective capacity in the most diverse spheres of life, from work, consumption and leisure, to intimacy.

Considering the growing role of the internet in the production of reflexivity, interactivity and electivity, this chapter discusses its relevance in the constitution of transnational configurations of adult heterosexual intimacy (e.g. erotic-sexual, emotional, romantic and conjugal) between Brazilian women and European men (*gringos*).[2] This Euro-Brazilian 'transnationalization of intimacy' (King, 2002) is carried out within the framework of the tourist stays of European men in the beach neighbourhood of Ponta Negra (city of Natal-RN, Northeast Brazil), mainly in the context of transactional sex (*programas*). More specifically, the analysis will be guided by two main objectives: (i) to understand the cyberspace processes, practices and contents through which gendered representations of hedonism and sensuality are projected to the tourist context, loading it erotically and making it the object of an intense transatlantic male tourist demand permeated by certain expectations of intimacy; (ii) to perceive the uses of the internet as an essential device in the genesis of many of the Euro-Brazilian relationships in Ponta Negra and in their maintenance, sometimes as a couple project, after the return of tourists to their home countries. The aim, therefore, is to show how the digital space works. Upstream, in the destination image construction of the tourist place and in the dissemination of the signs that organise the imagination that drives the European male tourist mobility, and downstream, in the intermediation of the passionate encounters and in the persistence, at distance, of some of the resulting intimate bonds.

Methodological Issues

The empirical data supporting the analysis presented in this chapter were provided within the framework of a broader study on transnational mobilities and configurations of intimacy between European tourists and Brazilian women (Sacramento, 2014). This was a multi-site study (Marcus, 1995) developed in Brazil and various European countries (e.g. Northern Italy and the Netherlands) over about a year, from November 2009 to October 2010. In this study, a qualitative methodological approach was followed, using ethnography as the guiding procedure. The process of collecting information was based mainly on participant observation and semi-structured interviews, complemented by a small survey of the socioeconomic characterisation of European tourists, and documentary research on tourist flows and transnational marriages. In the most specific case of the data supporting the discussion throughout this chapter, they resulted from participant observation, semi-structured interviews and ethnographic exercises in internet digital spaces. Although very succinctly, I try to explain hereafter these empirical research procedures.

I begin by highlighting participant observation as the central reference of data gathering work. Although it assumes a handicraft feature (Sardan, 1995) and does not obey rigid work plans or strict sampling criteria, participant observation has provided in-depth research and a large volume and density of information. In this way, I was able to access a wide range of experiences and discourses of the social actors who are protagonists of my object of study and to detailed elements about their cultural contexts. This information was recorded daily, in narrative format, in a field diary. In the end, the many pages of handwritten notes constituted a first, though disorganised and lacking analytical depth, effort to textually translate the observed reality and its multivocality. In addition to the field diary data, there is always another diffuse part of information and 'impressions' that pervade the researcher under the form of tacit (almost naturalised) knowledge, which *a posteriori* is mobilised, practically imperceptibly, in the scientific analysis and textualisation processes.

The centrality of participant observation in the fieldwork was also manifested in preparing the way for the use of other methodological procedures and even in the construction of the respective research instruments. This has clearly happened with the semi-structured interviews. The process leading up to these interviews took place in a certain way: first, informal conversations, attempts to empathise and making any adjustments to the interview script; and only then the more formal interview, usually subject to audio recording and lasting more than one hour. This standard orientation was perfectly practicable when approaching the majority of local women and tourists or resident tourists with stays of one, two, three months or more. On the contrary, their observance has become more difficult for tourists who spent only a week or two in Ponta Negra and for some *garotas de programa* (sex workers) in constant mobility between various tourist places. In these cases, the process from the first contacts, through the establishment of empathy, until the moment of the inquiry had to be abbreviated and compacted, which would eventually have a negative effect on some interviews. In compliance with the data saturation criterion (Saunders *et al.*, 2018), a total of 50 semi-structured interviews with European tourists and local women (in practically equal parts) were conducted. They were later transcribed and subjected to comprehensive content analysis (Bardin, 1995), with a view to producing inferences from their most significant elements and evidence.

More or less at the same time, I made ethnographic incursions into the internet – netnography (Kozinets, 2010) – in sites that I was identifying as privileged spaces for representation of Ponta Negra as a tourist destination and for intimacy construction, negotiation and expression of the social actors that I was getting to know on the field. Therefore, the internet represented another important ethnographic context, because in their travels and in the maintenance of intimate relationships at a distance, subjects make intensive use of new information and communication technologies. In this cyberspace approach I repeatedly surveyed discussion forums, blogs, social networks, chat and dating sites, as well as channels (especially YouTube) where audiovisual content is produced about Ponta Negra.[3] As a guiding principle, the criterion that I followed to consult these sites and content was their identification by the informants I came to know and follow, as privileged means of participation in processes of transnationalisation of intimacy and spaces where they access and/or expose tourist experiences in Northeast Brazil.

I have always tried to develop empirical research in the digital field as an exercise of continuity and complementarity with the work carried out in the other research contexts. As a medium for the circulation of images and interaction, the internet generates repercussions that extend beyond the screen and are expressed in many spheres of everyday life, making it almost irrelevant to establish any boundaries between the 'virtual' and the 'real' (Lemos, 1996; Lévy, 2001; Piscitelli, 2005; Wilson & Peterson, 2002). As Jungblut concludes (2004: 102), '[...] many of the acts produced by virtualisation mechanisms are concrete social facts, since they produce effects in reality and thus do not belong to the realm of the imaginary, do not disappear from the universe of social actions as soon as the technological mechanisms that allowed their "virtual" existence are turned off'. Like other anthropological works (Miller, 2011; Miller & Slater, 2004), the analysis that follows shows us the dense connectivity between online and offline social scenarios and, more concretely, the influence that the internet has been assuming in the informal promotion of tourist destinations, and in the redefinition of spaces, times, opportunities and processes of intimate relationships (Constable, 2003; Roca, 2011).[4]

From the 'Myths of Origin' to the Digital Projection of a Pleasure Geography

As in many other coastal places in Northeast Brazil, the beaches of Natal consolidated as mass tourism destinations in the last years of the 20th century (Fonseca & Lima, 2012; Sacramento, 2018a, 2018b). In addition to the development of the infrastructure and aerial connections, the intense tourism growth resulted from city marketing policies (Fonseca, 2005; Santos, 2010) outlined by the state government in articulation with the municipality of Natal. The production of the local tourist identity followed the strategic framework of the Brazilian Tourism Company/Brazilian Tourism Institute (EMBRATUR). Since the end of the 1960s, this federal agency for the promotion of the sector has disseminated representations about Brazil as an exotic and sensual country, repeatedly associating images of Carnival, idyllic beaches and bikini-clad mulattoes (*mulatas*) (Alfonso, 2006). In this promotional language, the primordial element was the corporeality of the mestizo woman, deeply sexualised in colonial discourses and practices, and later assumed as a postcolonial icon of the affirmation of Brazilian identity (Gomes, 2010; Ribeiro & Sacramento, 2009; Sacramento & Ribeiro, 2013; Sacramento, 2018b).

Since the earliest contacts with Europeans, Brazil has been constructed as a place populated by myths of origin around allegedly extraordinary sexuality (Parker, 1991) and is an object of Western fascination and desire. These myths intensified and gained greater amplitude in the framework of the overseas European imperialism of the eighteenth and nineteenth centuries (Stolcke, 2006). Later on, they were appropriated by independent Brazil as essential referents of discourses (e.g. political, literary, scientific, tourist) of national cultural production (Filho, 2011; Machado, 2009; Parker, 1991; Sommer, 2004). Thus, more than image-maker of the Brazilian nation, as Alfonso (2006) presents it, EMBRATUR was a box of resonating national identity elements with a long history (Sacramento & Ribeiro, 2013). Through this box, EMBRATUR produced and disseminated a semantic ordering for tourism based on cultural content already circulating in various fields of Brazilian society. As Gomes (2010) points out, by disseminating representations of Brazil as a 'mulatto paradise', EMBRATUR echoed the idealisations of the colonial imaginary about Latin America as a terrestrial paradise and reaffirmed the Brazilian identity outlined in the Gilberto Freyre's ideas on miscegenation, sexuality, and slavery (Freyre, 2006).[5]

Nowadays, the sexualised representations of Brazil are reproduced through a vast articulated complexity of cultural industries and information, and global communication systems, with special emphasis on the internet. The internet's role is particularly relevant in the broad and rapid circulation of the foundational images of Brazil referred to above. In the specific sphere of stereotypes that articulate nationality and sexuality, their relevance is such that cyberspace is identified by Piscitelli (2005) as the main contemporary vehicle of Brazilian touristic sexualisation and arrangement of international sexual landscapes. Considering its amplifying effects, Piscitelli (2005) notes that the images about the women of South America broadcasted in the virtual medium may be playing a role in the change of the international tourist circuits, increasing demand for the masculine accomplishment of sexually intimate experiences and marriage projects in the Brazilian Northeast to the detriment of the Southeast Asian sexual landscapes.

In the specific case of Ponta Negra, YouTube is one of the most privileged sites for registering the manifestations of hedonism that make up the tourist identity of the place in the global digital space. When inserting search terms (tags) such as 'Ponta Negra, Natal', there were around 10,100 results (at the date of 9 February 2012), and the volume of information increased considerably with the use of some keywords (e.g. beach) in Italian, English, Spanish, Norwegian and Swedish. By analysing at random a few dozen of these results, in particular their statistics, it is possible to detect the existence of a very strong tendency with regard to the nationality, gender, and age of the persons who view these materials. Brazil, Italy, Spain, Portugal, Norway, Sweden and the Netherlands are the countries with the most video views.[6] The main audience of these videos (people who see and comment) is men between the ages of 25 and 54 years.

A large part of these videos, as well as the respective comments, are added by tourists.[7] This aspect reveals the transnational scale of the identity composition of the place, its conversion into a 'space of flows' (Castells, 2002), and, on the other hand, the internet as 'metaphor for the social life as fluid' (Urry, as cited in Lemos, 2009: 30). Foreign tourists who participate actively in this process of the virtualisation (Molz, 2004) of Ponta Negra through YouTube, inserting images and/or written observations, are mostly European men, especially Italians. The content they offer online refers mainly to the spaces and times most associated with the passionate tourist landscapes, in particular, the beach and nightlife. The same happens in certain videos posted by domestic tourists and even native people. In these audiovisual elements there is frequent reference to highly recreational environments, surrounded by great agitation and intense male conviviality, where music and alcohol are frequently present. Tourists often emerge as a mix of filmmakers, narrators, and protagonists of the events. These tourists are usually in the company of Brazilian women with whom they develop an interaction based on the sensuality of the corporal performances – especially on the beach, where the bodies are shown in a particularly appealing manner – or, in other cases, based on a romantic complicity, reflecting intimate scenes of couples on vacation. The insertion of these personal contents on the internet can be partially understood in the context of a growing culture of the mediatic unveiling of the self. In this culture, the public display of intimacy in the windows of the digital space is stimulated, establishing a '[...] true festival of "private lives" who offer themselves unabashedly to the eyes of the whole world' (Sibilia, 2008: 27).

Certain videos focus unequivocally on scenarios of eroticism, passion and/or romance starring the gringos and their local female companions, usually in a climate of the more or less explicit exaltation of heterosexual masculine values. Sometimes, the narrative structure of these videos is organised into thematic sections based on the categories of gender and sexuality, as can be seen in the sequence of photographs of a group of six Italian tourists (added by C., 2008). In this particular case, the loaded materials revealed a sectioned structure with several titles and subtitles (in Italian) in which two parts can be implicitly identified. The first one, with the sound of Daniela Mercury's *Levada Brasileira* song, includes photos distributed in various categories, such as: *consigli utili* [useful advice] – posters alluding to 'sex tourism' and the use of condoms, and attention to the presence of transgenders; *la gente* [the people] – especially images of women on the beach; *la spiaggia di Ponta Negra* [the beach of Ponta Negra] – excerpts from everyday life on the beach and the relationships that occur there. The second part presents a song in which the powerful refrain '*cachaça!!!*' [sugarcane liquor] stands out and is composed of thematic sections whose titles (e.g. *stati d'ebbrezza* [drunk], *noi* [us]) and respective images centred on the group, configure a kind of tribute to virile camaraderie. Contrary to this, in many other audiovisual compositions, the erotic charge, the passions and homosocial manifestations associated with Ponta Negra are more blurred, immersed in images of the beach, the neighbourhood and the tourist attractions in the region.

Regardless of the settings and nuances of the posted materials, in almost all of them there tend to be glorified elements such as tropical exoticism, warm ambiance (from the thermic and social point of view), music and dance, recreational atmosphere, intense male conviviality, the female body and heterosexual intimacy. These components are presented as elementary constituents of an idyllically hedonic sensory regime, in which the moment (the present) and the place are conceived as the ultimate expression of the pleasures of life. In the brief narrative accompanying a video that reports a panoramic view of the beach daily life and where a tourist deliberately exposes himself to the camera, surrounded by some local women, the following written testimony is shared: 'I was in November 2006 in Ponta Negra near Natal, Brasil. Brasil is absolutely the place where the life is. There is no yesterday, no tomorrow – the life is now' (added by J., 2006). In the following comments, another youtuber refers to this hedonistic here and now[8] as the essence of what is Brazil: 'You've captured the essence of Brazil' (added by C., 2007). Another declares his strong sentimental connection to Ponta Negra and his desire to return: 'i love ponta negra!! i have been there on febraury 2006!! i have met the best and beautfiul [sic] girl in the world there! I will come back in ponta negra!' (added by M., 2007).

For many of the YouTube users, the alleged Brazilian essence tends to be more strictly and explicitly fixed in the rhythmic, musical eroticism of the mixed-race female corporeity, as can be seen in a short video called *Creu!!!*[9] *Che fisico!!!!* [*Creu!!!* What a physical!!!], posted online by an Italian man. In this video, there are images of a mulatto woman dancing to the sound of the song *Dança do creu* on the beach, clinging to the trunk of a palm tree in a performance marked by erotic-sexual movements. In the note appended as a caption, the author of the recording emphasises the singularity of the scene, showing astonishment and enthusiasm, as if the author was facing any tourist attraction: '*questo è ciò che può succedere sulla spiaggia di ponta negra - natal -rn- brasile in un caldo pomeriggio di dicembre a 35 gradi. spettacolo!!!*' [this is what can happen on the beach of Ponta Negra - Natal -RN- Brazil on a warm December afternoon at 35 degrees. Amazing!!!] (added by T., 2008).

The female corporeality, the music and the dance are also central elements in the recordings and comments on YouTube about the neighbourhood's nightlife: '*Una notte all' X. Il locale piu' bello e frequentato di Ponta Negra (Natal). In consolle Eddy dj (Italia) & Dj Pons (Spagna). Bella musica e belle ragazze tutte le sere*' [One night at the X (nightclub). The most beautiful and popular place in Ponta Negra (Natal). In the console, Eddy dj (Italy) & Dj Pons (Spain). Beautiful music and beautiful girls every night] (added by t., 2007). Sometimes, as in a video about the Miss election contest of the same nightclub, the erotic content of the images and/or the language used in the comments leads the site administration to flag the content in question and to impose restrictions on its visualisation: 'This content may contain material flagged by YouTube's user community that may be inappropriate for some users. To view this video please verify you are 18 or older by signing in or signing up'. This warning turns out to be itself an additional factor of erotisation of the content to which it refers.

Through narratives more or less impregnated with elements associated with feminine sensuality, in the overwhelming majority of the videos and observations posted on YouTube there emerges a clear eulogy of Brazilianness: *'il brasile è stupendo natal è fantastica'* [Brazil is gorgeous, Natal is fantastic] (added by F., 2009). In this praise, the importance of the intimacy sphere tends to be given particular importance, as is evident in the following gratitude statement: *'Natal mi ha dato tutto amore moglie e figlio ... Tutto maravilhoso como diz o brasileiros...'* [Natal gave me all love, wife and son ... All *maravilhoso* (wonderful), as the Brazilians say...] (added by M., 2011). In this context, the nostalgia that many demonstrate when referring to Brazil is understandable. They often use the word *saudade* (missing) and invoke elements of Brazilian culture (e.g. music) to illustrate their state of mind, as can be seen in a video titled *saudade do Brasil* (missing Brazil), followed by this comment: *'Dopo un viaggio in brasile, al rientro quello che si prova è espresso in questa magica canzone di Toquinho ... nostalgia. (regra tres)'* [After a trip to Brazil, what is felt upon the return is expressed in this magical song by Toquinho ... nostalgia.] (added by E., 2007). Nostalgia is sometimes directly linked to fun, intimacy and the alleged advantage in the supply and demand in the local market for heterosexual encounters: *'bella discoteca uomini pochi donne a flotte ... non vedo ora di tornarci ... saudade do brasil...'* [beautiful nightclub few men many women ... I cannot wait to go back ... missing Brazil...] (added by R., 2010).

Exposed to these and many other digital flows, almost all the tourists I met during the fieldwork in Ponta Negra told me that even before someone told them about Brazil and before they even considered choosing it as a leisure destination they had already incorporated some of the symbolic denominators of the country's identity, most particularly those that are closely associated with its sexualised tourist representations: 'Before coming, for me Brazil was ... beaches, sun, women' (Italian tourist, 34 years old, salesman). Increasingly, the internet provides many of the symbolic coordinates that structure the tourist's gaze and provide a synthetic preview of what they can experience, influencing the choice of destination to visit. In fact, the mass consumption practices of digital contents allow us to conceptually conceive the world without leaving home and access sensorial states that fit into what Campbell (2005: 77) identifies as 'imaginative hedonism'.

The Internet as a Constitution Space of Transatlantic Intimate Relationships

The insertion of Ponta Negra, like many other places, into the routes of mass tourism and the cartography of the international affective-sexual and matrimonial markets has been largely boosted by the internet. First of all, and as was evident in the previous section, there is the internet's capacity for amplification and massive diffusion of the aura of exoticism and sensuality that, historically, involves the identity of the Brazilian nation. But, at the same time, the internet also contributes, mainly through digital social networks, to the intensification of electivity in the sphere of private life and to providing wider socio-spatial scales and new possibilities for configuring intimacy and gender relations. In this time of increasing individual elective capacity (Roca, 2007; Roca et al., 2008), many Europeans, dissatisfied with gender identities and relationships in their countries, cross the Atlantic, moved by the representations of Brazil as a destination that, among other things, will ensure them new and better experiences of intimacy and access to forms of femininity considered unavailable at home.[10] Through mobility, these Europeans try to find in alterity what they claim not to find at home. Thus, they try to concretise at the transnational level the high expectations that currently accompany the most common conceptions about sex, romance, and conjugality (Beck & Beck-Gernsheim, 2004). Transposing ethno-sexual boundaries (Nagel, 2003), they hope to discover below the equator other forms of femininity and access heterosexual coexistence scenarios more suited to their subjectivities than those to be found in their daily lives.

Although not always the main means to provide the first references and to raise the awareness of Natal – or, specifically, Ponta Negra – the internet is frequently used to obtain information that, in general, ends up being identified as very important in making decisions about trips and the organisation of the stays at destinations like Ponta Negra: 'I heard the other people talking and then, through the internet, I was looking and I liked it. I spoke with friends who had already been here [Ponta Negra] and they told me that it was a *bello posto* [beautiful place], very different from Italy, of things in Italy' (Italian tourist, 25 years old, factory worker). Even if some of the content that flows in the digital space is produced by the tourist trade, its role in the diffusion of information and in the capture of external visitors is less dominant than that of the informal social circuits and the internet (Sacramento, 2018a). The majority of the Europeans did not know Ponta Negra through direct contact with official travel agencies or other institutions related to the tourism sector, nor did they even resort to these entities to organise their stay. The knowledge of and familiarity with Ponta Negra occurred mainly in tourists' closest circles of male sociability, followed by the internet, especially as a means of complementary information. The images incorporated in these two social spaces, together with the most common Brazilian concepts – in particular, the discourses that privilege the male gaze and produce the Brazil as 'male tourism landscape' (Pritchard & Morgan, 2000a, 2000b) – provided the essential symbolic resources to the prospective practices of imagination and to the individual expectations that have boosted the tourist experience.

Beyond using the internet to better know the tourist destination and the organisation of the trip, it is quite common for the European men, even in their respective countries, to use dating sites to get to know women from Natal and to initiate contacts at a distance. Then, once they go to Brazil they will seek to continue these relations.[11] The cases of two of my main informants, Gentile and Ambrosini,[12] are paradigmatic:

> Many women I met here, in Natal, I met first on the internet. When I'm in Italy, on the internet, I get the cell phone number and when I get here I call them for a date. I invite them to go to a party, to a place, to another ... I know their friends. There are many sites for this: *Orkut*, *Badoo* ... I know them all! You put your data, the photo and then you send a message to a woman and if she wants, you communicate with her. [...] Every week I talk to one, another ... (Italian tourist, 48 years old, mason)

> I've met more than 20 women through *Orkut*, *Par Perfeito*, *Match*, *Badoo* that I later found here in Natal. That's how I meet women who do not do a *programa* [transactional sex]. If it were not so, it was more difficult. You go downtown, there's a lot of beautiful women, but they do not talk to us because they see that we are foreigners and do not want us to think they [are] doing *programas*. [...] I also met on the net a woman who works at *Banco do Brasil*. I talked to her a lot on the net and then met her here. It was different because she already knew me and then she started introducing me to other friends, telling that I was a friend she met on the net. [...] When I come here, I select on the sites of women from this region. If I go to another country I am looking for women from the city where I am going. (Italian tourist, 43 years old, mason)

Likewise, the digital space allows many Brazilian women to establish a wide network of potential love companions on the other side of the Atlantic, who, as we have just seen, are also actively seeking partners in the global intimacy 'supermarket' that has been facilitated by the internet (Roca, 2011). The set of digital resources that these women use is broad and diverse: social networks (e.g. *Orkut*, *Facebook*), forums where companion search ads are posted (e.g. OLX), thematic chat rooms (dating, sex) in which the nationality of the actors is identified (e.g. *batepapo.uol*) and, increasingly, specific sites about relationships such as *Badoo*, where people from almost all over the world are registered. As an example, I transcribed from Portuguese into English one of the European companion search ads, inserted in OLX (section 'women looking for men' from Natal) by Rossana (24 years old), one of my informants in Ponta Negra: 'I am a beautiful woman of 22 years. I am looking for a serious gentleman. An educated European, good-looking and intelligent. Resident or not in Natal. I can travel and meet him personally, I work in the bank, I am charming, beautiful and cheerful. My email [xxxxxx] kisses'.

As there are few women in Ponta Negra who have personal computers, most of them access the internet at the small telecommunication *points* (*lan houses*) that exist along the beach promenade (*calçadão*) and throughout the neighbourhood. The field observations that I made on these *points* were particularly indicative of the agility of the female users in the appropriation of new technological possibilities. For example, they use chat rooms, dating sites, online translators and webcams to meet and communicate with potential European partners or to review others who have already been in Ponta Negra and with whom they have some kind of relationship. Sometimes the interactions initiated in the digital space evolve in such a way that the interlocutors end up meeting face to face, usually through the foreigner coming to Brazil. Besides the context/opportunity for first contact, the internet and the telecommunications technology, in general, are fundamental devices in the maintenance of long-distance relationships until physical reunion is possible, mitigating obstacles resulting from physical separation and, to a certain extent, reinventing the intimacy parameters (Sacramento, 2017). I was able to see at first hand the important roles of the internet in maintaining the passional bonds that began in the Northeast of Brazil on one of the days I spent with Gentile in Aosta (Northern Italy), after having met and regularly followed him in Ponta Negra:

> While we were talking, he has been preparing things for lunch. He had to be ready before 1 PM, at which time he agreed to talk in *Messenger* with his Brazilian girlfriend, with whom he is about to get engaged. He told me that they see each other and talk almost daily through the internet. She is 44 years old, from a city in the State of São Paulo, has been sep-arated for more than 10 years and has two children. They met in Ponta Negra a few years ago, at a time when she too was there for tourism. [...] Religiously, they coincide in Messenger at the appointed time. Gentile introduced us. I talked with her a little and left them alone. They spoke for about half an hour. (Field notes, Aosta, 10 October 2010)

In these processes and practices of mediated intimacy management, women are especially proactive. I noticed this, for example, when a domestic female tourist from Belo Horizonte (40 years old, public employee), who was a friend of an informant, asked me to translate a message written on a napkin that she would email to a Swedish tourist with whom she had a brief, but intense, affair (*chamego*) in Ponta Negra. This message read as follows: 'Hi, everything is fine? I hope so. I'm in Natal and I remembered you. When do you return to Natal?'. Finding the content very poor, the friend provided another message. This one declared passionately: 'Love, I am very eager to see you again. I could not forget you. I await news soon. Kisses from someone who fell in love with you'. After a short time, she told me that 'an email came from the Swedish' and that there is a possibility that they will meet again. This, like many other relationships initiated in Ponta Negra, remains at a distance and from time to time it is resumed in a face-to-face format through new male travel to Brazil and/or female travel to Europe, as was the case of Nilda:

> All day, all day we [she and her Dutch boyfriend] talked on the internet. Then he said: 'Do you want to come here?' Then I said: 'I do not have a passport (I have never travelled) and I have no money to pay for the ticket'. There, he: 'No, but I'll send to you'. So, I went, took my passport and came [to Holland] for 15 days this time. He also told me that he was going to send the ticket, and sent it over the internet. I went to get the ticket and I came. (Brazilian, 37 years old, unemployed, ex-cook)

Through these re-encounters and the conditions of interactivity and social proximity that the internet nowadays makes possible, some of the relationships evolve into more consistent intimacy configurations; towards conjugality. This presupposes certain flexibility in the organisation of the couple and in their strategies of mobility and residence, implying displacements of one or both spouses. The most common scenario is the so-called female 'marriage migration' to the European spouse's country. Less frequent situations involve male migration in the opposite direction and the successive seasonal displacements of the couple or one of the spouses, alternating stays of some months between Brazil and Europe (Sacramento, 2016a). This plasticity in the organisation of intimacy and citizenship is, to a large extent, stimulated by the current technological conditions, especially in transport and communications. This emphasises, once again, the ability of the internet and its extraordinary wealth of resources to creatively attenuate the constraints of physical distance.

Conclusion

In today's hypermediatic conditions we are permanently involved in a dense ecology of communications, information, and representations that significantly influences how we perceive the world and build our biographies (Orgad, 2012). The internet, in particular, has been assuming progressively more centrality in the most diverse dimensions of the daily life of many people. The Euro-Brazilian mobilities and configurations of intimacy considered throughout this chapter are an excellent example of this preponderance, showing us the dense digital imbrication of processes and practices that shape a wide diversity of manifestations of contemporary social life.

The European tourist transits towards Ponta Negra, made up mainly of men, are inseparable from the role of cyberspace in the amplification and dissemination of Brazil's global image as a pleasure destination and, more specifically, in the growing insertion of Natal and the Northeast of Brazil on the map of the main international contexts in which mass tourism is the main scenario of intimacy transnationalisation (Sacramento, 2016b). As it was possible to identify in the analysis of audiovisual elements of YouTube, Ponta Negra is digitally projected mainly under an aura of hedonism, sensuality, and eroticism. Thus, the hegemony of this representational register generates a powerful inductive effect in the imagination and desire exercises of the place, fuelling the (potential) tourists' expectations to have access to alternative forms of intimacy to those they found on the European continent. They expect to find on the other side of the Atlantic *warmer* women (less emancipated, more family-oriented and sexually uninhibited and intense) and, thus, be able to construct intimacy spaces more convergent with the hegemonic idealisations of what it is to be a man, at least from their perspective.

In addition to the content that preludes and promotes the transatlantic male tourist mobility, the internet offers innumerable mediation possibilities to the European-Brazilian passionate encounters and to establish and maintain relations that sometimes culminate in marriage. When it precedes tourist mobility, the online love approach is another factor influencing the decision to visit Ponta Negra, in view of a first face-to-face meeting. Besides promoting the encounter, cyberspace is the privileged means in the distance management of relationships that survive the ephemerality of the tourist stay and in its eventual consolidation as conjugal projects. The (potential) role of the internet and mass tourism in the socio-spatial expansion of the passional and marital markets is, therefore, evident. They both strengthen the individual elective capacity in the sphere of intimacy.

Acknowledgments

To the Centre for Transdisciplinary Development Studies (CETRAD-UTAD), an institution supported by national funds, through the FCT – Portuguese Foundation for Science and Technology under the project UID/SOC/04011/2019.

To the Centre for Research in Anthropology (CRIA), an institution supported by national funds, through the FCT – Portuguese Foundation for Science and Technology under the project é UID/ANT/04038/2019.

To FCT for the PhD scholarship SFRH/BD/60862/2009.

To Neil Carr and Liza Berdychevsky for their precious work of reviewing the translation from Portuguese to English.

Notes

(1) A relatively similar version of this text was published in Portuguese in *Quaderns-e* (Institut Català d'Antropologia).

(2) These women tend to be aged 25–30 years and belong, mostly, to the popular classes (working or dominated classes), according to the social space characterisation made by Bourdieu (2007 [1979]). With ages ranging from 35 to 45 years, the men come mainly from Mediterranean Europe (especially Italy). The tourists are not part of the most affluent social strata of their countries (Sacramento, 2014).

(3) In general, the information available on YouTube is considered public and access to such information does not require prior consent: 'An observational study of YouTube videos involves publicly posted and available content accessible to any Internet user. In this case, the information is not private, and it does not require any interaction with the subject to access it. [...] Anyone may view general YouTube videos, with or without a username or password. One would therefore not expect that the consent would be required to conduct an observational study of general YouTube videos' (Moreno *et al.*, 2013: 710). However, throughout the chapter and as far as possible, I try to maintain the confidentiality of the authors and specific locations of the YouTube content that are being analysed. All such material has been identified by a letter and year in this chapter – the author confirms she is happy with this.

(4) It is also pertinent to see the works of Ben-Ze'ev (2004), Kaufmann (2010) and Miller (2011), Sibilia (2008) and Silva and Takeuti (2010), on the new possibilities of interaction and mediated construction of intimacy provided by current electronic communication systems.

(5) For Freyre (2006), the fact that migratory colonisation flows from Portugal to Brazil integrate almost only men (especially in a more initial period) explains the inevitability of miscegenation as the inaugural landmark of Brazil's foundation. At the same time, the slave regime implanted by the Portuguese favored lust and miscegenation: 'There is no slavery without sexual depravity. It is the very essence of the regime. First, economic self-interest favors depravity by creating immoderate men's desire to possess as many offspring as possible. [...] Within such a moral atmosphere, created by the economic interest of the masters, how could one hope that slavery – whether Moorish, Negro, Indian, or Malay slaves – would act otherwise than in the sense of dissolution, libidinousness, lust? What was wanted was for women's wombs to generate. Those black women would produce brats [*moleques*]' (Freyre, 2006: 399).

(6) Each video often reaches tens of thousands of views, thus proving the fundamental role of the internet in the global projection of Ponta Negra as an international tourist destination.

(7) This is one of the many practices that integrate the 'tourist performances' referred to by Sheller and Urry (2004: 7). The video, like photography, seems to represent to the tourist the great support of the narrative of his experience, as well as the material proof of 'having been there' and of having, supposedly, captured the reality of the context (Abbink, 2004: 277).

(8) It reminds us of the presentism and the Dionysiac exuberance, irrepressible and inalienable, discussed in Maffesoli's works (1979, 1985).

(9) A Brazilian slang word that, in the semantic context in which it is used, is equivalent to the popular Portuguese expression *foda-se* (*fuck*), with a meaning related to amazement and admiration.

(10) Most of these men identify the emancipation of European women and their (alleged) exaggerated investment in a professional career, to the detriment of family life, as the main cause of what they perceive to be the major problems in the intimate sphere: women's selectivity in the processes of seduction and love conquest, and the difficulties in developing convergent bonds with the conjugal idealisations about affective-sexual complicity and the need for a permanent conciliation of family and work projects (Sacramento, 2018a, 2016a). In contrast, Brazil represents for them a geography of change. Unhappy with romantic relationships in Europe, they are encouraged by the possibility of finding on the other side of the Atlantic intimate arrangements more in line with their aspirations for conjugal and family life, and

with their notions of normalcy about what it is to be a man and to be a woman. The dominant representations of Brazilianness, extremely associated with feminine sensuality, especially a sexualised notion of Brazilian women as warm and affectionate (and, at the same time, more traditional and less emancipated than their European counterparts), help to widely foster the belief that the tropics will be an effective alternative to the Western 'chaos of love' (Beck & Beck-Gernsheim, 2004).

(11) Sometimes the beginning of a relationship at a distance is one of the most important reasons for visiting the city of Natal.

(12) To ensure the informants' anonymity pseudonyms are used.

References

Abbink, J. (2004) Tourism and its discontents: Suri-tourist encounters in Ethiopia. In S. Gmelch (ed.) *Tourists and Tourism: A Reader* (pp. 267–287). Long Grove: Waveland Press.

Alfonso, L. (2006) Embratur: Formadora de imagens da nação brasileira. MSc Thesis, Unicamp, Campinas.

Appadurai, A. (1996) *Modernity at Large: Cultural Dimensions of Globalization.* Minneapolis: University of Minnesota Press.

Bardin, L. (1995) *Análise de conteúdo.* Lisbon: Edições 70.

Beck, U. (2000) The cosmopolitan perspective: Sociology in the second age of modernity. *British Journal of Sociology* 51 (1), 79–105.

Beck, U. and Beck-Gernsheim, E. (2004) *The Normal Chaos of Love.* Cambridge: Polity Press.

Ben-Ze'ev, A. (2004) *Love Online: Emotions on the Internet.* Cambridge: Cambridge University Press.

Bourdieu, P. (2007 [1979]) *A distinção: Crítica social do julgamento.* Porto Alegre: Zouk.

Campbell, C. (2005) *The Romantic Ethic and the Spirit of Modern Consumerism.* London: Alcuin Academics.

Castells, M. (2002) *A era da informação: Economia, sociedade e cultura. A sociedade em rede* (vol. I). Lisbon: Fundação Calouste Gulbenkian.

Constable, N. (2003) *Pen Pals, Virtual Ethnography, and 'Mail Order' Marriages: Romance on a Global Stage.* Berkeley: University of California Press.

Filho, A.S. (2011) *Brésil: Terre de métissages – imaginaire et quotidien dans la société brésilienne.* Sarrebruck: Éditions Universitaires Européennes.

Fonseca, M. (2005) *Espaço, políticas de turismo e competitividade.* Natal: EDUFRN.

Fonseca, M. and Lima, R. (2012) Globalização, turismo e lazer na região metropolitana de Natal/RN. *Revista Turismo, Visão e Ação* 14 (3), 322–336.

Freyre, G. (2006 [1933]) *Casa-grande e senzala: Formação da família brasileira sob o regime da economia patriarcal.* São Paulo: Global.

Gomes, M. (2010) A (des)(re)construção do Brasil como um paraíso de mulatas. *Revista Eletrônica de Turismo Cultural* 4 (2), 48–70. See http://www.eca.usp.br/turismocultural/8.03_Mariana_Selister.pdf (accessed July 2020).

Jungblut, A. (2004) A heterogenia do mundo on-line: Algumas reflexões sobre virtualização, comunicação mediada por computador e ciberespaço. *Horizontes Antropológicos* 10 (21), 97–121.

Kaufmann, J.-C. (2010) *Sex@mour.* Paris: Armand Colin.

King, R. (2002) Towards a new map of European migration. *International Journal of Population Geography* 8, 89–106.

Kozinets, R. (2010) *Netnography: Doing Ethnographic Research Online.* London: Sage.

Lemos, A. (1996) As estruturas antropológicas do ciberespaço. *Textos de Cultura e Comunicação* 35, 12–27.

Lemos, A. (2009) Cultura da mobilidade. *Revista Famecos* 40, 28–35.

Lévy. P. (2001) *O que é o virtual?* Coimbra: Quarteto.

Machado, I. (2009) *Cárcere público: Processos de exotização entre brasileiros no Porto.* Lisbon: ICS.

Maffesoli, M. (1979) *La conquête du présent. Pour une sociologie de la vie quotidienne.* Paris: PUF.

Maffesoli, M. (1985) *A sombra de Dionísio: Contribuição para uma sociologia da orgia.* Rio de Janeiro: Graal.

Marcus, G. (1995) Ethnography in/of the world system: The emergence of multi-sited ethnography. *Annual Revue of Anthropology* 24 (1), 95–117.

Massey, D. (1994) *Space, Place and Gender.* Minneapolis: University of Minneapolis Press.

Miller, D. (2011) *Tales from Facebook.* Cambridge: Polity Press.

Miller, D. and Slater, D. (2004) Etnografia *on* e *off-line*: Cibercafés em Trinidad. *Horizontes Antropológicos* 10 (21), 41–65.

Molz, J. (2004) Playing online and between the lines: Round-the-world websites as virtual places to play. In M. Sheller and J. Urry (eds) *Tourism Mobilities: Places to Play, Places in Play* (pp. 169–180). London: Routledge.

Moreno, M., Goniu, N., Moreno, S. and Diekema, D. (2013) Ethics of social media research: Common concerns and practical considerations. *Cyberpsychology, Behavior, and Social Networking* 6 (9), 708–713.

Nagel, J. (2003) *Race, Ethnicity, and Sexuality: Intimate Intersections, Forbidden Frontiers.* Oxford: Oxford University Press.

Orgad, S. (2012) *Media Representation and the Global Imagination.* Cambridge: Polity Press.

Parker, R. (1991) *Bodies, Pleasures and Passions: Sexual Culture in Contemporary Brazil.* Boston: Beacon Press.

Piscitelli, A. (2005) Viagens e sexo on-line: A internet na geografia do turismo sexual. *Cadernos Pagu* 25, 281–327.

Pritchard, A. and Morgan, N. (2000a) Privileging the male gaze: Gendered tourism landscape. *Annals of Tourism Research* 27 (4), 884–905.

Pritchard, A. and Morgan, N. (2000b) Constructing tourism landscapes: Gender, sexuality and space. *Tourism Geographies* 2 (1), 115–139.

Ribeiro, F.B. and Sacramento, O. (2009) Imagens, erotismo e culturas *on the road*: Perspectivas sobre o Brasil como destino turístico. *Configurações* 5–6, 241–255.

Roca, J. (2007) Migrantes por amor. La búsqueda y formación de parejas transnacionales. *AIBR – Revista de Antropología Iberoamericana* 2 (3), 430–458.

Roca, J., Flores, L., Puerta, Y., Djurdjevic, M. and Masdeu, M. (2008) *Amor importado, migrantes por amor: La constitución de parejas entre españoles y mujeres de América Latina y de Europa del Este en el marco de la transformación actual del sistema de género en España.* Madrid: Ministerio de Trabajo y Asuntos Sociales – Instituto de la Mujer. See http://www.inmujer.es/eu/areasTematicas/estudios/estudioslinea2009/docs/766Amorimportado.pdf (accessed July 2020).

Roca, J. (2011) Amores glocales, noviazgos transnacionales. La búsqueda virtual de pareja mixta por parte de hombres españoles. *Revista de Antropología Social* 20, 263–292.

Sacramento, O. (2014) *Atlântico Passional: Mobilidades e Configurações Transnacionais de Intimidade Euro-Brasileiras.* PhD Thesis. ISCTE-IUL, Lisbon.

Sacramento, O. (2016a) Conjugalidades distendidas: Trânsitos, projetos e casais transatlânticos. *DADOS – Revista de Ciências Sociais* 59 (4), 1207–1240.

Sacramento, O. (2016b) Turismo e transnacionalização da intimidade nos trópicos globais. *Revista Turismo em Análise* 27 (2), 256–273.

Sacramento, O. (2017) *Mulé' tem que ficar esperta*: Turismo, encontros passionais e gestão feminina da intimidade no nordeste do Brasil. *Mana: Estudos de Antropologia Social* 23 (1), 137–165.

Sacramento, O. (2018a) From Europe with passion: Frameworks of the touristic male desire of Ponta Negra, in the North-East of Brazil. *Current Issues in Tourism* 21 (2), 210–224.

Sacramento, O. (2018b) The production of tourism in Ponta Negra, Northeast Brazil: Policies, representations and logics of desire. *Journal of Tourism and Cultural Change* 16 (2), 191–207.

Sacramento, O. and Ribeiro, F. B. (2013) Trópicos sensuais: A construção do Brasil como geografia desejada. *Bagoas* 10, 215–232.

Santos, T. (2010) *O city marketing em Natal/RN e a construção da imagem da cidade.* MSc Thesis. UFRN, Natal.

Sardan, J-P.O. (1995) La politique du terrain. Sur la production des données en anthropologie. *Enquête* 1, 71–109.

Saunders, B., Julius, S., Kingstone, T., Baker, S., Waterfield, J., Bartlam, B., Burroughs, H. and Jinks, C. (2018) Saturation in qualitative research: Exploring its conceptualization and operationalization. *Quality & Quantity: International Journal of Methodology* 52 (4), 1893–1907.

Sheller, M. and Urry, J. (2004) Places to play, places in play. In M. Sheller and J. Urry (eds) *Tourism Mobilities: Places to Play, Places in Play* (pp. 1–10). London: Routledge.

Sibilia, P. (2008) *O show do eu: A intimidade como espetáculo.* Rio de Janeiro: Nova Fronteira.

Silva, V. and Takeuti, N. (2010) Romance na *web*: Formas de experimentar o amor romântico num namoro virtual. *Revista Brasileira de Sociologia da Emoção* 9 (26), 398–455.

Sommer, D. (2004) *Ficções de fundação: Os romances nacionais da América Latina.* Belo Horizonte: UFMG.

Stolcke, V. (2006) O enigma das intersecções: Classe, 'raça', sexo, sexualidade. A formação dos impérios transatlânticos do século XVI ao XIX. *Estudos Feministas* 14 (1), 15–42.

Warf, B. (2013) *Global Geographies of the Internet.* Dordrecht. New York: Springer.

Wilson, S. and Peterson, L. (2002) The anthropology of online communities. *Annual Review of Anthropology* 31, 449–467.

7 Online Dating on the Move: At the Intersection of Sexuality, Tourism and Space Representation

Elsa Soro, Sheila Sánchez Bergara
and Jose A. Mansilla López

Sex and Tourism

It seems intuitive that during travel, people's behaviour changes. For instance consumer behaviour (CB) research in tourism studies (Horner & Swarbrooke, 2016) has scrutinised all factors affecting the consumption experience along all the stages of the travel journey by underpinning how purchasing during holidays is different from the experience of everyday consumption.

More recently, within the framework of the so-called 'experience economy' (Pine & Gilmore, 1998), emotions have been taken into account as crucial factors in consumer decision-making. With the advent of User Generated Content (UGC), destinations have been increasingly positioned around the feelings they generate. For this reason DMOs (Destination Marketing Organisations) are more and more interested in generating emotional links to a destination.

In turn, the holiday environment has been analysed as a liminal space related to 'pleasure seeking' practices, or even 'hedonistic' ones (Ryan & Robertson, 1997). Such behaviours are often imbricated with practices linked to risk, 'self-exploration and the construction of personal identity' (Carr, 2016: 193), such as hard drinking and drug consumption. Within this context, according to Pritchard and Morgan, 'young people are more likely to indulge in sexual encounters on holiday when they lose their inhibitions' (1996: 78). Furthermore, recent work on gender and sexuality in tourism has focused on sexual orientation as a basis for holiday choices (Waitt & Markwell, 2006).

The commercial relationship between sex and tourism has been the main focus of the multidisciplinary literature. In particular, this has focused on the socio-cultural-economic impacts of sex tourism. This is despite the fact that scholars have highlighted that sex and tourism is far more prevalent than sex tourism (Berdychevsky *et al.*, 2013). In this regard, the definition of sex tourism needs to be nuanced (Carr, 2016) since it is much more multifaceted than the simple 'purpose of effecting a commercial sexual relationship by the tourist with residents at the destination', as defined by the World Tourism Organization (1995).

In an attempt to focus on the intersection between sexuality, tourism and space representation, the present work adopts a nuanced approach within the sex and tourism framework. In this regard, it is noteworthy that within so-called mobilities studies, an emotional turn has emerged, as reported by Mai and King (2009) who interpret mobilities as informed 'by a variety of emotional, affective and sexual liaisons'.

Nowadays, the relationship between sexuality, affectivity and travel can no longer be disconnected from the digitalisation process that has entered all aspects of our lives, including tourism and travel. Social networks and online communities have truly shifted interactions, behaviour and experiences during travel and tourism. Among all those digital platforms, digital dating applications have especially reshaped personal and interpersonal interactions.

Geolocalised Dating

The increasing popularity of dating apps has made online dating a crucial catalyst for disclosing the association between sex, leisure and the experience of a place. Unlike traditional dating agencies and websites, dating apps are able to expose the location of the users and, by so doing, connect to others based on their proximity.

In fact, the advent of geolocalisation allows the tracking of devices by using GPS and this has led to a variety of different uses in many industries and sectors. For instance, within risk management, location can be leveraged to help those affected in case of disaster, by helping them to find the right information and by making sure their requests for help are sourced to the correct agencies. Furthermore, within the tourism industry, thanks to the geo-tagged photos available on online web services people contribute to the perception of destinations and, by so doing, tourists end up becoming the co-creator of destination marketing strategies (Prebensen *et al.*, 2014; Sigala, 2015)

Lastly, at an interpersonal level, people-nearby applications (PNAs) are playing an increasing role in the creation of new social relations, which has meaningful consequences in offline space too. In fact, such applications enable people to discover and meet new people in their physical proximity. Regardless of the scope of the encounter, the physical distance between two users has become a crucial factor. Particularly, in digital dating applications the offline space becomes a crucial factor in the ecology of potential partner choice.

Nevertheless, beyond the more evident interpretation of space as the mere distance between two potential partners, the concept of space is further problematised in the new ecosystem of mediated intimacy. In the case of the use of dating apps while away from home, users might give value not only to the distance to cover in order to reach the potential partner, but also to the same location and its sights. In other words, 'space' understood both as location and distance in dating apps can be thought of as a driver of (a different) use of the same application. If there is no doubt that hooking up and looking for a partner are among the first motives for using dating apps, nonetheless specific geographical contexts such as tourist location might partially shape the attitude through which users interpret the practice of online dating.

As mentioned above, the holiday environment is particularly 'pleasure seeking' and this has consequences for the way in which online dating is performed by players that populate such a context beyond the everyday, home environment. Having said that, the main idea that drives this work is that the quest for authentic experiences of the place and the contact with the local context are sought by users during mobility circumstances, are complementary goals of dating and hooking up. As a complementary idea, the work defends that the same condition of being on the move is positively valued by the dating apps users and they pay special attention to the setting of their profile picture, as a crucial factor of their identity.

After a short contextualisation of the literature on online dating by different disciplinary approaches to date, the chapter will touch upon mobility in space as a specific condition of the contemporary global scenario and how such conditions specifically engage with affectivity and intimacy. In order to interrogate how online dating is performed under mobility conditions findings from a triangulation between a netnography, informal face-to-face interviews and content analysis are presented and discussed. The conclusion of the chapter will point out the extent to which the findings support the main hypothesis, as well the study limitations and the future lines of research to be carried out.

From Hooking Up to Tinder Tourism

In recent years, a variety of disciplinary approaches have been focused on online dating and the hook-up culture. Most of the insights into online dating and mediated intimacy have been raised from media studies (Albury *et al.*, 2017; Cohen, 2015; David & Cambre, 2016; De Ridder, 2017; Duguay, 2017), psychology (Couch & Liamputtong, 2008; Lawson & Leck, 2006; Wang & Chang, 2010), gender studies (MacLeod & McArthur, 2018; Mason, 2016) and sociology (Hobbs *et al.*, 2016; Illouz, 2013) and common research topics can be tracked. For instance, scholars have examined online dating app affordances and use motivation in order to explore how the field of sex and intimacy has been transformed and which are the main discrepancies or similarities between offline and online behaviours.

Despite the common ground, each disciplinary approach shows its own specificity and perspective. From media studies, scholars have scrutinised online dating as an ultimate form of mediatisation (Couldry & Hepp, 2013) and by so doing they have shed light on the role of media in changes of sexuality. Within this framework, De Ridder (2017) has studied the way in which media have become infrastructures through which people's sexualities are lived. Similarly, David and Cambre (2016) have talked in terms of swipe logic[1] by means of interrogating the ironic disruption of intimacy of Tinder's interface.

Within a data culture framework, Albury *et al.* (2017) have raised awareness on privacy, security and ethics, especially considering the disclosure of localisation entailed by the use of mobile applications. Furthermore, Ranzini and Lutz (2017) have approached Tinder as a platform for self-representation, by considering both motivation and app affordances. Their study was aimed at exploring how authentically individuals present themselves on Tinder.

The exploration of motive and purpose in using dating apps has specifically been addressed by research in psychology. In this framework, Couch and Liamputtong (2008), Lawson and Leck (2006) and Wang and Chang (2010), in particular, have examined the reasons related to why people use dating websites. Kim *et al.* (2009), among others, have approached the psychological characteristics of internet dating service users.

The focus on users and population has also been led by gender, feminist studies and race perspectives. Such studies have generally considered dating apps to be 'hetero-normative spaces '. In particular, Mason (2016), from a cultural theory perspective, has researched the rhetoric of the 'female friendliness' of Tinder and how digital dating is racialised.

From a sociology perspective, Illouz (2013) has inquired into how capitalist culture is changing the way we make sense of love and intimacy. With regard to dating apps, she has understood internet structures in the search for a partner in the form of an economic transaction. On the other hand, Hobbs *et al.* (2016) have explored the experiences of dating app users in order to assess the extent to which a digital transformation of intimacy might be under way and how online dating can lead to so-called networked individualism.

If the transformation of the field of sex and intimacy has been relatively widely explored, we know little about how this field intersects practices related to all sorts of mobility conditions. Nevertheless, more recently, the interaction between dating apps and tourism has been approached and the specific phenomenon of the so-called 'Tinder tourism' has created interest not only in blogs and magazines but also in academic literature. In this regard, Leurs and Hardy (2018) have explored Tinder's potential to enhance the tourism experience, by demonstrating that Tinder tourists seek control of their own experience by using a non-traditional tourism app, which has implications for what the tourism industry can offer.

Taking into account these latest insights, the present work aims to focus on the intersection between dating apps and tourism. However, the approach of the study is not limited to the analysis of the use of dating apps during travel. What is at stake is the imbrication between digital intimacy and space, performed and represented.

Affects in the Age of Mobility

With the turn of millennium, a series of social, economic, political and cultural phenomena, such as the increase in travelling around the world, the spread of digital communication, and the disruption of low cost transport, led scholars from a variety of disciplinary approaches to consider 'the importance of mobilities for people's social and emotional lives' (Sheller, 2017: 5). In this regard, the first sentence of the crucial paper published by Sheller and Urry that appeared in the prestigious journal *Environment and Planning* was 'all the world seems to be on the move' (2006: 208).

New mobility theories link up with a variety of topics such as networked capital, affective geography and tourism and capture different types of movement and related spatial practices and mobility regimes. Within a mobility theory approach, mobility is scrutinised as a contingent and uneven condition. In this vein, phenomena such as tourism or migration are comprehended as wider situations tied to movement in space.

In turn, affective and sexual liaisons are informed by different forms of mobilities and journeys. This can lead scholars to argue for both a 'sexual turn' and an 'emotional turn' in mobility studies (Mai & King, 2009). In such a framework, affects and mobility arguably have a twofold intersection. On the one hand, those on the move by means of maintaining existing social ties. On the other hand, during travels of any means the urgency to create new bonds and a new sense of belonging *in situ* emerges. In the contemporary mediascape, such a quest for localness and community is meaningfully fostered by new technologies and social networks.

Within the type of changing scenario drawn above, the use of dating apps by the mobile collective in places and cities featuring significant flows of people 'on the move', emerges as an interesting ground for research. In this regard, at least two research lines are worth exploring.

First, how people use dating apps while on the move and whether functions other than dating emerge during such practices. Secondly, how travel and more generally, movements in space, can be a driver of attractiveness in profile rating. Consequently, on Tinder profiles, the relationship between self-presentation and the touristic space experience will be scrutinised.

Methodology: Data and Sample

In this chapter we examine the relationship between digital intimacy and space. In order to do this, the methodology used is mostly qualitative (Berg, 2007). A multi-method approach, including netnography, in-depth semi-structured interviews, informal conversations and dialogues with different actors and content analysis of Tinder profiles as a way of triangulation (Kozinets, 2009), has been conducted in order to empirically determine the propositions.

The first step in our work was a review of the extensive relevant bibliography (books or articles in relevant scientific magazines, news, statements, websites, apps and social networks) about mobility, tourism and leisure and mediated intimacy. This was followed by over 10 months of fieldwork, between 2018 and 2019. Five face-to-face interviews were carried out in the city of Barcelona. In addition, 10 online interviews with Tinder users were carried out, by creating a Tinder profile which specified the research purposes. During all the netnography period, researchers browsed hundreds of Tinder profiles so as to have insight about the profile set-up composition as a means of self-representation strategy.

As we are presenting an ongoing work, the sample of the interviewees is not totally extensive or representative. Responders were selected initially on the basis of their willingness to participate. For the interviews, a rough semi-structured guideline was used. Interview guidelines were constructed through literature studies. Interviews were transcribed and analysed using an inductive coding strategy. We truly believe that this methodology is best suited to this sort of research, because it allows the object of study to be approached from within and attempts to describe and interpret the social process, putting the focus on the participants and the context. Finally, the results presented in the chapter intentionally do not differentiate on the basis of age or gender. The assumption was to track if the condition of being on the move has consequences for how people date digitally regardless of their age and the gender they feel they belong to.

Following Sales (2015), we have elected to utilise Tinder as our flagship for dating practices. Nonetheless, a significant number of users interviewed indicated that they may use more than one platform at the same time for similar purposes. The netnography was conducted by the female researchers, so the respondents were mainly male, even if the researchers could, while surfing on the App, visit and contact both male and female profiles. The two profiles created by the researchers specified in the description that the purpose for using the App was to conduct research. Despite this clarification, many of the people with whom we were able to exchange messages initiated the contact by asking whether the research was for real. Also, on several occasions, when it was confirmed that the objective was to have a conversation/interview about the use of the App for research purposes, repondents did not respond again and in one case one of the researchers was blocked. On the other hand, another group of respondents did take a collaborative stance and selflessly agreed to participate in the investigation.

It is important to remark that all the people who could be contacted through messages to invite them to participate in the research were those with whom the researchers got a match. Thus, the selection of the final sample was the result of, on the one hand, the initial selection made by the researchers of the profiles proposed by the App and, on the other hand, those profiles that effectively gave a like to the researchers, thus allowing the match required by this application to contact people. The selection of profiles was made weekly, in most cases on Friday afternoons, to facilitate the possibility of contacting the potential participants. For one hour, the different profiles proposed by the App were reviewed and those who were supposed to be in a mobile situation, were selected with a 'like'.

During this part of the fieldwork, 16 people, 12 men and 4 women, were directly contacted after being informed by Tinder about the match. A message was sent to all of them explaining the purpose of the research in order to invite them to participate by answering a set of questions. The final sample consisted of 7 people, 6 men and one woman, between the ages of 33 and 43 years.

During the netnography, the researchers deliberately did not use surveys. Nonetheless, the guideline for the interview focused around three main topics:

- The reason for using the App.
- The use during mobility situations.
- Purposes of use other than dating whilst in a situation of mobility.

During the face-to-face interviews, the topics touched on were wider, on the basis of what the respondents wanted to highlight. The role of the interviewer was to guide respondents toward the topics and extract collateral data and information.

For the content analysis, both profile image and description have been taken into account. Since the general goal of each dating app user is to choose a specific scenography for staging an alleged desirable self, the profiles disclose a selection of identity elements, while hiding others in Eco's terms (1979). At this stage of the research, both the space typology and the kind of activity performed in such spaces were considered and classified.

Lastly, the geographical context of the research needs to be mentioned. The city of Barcelona is the place where the interviews were carried out and from where the dating profiles have been analysed.

Findings Discussion

Face-to-face interviews and netnography

Ninety per cent of the respondents admitted using Tinder while travelling (or under other mobility circumstances). In one case (female, 36 years old), she claimed to use Tinder especially (but not limited to) while travelling or during short or medium stays away from her habitual residence.

In the majority of cases, the main reason for using dating apps does not change during the trip, where it is the quest for a casual (or not casual) intimate (and sexual) relation. Nonetheless, during trips and away from the habitual residence, other reasons and drivers for the use emerge. They are, for the most part: meeting new people for sharing leisure activities; learning (or improving) the destination language; making new friends; getting in contact with local nightlife ('hanging out where locals hang out'). Conversely, two respondents reported they were contacted via Tinder by tourists and they were asked about local consumption habits, such as local food and drink establishments, and how to find an apartment to rent.

Despite the limitations explained in the methodological section of the chapter, significant insights into the topic emerged thanks to the netnography, beginning with the fact that the great majority use Tinder while travelling and more in general under mobility circumstances. Even if the main reason for using Tinder while travelling did not differ from the habitual use, more incentives in using dating app show up. The transitory idea of holidays, travelling and other situations tagged as 'away from home' seems to foster the use of the dating app as a medium to achieve random, casual, occasional relationships. One might argue that a kind of 'specularity' between the temporality of the mobility condition and the one of the dating has been established in order to possibly consider dating apps as a sort of app for travellers.

Scenography of self-presentation

The last part of the research includes the analysis of images and content of the profile presentations by more than 100 users analysed.

Table 7.1 Code scheme for content analysis

Space	Urban	Rural	Exotic	Familiar	Natural	Industrial	Heritage	Outdoor	Indoor	Touristic	Off the beaten track
Activity	Alone	Group	Pets	Adventure wilderness	Relax	Dining	Fitness	Winter sports	Summer and beach	Social Media	Nightlife

The assumption that has driven this part of the study was that travelling and having a 'life on the move' is one of the elements of a person's self to be shown while selecting a specific scenography for staging an alleged desirable self. This hypothesis arises from the observation of the self-presentation on Tinder throughout the time of the netnography study. In order to systematise the information, a code scheme has been used to analyse those Tinder profiles considered relevant for the topic (see Table 7.1).

It is worth noting that 70% of the profiles surfed have been considered significant in this respect, which means that they include travel and mobility either in the photos selected or the profile description. Both the space typology and the kind of activity performed in such spaces have been considered, since places have been continuously given new meanings according to the actions performed there by users.

Elsewhere (e.g. Soro, 2019) an extensive semiotics analysis of the discursive categories has been conducted. Following Greimas' (1970) assumption that the condition for grasping any meaning lies in an elementary system of relations articulated in the semiotic square, two opposite attitudes towards space and leisure have been highlighted, namely Ordinary vs. Extraordinary. From this basic opposition another two terms arise, called in Greimas' terminology contradictory stem, 'Not ordinary' and 'Not extraordinary' (1970). These four terms, each corresponding to a position on the square, will be broken down and different typologies of being a tourist or performing tourism will be identified.

For the specific purpose of the present chapter it is sufficient to identity the most popular scenography in Tinder profiles, represented either in images or in textual format. On one hand, well-known tourism sites, such as the Eiffel Tower, Machu Picchu, the Leaning Tower of Pisa or the Brooklyn Bridge have been reported as significantly present in the analysed sample. This category also encompasses the 'standard', but anonymous tourism locations (i.e. tropical beaches) where the users perform 'typical tourist ways of life', such as drinking cocktails at sunset or lying on a beach. On the other hand, a significant presence of scenography for staging the self-tied to nature, wilderness and exotic fauna was noticed. In such environments, users perform adventure activities such as hiking, diving, surfing, backpacking, etc. … Lastly, a number of urban settings were observed. In such scenarios, users are depicted as carrying out daily life activities, such taking the bus or the metro, and walking in the street. This kind of scenography, combined with a 'hipster' appearance, can be defined as 'cosmopolitan'.

Arguably, the significant presence of sites and activities in Tinder profiles might contribute to singling out which trends in tourism and travel are emerging. Classical tourism sites, the ones reproduced in millions of postcards, are no longer the only ones represented. New sceneries, both urban and natural, as a site for self-performance, shows new travellers preferences and lifestyles. Furthermore, regardless of the specific geographic references, the same condition of travelling deployed by profile picture seems to be considered as the bottom line of the supposed attractive self.

Conclusions

As mentioned in the methodological section, the main finding of the present work regards the city of Barcelona, since both the people interviewed and the profiles browsed have been sharing, temporarily or permanently, this environment The insights of the work resemble the geographical, social and cultural environment of the location; this being Barcelona, a city that is well known as an international hub for tourism and business, and for its creative and smart economy. This city matches the goals of the study that has been focused on geographical environments that involve significant flows of people, primarily tourists. Nonetheless, a comparison between different and similar geographical contexts, both touristic and not-touristic, could strengthen the relevance of the findings.

Aside from the geographical context, our study is subject to other limitations, providing ideal opportunities for future research on the imbrication between mediated intimacy, leisure and mobility condition. Firstly, our sample was relatively small and it does not address a specific segment of the population or consider cultural background, age or geographical origin of those interviewed. This makes the generalisation of the results problematic. In order to overcome this limitation, future research should engage a sample that is both wider and more segmented. As part of this, there needs to be a focus on gender in future studies.

Despite the limitations of the current study, the insights provided by it are partially aligned with its main hypothesis. Even though an exclusive use of the dating App while on the move is not shown by the findings, intimate liaisons appear to be informed by different forms of mobilities. The same transitory condition of being on the move arguably encourages the use of dating apps by widening and differentiating such use behind the 'prescribed' one.

Furthermore, this work has contributed to interpreting the relationship between sex and tourism as dynamic and multifaceted. In this vein, the chapter proposes a twofold and two-way research direction. On one side, those tourism narratives embedded in dating profile images can be considered as lens 'with which to interrogate dynamic social processes' (Minca & Oakes, 2014: 295) and, in particular, to read self-presentation strategies in online intimacy platforms. On the other side, those narratives of intimacy as deployed by dating devices might provide a platform to view new tourism and travel trends in the degree to which users employ tourism sites (both well known and off the beaten track) for setting up their profile compositions. As a consequence, the emergence of new tourism trends and niches (tourism and wildness, urban tourism, etc...) ultimately can be inferred by the presence of tourism spots and experiences in dating app profiles. Ultimately, future research might focus on how the domains of intimacy and mobility, as conditions that are typical of our times, mirror themselves and show mutual influences.

Acknowledgements

This project has received funding from the European Research Council (ERC) under the European Union's Horizon 2020 research and innovation programme (grant agreement No 819649 – FACETS).

Note

(1) With the 'swipe logic', the authors refer to 'the pace, or the increased viewing speed encouraged by the UI of this app, and that very pace that emerged as a prominent feature of the discourses examined both online and off-line' (David & Cambre, 2016: 2).

References

Albury, K., Burgess, J., Light, B., Race, K. and Wilken, R. (2017) Data cultures of mobile dating and hook-up apps: Emerging issues for critical social science research. *Big Data & Society* 4 (2), 1–11.

Berdychevsky, L., Gibson, H. and Poria, Y. (2013) Women's sexual behavior in tourism: Loosening the bridle. *Annals of Tourism Research* 42, 65–85.

Berg, B.L. (2007) *Qualitative Research Methods for the Social Sciences*. Boston: Pearson Education Inc.

Carr, N. (2016) Sex in tourism: Reflections and potential future research directions. *Tourism Recreation Research* 41 (2), 188–198

Cohen, L. (2015) World attending in interaction: Multitasking, spatializing, narrativizing with mobile devices and Tinder. *Discourse, Context & Media* 9, 46–54.

Couch, D. and Liamputtong P. (2008) Online dating and mating: The use of the internet to meet sexual partners. *Qualitative Health Research* 18 (2), 268–79

Couldry, N. and Hepp, A. (2013) Conceptualizing mediatization: Contexts, traditions, arguments. *Communication Theory* 23 (3), 191–202

David, G. and Cambre, C. (2016) Screened intimacies: Tinder and the swipe logic. *Social Media + Society* 2 (2), 1–11.

De Ridder, S. (2017) Mediatization and sexuality: An invitation to a deep conversation on values, communicative sexualities, politics and media. *Media@LSE Working Paper Series*.

Duguay, S. (2017) Dressing up Tinderella: Interrogating authenticity claims on the mobile dating app Tinder. Information. *Communication & Society* 20 (3), 351–367.

Eco, U. (1979) *Lector in Fabula*. Milano: Bompiani.

Greimas, A.J. (1970) *Du sens 1*. Paris: Seuil.

Hobbs, M., Owen, S. and Gerber, L. (2016) Liquid love? Dating apps, sex, relationships and the digital transformation of intimacy. *Journal of Sociology* 53 (2), 271–284.

Horner, S. and Swarbrooke, J. (2016) *Consumer Behaviour in Tourism*. London: Routledge.

Illouz, E. (2013) *Why Love Hurts: A Sociological Explanation*. Cambridge: Polity.

Kim, M., Kwon, K. and Lee, M. (2009) Psychological characteristics of internet dating service users: The effect of self-esteem, involvement, and sociability on the use of internet dating services. *Cyberpsychology & Behavior* 12 (4), 445–449.

Kozinets, R.V. (2009) *Netnography: Doing Ethnographic Research Online*. London: Sage Publications Ltd.

Lawson, H.M. and Leck, K. (2006) Dynamics of internet dating. *Social Science Computer Review* 24 (2), 189–208.

Leurs, E. and Hardy, A. (2018) Tinder tourism: Tourist experiences beyond the tourism industry realm. *Annals of Leisure* 22 (2), 323–341.

MacLeod, C. and McArthur, V. (2018) The construction of gender in dating apps: An interface analysis of Tinder and Bumble. *Feminist Media Studies* 19 (6), 822–840.

Mai, N. and King, R. (2009) Love, sexuality and migration: Mapping the issue(s). *Mobilities* 4 (3), 295–307.

Mason, C.L. (2016) Tinder and humanitarian hook-ups: The erotics of social media racism. *Feminist Media Studies* 16 (5), 822–837

Minca, C. and Oakes, T. (2014) Tourism after the postmodern turn. In A. Lew, C.M. Hall and A. Williams (eds) *The Wiley Blackwell Companion to Tourism* (pp. 294–303). Hoboken, NJ: Wiley-Blackwell.

Pine II, B.J. and Gilmore, J.H. (1998) Welcome to the experience economy. *Harvard Business Review* 76 (4), 97–105.

Prebensen, N., Chen, J. and Uysal, M. (2014) *Creating Experience Value in Tourism*. Wallingford: CABI.

Pritchard, A. and Morgan, N. (1996) Sex still sells to generation X: Promotional practice and the youth package holiday market. *Journal of Vacation Marketing* 3 (1), 69–80.

Ranzini, G. and Lutz, C. (2017) Love at first swipe? Explaining Tinder self-presentation and motives. *Mobile Media & Communication* 5 (1), 80–101.

Ryan, C. and Robertson, E. (1997) New Zealand student-tourists: Risk behaviour and health. In S. Clift and P. Grabowski (eds) *Tourism and Health: Risks, Research and Responses* (pp. 119–138). London: Pinter.

Sales, N. (2015) Tinder and the dawn of the 'dating apocalypse.' *Vanity Fair*. Accessed 31 July 2020 http://www. vanityfair.com/culture/2015/08/tinder-hook-up-culture-end-of-dating.

Sheller, M. (2017) From spatial turn to mobilities turn. *Current Sociology* 65 (4), 623–639.

Sheller, M. and Urry, J. (2006) The new mobilities paradaigm. *Environment and Planning A: Economy and Space* 38 (2), 207–226

Sigala, M. (2015) From demand elasticity to market plasticity: A market approach for developing revenue management strategies in tourism. *Journal of Travel and Tourism Marketing* 35 (1), 1–4.

Soro, E. (2019) Sex of place: Mediated intimacy and tourism imaginaries. *Digital Age in Semiotics & Communication* 2, 92–101.

World Tourism Organization (1995) *WTO Statement on the Prevention of Organized Sex Tourism*. Cairo, Egypt: The General Assembly of the World Tourism Organization

Waitt, G. and Markwell, K. (2006) *Gay Tourism: Culture and Context*. New York: The Haworth Hospitality Press.

Wang, C. and Chang, Y. (2010) Cyber relationship motives: Scale development and validation. *Social Behavior & Personality: An International Journal* 38 (3), 289–300.

Part 2: Fifty Shades of Grey of Sex in Tourism: Romance Tourism, Sex Tourism or Exploitation Tourism?

8 Sex Tourism Beyond the Human

S. Emre Dilek

Introduction

After reviewing the existing literature on sex tourism, it can be concluded that the characteristics of sex tourism include (a) international travel from developed to developing countries, (b) the consumption of paid-for sex and (c) inequality. There are differences in power between sex tourists (the buyers) and sex workers (the sellers), which may be based on gender, race, social class, economic welfare and nationality (Brennan, 2004; Taylor, 2010). These differences become commodified inequalities. Buyers also eroticise these differences as part of paid-sex experiences by means of sex tourism. Consequently, sex tourism may be defined as a phenomenon that describes a person travelling away from his or her community to engage in commercial sexual relations, usually with prostitutes. In brief, sex tourism is described as a '*sexual Disneyisation*' in which sex tourists' desire opportunities for sexual contacts and are looking for sexual experiences that go beyond the realm of their everyday lives.

This chapter asks '*what will sex tourism look like in the future?*' looking in particular at how the industry is going beyond humankind and using non-human animals and robots, as well as sex in cyberspace. After establishing the framework for the relationship between sex and tourism, the chapter scrutinises the various types of sex tourism, including sex with humans, non-human animals, technological tools and sex in cyberspace.

Although sex has played a part in tourism since the earliest days of travel (McKercher & Bauer, 2003; Yeoman & Mars, 2012), the modern 'sex tourism' industry is one of the most controversial in the world. The term sex tourism usually brings to mind the image of Western businessmen being herded onto buses and into 'juicy bars' in South Korea or 'go-go bars' in Thailand. However, it can actually take many different forms in a variety of locations (Davidson & Taylor, 2005). Modern day sex tourism is defined as travel for the purpose of engaging in sexual activity, not only with human prostitutes but also with non-human prostitutes such as robots and animals. One of the purposes of this chapter is to develop an understanding of the sex tourism phenomenon beyond the human. In this context, after talking about the relationship between sex and tourism and sex tourism in which people are the main actors, the framework of the study was determined in three basic questions: (1) Where are the non-human animals in sex tourism? (2) How do technological tools transform sex tourism? (3) Does cyberspace (virtual reality) bring a different dimension to sex tourism?

The subject of sex robots is attracting an increasing amount of attention in current discussions about technology, the future of human relationships, and tourism (Scheutz & Arnold, 2016). At the same time, animals are increasingly being commoditised as sex slaves and sexual performers in the tourism industry (Fennell, 2012). The three main providers of sex tourism can therefore be classified as: (1) humans (local men, women and children), (2) non-human animals (orangutans, dogs and donkeys, among others) and (3) technological tools (robots, androids, dolls and virtual reality). Alongside this, many authors emphasise the five basic dimensions of sex tourism: legal, political, ethical, economic and sociocultural (Ghorbani et al., 2014; Hall, 1998; Leheny, 1995). The technological dimension should also be added to this list because of the use of technological tools in sex tourism. This, of course, marks a blurring of the distinction between dimensions and providers.

'Sex' and 'tourism' must be considered in terms of both the providers and the dimensions of the sex tourism industry. This chapter considers how non-human animals, robots and sex in cyberspace are used in the sex tourism industry, with particular attention paid to the following questions based on Ryan and Hall's work (2001: X): Even though the tourism stakeholders might proclaim that prostitution is immoral, (a) how aware are stakeholders that sex has a market value; (b) why do they/do they not make an effort to develop sex tourism beyond the human?

Framing the Sex-Tourism Relationship

There has long been a very close relationship between tourism and sex (Littlewood, 2002; McKercher & Bauer 2003). Since antiquity, tourism and travel have taken people out of normality, both temporally and spatially, including sexual escapades (Casson, 1994). Interest in sex tourism-related activities seems to be increasing, especially in Third World countries and including sexual interactions between western tourists and third world women and men (Garrick, 2008; Taylor, 2001).

Tourism allows people to escape from the troubles, limitations, rules and pressures of everyday life. While the normal lives of people are often expressed in terms of work and everyday difficulties, tourism and travel are described in terms of freedom and hedonistic experiences (Krippendorf, 1987; Uriely, 2005). In other words, in becoming a tourist, one is temporarily feted and free (or at least perceived to be free) from the usual constraints of work, family and social expectations (Ryan & Hall, 2001).

The four Ss of tourism – *'sun, sand, sea and sex'* – are often regarded as synonymous with the supposedly globalising and homogenising nature of international mass tourism (Campbell *et al.*, 1999; Richards & Reid, 2016; Ryan & Hall, 2001). The modern tourism industry uses sexuality in its marketing, generating an image of tourism that encourages more relaxed attitudes towards sexuality while travelling (Diken & Laustsen, 2004; Thomas, 2005). Set against this backdrop, sex tourism is a protean term that attempts to capture the wide variety of leisure travel that has as a part of its purpose the purchase of sexual services.

Sexuality is both a natural and social phenomenon, with different sexualities arising at different times and in different places (Bailey *et al.*, 2016). Sexual relations in tourism are influenced by factors such as the place of the sexual partner in relation to the tourist's own culture, the tourist's individual characteristics, the status of sexuality in their everyday lives, the culture of the tourism destination and the social positions of the parties involved. Thus, this can generate different effects, goals and meanings for the different parties involved (Piscitelli, 2007).

The traditional image of sex tourism that comes to mind is that of male tourists from developed countries travelling for the purpose of experiencing non-committal heterosexual sex in a tourism destination in a developing country (McKercher & Bauer, 2003; Oppermann, 1999). In most cases, the macro and micro properties of this phenomenon are clear (Davidson, 2001). On the micro level, sex tourism has a hugely negative impact on the people who are forced to sell their bodies, while the reproduction and preservation of existing power imbalances between genders, social classes and nationalities is the negative macro effect of this industry (Choorichom, 2011; Pettman, 1997; Yeoman & Mars, 2012). Sex tourism activities are still considered controversial due to their negative impacts, in particular, safety and security concerns, social conflict and health issues (Leong Chong, 2014).

Sex Tourism with Humans

Sex tourism, as an identifiable concept, emerged in the late 20th century as a controversial aspect of Western tourism and globalisation. Sex tourism highlights the convergence between prostitution and tourism, links the global and the local and draws attention to both the production and consumption of sexual services.

> I pay for sex because that is the only way I can get sex. I am not ashamed of paying for sex. I pay for food. I pay for clothing. I pay for shelter. Why should I not also pay for sex? (Loebner, 1998: 221)

Around the world, millions of men, women and children are being exploited for sex trafficking (Carolin *et al.*, 2015). Sex trafficking is defined as '*the recruitment, harboring, transportation, provision, or obtaining of a person for the purpose of a commercial sex act*' (U.S. Department of State, 2015: 7) and is a critical issue facing the hospitality and tourism industry. Almost every part of the world experiences sex tourism. Prostitution is legal in 49 countries while a further 12 countries have limited laws allowing some aspects of prostitution, and 39 countries have laws making prostitution illegal (Carolin *et al.*, 2015; Pettman, 1997).

Sex tourism is defined as travelling with the primary motivation of engaging in commercial sexual relations (Kibicho, 2009). Even if not all tourism to sex tourism hubs is driven by a motivation to engage in sex, every year, millions of travellers visit the sex tourism hubs of underdeveloped or developing nations in search of sex, intimacy, exoticism and sexually driven adventure and/or freedom from social constraints. Some of the key areas globally include the Philippines, the Dominican Republic and Thailand, which are sex tourism destinations for tourists from Australia, Europe, Japan and the USA (Brooks & Heaslip, 2019). It is estimated that 250,000 Australian tourists visit Asia for sex with a minor each year, while 25% of sex tourists come from the United States (Equality Now, 2009). Men are more commonly sex tourists, with most being middle or upper class (Bender & Furman, 2004; Brooks & Heaslip, 2019). Many sex tourists seek an experience beyond the realm of their everyday lives without the usual consequences or costs that accompany inappropriate sexual behaviours in their home environment. These motivations drive the commercial sexual exploitation of people around the world (UCSB, 2018).

While sex tourism has become a popular recreational activity for Americans and other affluent Western travellers, the industry itself is linked to the fastest growing criminal enterprise in the world. Sex trafficking is a lucrative industry worth an estimated US$99 billion a year (ILO, 2014), with at least 20.9 million people being bought and sold worldwide into commercial sexual servitude, forced labour and bonded labour (ILO, 2012). Within this population, an estimated 2 million children aged 11 to 17 are exploited every year in the global commercial sex trade (ECPAT, 2016; UNICEF, 2005). Women and girls make up 96% of victims of trafficking for sexual exploitation (UNODC TIP Report, 2016).

Sex Tourism with Non-Human Animals

Millions of animals have been used in the tourism industry for human enjoyment and benefit (Fennell, 2014). Sexual relations between humans and non-human animals, sometimes referred to as bestiality, is perhaps the least understood of all human-animal interactions (Jory et al., 2002) and one of the areas where animals are commodified in the tourism industry.

> Pony was a cash machine and a source of luck. Men could pay a certain amount of money to the house owner to have sex with her. (Fridman, 2015)

Non-human animals are being commoditised in various ways in the tourism industry, as performers and competitors, for forced labour, wildlife viewing and recreational hunting (i.e. killed for sport) (Fennell, 2012). One of the areas in which animals are used is sex tourism. Awareness of human sexual contact with animals dates back as far as Biblical times (Aggrawal, 2009). The range of sexual behaviours engaged in with animals includes not only coitus but also behaviours such as fellatio, cunnilingus, the masturbation of animals, anal intercourse, exhibitionism, frotteurism and voyeurism (London & Caprio, 1950; McNally & Lukach, 1991; Peretti & Rowan, 1983). Stephanie Feldstein, from the activism organisation Change.org (2010), has reported on sexualised animal companionship in the tourism industry; referred to as bestiality tourism (Fennell, 2012). Sexual relations between humans and non-human animals have existed since the dawn of human history in every place and culture in the world (Miletski, 2005). Even more important are the reports that bestiality is still an integral part of many people's lives, whether in myth, art, literature or as actual sexual behaviour (Navarro & Tewksbury, 2015). There is arguably a need to examine the position of non-human animal sex in tourism (Carr, 2016). Although no one knows how prevalent sexual behaviour with animals is, bestiality is unquestionably among us (Miletski, 2005). The term bestiality is defined as the *sexual attraction of a human toward a nonhuman animal, which may involve the experience of sexual fantasies about the animal or the pursuit of real sexual contact with it* (Aggrawal, 2011; Alvarez & Freinhar, 1991). In a simple way, 'it is defined as the sexual coupling of a human with a non-human animal' (Carr, 2014: 68).

Although no reliable statistics exist on the number of people engaging in bestiality around the world, and which animals are chosen for such activities, there have been some reports in the media concerning '*sex tourism with non-human animals*', in which people travel to destinations such as Hungary, Serbia, Romania and Germany where so-called '*animal brothels*' are not illegal (Blake, 2013; Fennell, 2012; Markwell, 2015; Martin, 2017; Newsroom, 2017).

The globalisation of sex tourism implies not only the proliferation of sex tourism into ever more regions of the world but also its varied forms of development. Animal sex tourism (AST) is a touristic phenomenon that has developed around the practice of sexual acts with animals

(Panko & George, 2018). There have been reports, for example, of tourists travelling to Denmark for this purpose, with Danish animal rights advocates strongly opposing the industry (Tange, 2015). Such practices have since been made illegal, following a vote on the matter in the Danish parliament on 1 July 2015 (Staples, 2015). Despite the passing of this legislation in Denmark, tourists continue to arrive for the purpose of engaging in sexual intercourse with animals and participating in other animal sex tourism activities (Pierce, 2015).

In other countries, sexual relations between animals are displayed as part of a 'show'. For example, in Tijuana, Mexico, people can pay to watch sexual intercourse between donkeys (Love Travel Life, 2012). In Indonesia, orangutans are forced to 'work' as sex workers and are marketed particularly at tourists (Mishra, 2015). The example of a female orangutan called Pony (as noted above) is at the more extreme end but demonstrates the complete lack of animal rights and welfare in the sex tourism industry. If non-human animals are not generally seen as sentient beings and lack the legal rights of humans, can we apply a humanistic label like 'employee or worker' to them, as in the case of Pony (Carr & Broom, 2018)? Pony was found, aged six or seven, living in Kareng Pangi village, in Central Kalimantan, Indonesia, where she was being used as a sex slave and sold as a prostitute by her owner. When Pony was discovered, it was unclear how long she had been living there. Pony's owner refused to release her as she was a very lucrative source of income and seen as a good luck charm. Efforts were made by the Borneo Orangutan Survival (BOS) Foundation and the Central Kalimantan Conservation and Natural Resources Authority (BKSDA), alongside the police and military forces, to persuade the owner to give Pony to the BOS Foundation, with eventual success. However, living for so long with humans and being treated so appallingly by them meant that it was not easy for Pony to live as a wild orangutan. In 2013, aged 17, Pony was finally given the chance to start again on a pre-release island before being relocated to Kaja Island, where she now lives with seven other female orangutans (Fridman, 2015).

As the number of activities involving animals in tourism has grown, so too has the understanding of the animals involved and the potential impacts of interaction between tourists and animals. Animal sex tourism is a form of tourism (Fennell, 2012) in which sex tourists travel in search of authentic sexual experiences, such as sexual intercourse, with non-human animals. Authenticity, a search for pure objects of consumption (MacCannell, 1973), may refer to either, or both, the authenticity of the observed tourist object or the authenticity of the tourist's first-person experience. Seeking of authentic sexual experiences with non-human animals indicates that activity-related authenticity, defined as 'existential authenticity' by Wang (1999), is important in this case. It refers to a potential existential state of being that is to be activated by tourist activities. Since the concept of existential authenticity can explain a wider spectrum of tourist phenomena than the conventional concept of authenticity, it opens up a broad viewpoint for the justification of authenticity-seeking as the foundation of animal sex tourism motivation (Steiner & Reisinger, 2006; Wang, 1999). An edited book by Markwell (2015) entitled, *Animals in Tourism: Understanding Diverse Relationships,* contains a chapter on the exploitation of both humans and animals in Thailand. The chapter, written by Bone and Bone (2015), infers the striking similarities between the mistreatment of women and elephants in the sex and elephant tourism markets. They explain that women and animals are oppressed in similar ways via containment and control for tourist enjoyment. In other words, the authors point to the subjects as merely a product to be consumed by the tourist gaze and call for people to act responsibly with the 'other' (animals and women). Even if tourism allows people to distance themselves from their norms (i.e. that tourism activities are non-ordinary, free from the constraints of daily life) it is clear that individuals participating in tourism must respect everyone and everything else. Otherwise, the tourist experience cannot go beyond an inauthentic and artificial experience. In this regard, animal sex tourism is an artificial tourism experience produced by and for the tourist gaze and human enjoyment and it is contrary to existential authenticity. However, as Urry (1990) argued, human sexual encounters in contemporary society have become increasingly artificial. Thus, 'the superficiality of sexual encounters may facilitate experimentation with non-human animals' (Panko & George, 2018: 183).

Sex Tourism with Technological Tools

Technology has changed in our lives. Many types of social activity now involve technology and it can also be connected with some concrete technological tools that affect the link between sex and tourism; see, for example, Jason Lee's book entitled '*Sex Robots: The Future of Desire*'. He addressed how robots will affect our humanity and in particular our sexuality (Lee, 2017).

> Robot sex is safer sex, free from the constraints, precautions and uncertainties of the real deal. (Yeoman & Mars, 2012: 370)

The words 'sex' and 'tourism' together conjure up images of red-light districts, prostitution and exploitation (Ryan, 2000). However, what about sex with robots? The traditional view of sex tourism that only includes human or non-human individuals requires revision. Robot sex arguably offers a solution to a host of problems associated with the sex trade. Given the rise of incurable STIs (Sexual Transmitted

Infections) around the world, including emergent strains of gonorrhoea and HIV (Human Immunodeficiency Virus)/AIDS (Acquired Immune Deficiency Syndrome), and the problems associated with human trafficking and sex tourism, it is likely that we will see an increase in demand for alternative forms of sexual expression (Yeoman & Mars, 2012). For example, '*Lumidolls*', the world's first brothel staffed entirely by robot sex workers, opened in Barcelona, Spain, near the city's popular tourist spots in February 2017 (Lockett, 2017). Customers can choose what their dolls wear and can watch pornography featuring them. The brothel allows men to live out their fantasies without having to persuade real women, girls or children to indulge them (Naff, 2017). The company now has plans to expand all over the world.

A recent international conference at the University of London entitled, '*Love and Sex with Robots*' attracted experts from around the world to consider the future of societies in which sex robots become the new norm (Cheok & Levy, 2018). In the report '*The Future of Sex*' by Ian Pearson, he outlines '*a future in which robotic brothels and strip clubs with computer-controlled dancers are normal*' and claims that '*sex with humans could soon be a thing of the past*' (Rodriguez, 2017: 20).

The future of sex tourism lies in robot prostitutes according to Yeoman and Mars (2012), as not only do robots not spread diseases but they also cannot be sold into sex slavery. These are just two of the advantages of robot prostitutes, which are expected to overtake their human competitors in the sex tourism market by the year 2050 (Yeoman *et al.*, 2011).

However, such scholarly contributions have not, thus far, adequately disseminated the rapidly developing discussions around the newest sex robots introduced to the market. In the case of human-robot interaction, the emerging role of sex robots has piqued public interest and sparked discussions around robotic design, societal norms, and the status of human-robot sex vis-a-vis human relationships (Scheutz & Arnold, 2016). On the other hand, this issue is of particular interest to the media and the predictions that have been made about the future of robot sex have stimulated provocative public debates about technology and the changing qualities of human communication and social relationships (Danaher & McArthur, 2017; Horton, 2015; Scheutz & Arnold, 2016). According to futurologist Dr Pearson, not only will technology allow humans to merge with computers, this will also lead to the creation of an entirely new species called '*Homo Optimus*' (Griffiths, 2016). Pearson makes the following predictions about the future of sex (Pearson, 2015: 2):

- By 2030, most people will have some form of virtual sex as casually as they browse pornography today.
- By 2035, the majority of people will own sex toys that interact with virtual reality sex.

- We will start to see some forms of sex robots appearing in households as soon as 2025.
- We will start to see human-robot sex overtaking human-human sex in 2050.
- Leisure spending on sexual technological tools could grow by a factor of five, and the sex market in 20 years could be three times bigger than it is today and seven times bigger by 2050.
- Love and the act of sex will become increasingly separate, and relationships will be about more than just sex via new technological tolls such as virtual and augmented reality.

In a rapidly changing world, many aspects of our lives are being transformed by technology, including how we feel and express our sexuality. Owsianik and Dawson (2016) stated that robotics, virtual reality and extraordinary scientific innovations are expanding and tried to explain how people can experience sexuality through the five senses. They make a prediction of five dimensions about the future of the sex landscape (Figure 8.1).

Remote sex is sex between two or more people who are not in the same place, yet are connected through the internet. People often use

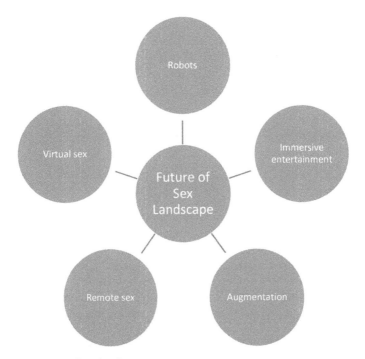

Figure 8.1 Future of sex landscape
Source: Owsianik and Dawson (2016: 2)

electronic sex toys, operated by computers or devices that use data, to boost the experience and share pleasure. They transmit sensations through touch sensors to help long-distance partners arouse each other in real time. **Virtual sex** happens when people connect through communication devices and share sexual content. This includes typed messages as well as video and voice chats both online and over the phone. Three-dimensional worlds developed by computers are an increasingly popular place to have virtual sex by using avatars, which are digital representations of players. **Robots** are machines intended to make human lives better, but some fear they will steal our jobs and our hearts. Human-like robots are called androids, while female robots are gynoids. Advances in robot sex technologies are taking them into the more complex domains of sex, emotions and love. **Immersive entertainment** is technology that blends the physical world with virtual or simulated worlds created by computers. The point is to make users feel they are truly part of the action in a created environment. One form is virtual reality, which is when someone fully enters 3D environments, usually by wearing a headset. **Human augmentation** is using technology to improve what the human body is capable of doing and how it appears. Augmented reality, implants and wearable computers are meant to push biological limits. Each of these aspects has had an impact on the sex tourism industry. Owsianik and Dawson (2016) delve into each of them, revealing how breakthroughs are moving us past the threshold of thinking technology isolates us. From this point of view, the future of sex tourism and the situation of prostitutes can be visualised. It can be suggested that a robotic prostitute will be a solution for existing problems in the sex tourism industry such as human trafficking, child abuse, non-human animal abuse and the degradation of humans. Other technological innovations will also help to minimise the spread of sexual diseases and sexually transmitted infections (Owsianik & Dawson, 2016).

Sex Tourism in Cyberspace

Starrs (1997: 212) stated that 'Cyberspace has a recognizable geography, but it remains an elusive space, rather than a community ... the formation of community requires contact and individual identity merging into shared goals'. In other words, he appears to conclude that cyberspace shares many resemblances with real space, in that it is somehow recognisable. He goes on to equate the geography of cyberspace to a mirror, in that it reflects similar evolutions in real space and abides by the will of its human creators. The term 'cyberspace' is used interchangeably with specific technologies (especially the internet and the World Wide Web) and their effects (Warf, 2001). One of the effects is the transformation of sexuality.

Advances in technology, in all its various forms, frequently has direct and lasting impacts on tourism (Guttentag, 2010). Developments in information and communication technology are increasingly transforming spatial relationships in tourism from the local into the global dimension. The virtual reality (VR) technology developed in this context is an important tool in this transformation. VR is defined as the use of a computer-generated 3D environment – called a 'virtual environment' (VE) – that one can navigate and possibly interact with, resulting in the real-time simulation of one or more of the user's five senses (Guttentag, 2010). A VR experience can be described in terms of its capacity to provide physical immersion, which refers to the extent to which a user is isolated from the real world and experiences within it (Gutiérrez *et al.*, 2008). VR allows for interactions and reactions and can include virtual trips or voyages to fantasy worlds that are inconceivable in reality. In this context, VR programmes may be developed that transport the (cyber) sex tourist to the sights, sounds and sensations of the virtual fantasy world (Kibicho, 2009).

Sex tourism examines the issues that emerge from sex worker-client interactions and from tourists visiting 'sex destinations' (Hall & Ryan, 2005). However, Kohm and Selwood (1998) draw attention to the development of virtual sex tourism, arguing that the internet opens up a whole range of new questions as customers will no longer need to physically travel, but nonetheless may be considered cyberspace tourists, or even cyberspace sex tourists. The virtual/cyber-sex tourist will avoid many of the issues associated with tourism, and sex tourism in particular, such as loss of time, long queues and language problems, as well as the risks of potential violence, accidents and threats by engaging in virtual sex tourism (Kibicho, 2009; Kohm & Selwood, 1998). In addition, Earle and Sharp (2016) emphasise that virtual sex tourism may be a solution to the problem of sexual deviance. This is because virtual environments can be navigated from the anonymity and safety of home and are usually perceived as risk-free (Cheong, 1995). On the other hand, gender exploitation in cyberspace includes gender-humiliating comments, sexual remarks, dirty jokes, insulting erotic or pornographic pictures and the like. These messages can be targeted directly to a particular person or potential receivers generally. Unwanted sexual attention assumes personal communication between a harasser and victim involves sending messages that refer to or ask about a victim's intimate subjects (i.e. sex organs, sex life), or invite them to talk about or engage in sex-related activities (Barak, 2005). In fact, Asquith and Turner (2008) suggest that sexual exploitation encompasses various forms of sexual abuse, including prostitution, child pornography and child marriage, and is used variously to mean any one or all of these.

Much of the literature on the subject of cybersex is inclined towards the debates of its advantages and disadvantages (Ben-Ze'ev, 2004;

Harton & Boedeker, 2005; Ross *et al.*, 2007) Some people consider cybersex in the virtual environment to be a physically safe way for young people, such as teenagers, to experiment with their sexual thoughts and emotions (TanimoonwoFasugba-Idowu & Aishah Hassan, 2013). Moreover, cybersex in the virtual environment is financially less demanding than in real life (Daneback *et al.*, 2005). In addition, people with long-term ailments (including HIV/AIDS) can engage in cybersex as a way to safely achieve sexual gratification without putting their partners at any health risks (TanimoonwoFasugba-Idowu & Aishah Hassan, 2013). These are among some of the perceived advantages of cybersex. On the other hand, the disadvantages of cyber-sexual activity can be divided into three categories, with moral, social, psychologic and religious implications. Cyberspace has created a platform for children to learn sexual information that should be out of their reach until they are adults. Indirect victimisation is a consequence of cyber communication that is sexual in nature that occurs between adults and children. In this context, cybersex is morally unacceptable (Lanning, 2010). Social effects of cybersex not only influence the individuals that engage in it but also their partners and children as well (Goldberg *et al.*, 2008). The children and partners of people that engage in cybersex become socially and psychologically affected to the point that they may need therapy (Goldberg *et al.*, 2008; TanimoonwoFasugba-Idowu & Aishah Hassan, 2013). In addition, the effects of cybersex on a social and moral level make the activity illicit in religious terms because it leads to fornication, adultery, paedophilia and other forms of sexual sin, as defined by various conservative religious rulings (TanimoonwoFasugba-Idowu & Aishah Hassan, 2013).

There is uncertainty as to the real impact of virtual sex in cyberspace on sex tourism. It may be argued that virtual reality sex tourism will not entirely replace the real sex tourism experience. For instance, the manager of a brothel in Las Vegas said, *'People are going to visit the top sex tourism city so that they can masturbate alone in a room? VR sex is a gimmick! We need human touch!'* (Bowles, 2016). However, the combination of the real and the virtual may lead to increasing diversity and complexity, adding to the richness of tourist destinations in terms of their tourist products and available alternatives (Kibicho, 2009). Žižek (1996) asked, *'Will virtual sex or virtual sex tourism be the ultimate freedom or the ultimate form of oppression? Only time will tell'*.

Conclusion and Discussion

Sex tourism is one of the most emotive and sensational issues in tourism. Cohen (1988), in his groundbreaking study, was the first to raise questions about who was exploiting whom in his analysis of love letters sent by Europeans to their 'Thai girlfriends'. Since then, several scholars have studied various aspects of sex tourism (Bandyopadhyay, 2013; Sanders-McDonagh, 2017). However, transformations in sex tourism in parallel with technological developments differentiate the aspects of sex tourism. In other words, now the sex tourism industry goes beyond being a traditional industry, where human or non-human animals are commodified as sex workers, with the use of different technologies such as virtual and augmented reality sex tools and robots. In other words, the sex tourism industry has diversified beyond the traditional conceptualisations that label it as a predominantly patriarchal form of exploitation and leisure (Garrick, 2008). In this chapter, it is recognised that not only human and non-human animals are a part of sex tourism, but also technological tools and cyberspace have become a tool of sex tourism. The transformations created by these tools have been discussed in the chapter. Because technologies are becoming an increasingly integral part of the human condition the traditional view of sex tourism needs revision (Yeoman & Mars, 2012). As part of the above discussions, there is much talk of sex with robots in the future (Pearson, 2017). Sex robots are gaining a significant amount of attention in current discussions about technology and the future of human relationships (Scheutz & Arnold, 2016). Human trafficking, sexually transmitted infections/diseases, beauty and physical perfection, the pleasure gained from sex toys, emotional connections with robots and the importance of sex are all driving forces behind this increase in the use of sex robots (Yeoman & Mars, 2012). When sex tourism goes beyond humankind, it may become like a '*sexual Disneyisation*', with sex tourists desiring opportunities for sexual contact and sexual experiences that go beyond the realm of their everyday lives (Ryan, 2000; Yates, 2016). While companies like True Companion and MacMil Cybernetics have attempted to create robotic sex partners (Roxxxy/Rocky and Susie Software/Harry Harddrive, respectively), a look at the accomplishments of the larger robotics industry shows great progress in creating human-like robots. As a result of these developments, the sex tourism industry will be able to go beyond the human-human or human-animal relationship and be transformed into an industry where human-robot relationships become more prominent in the future. In fact, Levy (2007: 151) stated, in his book *Love + Sex with Robots*, that 'Humans will fall in love with robots, humans will marry robots, and humans will have sex with robots, all as (what will be regarded as) "normal" extensions of our feelings of love and sexual desire for other humans'. Aligning with this view, Owsianik and Dawson (2016) have claimed that one in 10 young adults will have had sex with a humanoid robot by 2045.

Apart from sex robots, other important points that can shape the future of sex tourism are virtual reality (VR) and augmented reality (AR) technologies. However, virtual and augmented reality do not replace direct social and cultural experience, memorable interaction with the physical environment, or real sex tourism experiences. Yet the debate surrounding the real impact of VR and AR on sex tourism continues. For example, Kibicho (2009) stated that VR technology may depress demand for real sex tourism. This argument is based on the fact that VR is increasingly rendering homes and even offices as secure bases for sexual and other leisure activities. Online virtual worlds like *Second Life* and *Red Light Center* attract millions of users searching for virtual sex partners (Pearce *et al.*, 2015). While *Red Light Center* was created specifically for sex, the more mainstream *Second Life* allows players to purchase external add-ons like genitals and sex acts for an X-rated experience. In addition, with certain 3D sex games supporting virtual reality headsets and interactive sex toys, realism intensifies. In this regard, it may be said that sex tourism will be able to change and facilitate people having sex with whoever they want, at any time or place they want, and at any age they want in the virtual environment. Owsianik and Dawson (2016) predict that people will regularly pair virtual reality and haptic sex toys to fully immersive themselves in adult entertainment by 2020. This prediction is not completely realistic for now, however, it is likely to be realised in the coming years. In other words, virtual sex vacations might be in the offing, with cybersex tourists able to avoid loss of time, potential violence, risks of accidents, language problems, the threat of diseases and other cumulative expenses associated with sex tourism in the *real* world. All in all, there is no doubt that the robots, VR/AR technologies and the internet have created a paradigm shift across the sex tourism industry, with a range of impacts on the way the industry is organised and operated, and on how sex tourists behave (Kibicho, 2009). Tourism research on the diffusion of robotics and artificial intelligence is rather limited and mainly conceptual/experimental at this stage (e.g. Diallo *et al.*, 2015; Navarro *et al.*, 2015; Yeoman & Mars, 2012). Nevertheless, tourism practices are rapidly evolving in this direction, creating a gap in relevant research that will need to be explored in the coming years (Alexis, 2017).

In addition to focusing on technology about sex tourism, people exhibit a wide spectrum of sexual attractions, and for some, this attraction extends to non-human animals. Given the capacity of the internet to connect people with shared interests and proliferation of pornographic sites, some of which include animal-human sex, it is not impossible that such tourism could continue to grow, if at very low levels (Markwell, 2015). A whole sub-culture of people is engaging in sexual activity with non-human animals (they call themselves 'zoos'); there are internet forums dedicated to sharing stories and exchanging advice; there are organised bestiality events and animal sex farms where, like a whore house, a group of animals is available for the taking (Pierce, 2015). While the majority would find this form of tourism activity abhorrent, tourism scholars should not shy away from examining it as another form of animal-human interaction, looking beyond bestiality/zoophilia. This includes the presentation of sex between animals in the zoo environment; a place that is associated with the sterilisation of animal behaviour for the public gaze, ensuring that the consumption of food by carnivores takes place backstage, just as does sex (Carr, 2016).

References

Aggrawal, A. (2009) References to the paraphilias and sexual crimes in the Bible. *Journal of Forensic and Legal Medicine* 16 (3), 109–114.

Aggrawal, A. (2011) A new classification of zoophilia. *Journal of Forensic and Legal Medicine* 18 (2), 73–78.

Alexis, P. (2017) R-Tourism: Introducing the potential impact of robotics and service automation in tourism. *Ovidius University Annals, Series Economic Sciences* 17 (1), 211–216.

Alvarez, W.A. and Freinhar, J.P. (1991) A prevalence study of bestiality (zoophilia) in psychiatric in-patients, medical in-patients, and psychiatric staff. *International Journal of Psychosomatics* 38 (1–4), 45–47.

Asquith, S. and Turner, E. (2008) *Recovery and Reintegration of Children from the Effects of Sexual Exploitation and Related Trafficking*. Geneva: The Oak Foundation Child Abuse Programme.

Bailey, J.M., Vasey, L., Diamond, L.M., Breedlove, S.M., Vilain, E. and Epprecht, M. (2016) Sexual orientation, controversy, and science. *Psychological Science in the Public Interest* 17 (2), 45–101.

Bandyopadhyay, R. (2013) A paradigm shift in sex tourism research. *Tourism Management Perspectives* 6, 1–2.

Barak, A. (2005) Sexual harassment on the Internet. *Social Science Computer Review* 23 (1), 77–92.

Bender, K. and Furman, R. (2004) The implications of sex tourism on mens' social, psychological, and physical health. *The Qualitative Report* 9 (2), 176–191.

Ben-Ze'ev, A. (2004) *Love Online: Emotions on the Internet*. Cambridge: Cambridge University Press.

Blake, M. (2013) Bestiality brothels are 'spreading through Germany' warns campaigner as abusers turn to sex with animals as 'lifestyle choice'. *Daily Mail*. See http://www.dailymail.co.uk/news/article-2352779/Bestiality-brothels-spreading-Germany-campaigner-claims-abusers-sex-animals-lifestyle-choice.html (accessed June 2018).

Bone, K. and Bone, J. (2015) The same dart trick: The exploitation of animals and women in Thailand tourism. In K. Markwell (ed.) *Animals and Tourism: Understanding Diverse Relationships* (pp. 60–74). Bristol: Channel View Publications.

Bowles, N. (2016) Las Vegas brothel: Virtual reality porn is a gimmick, we need human touch. *The Guardian*. See https://www.theguardian.com/technology/2016/apr/20/las-vegas-brothels-virtual-reality-porn (accessed June 2018).

Brennan, D. (2004) *What s Love Got to Do With It?: Transnational Desires and Sex Tourism in the Dominican Republic*. Durham and London: Duke University Press.

Brooks, A. and Heaslip, V. (2019) Sex trafficking and sex tourism in a globalised world. *Tourism Review* 74 (5), 1104–1115.

Campbell, S., Perkins, A. and Mohammed, P. (1999) Come to Jamaica and feel all right: Tourism and the sex trade. In K. Kempadoo (ed.) *Sun, Sex, and Gold: Tourism and Sex Work in the Caribbean* (pp. 125–156). Lanham, MD: Rowman and Littlefield Publishers.

Carolin, L., Lindsay, A. and Victor, W. (2015) Sex trafficking in the tourism industry. *Journal of Tourism and Hospitality* 4 (4), 166–172.

Carr, N. (2014) *Dogs in the Leisure Experience*. Wallingford: CABI.

Carr, N. (2016) Sex in tourism: Reflections and potential future research directions. *Tourism Recreation Research* 41 (2), 188–198.

Carr, N. and Broom, D. (2018) *Tourism and Animal Welfare*. Wallingford: CABI.

Casson, L. (1994) *Travel in the Ancient World*. Baltimore: The John Hopkins University Press.

Cheok, A.D. and Levy, D. (eds) (2018) *The Proceedings International Conference on Love and Sex with Robots, LSR 2017*. London, UK.

Cheong, R. (1995) The virtual threat to travel and tourism. *Tourism Management* 16 (6), 417–422.

Choorichom, J. (2011) Factors influencing the selection of Hotels/Resorts in LantaYai Island, Krabi, Thailand by international travelers. *International Humanities, Social Sciences and Arts* 4 (2), 125–148.

Cohen, E. (1988) Tourism and AIDS in Thailand. *Annals of Tourism Research* 15 (9), 467–486.

Danaher, J. and McArthur, N. (eds) (2017) *Robot Sex: Social and Ethical Implications*. London: MIT Press.

Daneback, K., Cooper, A. and Mansson, S.A. (2005) An Internet study of cybersex participants. *Archives of Sexual Behavior* 34 (3), 321–328.

Davidson, J.O.C. (2001) The sex tourist, the expatriate, his ex-wife and her 'Other': The politics of loss, difference and desire. *Sexualities* 4 (1), 5–24.

Davidson, O.J. and Taylor, J.S. (2005) Travel and taboo: Heterosexual sex tourism to the Caribbean. In E. Bernstein and L. Schaffner (eds) *Regulating Sex: The Politics of Intimacy and Identity* (pp. 83–99). New York, NY: Routledge.

Diallo, A.D., Gobee, S. and Durairajah, V. (2015) Autonomous tour guide robot using embedded system control. *Procedia Computer Science* 76, 126–133.

Diken, B. and Laustsen, C.B. (2004) Sea, sun, sex and the discontents of pleasure. *Tourist Studies* 4 (2), 99–114.

Earle, S. and Sharp, K. (2016) *Sex in Cyberspace: Men who Pay for Sex*. London and New York: Routledge.

ECPAT (End Child Prostitution, Child Pornography and the Trafficking of Children) (2016) *Global Study on Sexual Exploitation of Children in Travel and Tourism*. See http://www.globalstudysectt.org/wp-content/uploads/2016/05/Global-Report-Offenders-on-the-Move-Final.pdf (accessed June 2018).

Equality Now (2009) United States: Sex tourism; Big Apple oriental tours acquitted of state criminal charges: federal action needed to prosecute G. F Tours and other US based sex tour operators. See www.equalitynow.org/action-alerts/sex-tourism-big-apple-oriental-tours-acquitted-statecriminal-charges-federal-action (accessed June 2019).

Feldstein, S. (2010) Outlaw sex with animals in the Sunshine State. *Change.org*. See https://www.change.org/p/outlaw-bestiality-in-the-sunshine-state/u/62315 (accessed August 2020).

Fennell, D.A. (2012) *Tourism and Animal Ethics*. London: Routledge.

Fennell, D.A. (2014) Exploring the boundaries of a new moral order for tourism's global code of ethics: An opinion piece on the position of animals in the tourism industry. *Journal of Sustainable Tourism* 22 (7), 983–996.

Fridman, M. (2015) Pony's new life, *Borneo Orangutan Survival Foundation Article*. See http://orangutan.or.id/ponys-new-life-2/ (accessed July 2018).

Garrick, D. (2008) Excuses, excuses: Rationalisations of Western sex tourist in Thailand. *Current Issue in Tourism* 8 (6), 497–509.

Ghorbani, A., Ghorbani, A. and Sharifi, S. (2014) Investigation of legal and cultural dimensions of sex tourism. *Singaporean Journal of Business, Economics and Management Studies* 51 (1448), 1–4.

Goldberg, P.D., Peterson, B.D., Rosen, K.H. and Sara, M.L. (2008) Cybersex: The impact of a contemporary problem on the practices of marriage and family therapists. *Journal of Marital and Family Therapy* 34 (4), 469–480.

Griffiths, S. (2016) Is technology causing us to 'evolve' into a new SPECIES? Expert believes super humans called homo optimus will talk to machines and be 'digitally immortal' by 2050. *Daily Mail*. See http://www.dailymail.co.uk/sciencetech/article-3423063/Is-technology-causing-evolve-new-SPECIES-Expert-believes-super-humans-called-Homo-optimus-talk-machines-digitally-immortal-2050.html (accessed July 2018).

Gutierrez, M., Vexo, F. and Thalmann, D. (2008) *Stepping into Virtual Reality*. London: Springer Science & Business Media.

Guttentag, D.A. (2010) Virtual reality: Applications and implications for tourism. *Tourism Management* 31 (5), 637–651.

Hall, C.M. (1998) The legal and political dimensions of sex tourism: The case of Australia's child sex tourism legislation. In M. Oppermann (ed.) *Sex Tourism and Prostitution: Aspects of Leisure, Recreation, and Work* (pp. 87–96). New York, NY: Cognizant Communication Corporation.

Hall, C.M. and Ryan, C. (2005) *Sex Tourism: Marginal People and Liminalities*. London and New York: Routledge.

Harton, H.C. and Boedeker, E.C., Jr. (2005) On the Many Advantages of Cybersex. [Review of the book *Love Online: Emotions on the Internet*. A. Ben-Ze'ev]. *PsycCRITIQUES* 50(4).

Horton, H. (2015) By 2050, human-on-robot sex will be more common than human-on-human sex, says report. *The Telegraph*. See http://www.telegraph.co.uk/technology/news/11898241/By-2050-human-on-robot-sex-will-be-more-common-than-human-on-human-sexsays-report.html (accessed July 2018).

ILO (International Labour Office) (2012) *ILO Global Estimate of Forced Labour: Results and Methodology*. See http://www.ilo.org/wcmsp5/groups/public/---ed_norm/---declaration/documents/publication/wcms_182004.pdf (accessed June 2018).

ILO (International Labour Office) (2014) *Profits and Poverty: The Economics of Forced Labour*. See http://www.unodc.org/documents/data-and-analysis/glotip/2016_Global_Report_on_Trafficking_in_Persons.pdf (accessed June 2018).

Jory, B., Fleming, W. and Burton, D. (2002) Characteristics of juvenile offenders admitting to sexual activity with nonhuman animals. *Society & Animals* 10 (1), 31–45.

Kibicho, W. (2009) *Sex Tourism in Africa: Kenya's Booming Industry*. Farnham: Ashgate.

Kohm, S. and Selwood, J. (1998) The virtual tourist and sex in cyberspace. In M. Oppermann (ed.) *Sex Tourism and Prostitution: Aspects of Leisure, Recreation and Work* (pp. 123–131). New York, NY: Cognizant Communication Corporation.

Krippendorf, J. (1987) *The Holiday Makers: Understanding the Impact of Leisure and Travel*. London: Heinemann.

Lanning, K.V. (2010) *Child Molesters: A Behavioral Analysis for Professionals Investigating the Sexual Exploitation of Children*. Washington, DC: National Center for Missing & Exploited Children with Office of Juvenile Justice and Delinquency Prevention.

Lee, J. (2017) *Sex Robots: The Future of Desire*. Cham, Switzerland: Springer.

Leheny, D. (1995) A political economy of Asian sex tourism. *Annals of Tourism Research* 22 (2), 367–384.

Leong Chong, K. (2014) The impact of sex tourism on Hotel Selection. *International Journal of Tourism Sciences* 14 (3), 106–115.

Levy, D. (2007) *Love + Sex with Robots: The Evolution of Human-Robot Relationships*. New York, NY: Harper.

Littlewood, I. (2002) *Sultry Climates: Travel and Sex*. Cambridge: Da capo Press.

Lockett, J. (2017) World's first brothel staffed entirely by robot sex workers now looking for investors to go global. *The Sun*. See https://www.thesun.co.uk/news/4131258/worlds-first-brothel-staffed-entirely-by-robot-sex-workers-now-looking-for-investors-to-go-global/ (accessed July 2018).

Loebner, H. (1998) Being a John. In J. Elias, V. Bullough, V. Elias and G. Brewer (eds) *Prostitution: On Whores, Hustlers, and Johns* (pp. 221–226). Amherst, NY: Prometheus Books.

London, L.S. and Caprio, F.S. (1950) *Sexual Deviations*. Washington: Linacre Press.

Love Travel Life (2012) The World's Top Sex Shows (part 2/2): Tijuana's Donkey Shows. *The alternative lifestyle blog for travellers.* See http://www.lovetravellife.com/the-worlds-top-sex-shows-part-23-tijuanas-donkey-shows/ (accessed July 2018).

MacCannell, D. (1973) Staged authenticity: Arrangements of social space in tourist settings. *American Journal of Sociology* 79 (3), 589–603.

Markwell, K. (2015) Birds, beasts and tourists: Human-animal relationships in tourism. In K. Markwell (ed.) *Animals and Tourism: Understanding Diverse Relationships* (pp. 1–23). Bristol: Channel View Publications.

Martin, D. (2017) Sick Brits 'travelling to Serbia for sex with dogs at animal brothels for as little as £60'. *Mirror.* See https://www.mirror.co.uk/news/world-news/sick-brits-travelling-serbia-sex-11360625 (accessed June 2018).

McKercher, B. and Bauer, T.G. (2003) Conceptual framework of the nexus between tourism, romance, and sex. In T.G. Bauer and B. McKercher (eds) *Sex and Tourism: Journeys of Romance, Love, and Lust* (pp. 3–17). New York: The Haworth Hospitality press.

McNally, R.J. and Lukach, B.M. (1991) Behavioral treatment of zoophilic exhibitionism. *Journal of Behavior Therapy and Experimental Psychiatry* 22 (4), 281–284.

Miletski, H. (2005) A history of bestiality. In A.M. Beetz and A.L. Podbersek (eds) *Bestiality and Zoophilia: Sexual Relations with Animals* (pp. 1–22). Oxford: Purdue University Press.

Mishra, R. (2015) Meet Pony – An orangutan who was forced to be a sex slave! *India.* See http://www.india.com/whatever/meet-pony-an-orangutan-who-was-forced-to-be-a-sex-slave-human-cruelty-touched-a-new-low-with-animal-prostitution-406822/ (accessed July 2018).

Naff, C.F. (2017) The future of sex. *The Humanist* 77 (4), 12–19.

Navarro, A.S.P.H., Monteiro, C.M.F. and Cardeira, C.B. (2015) A mobile robot vending machine for beaches based on consumers' preferences and multivariate methods. *Procedia – Social and Behavioral Sciences* 175, 122–129.

Navarro, J.C. and Tewksbury, R. (2015) Bestiality: An overview and analytic discussion. *Sociology Compass* 9 (10), 864–875.

Newsroom, T. (2017) These countries are into sex with animals. *Themanews.* See http://en.protothema.gr/these-countries-are-into-sex-with-animals-photos/ (accessed June 2018).

Oppermann, M. (1999) Sex tourism. *Annals of Tourism Research* 26 (2), 251–266.

Owsianik, J. and Dawson, R. (2016) Future of sex report. See https://futureofsex.net/Future_of_Sex_Report.pdf (accessed June 2019).

Panko, T.R. and George, B.P. (2018) Animal sexual abuse and the darkness of touristic immorality. In M. Korstanje and B. George (eds) *Virtual Traumascapes and Exploring the Roots of Dark Tourism* (pp. 175–189). Hershey, PA: IGI Global.

Pearce, C., Blackburn, B.R. and Symborski, C. (2015) *Virtual Words Survey Report: A Trans-World Study of Non-Game Virtual Worlds – Demographics, Attitudes, and Preferences.* See http://cpandfriends.com/wpcontent/uploads/2015/03/vwsurveyreport_final_publicationedition1.pdf (accessed October 2019).

Pearson, I. (2015) The Future of Sex Report: The Rise of Robosexuals. *Futurizon, in partnership with Bondara.* See http://graphics.bondara.com/Future_sex_report.pdf (accessed July 2018).

Pearson, I. (2017) The Future of Valentine's Day: A Futurizon Report for Sparkling Strawberry. *Futurizon.* See https://pressat.co.uk/media/uploads/2cc8a55e5d1ec44fc6b94d9f4138d8d8.pdf (accessed July 2020).

Peretti, O. and Rowan, M. (1983) Zoophilia: Factors related to its sustained practice. *Panminerva Medica* 25 (2), 127–131.

Pettman, J.J. (1997) Body politics: International sex tourism. *Third World Quarterly* 18 (1), 93–108.

Pierce, J. (2015) Sex with animals. *Psychology Today.* See https://www.psychologytoday.com/us/blog/all-dogs-go-heaven/201504/sex-animals (accessed June 2019).

Piscitelli, A. (2007) Shifting boundaries: Sex and money in the north-east of Brazil. *Sexualities* 10 (4), 489–500.

Richards, T.N. and Reid, J.A. (2016) Gender stereotyping and sex trafficking: Comporative review of research on male and female sex tourism. In J.A. Reid (ed.) *Human Trafficking: Context and Connections to Conventional Crime* (pp. 124–144). New York, NY: Routledge.

Rodriguez, C. (2017) Sex-Dolls brothel opens in Spain and many predict sex-robots tourism soon to follow. *Forbes*. See https://www.forbes.com/sites/ceciliarodriguez/2017/02/28/sex-dolls-brothel-opens-in-spain-and-many-predict-sex-robots-tourism-soon-to-follow/#32f879874ece (accessed July 2018).

Ross, M.W., Rosser, B.S., McCurdy, S. and Feldman, J. (2007) The advantages and limitations of seeking sex online: A comparison of reasons given for online and offline sexual liaisons by men who have sex with men. *Journal of Sex Research* 44 (1), 59–71.

Ryan, C. (2000) Sex tourism: Paradigms of confusion. In S. Clift and S. Carter (eds) *Tourism and Sex: Culture, Commerce and Coercion* (pp. 23–40). London and New York: Pinter.

Ryan, C. and Hall, C.M. (2001) *Sex Tourism: Marginal People and Liminalities*. London: Routledge.

Sanders-McDonagh, E. (2017) *Women and Sex Tourism Landscapes*. New York, NY: Routledge.

Scheutz, M. and Arnold, T. (2016) Are we ready for sex robots? In *The 11th ACM/IEEE International Conference on Human Robot Interaction* (pp. 351–358).

Staples, D. (2015) Animal-sex tourism crackdown: Denmark bans bestiality. *RT News* See http://rt.com/news/252065-denmark-bans-animal-sex/ (accessed July 2018).

Starrs, F. (1997) The sacred, the regional, and the digital. *Geographical Review* 87 (2), 193–218.

Steiner, C.J. and Reisinger, Y. (2006) Understanding existential authenticity. *Annals of Tourism Research* 33 (2), 299–318.

Tange, A. (2015) Denmark bans bestiality in move against animal sex tourism. *Reuters*. See http://uk.reuters.com/article/2015/04/21/uk-denmark-bestiality-idUKKBN0NC1Z620150421 (accessed July 2018).

TanimoonwoFasugba-Idowu, G. and Aishah Hassan, S. (2013) Cybersex: Advantages and disadvantages. *Journal of Humanities and Social Science* 14 (3), 60–65.

Taylor, J.S. (2001) Dollars are a girl's best friend? Female tourists' sexual behaviour in the Caribbean. *Sociology* 35 (3), 749–764.

Taylor, J.S. (2010) Sex tourism and inequalities. In S. Cole and N. Morgan (eds) *Tourism and Inequality: Problems and Prospects* (pp. 49–66). Wallingford: CABI.

Thomas, M. (2005) What happens in Tenerife stays in Tenerife': Understanding women's sexual behaviour on holiday? *Culture, Health and Sexuality* 7 (6), 571–584.

U.S. Department of State (2015) Trafficking in Person Report. See https://www.state.gov/documents/organization/245365.pdf (accessed June 2018).

UCSB (2018) *Sex Tourism*. UCSB Department of Sociology. See http://www.soc.ucsb.edu/sexinfo/article/sex-tourism (accessed July 2018).

UNICEF (2005) Children out of Sight, out of Mind, out of Reach. See https://www.unicef.org/media/media_30453.html (accessed June 2018).

UNODC (United Nations Office on Drugs and Crime) (2016) Global Trafficking in Persons Report. See http://www.unodc.org/documents/data-and- analysis/glotip/2016_Global_Report_on_Trafficking_in_Persons.pdf (accessed June 2018).

Uriely, N. (2005) The tourist experience: Conceptual developments. *Annals of Tourism Research* 32 (1), 199–216.

Urry, J. (1990) The 'consumption' of tourism. *Sociology* 24 (1), 23–35.

Wang, N. (1999) Rethinking authenticity in tourism experience. *Annals of Tourism Research* 26 (2), 349–370.

Warf, B. (2001) Segueways into cyberspace: Multiple geographies of the digital divide. *Environment and Planning B: Planning and Design* 28 (1), 3–19.

Yates, A. (2016) An introduction to the world of sex tourism. *Health & Disease.* See https://kinseyconfidential.org/sex-tourism-sex-tourists/ (accessed July 2018).

Yeoman, I. and Mars, M. (2012) Robots, men and sex tourism. *Futures* 44 (4), 365–371.

Yeoman, I., Robertson, M. and Smith, K. (2011) A Futurist View on the Future of Events. See www.tomorrowstourist.com/pdf/thefuturistviewonthefutureofevents.pdf (accessed May 2019).

Žižek, S. (1996) Sex in the age of virtual reality. *Science as Culture* 5 (4), 506–525.

9 Sex Tourism in the Caribbean: A Case Study of Negril Beach Boys

Amanda Jenkins, Roya Rahimi and Peter Robinson

Introduction

Although 'female sex tourism' is now a phenomenon and is gaining more attention in academic research, the topic remains largely taboo. The current chapter is based on observation and discourse analysis between the relationships of unaccompanied female tourists to Negril, Jamaica, and the sexual behaviour and attitudes of the 'Beach Boys' in the destination.

The main objectives of this chapter are to:

- Analyse lived experiences of female sex tourists to Jamaica through observation and discourse.
- Synthesise the impact of female sex tourism on the destination.
- Identify inter-relationships between the female sex tourism industry and the economic development of Jamaica as a tourism destination.

Although Jamaica is primarily promoted as a beach destination, some tourists do have sexual relationships with locals at destinations. Urry (2002) argued travels involving sex have always interconnected. Western women who become romantically involved with Caribbean men during their vacation are now a valid topic of discussion (Weichselbaumer, 2012). Especially as the practice usually takes place in 'post-colonial' countries, the hypothesis challenges past and current theories about women who travel for sex, investigating and considering traditional and contemporary discourse on the role of power and neo-colonialism. While there is a high degree of justification on discourses regarding this underground tourism sector, they tend to highlight a destination's colonial past and the power relationships that exist. It is against this background that the current chapter critically evaluates the impact of female sex tourism on the Island of Jamaica and its effect on the country's development.

Jamaica's population is estimated to be over 2.6 million (Jamaica Tourist Board [JTB], 2017). In 2015, the overall tourism sector contributed JMD481.6 billion to the country's Gross Domestic Product (GDP) (World Travel and Tourism Council [WTTC], 2016). Notwithstanding, in the first six months of 2016 the destination received 2.8 million international visitors (Jackson, 2016). Sugar, bananas and bauxite, which were the primary export commodities, have been replaced by tourism (Beckford, 2002) as the primary contributor to Jamaica's GDP (the Food and Agriculture Organization (FAO), 2019). Statistics show that, in 2015, 89% of arrivals visited Jamaica for leisure, spending approximately US$2.4 billion in the key resort areas of Montego Bay, Ocho Rios and Negril (JTB, 2016). However, Jamaica continues to combat serious social issues such as, high levels of crime and high unemployment (Johnson, 2019). Additionally, several external shocks, including the global financial crisis in 2008, further weakened Jamaica's economy (Kouame & Reyes, 2010), making the destination one of the slowest growing developing countries in the world. Although economic growth rates have increased significantly, they are still too low to eradicate poverty (World Bank, 2016).

Sex Tourism in Negril

The representation of sex and sexualities are central to modern-day tourism (Ryan & Hall, 2001), as many tourists appreciate a destination's sensual and sexual appeal (Spiteri, 2014). Additionally, to attract more visitors, many countries specifically target tourists wanting to escape reality (Spiteri, 2014). According to Spiteri (2014), sex is expressively used as much as Sun, Sand and Sea in destination marketing campaigns. While representation says a great deal about the images, topographies and realities of the sector, Ryan and Hall (2001) concurred that the popular representation of mass tourism contains a fourth 'S' which signifies sex. Within this context, the behaviour of tourists is strongly connected to, and contingent upon, the marketing activities of destination marketing organisations (DMOs) (Pearce, 2005). However, Bandyopadhyay and Nascimento (2010) argued that the image of Jamaica as a sex tourist destination is not a direct outcome of tourism representations alone. Rather, it is intricately linked to political, historical and cultural practices.

Traditionally, when spoken about, sex tourism has normally been situated in a negative framework that focuses on the exploitative and neo-colonialist nature of it (Glover, 2006; Herold et al., 2001; Taylor, 2006). The term usually invokes images of older men, in less than perfect shape, who travel to developing countries such as Thailand for soliciting sex (Bloor et al., 2000; O'Connell Davidson, 1996), and 'other' alternative morally dubious experiences (Rao, 2003; Truong, 1990).

Figure 9.1 Billboard when arriving into Negril

However, the term 'romance tourism' is often used to refer to 'female sex tourism' (Klein, 2015); women who travel to have sex with local men. Its popularity is argued to be facilitated by the appeal of exotic holiday settings for some women. Sex tourism is a key characteristic of Negril's tourism industry (Rhiney, 2012). Urry (2002) argued the tourist gaze produces an anticipation of impending pleasures. Furthermore, pleasures considered taboo back in the visitor's home country are indulged in when they are on holiday (Aston, 2008). A welcome to Westmoreland billboard (see Figure 9.1) stands erect upon entering Negril, with the words 'LIVE FOR NOW' written below. According to Kinnaird and Hall (1994) the production of language is representative of the destination. Female visitors can have a choice of local men anywhere along Negril's Seven Mile Beach and its vicinity.

The topic of 'sex tourism' has become increasingly accepted by politicians and tourism academics (Ryan & Hall, 2001; Taylor, 2001). Female behaviour is now, at times, incorporated into male dominated patterns (Pritchard & Morgan, 2000), although less attention has traditionally been paid to female sex tourism (Oppermann, 1998; Ryan, 2000). While the number of women travelling for sex is relatively small in comparison to men who travel for sex (Sanchez-Taylor, 2000), some women do travel for sex in almost the same way as men do (Bauer, 2014; Jeffreys, 2003). However, the phenomenon remains quite under-researched in comparison to men (Spiteri, 2014). Sex tourism in the Caribbean is unlike that in Thailand. For example, in the Caribbean, female sex tourists are reputedly more prominent than their male counterparts (Meisch, 1995; Pruitt & LaFont, 1995). Each year, an estimated 600,000 women travel from 'developed' countries to engage in sex tourism (Bindel, 2006).

Thousands of women, mostly from North America and Europe, travel to Jamaica each year, in search of young Jamaican boyfriends (Martin, 2006). A survey of 240 female tourists in Negril and the Dominican Republic revealed almost one third had sexual relationships with local males during their holiday (O'Connell Davidson & Sanchez Taylor, 1999). Additionally, a great number of female tourists admitted to the exchange of money or material goods for sex. Based on personal observation in Negril and other anecdotal evidence, women who were on vacation with their partner were also having sex with local men.

Negril was created especially as a place for hosts to sell and visitors to consume. It is now a key tourist destination where mostly white, wealthy female tourists visit for the sole purpose of having sex with young black men (Bindel, 2006). While enacting novelised and embellished models of extensive power relations (Taylor, 2006), Sanchez-Taylor (2000) argued that 'female sex tourists' to Negril are able to contravene sexual, racialised and age boundaries without the reprisals they would encounter in their home country. The local men who engage in sex tourism are often referred to as 'Beach Boys', 'Rent a Rasta', 'Rent a Dread', 'Gigolo' and 'Rent a Lion', among other terms (Ajagunna, 2006; de Albuquerque, 1998; Herold *et al.*, 2001; Ryan & Hall, 2001). The various appellations for 'Beach Boys' are used interchangeably throughout the chapter. Echtner and Ritchie (1993) asserted that the 'Beach Boys' are a part of the destination image. For the local men who engage in female sex tourism, the sector is a means to generate income or other commodities (Rhiney, 2012).

'Beach Boys' in these tourist destinations are mainly concerned with making money and usually target women past the ages of 40 or those who are younger and overweight (Herold *et al.*, 2001). These women are perceived to have had fewer sexual partners (Ryan, 2000) because men in 'First World' countries prefer slender, younger women. It must be noted that some female sex tourists do fall in love with the 'Beach Boys' and continue to provide economic benefits long after their departure (Herold *et al.*, 2001). Many women return regularly, bringing money and gifts (Herold *et al.*, 2001). In addition, some 'Beach Boys' are provided with the opportunity to travel overseas and visit several countries (Bauer, 2014; Herold *et al.*, 2001).

Neo-colonialism and Power Relations

Sex tourism is not new to the Caribbean but is a product of slavery. Since the 16th century, prostitution in the Caribbean has been intricately tied to European colonisers (Mullings, 1999) who exerted much power over those colonised (Boehmer, 2005). They controlled not only the wealth and political positions but also the rights to rape women and men whom they considered 'inferior' (Mullings, 1999; Sanchez-Taylor, 2000; Spencer & Bean, 2016). The post-colonial understandings of exploitation are not entirely untouched by a touristic predisposition as they are shaped by the romanticised travel tales of a colonial era (Strain, 2003). Power relationships that take place in less developed countries are intricate in nature (Taylor, 2001) and are based on unequal and mobile relations (Foucault, 1990).

Historically, colonisers were considered supreme over 'other races' and sexual relationships between white women and black men were forbidden (Meszaros & Bazzaroni, 2014). The preconceived fantasies about the excessive sexual appetites and prowess of black men were feared (Hall, 1997). Mercer (1994: 185) argued 'the primal fantasy of the big, black penis projects the fear of a threat not only to white womanhood, but to civilisation itself, as the anxiety of miscegenation, eugenic pollution and racial degeneration is acted out through white male rituals of racial aggression'. In contrast, black women were labelled as 'exotic' and sexual fantasies linked to them were legitimised by the colonisers (Wonders & Michalowski, 2001). Today, stronger relationships exist between first world tourists and members of the host population in less developed countries. Notwithstanding, these relationships are construed to be still colonial and imperialistic (Cheong & Miller, 2000).

The concept of core-periphery relationships is used within dependency theory as it highlights unequal and often exploitive relationships (Mowforth & Munt, 1998), especially in neo-colonial developing countries dependent on tourism (Smith *et al.*, 2010). Sanchez-Taylor (2000) argued that western women who practise sex tourism use their economic advantage and racialised identity to exert power and control over local men. The main reasons identified by 'Beach Boys' for becoming involved in sex tourism include unemployment, family problems, pleasure, adventure, money, and perceived reputation (Oriade, 2012). However, female tourists and the 'Beach Boys' of Jamaica often see their relationship as being more about romance than sex (Pruitt & LaFont, 1995; Spencer & Bean, 2016). In particular, the 'Beach Boys' typically consider themselves romantic companions rather than just sex partners (Spencer & Bean, 2016).

Female sex tourists perceive Caribbean men to be closer to nature and more emotional than white men (Taylor, 2006). Many female sex tourists have brief sexual encounters after a night out at a reggae bar. This may encompass temporary accommodation arrangements that include the Jamaican man staying at a hotel for a few days or weeks (Babb, 2014). The 'Beach Boys' frequently see themselves as simply giving the tourist 'a hand' to show them a 'good time' (de Albuquerque, 1998). The spaces of anonymity and sexual freedom offered by tourism are among the main places where tourists and locals form intimate relationships (Berdychevsky *et al.*, 2013; Cabezas, 2006). It is within this context that the service experience sometimes offers an intimacy that can lead to sexual intimacy (Andrews *et al.*, 2007). The tourism sector is composed of various independent, inter-related service providers, which includes informal sex workers (Leiper, 1990). Even those employed formally in various tourism sectors, at times, supplement their small wages by having intimate relationships with guests (O'Connell Davidson & Sanchez-Taylor, 2005). Jamaican activist Ellis (2007) contended that for the 'Beach Boys' of Negril, white female sex tourists represent hope, aspiration, and an achievement.

Methodology

Micro-ethnography is an established method that employs an ethnographic approach over a shorter duration (Creswell, 2007) than traditional ethnography. Additionally, the method focuses on one location or a single social situation to explain a phenomenon (Spradley & Baker, 1980). With micro-ethnography, the researcher must locate what is being studied in the context of the wider society or focus on studying what people do (Hammersley, 2006). Fieldwork, according to Preissle and Grant (2008), is the study of something in its natural environment and potentially one of the oldest forms of human inquiry. Furthermore, it produces information from natural, real time occurrences and provides real time explanatory insights (Arnould & Wallendorf, 1994). Amaratunga *et al.* (2002) suggested where research concerns human meanings and the interactions of 'female sex tourists' with local 'Beach Boys' observation is unsurpassed from an insider's perspective.

Additionally, familiarity with a tourism site helps in the design of a good research project, and the interpretation of the data (Bowen, 2002). Given Jenkins' Jamaican heritage and excellent rapport with the locals, it did not prove difficult finding local participants who were willing to discuss the sensitive topic of female sex tourism. Approximately ten participants, mostly natives of Negril, contributed to the discussions on the topic. In addition, observation was conducted over two consecutive weeks along Negril's Seven Mile Beach in 2017. Veal (2006) argued that the phenomenon of female sex tourism observed as it unfolds in its natural setting is not by any means obtrusive as the researcher is not involved with those being observed. Rather, they 'simply seeks to describe the phenomenon of interest and develop explanations and understandings in the process' (Veal, 2006: 193).

Ethnography is 'an impressionistic, reflexive method, which is flexible in techniques and approach rather than a set of specific procedures' (O'Gorman *et al.*, 2014: 51), that allows the researcher to enter the field and observe human interactions (Preissle & Grant, 2008). Therefore, it facilitated observation of the phenomenon of female sex tourism as it unfolded in its natural setting. Notwithstanding that tourism research can require statistics to get insights into aspects such as migration trends, Phillimore and Goodson (2004) argued that understandings of the scope of tourism and its social and cultural implications need to be interpreted based on the meanings people bring to them. Micro-ethnography allowed for the observation of the 'Beach Boys' and female tourists interactions. Additionally, the researchers' cultural heritage helped to analyse and describe Jamaican beliefs, practices and experiences.

The primary data include notes from observation and recorded conversations with approximately 10 locals in Negril, over the duration of two weeks. All participants were told of the nature of the study and of their right to withdraw at any time. Conversations were recorded using a mobile phone and by note taking. Secondary data consists of books, academic journals, newspaper articles, movies and YouTube videos. Fielding *et al.* (2008) suggest YouTube videos to be an essential research tool, as they are a passive means to collect data that provide an easy and convenient way to observe behaviour. While the sample sizes used in qualitative research are said to be small and do not, consequently, provide any statistical grounds for direction (Punch, 2006), the direct experience and exploration within an actual social or cultural setting (Atkinson *et al.*, 2001) is paramount for social research (Holloway *et al.*, 2010).

According to Mulhall (2003), ethnographers each have their own strategy of how they record data from observations. However, Kawulich (2005) argued field notes should be the primary way of capturing data from participant observations. As such, notes were jotted down to remember key events and dialogue then written up in detail privately. The following field notes' structure, which was used in this study, was adapted from Mulhall (2003):

- Description of buildings and surroundings.
- Description of people and how they acted and dressed.
- Description of daily process of activities.
- Description of beach parties and special events.
- Conversations between participants.
- Reflective diary on the researcher's thoughts.

Taking notes, thinking, learning and gaining trust, allowed for subjective knowledge to be replicated (Atkinson *et al.*, 2001), for richer data analysis. Data obtained from observations are usually more accurate than other data because the observer can see what participants may not (Sapsford & Jupp, 2006). Notetaking of the social and cultural framework allowed for examination of participants actions. The conversations which ensued pertaining to the topic of female sex tourism were with residents of Negril which included a masseuse, watercraft operators, men involved in sex tourism, a couple of hotel proprietors, hotel employees and local business owners. Jordan and Gibson (2004: 225) argued that 'allowing people to tell their own stories generates data that are rich with description, and the real value of qualitative data lies in this richness'. Despite the methods employed, it was still impossible to record everything that happened.

Although the British Psychological Society (BPS) advises researchers to obtain the consent of participants whenever possible (BPS, 2014) due to the stigma associated with, and sensitive nature ascribed to female sex tourism, participants were observed unbeknownst to them. For the purpose this paper, pseudonyms are used for locals who took part in the conversations.

Various forms of discourse analysis are used by tourism researchers to critically investigate tourist's motivations, experiences and practices. Discourse analysis can include textual data, interview transcripts, and photographs to assess how different groups of people understand their world (Hannam, 2002). Jørgensen and Phillips (2002) argued reality cannot be understood outside of discourse as the discourse becomes the object of analysis. In agreement with Sapsford and Jupp (2006), primary data gathered through less-structured observation produced detailed findings on behaviour as part of an all-round description. The main objective of the data analysis is to work with what has been said, or written, and to identify dissimilar discursive illustrations of reality (Jørgensen & Phillips, 2002). Hannam and Knox (2005) suggested the organisation of data facilitates the observation of certain relationships or themes. Consequently, in this study, following a discourse analysis, the data were compared and analysed for emerging trends.

Description of the Research Setting

Negril, where the study was based, was a remote fishing village until the late 1960s, whose primary visitors were hippies from North America. Traditionally, it was customary for tourists to stay with locals or on the beach in tents. Since then, Negril has grown to become one of Jamaica's largest and most rapidly expanding tourist resort towns (Rhiney, 2012). A beach cottage was rented by the first author adjacent to the beach. By morning the advertised picturesque 'tropical paradise' revealed it was not only inclusive of sun, sand and sea but a myriad of sex, drugs and reggae.

The fishermen of Negril still come in with their catch of the day (as they did 30 years ago). However, their brightly painted little wooden boats are now more numerous and no longer rowed by fishermen using their hand carved wooden oars. Instead, they are powered by high performance outboard marine engines (Figure 9.2). Historically, both sides of Negril's main strip consisted of only a few small wooden houses. Today, the same strip is lined with small rental cottages in between major brand hotels (Figure 9.3).

In the early 1900s, Negril was a remote, sparsely inhabited coastal village (Larsen, 2008). The tourism industry played an insignificant role

Figure 9.2 Fishing village in Negril

Figure 9.3 Negril's seven mile beach

in the region's economy (Rhiney, 2012). However, by the 1970s Negril's economy diverted away from fishing and agriculture and towards tourism. This saw the construction of several small and medium sized hotels, guest houses and resort cottages to meet tourist demand (Pariser, 1996). Rhiney (2012) argued that because of tourisms' rapid and unplanned development in Negril, several social and economic problems have emerged, including sex tourism.

Findings

Jenkins met Troy, who is a security guard contracted to various hotels around Negril. It was along Negril's Seven Mile Beach while seeking shelter from the scorching afternoon sun, Jenkins rested on the grounds of a picturesque beachfront villa along the strip. A conversation ensued initially about the villas rates and availability. However, the conversation with Troy progressed to white women who travel to Negril for sex as, like sand on the beach, they were everywhere. Troy was told of the study, and he agreed to share views on the topic although under the condition of complete anonymity. With no other people in proximity, the atmosphere was extremely relaxed and our conversation ensued. Following, is an excerpt of Troy's view about female sex tourists in Jamaica:

> A lot of them are here for Jamaican guys, you know, they are here, some of them here to have fun, some are here because then, for different stuff you know. Mostly, some of them mostly here for fun you know, mostly here for fun. They say they know that Jamaicans have the long bamboo [chuckles], the long bamboo. But most people are not going to talk you know, some are afraid to approach, some will come to you straight. They maybe start a conversation first you know, to see if you are that person who is more open, you know. They go around, and you know, they put it to you, to see if you are that fun person, if you have that side to you, you know. And if they say hey, I am here for that, I am here to have fun you know. And, I will be working, I am working in a hotel and, I have a woman approach me you know, I even have men approach me and say they will pay me to do that to their wife, seriously. Seriously, it happens you know, it happens.

> Sometimes it is risky because you know, our job you know, if you get caught, we lose our job in an instant you know. Yes, yes, our employer, you know our employer, they tell us hey, if you do that you will get into trouble you know. So maybe some of the guys who are riskier, they don't care about losing their work, they will go ahead and do it you know. But the smarter ones will say, hey we can link up later. We can pay for a room at a different cheap place local, you know, and we can go ahead and, you know. They will pay. They will pay the guys you know. But I never go that far before [chuckles], I never go that far before. I am worrying about my job, it's really hard to get a job here. And when I get it, I just want to hold onto it until something better comes, some better opportunities. (Troy)

Natty B is a popular Rastafarian musician and owner of a small, thatched seafood restaurant and juice bar along Negril's Seven Miles Beach. He was reluctant to have our conversation recorded but agreed to me taking handwritten notes. On his view of female sex tourists to Negril Natty B stated, 'the average age of female sex tourists to Negril are between the ages of 50 years to 70 years who come to Negril come looking for "fun" arrive in the country at 3pm and by 6pm they are having sex with someone they met on the beach'. The majority of Beach Boys see female tourists as a means to travel overseas as well as to provide material needs (Brewis, 2007).

Observation and general conversations highlighted that some female sex tourists' relationships end in marriage. Some local males may then migrate to the visitor's home country or the female visitor may take up residence in Jamaica. A conversation with a hotel employee revealed a recent wedding between an obese white female tourist and a 'Beach Boy'. The groom's lack of affection towards the bride during the ceremony was obvious and at the end of the ceremony the bride could be seen crying while discarding her wedding dress in the ocean. She wept with the realisation that her dream was nothing but a fallacy. Even marriages constructed in paradise may not last a lifetime, but it is interesting to ask how many do, and why? Natty B spoke of a female sex tourist and a 'Beach Boy' who, 'are still together after thirteen years of marriage and the relationship is still going strong, yeah man, yeah man [smiles]'.

Jamaican men are said to have incredible negotiation skills (the gift of the gab) and are therefore able to convince female sex tourists they are truly in love (Natty B). 'Flattery is just one of the main seduction strategies used' by 'Beach Boys' (Herold *et al.*, 2001: 986). Consequently, rather than just having a little 'fun', as some women set out to do, many become emotionally involved. Some women end up leaving their husbands and disconnecting from family members. Furthermore, 'it is not uncommon for female sex tourists to be in Jamaica with a 'Rent a Dread' while having their husbands send money via Western Union' (Natty B). On a micro level, 'female sex tourists provide much economic benefits to the "Beach Boys" of Negril and the community. In addition, many "Beach Boys" are given the opportunity to travel overseas. Often times an airplane ticket is considered as the least of generosities' (Natty B). Natty B adds that he himself has travelled to various countries. 'Many Beach Boys are provided with properties, cars and set up in a business of their choice and many female sex tourists continue to send money once they are back in their country' (Natty B).

'Natty B's' overwhelming concern was, however, the many female sex tourists who are abused, both mentally and physically, by some of the 'Beach Boys'. 'When the men are no longer interested in a relationship, they become physically abusive' (Natty B) and this generates a negative image for the non-violent 'Rent a Dreads' on the beach. He feared that if the abuse of visitors continued the violence could result in less female sex tourists coming to Negril. 'Some of the men, just use the women then beat them up badly when they don't need them anymore' (Natty B). 'Some of these Rasta's will beat the f**k out of them sometimes, 99% of the time, man they f**k them up, yeah man they get their money and they f**k them up. They beat them, they don't like them again, and they just go onto the next one' (Tony, local proprietor). Research by Taylor (2001) revealed that several American and European women who returned to Jamaica to live or get married to a 'Beach Boy' they met whilst on holiday ended up in exceedingly abusive relationships.

In contrast, only a handful of such relationships have a fairytale ending as the 'Beach Boys' of Negril are usually in it for the financial security it can afford them. When a tourist dates a guy on the street the relationship is complicated. The guy is a part of the visitors' holiday package and the visitor is a part of the 'Beach Boy's' earnings (Ellis, 2007).

Negril's unique selling point

Much research is needed to better understand the challenges associated with female sex tourism (Johnson, 2016), especially in post-colonial destinations where the practice continues to grow. Bindel (2006) argued that the practice is not without victims because, at the very least, there is abuse of racial and economic power as wealthy, western, white women continue to flock to Negril for sun and some adult fun. Jamaican masculinities appear to be social constructions related to the ways in which slavery, colonialism, and now globalisation have produced identity enactments (Hall, 1997). 'Women basically come to Negril looking for "fun"' (Natty B). However, Bindel (2006) argued that 'young men having to perform like studs for a plate of rice and peas is exploitation, not fun'. However, the relationships that exist between female sex tourists and Negril 'Beach Boys' appear to be constructed through a dialogue of romance (Pruitt & Lafont, 1995), including long-term relationships.

Donald is a watersports operator and tour guide who has worked on the beach for many years. He also identified the majority of female sex tourists to Negril to be aged 50 and upwards, with it not being unusual to see females in their seventies romantically involved with local males. The 'majority of females almost never ask the age of the partner until after they become sexually involved' (Donald). Most of the female sex tourists were observed to be significantly older than their local partner.

The majority of female sex tourists are aware that the 'Beach Boys' have multiple partners. 'The women who come to Negril, come to party and have "fun", besides they say Jamaican men give better loving' (Donald). Within this context, female sex tourists complain that their spouses are not as affectionate as their Jamaican counterparts. The locals suggested that this was because the cold weather affects their spouse's sexual performance. 'Jamaican men have greater stamina which allows the women dem to cum nuff' [have multiple orgasms] (Local C). In comparison, all the local men with whom conversations were held believed the reason behind Jamaica's popularity as a female sex tourist destination to be the destinations' warm tropical climate, the size of Jamaicans penises and their prolonged erection. Findings further revealed that female sex tourists that go to Negril are attracted to men of a lower socioeconomic standing. In relation to this, many natives were heard questioning the women's choice of men.

The findings suggest that the primary attraction of Negril is the 'offerings' of 'Beach Boys' 'supposedly' endowed with extra-large penises. Additionally, the study identified Negril as a choice destination for wealthy, black and white women looking to have sex. A local hotel proprietor stated, 'Negril is the Disney World for adults'. Just as Disneyland is for the rich, the development of tourist-related prostitution is facilitated by the introduction of wealthy tourists to poor local communities. Female sex tourists describe these destinations as 'sexual paradise' or 'Fantasy Island'; the place where sexual dreams come true (O'Connell Davidson & Sanchez Taylor, 2005). According to Tepanon (2006), female sex tourists' travel includes an escape from a mundane environment to gain personal and/or psychological rewards. Most women who travel to Negril look for a holiday experience with black men who flatter and seduce them (Klein, 2015). By using both the concepts of 'Rude Boy'[1] and 'Rasta' enactments[2] of masculinity, Negril 'Beach Boys' capitalise on their desirability to female tourists, while at the same time conforming to tourists' preconceived expectations of the destination (Spiteri, 2014).

Known to tourists and locals alike as Dr Love, he was approximately 55 years old, tall, slim, with a muscular body and hair worn in dreadlocks. To gain further publicity about his services, he requested his alias name of Dr Love be used in the research findings. Dr Love considered himself a sex doctor and documented his other profession as a marketing representative, promoting his services at local hotel establishments. He is nestled in between major hotel chains along Negril's Seven Beach, and has resided and worked at the same spot for two decades. Figures 9.4 and 9.5 show a few of Dr Love's extensive wood carvings of the male anatomy, which he has for sale. He identified the one in the top right of Figure 9.5 as an identical replica of his love

Figure 9.4 Woodcarving replica of 'Dr Love's' penis

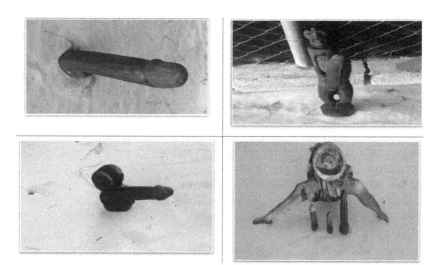

Figure 9.5 Dr Love's woodcarvings

muscle. de Albuquerque (1998), and many people living in Jamaica, agree that western women are sexually attracted to Jamaican men because of the racial stereotype regarding penis size.

Although Dr Love was overly persistent about providing a free viewing of his actual penis the offer was politely declined. Dr Love stated, his 'surgery' (where he also lives), is 'a place where women in need of healing from all over the world come to. The doctor makes them feel better [chuckle], I just take them right back there to my office [pointing to a shack not far from the exhibited carvings]'. When questioned about remuneration for his services rendered to the female sex tourists, Dr Love replied, 'they pay me as to how good I make them feel [chuckle]'. As a means of encouraging female sex tourists to fall in love with them, 'Beach Boys' try and provide a pleasurable sexual experience (Herold *et al.*, 2001).

According to Dr Love, most of his 'patients' are by referral from previous clients and he usually services around 10 'patients' a day. The original wooden shack he once operated out of was recently destroyed by law enforcement when a tourist failed to return home. The tourist's family filed a missing person's report and when the police went searching for the missing woman she was found living with Dr Love. Although the original shack no longer exists, Dr Love remains at the same spot, 'operating' now out of a makeshift tent made with coconut leaves. He also spoke of several trips taken overseas, with all expenses paid for courtesy of female sex tourists who had visited Negril. As part of his notoriety, he proudly displays to passersby an article, which includes a photo of himself, that featured in Jamaica's official Tourist Board magazine. 'They just love the medicine the doctor gives them and because I give to them good love, they show their appreciation [chuckle] for me making them feel better' (Dr Love). Research findings highlighted that many 'Beach Boys' from Negril who immigrated overseas returned to Jamaica to pick up where they left off on the beach. Due to limitations of the study, research was not carried out to identify the reasons for them returning. Furthermore, there is a dearth of published academic research to explain this phenomenon from the 'Beach Boys' perspective. Alongside the returning 'Beach Boys', it is clear that many female sex tourists return to Jamaica, some as often as every four months.

Conclusion

Observation of the locals observing the guests and the guests observing the hosts revealed the relationships between female sex tourists and the 'Beach Boys' of Negril are constructed through a dialogue of romance and long-term relationships (Pruitt & Lafont, 1995). However, Hall (1997) argued that Jamaican masculinities are social constructions related to the ways in which slavery, colonialism, and now globalisation have produced identity enactments. While most days consisted of doing observation, reflection was central to the study. Maslow, in his Hierarchy of Needs, highlights the first step to self-actualisation as meeting one's biological and physiological needs, which includes sex (Maslow & Lewis, 1987). Although the Hierarchy of Needs relates to the workplace, the chapter demonstrates that the same philosophy applies to the 'Beach Boys' of Negril because, they are at work, fulfilling certain basic needs.

To conclude, it is suggested that female sex tourism in Jamaica helps to facilitate the self-actualisation of the 'Beach Boys' in contrast to the lesser self-actualisation of female sex tourists. de Albuquerque (1998) contended that most female tourists to Jamaica want casual sex rather than romance and only a small number fall in love with a 'Beach Boy', although some tourists and 'Beach Boys' do define their relationship as one of romance. It is the 'Beach Boys' who decide which women to establish a relationship with by making the first approach.

The observation of the 'Beach Boys' in Negril highlighted that female tourists to the destination were viewed as a potential source of revenue. Therefore, each of these women was subjected to continuous sexual advances by men who appeared to be anywhere between their early twenties and mid-sixties. Although, research by Herold et al. (2001) indicated there were few 'Beach Boys' older than 25, several older local males were observed frolicking with female tourists on numerous occasions. Herold et al. (2001) have argued that because female sex tourists have more wealth than the 'Beach Boys' they are manipulated by the latter for financial gain. However, it is apparent that at least some of the relationships between female sex tourists and the local men were romantic in nature. Furthermore, the female sex tourists observed showed overt ownership of their Jamaican 'Beach Boy' and the men seemed subservient. 'At a psychological level, Third World countries are forced into the "female" role of servitude of being "penetrated" for money, often against their will; whereas the outgoing, pleasure seeking, "penetrating" tourists of powerful nations are cast in the "male" role' (Graburn, 1983: 441). Even when natives enter into sexual relationships with whites as equal partners, the relationships are still considered to have been established based on economic and racialised inequalities (Archer-Straw, 2000).

Notwithstanding, female sex tourism has had a positive effect on Jamaica's economic development, particularly in terms of foreign exchange (Richards, 2013). However, the sector is not without victims because, at the very least, there is abuse of racial and economic power involved in the relationships (Bindel, 2006). The 'Beach Boys' hustling on the beach in Negril are constructed gendered identities with an emphasis on sexual prowess, animalism, and natural instincts (Phillips, 2008). This commodification of differences has made it possible for sex tourists to construct and consume 'others' (Clift & Carter, 2000).

Notes

(1) 'Rude Boy' – Jamaican gangster boys who are considered 'rude' because of their attitudes.
(2) Rasta – men who wear dreadlocks and practice Rastafarianism.

References

Ajagunna, I. (2006) Crime and harassment in Jamaica: Consequences for sustainability of the tourism industry. *International Journal of Contemporary Hospitality Management* 18 (3), 253–259.

Amaratunga, D., Baldry, D., Sarshar, M. and Newton, R. (2002) Quantitative and qualitative research in the built environment: Application of 'mixed' research approach. *Work Study* 51 (1), 17–31.

Andrews, H., Roberts, L. and Selwyn, T. (2007) Hospitality and eroticism. *International Journal of Culture, Tourism and Hospitality Research* 1 (3), 247–262.

Archer-Straw, P. (2000) *Negrophilia: Avant-Garde Paris and Black Culture in the 1920s.* London: Thames and Hudson.

Arnould, E.J. and Wallendorf, M. (1994) Market-orientated ethnography: Interpretation building and marketing strategy formation. *Journal of Marketing Research* 31 (4), 484–504.

Aston, E. (2008) A fair trade? Staging female sex tourism in sugar mummies and trade. *Contemporary Theatre Review* 18 (2), 180–192.

Atkinson, P., Coffey, A., Delamont, S., Lofland, J. and Lofland, L.H. (2001) Editorial introduction. In P. Atkinson, A. Coffey, S. Delamont, J. Lofland and L.H. Lofland (eds) *Handbook of Ethnography* (pp. 1–7). London: Sage.

Babb, F.E. (2014) Review of 'Sexuality, women, and tourism: Cross-border desires through contemporary travel'. *Anthropological Quarterly* 87 (2), 579–582.

Bandyopadhyay, R. and Nascimento, K. (2010) 'Where fantasy becomes reality': How tourism forces made Brazil a sexual playground. *Journal of Sustainable Tourism* 18 (8), 933−49.

Bauer, I. (2014) Romance tourism or female sex tourism? *Travel Medicine and Infectious Disease* 12 (1), 20−28.

Beckford, C.L. (2002) Decision−making and innovation among small–scale yam farmers in central Jamaica: A dynamic, pragmatic and adaptive process. *The Geographical Journal* 168 (3), 248−259.

Berdychevsky, L., Poria, Y. and Uriely, N. (2013) Hospitality accommodations and women's consensual sex. *International Journal of Hospitality Management* 34, 169−171.

Bindel, J. (2006) This is not romance *The Guardian*. See www.theguardian.com/commentisfree/2006/aug/09/comment.gender (accessed February 2017).

Bloor, M., Thomas, D., Abeni, C., Goujon, D., Hausser, M., Hubert, D., Kleiber, D. and Nieto, J. (2000) Sexual risk behavior in a sample of 5676 young, unaccompanied travelers. In S. Clift and S. Carter (eds) *Tourism and Sex: Culture, Commerce and Coercion* (pp.157–167). New York: Pinter.

Boehmer, E. (2005) *Colonial and Postcolonial Literature: Migrant Metaphors*. Oxford: Oxford University Press.

Bowen, D. (2002) Research through participant observation in tourism: A creative solution to the measurement of consumer satisfaction/dissatisfaction (CS/D) among tourists. *Journal of Travel Research* 41 (1), 4−14.

Brewis, V. (2007) In T. Fishleigh (ed.) *Rent a Dread,* LINK International Productions. See https://www.youtube.com/watch?v=KtU3m2M1Ivs (accessed February 2017).

British Psychological Society (BPS) (2014) *Code of Human Research Ethics*. British Psychological Society.

Cabezas, A. (2006) The eroticization of labor in Cuba's all-inclusive resorts: Performing race, class and gender in the new tourist economy. *Social Identities* 12 (5), 507–521.

Cheong, S. and Miller, M. (2000) Power and tourism: A Foucauldian observation. *Annals of Tourism Research* 27 (2), 371−390.

Clift, S. and Carter, S. (2000) Tourism, international travel and sex: Themes and research. In S. Clift and S. Carter (eds) *Tourism and Sex Culture, Commerce and Coercion* (pp. 1−19). London: Pinter.

Creswell, J.W. (2007) *Qualitative Inquiry and Research Design: Choosing among Five Approaches* (2nd edn). Thousand Oaks, CA: Sage.

de Albuquerque, K. (1998) Sex, beach boys, and female tourists in the Caribbean. *Sexuality and Culture* 2, 87–111.

Echtner, C.M. and Ritchie, J.B. (1993) The measurement of destination image: An empirical assessment. *Journal of Travel Research* 31 (4), 3−13.

Ellis, B. (2007) in, Fishleigh, T. *Rent a Dread,* LINK International Productions. See https://www.youtube.com/watch?v=KtU3m2M1Ivs (accessed February 2017).

Fielding, N., Lee, L.M., and Blank, G. (2008) *The SAGE Handbook of Online Research Methods*. Thousand Oaks, CA: Sage Publications Ltd. See https://www.dawsonera.com/readonline/9781446206607 (accessed February 2017).

Food and Agriculture Organization (FAO) (2019) *FAO in Jamaica, Bahamas and Belize* [online]. See http://www.fao.org/jamaica-bahamas-and-belize/fao-in-jamaica-bahamas-and-belize/jamaica-at-a-glance/en/ (accessed October 2019).

Foucault, M. (1990) *The History of Sexuality: An Introduction*. New York: Vintage.

Glover, K. (2006) Human trafficking and the sex tourism industry. *Crime and Justice International* 22 (92), 4.

Graburn, N. (1983) Tourism and prostitution. *Annals of Tourism Research* 10, 437–442.

Hall, S. (1997) The spectacle of the 'Other'. In S. Hall (ed.) *Representation: Cultural Representations and Signifying Practices* (pp. 223−290). London: Sage.

Hammersley, M. (2006) Ethnography: Problems and prospects. *Ethnography and Education* 1 (1), 3−14.

Hannam, K. (2002) Coping with archival and textual data. In P. Shurmer-Smith (ed.) *Doing Cultural Geography* (pp. 189–197). London: Sage.

Hannam, K. and Knox, D. (2005) Discourse analysis in tourism research a critical perspective. *Tourism Recreation Research* 30 (2), 23–30.

Herold, E., Garcia, R. and DeMoya, T. (2001) Female tourists and beach boys: Romance or Sex Tourism? *Annals of Tourism Research* 28 (4), 978–997.

Holloway, I., Brown, L. and Shipway, R. (2010) Meaning not measurement: Using ethnography to bring a deeper understanding to the participant experience of festivals and events. *International Journal of Event and Festival Management* 1 (1), 74–85.

Jackson, S. (2016) Jamaica Visitor Arrivals Hit Record at Half Year. *Jamaica Gleaner*. See http://jamaica-gleaner.com/article/business/20160907/jamaica-visitor-arrivals-hit-record-half-year (accessed February 2017).

Jamaica Tourist Board (JTB) (2016) *Annual Travel Statistics 2016*. See http://www.jtbonline.org/wp-content/uploads/Annual-Travel-Statistics-2016.pdf (accessed June 2017).

Jamaica Tourist Board (JTB) (2017) *Tourism Information Publishing Site (TIPS)*. See http://www.jtbonline.org/?s=jamaica+population (accessed February 2017).

Jeffreys, S. (2003) Sex tourism: Do women do it too? *Leisure Studies* 22 (3), 223–238.

Johnson, L.C. (2016) 'Men at risk': Sex work, tourism, and STI/HIV risk in Jamaica. *Culture, Health & Sexuality* 18 (9), 1025–1038.

Johnson, H. (2019) Between fame and infamy: The dialectical tension in Jamaica's nation brand. In H. Johnson and K. Gentles-Peart (eds) *Brand Jamaica: Reimagining a National Image and Identity* (pp. 1–30). LINCOLN: University of Nebraska Press.

Jordan, F. and Gibson, H. (2004) Let your data do the talking: Researching the solo travel experiences of British and American woman. In L. Goodson and J. Phillimore (eds) *Qualitative Research in Tourism: Ontologies, Epistemologies and Methodologies* (pp. 215–235). London: Routledge.

Jørgensen, M. and Phillips, L. (2002) *Discourse Analysis as Theory and Method*. London: Sage.

Kawulich, B. (2005) Participant observation as a data collection method. *Qualitative Social Research* 6 (2), 1–28.

Kinnaird, V. and Hall, D. (eds) (1994) *Tourism: A Gender Analysis*. Chichester: Wiley.

Klein, H. (2015) Female sex tourism in the Caribbean–A 'fair trade' or a new kind of colonial exploitation? – Tanika Gupta's sugar mummies and Debbie Tucker green's trade. *Gender Studies* 14 (1), 154–170.

Kouame, A. and Reyes, M.I. (2010) The Caribbean region beyond the 2008-09 Global financial crisis. *Conference on Economic Growth, Development and Macroeconomic Policy*. Seehttps://www.imf.org/external/np/seminars/eng/2010/carib/pdf/kourey.pdf (accessed October 2019).

Larsen, S.C. (2008) Negril in the News: Content analysis of a contested paradise. *Caribbean Geography* 15 (1), 35–58.

Leiper, N. (1990) The business of tourism and the partial industrialisation of tourism systems: a management perspective. *Tourism System: An Interdisciplinary Perspective*. Palmerston North: Massey University.

Martin, L. (2006) Focus: Sex, sand and sugar mummies in a Caribbean beach fantasy: A controversial new Royal Court play will explore sex tourism in Jamaica, where lonely women flock for flings with young black men. But what's the truth about these real-life Shirley Valentines? *The Observer*. See https://search-proquest-com.ezproxy.wlv.ac.uk/docview/250390098?pq-origsite=summon (accessed June 2018).

Maslow, A. and Lewis, K.J. (1987) Maslow's hierarchy of needs. *Salenger Incorporated* 14, 987.

Meisch, L.A. (1995) Gringas and otavalenos: Changing tourist relations. *Annals of Tourism Research* 22, 441–462.

Mercer, K. (1994) *Welcome to the Jungle*. London: Routledge.

Meszaros, J. and Bazzaroni, C. (2014) From taboo to tourist industry: The construction of interracial intimacies between Black men and White women in colonial and contemporary times. *Sociology Compass* 8 (11), 1256–1268.

Mowforth, M. and Munt, I. (1998) *Tourism and Sustainability: New Tourism in the Third World*. London: Routledge.

Mulhall, A. (2003) In the field: Notes on observation in qualitative research. *Journal of Advanced Nursing* 41, 306–313.

Mullings, B. (1999) Globalization, tourism, and the international sex trade. In K. Kempadoo (ed.) *Sun, Sex, and Gold: Tourism and Sex Work in the Caribbean* (pp. 55–80). Lanham: Rowman and Littlefield.

O'Connell Davidson, J. (1996) Sex tourism in Cuba. *Race and Class* 38 (1), 39–48.

O'Connell Davidson, J. and Sanchez Taylor, J. (1999) Fantasy Islands: Exploring the demand for sex tourism. In K. Kempadoo (ed.) *Sun, Sex and Gold: Tourism and Sex Work in the Caribbean* (pp. 37–54). Lanham: Rowman and Littlefield.

O'Connell Davidson, J. and Sanchez Taylor, J. (2005) Travel and taboo: Heterosexual sex tourism to the Caribbean. In L. Schaffner and E. Bernstein (eds) *Regulating Sex: The Politics of Intimacy and Identity* (pp. 83–99). London: Routledge.

O'Gorman, K., MacLaren, A. and Bryce, D. (2014) A call for renewal in tourism ethnographic research: The researcher as both the subject and object of knowledge. *Current Issues in Tourism* 17 (1), 46–59.

Oppermann, M. (1998) *Sex Tourism and Prostitution*. New York: Cognizant Communication Corp.

Oriade, A. (2012) Sex tourism. In P. Robinson (ed.) *Tourism: The Key Concepts* (pp. 185–187). London: Routledge.

Pariser, H. (1996) *Jamaica: A Visitor's Guide* (3rd edn). Edison: Hunter Publishing.

Pearce, P. (2005) *Tourist Behavior: Themes and Conceptual Schemes*. Clevedon: Channel View Publications.

Phillimore, J. and Goodson, L. (2004) Progess in qualitative research in tourism: Epistimology, ontology and methodology. In L. Goodson and J. Phillimore (eds) *Qualitative Research in Tourism: Ontologies, Epistemologies and Methodologies* (pp. 3–29). London: Routledge.

Preissle, J. and Grant, L. (2008) Fieldwork traditions: Ethnography and participant observation. In K. deMarrais and S.D. Lapan (eds) *Foundations for Research: Methods of Inquiry in Education and the Social Sciences* (pp. 161–180). London: Lawrence Erlbaum Associates.

Phillips, J. (2008) Female sex tourism in Barbados: A postcolonial perspective. *Brown Journal of World Affairs* 15 (2), 201–211.

Pritchard, A. and Morgan, N.J. (2000) Privileging the male gaze: Gendered tourism landscapes. *Annals of Tourism Research* 27 (4), 884–905.

Pruitt, D. and LaFont, S. (1995) For love and money: Romance tourism in Jamaica. *Annals of Tourism Research* 22 (2), 422–440.

Punch, K.F. (2006) *Developing Effective Research Proposals* (2nd edn). London: Sage.

Rao, N. (2003) The dark side of tourism and sexuality: Trafficking of Nepali girls for Indian brothels. In T.G. Bauer and B. McKercher (eds) *Sex and Tourism: Journeys of Romance, Love, and Lust* (pp. 155–166). New York: The Haworth Hospitality.

Rhiney, K.C. (2012) The Negril tourism industry: Growth, challenges and prospects. *Caribbean Journal of Earth Science* 43, 25–34.

Richards, G. (2013) Creativity and tourism in the city. *Current Issues in Tourism* 17 (2), 119–144.

Ryan, C. (2000) Sex tourism: Paradigms of confusion? In S. Clift and S. Carter (eds) *Tourism and Sex: Culture, Commerce and Coercion* (pp. 23–40). London: Pinter.

Ryan, C. and Hall, C.M. (2001) *Sex Tourism: Marginal People and Liminalities*. London: Routledge.

Sanchez-Taylor, J. (2000) Tourism and 'embodied' commodities: Sex tourism in the Caribbean. In S. Clift and S. Carter (eds) *Tourism and Sex: Culture, Commerce and Coercion* (pp. 41–53). London: Pinter.

Sapsford, R. and Jupp, V. (2006) *Data Collection and Analysis* (2nd edn). London: Sage.

Smith, M., MacLeod, N. and Robertson, M.H. (2010) *Key Concepts in Tourist Studies*. Los Angeles: Sage.

Spencer, A. and Bean, D. (2016) Female sex tourism in Jamaica: An assessment of perceptions. *Journal of Destination Marketing & Management* 6 (1), 13−21.

Spiteri, S. (2014) Female Sex Tourism in Jamaica: An Arena for Adaptation and Recreation for Marginalized Men. Doctoral dissertation. McMaster University.

Spradley, J. and Baker, K. (1980) *Participant Observation*. Vol. 195. New York, NY: Holt, Rinehart and Winston.

Strain, E. (2003) *Public Places, Private Journeys: Ethnography, Entertainment and the Tourist Gaze*. New Jersey: Rutgers.

Taylor, J.S. (2001) Dollars are a girl's best friend? Female tourists' sexual behaviour in the Caribbean. *Sociology* 35 (3), 749−764.

Taylor, J. (2006) Female sex tourism: A contradiction in terms? *Feminist Review* 83 (1), 42−59.

Tepanon, Y. (2006) Exploring the Minds of Sex Tourists: The Psychological Motivation of Liminal People. Doctoral dissertation. Virginia Polytechnic Institute and State University.

Truong, T. (1990) *Sex, Money and Morality: Prostitution and Tourism in Southeast Asia*. London: Zed Books.

Urry, J. (2002) *The Tourist Gaze* (2nd edn). London: Sage.

Veal, A. (2006) *Research Methods for Leisure and Tourism: A Practical Guide* (3rd edn). Essex: Pearson Education Limited.

Weichselbaumer, D. (2012) Sex, romance and the carnivalesque between female tourists and Caribbean men. *Tourism Management* 33 (5), 1220−1229.

Wonders, N. and Michalowski, R. (2001) Bodies, borders, and sex tourism in a globalized world: A tale of two cities: Amsterdam and Havana. *Social Problems* 48 (4), 545−571.

World Bank (2016) *Jamaica*. See http://www.worldbank.org/en/country/jamaica (accessed February 2017).

World Travel and Tourism Council (WTTC) (2016) *Travel and Tourism Economic Impact 2016: Jamaica* See http://www.wttc.org/-/media/files/reports/economic-impact-research/countries-2016/jamaica2016.pdf (accessed February 2017).

10 Sex Tourism and Girls' Education: Reflective Voices of 'Girls' in Mtwapa, Kenya

George Ariya and Ruth Nyamasyo

Introduction

Since the World Conference for Education for All in 1990, developing countries have committed to expanding and ensuring access to quality basic education (Uwezo, 2015). However, millions of girls in Sub-Saharan Africa, including Kenya, do not have access to schools despite concerted efforts to push the cause forward (World Bank, 2018). Previous research indicates that customs, poverty, violence and fear are some of the reasons why girls stay out of school (UNESCO, 2012). When many parents cannot afford school fees for all the household children, it is often the case that girls are denied education in preference to boys (Grown *et al.*, 2005). As a result, just over two thirds of girls complete their primary education and 4 in 10 complete lower secondary school in Sub-Saharan Africa (World Bank, 2018). Girls who drop out of school early are likely to marry early, have children early or tend to seek precarious jobs for their survival. They also lack socio-emotional skills that a functional education system ought to provide. Could it be then that sex tourism acts as an alternative source of survival and easily accessible employment opportunity for girls? In a country like Kenya, where formal employment for youths has become elusive even to university graduates, could sex tourism be an alternative source of employment? This chapter attempts to raise reflective voices of young girls participating in sex tourism in Mtwapa in the coastal region of Kenya in relationship to their childhood education.

The relationship between sex tourism and the education of girls cannot be underestimated. While education is regarded as a determinant for economic development that can address socioeconomic and political inequalities (Galor & Moav, 2004; Manyasa, 2015; Wodon *et al.*, 2018), sex tourism can also provide an alternative source of livelihood and does not require education qualifications in order to participate. Some studies argue that this is due to the gendered nature of the tourism industry, where women and children are literally regarded as men's leisure (Clift & Carter, 2000). Further, compounding factors such as acute poverty, tourists seeing women in less economically developed countries as sexually available and an international system that promotes sex tourism have acerbated sexual exploitation (Jeffreys, 1999).

While feminist tourism scholars argue that tourism exploits women mainly in developing countries due to power imbalances (between rich and poor nations), the motivations of locals and tourists are less clear cut than expected (Cabezas, 2004; Cohen, 1971; de Albuquerque, 1998; Herold et al., 2001). The major divide is between feminists perceiving sex tourism as sexual domination and the essence of women's oppression, and those who maintain that women can strengthen their societal position through sex tourism (Outshoorn, 2004).

Most research on sex tourism and romance tourism has focused on the sexual and romantic relations between tourists and locals, local intentions to participate or the consequences of participation (Herold et al., 2001; Meisch, 1995; O'Connell Davidson, 1996; Pruitt & LaFont, 1995). Other researchers have discussed how sex tourism negatively affects a society, as in Ghana (Teye et al., 2002). This could be due to the metaphorical view that poor destinations sell themselves (female role of servitude) to the rich pleasure-seeking tourist-generating countries in order to earn a living (Graburn, 1983). Kibicho (2009), while referring to Kenya's coastal region, reasoned that sex tourism was a significant part of the national tourism industry in terms of its economic role.

While the majority of sex tourism research demonstrates the silencing of women's power, this chapter raises the voices of young girls participating in sex tourism in Mtwapa Kenya. The chapter explores young girls' motives to participate in sex tourism instead of pursuing formal education and whether this could be a 'forced choice' based on their socioeconomic circumstances. The 'girls' referred to in this study are contextualised to mean young adult women of 18 years and above who are in theory mature enough to make personal decisions regarding their lifestyle. The chapter is based on a reflection of the girls' past to explain their choice to participate in sex tourism as opposed to formal basic education.

Literature Review

Sex and tourism literature has mainly been focused on the undesirable nature of sex tourism (Ryan, 2002), power relationships emanating from the interactions between tourists and locals (Cabezas, 2004; Cohen, 1982; Sánchez, 2006), sexual behaviour among tourists themselves, that is, mainly on casual sex among students (Apostolopoulos *et al.*, 2002; Litvin, 2010; Mewhinney *et al.*, 1995), and the sexual experiences of gay and lesbian people in the tourism experience (Altman, 2008; López & Van Broeck, 2010; Visser, 2010) rather than heterosexual people (Berdychevsky *et al.*, 2010). However, much of the sex tourism industry is geared toward the idea of a romantic gateway for heterosexual couples (Hatvany, 2011).

Sex tourism can be easily associated with prostitution. Studies have indicated that sex tourism is more than just the provision of sex for the exchange of money in an exotic place. According to Ryan and Hall (2001), sex tourism is conceptualised as tourism for which the main motivation, or at least part of the aim of the trip, is to consummate or engage in commercial sexual relations. In this context, sex tourists are perceived as travellers mainly from developed countries to undeveloped or developing nations with the purpose of purchasing sex. The UNWTO (2011) describes sex tourism as undertakings of domestic or international persons visiting a destination for the purpose of engaging in a sexual relationship with a local resident. The parties in this relationship can be male or female. However, some researchers, like Jago (2003), argue that a female sex tourist is often described as a romance tourist, even if the result is comparable to the behaviour on male sex tourists.

Sex tourism is also regarded as an economic and political phenomenon since there must be a market and sex transactions must have indirect and/or direct social and political legitimacy (Outshoorn, 2004). Oppermann (1998) further argues that sex tourism simply occurs because the opportunity arises or because tourists meet like-minded individuals. In terms of market demand, sex tourism is regarded as a very lucrative and growing industry. This is especially the case related to the number of men and women travelling to foreign destinations (Southeast Asia, Cuba, the Dominican Republic, Costa Rica, Brazil, Eastern Europe), particularly those situated within the third world (Tunisia, South Africa, The Gambia, Kenya) (Clancy, 2002; Law, 2000; Ryan & Hall, 2001). This study follows the definition of sex tourism as domestic or international tourists visiting a destination for the sole or partial purpose of engaging in a sexual relationship with a 'local resident' (Ryan & Hall, 2001; UNWTO, 2011). The authors believe that purchasing sexual services does not have to be the sole purpose of the trip, the pay is not purely monetary, the local resident must not necessarily be a woman and locals need not necessarily be brought up at the destination where sex tourism occurs.

Motivations for sex tourism

Many scholars (de Albuquerque, 1998; Decosta, 2012; Herold *et al.*, 2001; Jeffreys, 1999; Pruitt & LaFont, 1995) have argued that motivations towards romantic or sex tourism are often ambiguous and all different kinds of relations between them are possible. According to Jeffreys (1999), sex tourism is founded on three factors, including acute poverty, tourists socialised into seeing women in less economically developed countries as sexually available and an international system that promotes sex tourism, of which the tourism industry is an integral part. Tourists, for example, are motivated to be involved in relations with locals mainly due to a search for, or maintenance of, a romantic love relation, and sexual excitement and novelty (de Albuquerque, 1998). Pruitt and LaFont (1995) argue that sometimes tourists desire concepts of a simple experience, a friendship, romance, companionship, which culminates in sex, making motivation for sex tourism highly intertwined, with vague borders in between.

From the local people's perspective, a broad range of different motivations to be involved with tourists, sexually or romantically, have been identified. It can be about direct or indirect financial gain, recreation, travel, marriage and/or migration. Often the long-term social-economic benefits are taken into account (Herold *et al.*, 2001). While the situation of sex tourism workers has often been linked to poverty (see Jeffreys, 1999) and the dependence on the tourism industry to earn a living, the establishment of relations with tourists (whether the focus might be on sex or other activities/services) seems to have a strong relation with migration, especially in the case of places where finding satisfying work is difficult or poverty is present (Cohen, 1971). However, there are other contexts. For example, where it is hard to establish sexual or romantic encounters, leading to the motivation of locals to engage in sexual encounters with tourists. In Egypt, for example, there is a strict cultural control on pre-marital sex for women. Therefore, local men look for sexual or romantic contacts with tourists. In this case, the primary reason for these men to engage in sex tourism is mostly hedonistic (Decosta, 2012). Benefits could be more sexual, romantic or emotional, while economic aspects in some contexts are secondary.

Sex tourism as a source of women's livelihood

Studies have shown that tourism growth, and its size and flexibility, give it enormous potential to advance women economically, socially and politically (Ghodsee, 2005). This is because tourism is a disproportionately important employer for women, especially in less developed countries, and can spur their own lives, and those of their families and communities (UNWTO, 2011). Despite this, women's tourism labour, including labour in sex tourism, remains underexplored and it is difficult to estimate the number of women employed, both formally and informally, in the tourism industry. Furthermore, insufficient attention, in terms of empirical research, has been devoted to exploring how tourism can empower women (Swain & Momsen, 2002; UNWTO, 2011). Other studies argue that tourism employment is far from gender balanced in that it favours men over women. Rather, it promotes women's economic and sexual exploitation through employment practices that abuse precarious workers through denial of employment rights, stable employment, social benefits, sustainable wages and suitable working conditions (Women First, 2010). There is also a growing public debate on the perceived objectification of women in tourism and women's willingness to participate in certain aspects of tourism encounters to supplement their source of livelihood.

Prostitution, and other forms of tourist-host sexual-economic exchange, are among a wide range of activities taking place at tourism destinations as a source of employment in both the formal and informal sectors. Sometimes even workers employed in the formal tourism industries, such as hotels, restaurants, entertainment venues and the travel trade, supplement their low wages by entering into sexual-economic exchanges with tourists. For example, studies in Jamaica and the Dominican Republic established that increased unemployment rates and poverty have gradually forced locals to scavenge a living in the informal sex tourism economy (Anderson & Witter, 1994). There are also many examples of sexual encounters where no commercial transaction is involved, which provide a different perspective on the interpersonal sexual dynamic (sometimes with long-term relationships) in tourism (Berdychevsky et al., 2010; Eiser & Ford, 1995; Thomas, 2005). Yet a 'double standard' is often applied to male and female tourist-local sexual encounters in academic discourse, with male tourists mainly being described as 'sex tourists' but female tourists being described as engaging in 'romance tourism' (Herold et al., 2001; Pruitt & LaFont, 1995).

Although many tourism stakeholders claim that prostitution is immoral, they are all aware that sex has a market value (Ryan & Hall, 2001). Furthermore, even though sex tourism is perceived largely as having a negative impact on society, it can generate income for both the destination and individuals engaged in the field. Studies like those undertaken by Kibicho (2005) support the notion that women who engage in sex tourism have been able to earn a better living and maybe buy a (new) house and/or provide education for their children. This is because 'earnings from prostitution are often more than from other alternative employment opportunities open to women with low levels of education in developing countries' (Kibicho, 2005: 276).

Study Setting and Methodology

The study on which this chapter is based was situated in Mwapa in Kilifi County within Kenya's North Coast region. Within this area, and generally across the coastal regions of Kenya, there has been a steady rise in school dropouts as girls (especially from poor families) fall prey to sex tourism (UNICEF, 2006). Due to high numbers of commercial sex workers in this area, there is stiff competition among the girls, erratic income from sex tourism and sometimes police harassment. Clubs in the area do not take any notice of age restrictions for entry and sale of alcoholic drinks (ILO, 2007). These compounding factors encourage the habit of girls grouping together to protect 'territorial areas' of operation.

The research took place between May and July 2016. The study adopted an informative practice and observation approach to the behavioural patterns of the five selected respondents. The baseline of the research was to elicit reflective voices of sex girls in Mtwapa town who had dropped out of school to pursue sex tourism in terms of their profiles, experiences and challenges in sex tourism in relation to their education. The research employed a qualitative paradigm using a range of ethnographic methods to gather data (Charmaz, 2006). The study adopted purposive, snowball and network sampling techniques to identify the respondents. Purposive sampling was used to identify the respondents who had dropped out of school to engage in sex tourism while snowball and network techniques were further employed to identify more respondents. We conducted in-depth unstructured interviews with face-to-face encounter as well as participant observation to establish rapport, which is essential for achieving trustworthiness that can be evaluated based on the principles of dependability, credibility, transferability and confirmability (Decrop, 2004; Gubrium & Holstein, 2002). This was complemented with follow-up questions to elicit continuation, elaboration, clarification and steering probes (Rubin & Rubin, 2005).

All interviews were conducted by the second author in English, with assistance from the first author, to minimise the risk to trustworthiness caused by potential biases and tensions linked to gender differences. Previous research (Catania et al., 1996) suggests that, in sex tourism research, matching interviewers and participants on gender elicits higher cooperation, especially in sensitive questions. Catania (1999) further recommends that greater similarity between interviewee and interviewer in terms of age, gender and social class might yield more comfort and, thus, higher self-disclosure on behalf of the participant. To explore such a sensitive topic, the second researcher first developed an unintimidating and ice-breaking interview opening by engaging in the Swahili language. It was like a process of discovery (learning what is happening), as explained by Lofland (1971). The place of interview was set according to participants' preferences and all interviews were conducted at night. The questions were realistic to provide participants own accounts of their points of view and experiences. After every interview (which lasted between one and one and a half hours), we had to reflect and document information before engaging the next participant. Anonymity, informed consent and confidentiality were guaranteed to the participants. Therefore, in this chapter we used pseudonyms instead of the real names of the participants.

In this research, Braun and Clarke's (2006) theoretical thematic analysis was utilised to capture the participants' reflective experiences and challenges regarding their involvement in sex tourism as opposed to pursuing formal education. We looked at the latent level of what was said by the participants during the interviews. This involved familiarisation with the data corpus to generate initial extracts for coding. We did this by hand initially, working through hard copies of the transcripts with pens and highlighters. We then searched for themes to capture something significant about our research question. Our themes were predominantly descriptive. We then reviewed, modified and developed preliminary themes and gathered all data relevant to each theme, as recommended by Bree and Gallagher (2016). We refined the themes to identify the 'essence' of what each theme is about (Braun & Clarke, 2006: 92). The researchers organised the identified themes into meaningful narratives to provide a structural synthesis of the core elements of the experiences described. The analysis was more top-down than bottom-up and was driven by interview questions.

Findings and Discussion

The girls in the streets of Mtwapa

Streets of Mtwapa on the Kenya's North coast are liminal spaces dotted with young and unemployed girls hanging around the streets, clubs and eateries during the day and at night in search of tourists that they referred to as 'clients'. Such scenarios have been witnessed by other researchers, such as on West African beaches (Ebron, 2002) and the Caribbean, where they are described as 'gigolos' for men (Brennan, 2004; Cabezas, 2004; Pruitt & LaFont, 1995). Mtwapa streets serve as the main point of contact and interaction between the girls and clients, a symbol of social inequality between the struggling girls and the more privileged clients and an intersectional space where locals, tourists and migrants engage in lifestyles they normally would not pursue in their native home environment. It is a life stage transition phase for the girls.

Having a general conversation about sexual-economic exchange in Mtwapa it seems moral, acceptable with a positive reputation. Here, sexual-economic exchange is a normal way for the girls to earn a living, something of which they are proud of and not ready to quit anytime soon. Using scholarly literature words of categorisation such as 'prostitutes' or 'commercial sex workers' seemed inappropriate. To my interviewees, this was their legitimate source of livelihood; a sexual-economic exchange. Use of such terms has been questioned and rejected in other research by Bergan (2011), Berman (2017), Tami (2008) and Venables (2009).

The girls have attained low levels of education (the large majority hardly completed primary school), which is a hindrance to securing formal tourism and hospitality-related employment. Most of the tourism and hospitality related businesses on the Kenyan coast employ highly educated Kenyans (Chege, 2014, 2017, 2019). The girls have little choice but to receive money, meals, drinks and sometimes transport rewards in exchange for their services of romance/sex. They have expanded their social networks, created their own territories – there is heavy competition amongst them although not in front of clients – and seemed to have been in the trade for some time despite their age, which ranges from 18 to 21 years. Like the beach boys on Kenya's coast (see Chege 2015, 2017), the girls support their family members – younger siblings, parents, children and sometimes their life partners – to improve their standard of living.

Abandoned, orphaned, girls raised without parental love, girls from extremely large families and those from poor backgrounds are the ones mostly found wandering the streets of Mtwapa day and night. They wear short, skimpy, styled and matching Western skirts or dresses, uncharacteristic of the dressing culture of Kenya's coastal women, to lure clients or possibly as symbols of upward social mobility. They also form part of Mtwapa's informal economy, which seemed slow during the day and active in the night until dawn. Sometimes they approach both local tourists and international tourists who represent possible clients. Once sex tourists have been approached, they exploit this opportunity to negotiate with the girls for sex. It was easy for tourists to access these girls involved in the sex business since they mainly practiced street sex. In Mtwapa there are also brothels dedicated to providing sex, escorts where tourists contact the girls by phone or via hotel staff or brokers, private premises, clubs, pubs and bars. Girls sometimes act as beer girls to gain contact with clients. During the low tourist season for international tourists, domestic tourists supplement their clientele base.

According to a study by UNICEF (2006) on *The Extent and Effect of Sex Tourism and Sexual Exploitation of Children at the Kenyan Coast*, girls were initiated into the sex industry from the age of 12–13 years. This research established that the age of initiating many girls into the sex business is between 12 and 14 years, as reported by the interviewees. The desire to please international tourists by being more westernised and innocent, being more fashionable and stylish appears to have a bearing on entry into sex work. International tourists mainly perceive young girls as innocent and more appealing.

According to Kibicho (2004), the street sex trade is the most prevalent and conspicuous form of prostitution in Kenya and the business makes up about 60% of Kenya's sex trade. Almost 94% of the commercial sex workers in this group are within the poverty sex trade, where a commercial sex worker solicits customers while waiting at street corners or walking on a street. They are usually dressed in suggestive clothing, exposing their bodies.

The allure of sex tourism or formal education

The narratives of our interviewees – with both locals and immigrants – depict girls growing up in dire need of basic life necessities, their early childhood interaction and proximity with tourists, struggling to attend school and early life perception that formal education could not provide households' with an income. To elaborate this, consider Joy's story (she was found standing alone by the researcher outside Casaurina club in Mtwapa, aged 18):

> I did not have sincere female friends since I was young, I could only confide in boys. I grew up alone in the streets of Mtwapa after I lost my mother at the age of ten who left without ever telling me where I came from or who really was my biological father [She sighs]. When I was young, I could see my mother bring different men in our single room I called home and she could force me to call them 'father!' failure to which she could punish me brutally. I could not trust any female friends because they made up stories including my own mother so I just trusted men and in most cases older ones. I could tell them my inner most secrets. Some would buy me sweets and food and sometimes I could take money home ... so, that's why I am here alone waiting for potential clients [sex tourists].

Some of the interviewees had come from as far away as Uganda to engage in sex tourism. Beth (aged 21 but without legal identification documents), who is in Kenya illegally, with the aid of a translator, who happens to be her Ugandan boyfriend but fluent in English unlike Beth, narrated her experience to the researcher:

> I have been in Kenya since the year 2013. I was promised a well-paying job in Kenya so I dropped out of school in Uganda since I come from a very poor background; my parents had difficulties in paying my school fees and buying food for us. I am a third born from a family of nine [she looks deep into my eyes as if I am supposed to note something], so I accepted the offer considering I would get back to my country and help my parents. Being under age, I did not have an identification card, which I was told would not be a problem. I kept worrying how I would exit Uganda without national identification. After a month, my friend [whom she refuses to reveal] came to my home and took me with her. She handed me a fake Ugandan identity card which she said it would help me at the Kenya-Uganda border. From Kampala, I went to Nairobi

and connected with another bus straight to Mtwapa. I don't know many people here since I can only communicate in Kiganda [she smiles]. I only talk to Japheth and my friend who brought me here. I have mastered numbers, so if a client comes I can say two hundred shillings, five hundred and one thousand shillings [she looks down]. At times, clients start talking much and I cannot understand but I call Japheth to help me. Sometimes I am afraid of being caught by the police here without any identification document [her facial expression seems to portray fears too]. I love Mtwapa, business here is good, there are many clients [sex tourists], since sometimes I take home as much as ten thousand Kenya shillings. When I get back to Uganda I will be a millionaire [she laughs sarcastically] but I will come back to Kenya, Mtwapa is the place to be [she concludes and moves away].

Beth tells the researcher how sometimes it is unsafe at night for the girls. She gives an incident that she said had happened recently where young men from Kisauni (a region in Mombasa) came to Mtwapa and started fighting residents, including commercial sex workers and everyone else they met on the way. Many of them got hurt badly and were admitted to hospitals.

From the narratives, socioeconomic factors like poverty formed one of the reasons why the girl child is forced to drop out of school to engage in sex tourism. Girls are introduced into the sex industry in different ways. Some are lured away from poor backgrounds by recruiters and their peers who promise them jobs in cities or other countries. Once away from their families, these girls are forced to have sexual liaisons with sex tourists. Parental upbringing is also a contributing factor as girls may copy what their parents do, as in Beth's case. Involvement in sexual-economic relationships as a much faster income-generating activity proved to be the most viable alternative for the girls to provide for themselves and their dependents, with a possibility to improve their future economic lives.

Gender inequality is also a major cause of girls moving to cities to engage in commercial sex. In many traditional African societies, girls and boys do not have an equal chance to pursue an education. In large African family units, parents differentially treat their children based on gender. They tend to favour education for boys rather than girls. Consider Rachael's narrative (aged 19):

We are five members in my family and being the only girl I would be the house help of the family when we were growing up. My brothers were favoured by my both parents than myself [sic]. I could be blamed for their mistakes and I could not take it anymore. I quit school and came to Mombasa, I got a job as a house help but it was not well paying, so I started a mission of finding a Mzungu [local name for a white man]. I used to walk along the beaches hoping to have one eventually. One morning, I met a girl on the beach who gave me an easier way of accessing a Mzungu, she took me to a beach hotel and we placed an order of two glasses of juice and waited for our bait. Being a lucky day for me, a waiter approached us with an extra glass of juice. I got furious since I had not placed an order for it. She then told me that it had been bought for me by a white man who was seated next to us. He wanted my phone number, which I did not hesitate to give out. Things went on a little bit fast since that night I slept in his hotel room [she laughs cynically]. He gave me sixty dollars the following day, plus other gifts. We would meet every day, show him around and sleep in his hotel room until he left for Germany. After he left, I had to find another Mzungu since I was so much used to that life and that became the trend up to date, but right now international tourists are at low peak so we are just surviving upon the local tourists who do not pay much but the season peaks as from August to December and we are looking forward to good business come August. You can join us too [she invites the researcher jokingly].

Studies by McLeod (1982) and Middleton (1993) stated that, from a social point of view, women and girls are never given equal opportunities to their male counterparts in many societies. Girls then perceive themselves as inferior to boys in society. This power differential between girls and boys in many instances compels young girls to become involved in transactional sex. This scenario also provides a reason for girls to drop out of school and engage in commercial sex as men's objects.

The sex tourism business in Mtwapa is dependent on low and peak seasons. From January to July, the girls rely on local tourists who do not pay as much as international visitors but from August to December business booms due to the increased inflow of international tourists in the region. The interviewees informed the researcher that Mtwapa is a good target market for a commercial sex business since there is freedom (one can work freely day and night without being questioned or harassed by anyone). They denied having any personal challenges but, upon assuring Ericka (aged 19) that she cannot be exposed to the public and the information she gives is strictly for educational purposes, she shared this:

'Sometimes we are not even paid by the clients we take in [she shakes her head]. They assault you sexually a whole night promising large sums of money but the following day they refuse to pay even a penny. When you insist they start acting up; tearing your clothes or even confiscating them, you are forced to call a friend to bring you clothes or risk walking naked in the streets. Some clients are also so brutal in bed; they bruise you in the name of 'I'm paying for this madam!' [She imitates a male voice]. Others beat you up and the next morning you are in no state to have any other client. You are left nursing injuries [she regrets]. It is never an easy business [she concludes and sadly walks away].

The next participant was a Ugandan commercial sex worker in a group of four others and could speak very fluent English. Upon asking about her experiences in the sex business and the challenges she faces, Janet (aged 20) paused and looked at the researcher saying;

'Business is good and I am happy. I have no challenges at all. I love Kenyan money because when I take it to Uganda it is much. I am able to sustain myself here, do shopping, buy good clothes, eat well and live in a good house from the wages I get. I love what I do here [she remarks with confidence]. So far I have not encountered any major hitch here, I have heard of some girls here complaining about clients mistreating them but I think it depends [on] how you present yourself to them, I cannot compare this life with life in school back in Uganda [she boasts].

The final respondent, Jane, declined to divulge any information about her education level or studies but instead talked about her experience: 'I am earning more than those who have gone to school [she proudly says with a smile]'. When the interviewees were asked about the possibility of going back to school given a chance, they all refused and argued that 'Mtwapa is where they belong and they have nowhere else to go' Rachael and Joy stated. 'Learning is a waste of time' Beth and Janet concluded. They seemed to be happy with the business they engage in despite the challenges some of them have faced during their encounters with clients. 'No one can pay me as much as I get here' says Janet. Again, she mockingly tells the researcher: 'Finish school and tell me where studies will take you, maybe I will be richer than you [she says confidently]'.

The participants felt education was meaningless, a waste of time and resources. Their perception was that sex tourism could pay more than education, and improve their living standards and social status, especially when they were working with foreign tourists. They had accepted their state as casual sex workers and seemed to be proud of engaging in the business. According to ILO (2007), the reason why children leave school to engage in commercial sex is due to lack of money to pay school fees. Hence, they engage in commercial sex work as a source of income to support their families. The current study corroborates this. For example, while Beth dropped out of school because her parents had difficulties in raising sufficient money to pay the school fees and to buy food for the family, her final emphasis was that education could not offer financial prosperity, which sex tourism seemed to offer. The allure of a good life through sex tourism outweighed the pursuit of education. Peer influence is another reason why girls drop out of school to engage in sex work (ILO, 2007). Indeed, some girls are pushed towards commercial sex by their peers who are in the sex business and present an enviable image of financial wealth and stability. Some girls, after getting pregnant and being forced out of school, opt to engage in commercial sex to support their babies.

Conclusion

The study on which this chapter is based was conducted to determine the influence of sex tourism on girls' education in Mtwapa Kenya by giving voice to the experiences of the girls involved in the sex trade through their narratives. Finding commercial sex workers who would agree to be part of the study was a big challenge. A number of girls refused to be part of the study. The participants who voluntarily agreed to take part in the study chose commercial sex as a primary source of income and as a means to support their family. It is seen as perhaps the most realistic hope for lifting the girl and her family out of poverty, or at least to gain a better standard of living. As they engage in the business, sexual-economic transactions are also perceived as prestigious. The aspiration for an individual girl or a young woman of having a 'Mzungu' boyfriend of whatever age was a fantasy for many. Girls trafficked from other countries due to the allure of better jobs ended up being engaged in commercial sex work. The study also established that some commercial sex workers are assaulted by their clients after providing sexual services. Despite their experience, the interviewees were proud of their involvement in the sex business. They valued being in commercial sex work more than education and mainly believed that sex tourism pays more than pursuit of education.

This study contributes to the growing body of sex tourism research, especially in Kenya. While previous studies (see Bergan, 2011; Chege, 2014, 2015, 2017, 2019; Kibicho, 2004; Mannava et al., 2013; Meiu, 2015) focused on sex tourism and Kenya's beach boys, the current study raises the voices of girls in the sex tourism industry in Kenya's coastal region.

The authors recommend that families should provide equal opportunities to both girls and boys in areas such as education despite hard family economic conditions. The study also raises questions about the abolitionist approach to the sex tourism industry on Kenya's coast, where the government criminalises sex tourism yet the public perception at tourism destinations like Mtwapa is that the trade does not necessarily have to be legal. With the current popular general consensus in Kenya, that states of poverty, inequalities and general social-economic malaise are greater today than they were 60 years ago (Chege, 2017), an upsurge in sexual-economic exchanges could ensue in future. As a last resort, a national sex tourism policy framework that recognises sex workers like any other informal work in Kenya should be enacted and operationalised and willing participants be issued with operating licenses to improve their dignity, reduce client assaults, enable payment of taxes and prevent the exploitation of underage girls. The current condition in Kenya is that of a general conservative attitude towards public discussion of sexuality, as previously also noted by Chege (2014) and Kibicho (2004), and the subject is avoided and public understanding of the phenomenon is still shaped and heard through the moral views and discourses of a few social actors.

References

Altman, D. (2008) AIDS and the globalization of sexuality. *Social Identities* 14 (2), 145–160.

Anderson, P. and Witter, M. (1994) Crisis, adjustment and social change: A case study of Jamaica. In E. Le Franc (ed.) *Consequences of Structural Adjustment: A Review of the Jamaican Experience* (pp. 1–55). Kingston: Canoe Press

Apostolopoulos, Y., Sönmez, S. and Yu, C.H. (2002) HIV-risk behaviours of American spring break vacationers: A case of situational disinhibition? *International Journal of STD & AIDS* 13 (11), 733–743.

Berdychevsky, L., Poria, Y. and Uriely, N. (2010) Casual sex and the backpacking experience: The case of Israeli women. In N. Carr and Y. Poria (eds) *Sex and the Sexual during People's Leisure and Tourism Experiences* (pp. 105–118). Newcastle: Cambridge Scholars Publishing.

Bergan, E.M. (2011) 'There's No Love Here' Beach Boys in Malindi, Kenya. Masters Dissertation. University of Bergen.

Berman, N. (2017) *Germans on the Kenyan Coast*. Bloomington and Indianapolis: Indiana University Press.

Braun, V. and Clarke, V. (2006) Using thematic analysis in psychology. *Qualitative Research in Psychology* 3, 77–101.

Bree, R. and Gallagher, G. (2016) Using Microsoft Excel to code and thematically analyse qualitative data: A simple, cost-effective approach. *All Ireland Journal of Teaching and Learning in Higher Education* 8 (2), 2811–2814.

Brennan, D. (2004) *What's Love got to do with it? Transnational Desires and Sex Tourism in the Dominican Republic*. Durham, NC and London: Duke University Press.

Cabezas, A.L. (2004) Between love and money: Sex, tourism, and citizenship in Cuba and the Dominican Republic. *Journal of Women in Culture and Society* 29 (4), 987–1015.

Catania, J.A. (1999) A framework for conceptualizing reporting bias and its antecedents in interviews assessing human sexuality. *The Journal of Sex Research* 36 (1), 25–38.

Catania, J.A., Binson, D., Canchola, J., Pollack, L.M. and Hauck, W. (1996) Effects of interviewer gender, interviewer choice, and item wording on responses to questions concerning sexual behavior. *The Public Opinion Quarterly* 60 (3), 345–375.

Charmaz, K. (2006) *Constructing Grounded Theory: Practical Guide Through Qualitative Analysis*. London: Sage Publications.

Chege, N. (2014) Male Beach Workers and Western Female Tourists: Livelihood Strategies in Kenya's South Coast Region. PhD Thesis. University of Lausanne.

Chege, N. (2015) 'What's in it for me?' Negotiations of asymmetries, concerns and interests between the researcher and research subjects. *Ethnography* 16 (4), 463–481.

Chege, N. (2017) Towards a deeper understanding of the meaning of male beach worker – female tourist relationships on the Kenyan coast. *Journal of Arts and Humanities* 6 (2), 62–80.

Chege, N. (2019) 'If you give me time I can love you': A pregnant researcher among male beach workers on Kenya's liminal south coast beaches. *Anthropology Matters Journal* 19 (1), 1–34.

Clancy, M. (2002) The globalization of sex tourism and Cuba: A commodity chains approach. *Studies in Comparative International Development* 36 (4), 63–88.

Clift, S. and Carter, S. (eds) (2000) *Tourism and Sex: Culture, Commerce and Coercion.* London: Pinter.

Cohen, E. (1971) Arab boys and tourist girls in a mixed Jewish-Arab community. *International Journal of Comparative Sociology* 12 (4), 217–233.

Cohen, E. (1982) Thai girls and farang men: The edge of ambiguity. *Annals of Tourism Research* 9 (3), 403–428.

de Albuquerque, K. (1998) Sex, beach boys and female tourists in the Caribbean. *Sexuality and Culture* 2, 87–111.

Decosta, P.L. (2012) A review of 'Sex, tourism and the postcolonial encounter: Landscapes of longing in Egypt'. *Tourism Geographies* 14 (3), 524–528.

Decrop, A. (2004) Trustworthiness in qualitative tourism research. In J. Phillimore and L. Goodson (eds) *Qualitative Research in Tourism: Ontologies, Epistemologies and Methodologies* (pp. 156–169). London: Routledge.

Ebron, P.A. (2002) *Performing Africa.* Princeton and Oxford: Princeton University Press.

Eiser, J.R. and Ford, N. (1995) Sexual relationships on holiday: A case of situational disinhibition? *Journal of Social and Personal Relationships* 12 (3), 323–339.

Galor, O. and Moav, O. (2004) From physical to human capital accumulation: Inequality and the process of development. *The Review of Economic Studies* 71 (4), 1001–1026.

Ghodsee, K.R. (2005) *The Red Riviera: Gender, Tourism, and Postsocialism on the Black Sea.* Durham: Duke University Press.

Graburn, N.H.H. (1983) Tourism and prostitution. *Annals of Tourism Research* 10, 437–456.

Grown, C., Gupta, R. and Kes, A. (2005) *Taking Action: Achieving Gender Equality and Empowering Women-UN Millennium Project Task Force on Education and Gender Equality.* London: Earth Scan.

Gubrium, N.J. and Holstein, J.A. (2002) *Handbook of Interview Research: Context and Method.* Thousand Oaks: Sage Publications.

Hatvany, O. (2011) Lack of safety net for LGBT couples causes stress. *Psych Central.* See https://psychcentral.com/lib/lack-of-safety-net-for-lgbt-couples-causes-stress/ (accessed March 2019).

Herold, E., Garcia, R. and DeMoya, T. (2001) Female tourists and beach boys: Romance or sex tourism? *Annals of Tourism Research* 28 (4), 978–997.

ILO (2007) *ABC of Women Workers' Rights and Gender Equality* (2nd edn). Geneva: ILO.

Jago, L. (2003) Sex tourism: An accommodation provider's perspective. In T.G. Bauer and B. McKercher (eds) *Sex and Tourism: Journeys of Romance, Love, and Lust* (pp. 85–94). New York: Haworth Hospitality Press.

Jeffreys, S. (1999) Globalizing sexual exploitation: Sex tourism and the traffic in women. *Leisure Studies* 18 (3), 179–186.

Kibicho, W. (2004) Tourism and the sex trade: Roles male sex workers play in Malindi, Kenya. *Tourism Review International* 7, 129–144.

Kibicho, W. (2005) Tourism and the sex trade in Kenya's costal region. *Journal of Sustainable Tourism* 13 (3), 256–280.

Kibicho, W. (2009) *Sex Tourism in Africa: Kenya's Booming Industry.* Farnham: Ashgate.

Law, L. (2000) *Sex-Work in Southeast Asia: The place of Desire in a Time of HIV/AIDS.* London: Routledge.

Litvin, S.W. (2010) A comparison of student spring break and their 'normal' behaviors: is the hype justified? *Tourism Review International* 13 (3), 173–181.

Lofland, J. (1971) *Analysing Social Situations: A Guide to Qualitative Observation and Analysis.* Belmont, CA: Wadsworth Publishing.

López, Á.L. and Van Broeck, A.M. (2010) Sexual encounters between men in a tourist environment: A comparative study in seven Mexican localities. In N. Carr and Y. Poria (eds) *Sex and the Sexual During People's Leisure and Tourism Experiences* (pp. 119–142). Newcastle: Cambridge Scholars Publishing.

Mannava, P. Geibel, S., King'ola, N., Temmerman, M. and Luchters, S. (2013) Male sex workers who sell sex to men also engage in anal intercourse with women: Evidence from Mombasa, Kenya. *PLoS One* 8 (1), e52547.

Manyasa, E. (2015) Schooling without learning: The long-term implications of free primary education for income and welfare inequalities in Kenya. In N. Aworti and H. Musahara (eds) *Implementation of Millennium Development Goals: Progress and Challenges in some African Countries* (pp. 33–59). Ossrea: Addis Ababa.

McLeod, E. (1982) *Women Working: Prostitution Now.* London: Croom Helm.

Meisch, L. (1995) Gringas and otavalenos: Changing tourists' relations. *Annals of Tourism Research* 22 (2), 441–462.

Meiu, G.P. (2015) 'Beach-boy elders' and 'young big-men': Subverting the temporalities of ageing in Kenya's ethno-erotic economies. *Ethnos* 80, 472–496.

Mewhinney, D.M., Herold, E.S. and Maticka-Tyndale, E. (1995) Sexual scripts and risk-taking of Canadian university students on spring break in Daytona Beach, Florida. *The Canadian Journal of Human Sexuality* 4 (4), 273–288.

Middleton, S. (1993) *Educating Feminist: Life Histories and Pedagogy.* New York: Teachers College Press.

O'Connell Davidson, J. (1996) Sex tourism in Cuba. *Race and Class* 38 (1), 39–48.

Oppermann, M. (1998) Who exploits whom and who benefits? In M. Oppermann (ed.) *Sex Tourism and Prostitution: Aspects of Leisure, Recreation, and Work* (pp. 153–160). New York: Cognizant Communications Corporation.

Outshoorn, J. (2004) *Politics of Prostitution: Women's Movement, Democratic States and the Globalisation of Sex Commerce.* Cambridge: Cambridge University Press.

Pruitt, D. and LaFont, S. (1995) For love and money: Romance tourism in Jamaica. *Annals of Tourism Research* 22 (2), 422–440.

Rubin, H.J. and Rubin, I.S. (2005) *Qualitative Interviewing: The Art of Hearing Data.* Thousand Oaks: Sage Publications.

Ryan, C. (2002) Equity, management, power sharing and sustainability-issues of the 'new tourism'. *Tourism Management* 23 (1), 17–26.

Ryan, C. and Hall, C.M. (2001) *Sex Tourism: Marginal People and Liminalities.* London: Routledge.

Sánchez, T.J. (2006) Female sex tourism: A contradiction in terms? *Feminist Review* 83 (1), 42–59.

Swain, M.B. and Momsen, J.H. (eds) (2002) *Gender/Tourism/Fun(?).* New York: Cognizant Communication Corporation.

Tami, N. (2008) Romancing Strangers: The Intimate Politics of Beach Tourism in Kenya. PhD Thesis. University of Illinois at Urbana-Champaign.

Teye, V., Sirakaya, E. and Sönmez, S.F. (2002) Residents' attitudes toward tourism development. *Annals of Tourism Research* 29 (3), 668–688.

Thomas, M. (2005) 'What happens in Tenerife stays in Tenerife': Understanding women's sexual behaviour on holiday. *Culture, Health & Sexuality* 7 (6), 571–584.

UNESCO (2012) *Education for all Global Monitoring Report 2011/2012.* Paris: UNESCO.

UNICEF (2006) *The Extent and Effect of Sex Tourism and Sexual Exploitation of Children on the Kenyan Coast.* Nairobi: UNICEF.

UNWTO (2011) *Global Report on Women in Tourism.* See http://ethics.unwto.org/en/content/global-report-women-tourism (accessed March 2019).

Uwezo (2015) *Are Our Children Learning? The State of Education in Kenya in 2015 and Beyond.* Nairobi: Twaweza East Africa.

Venables, E. (2009) 'If you give me some sexing, I might talk to you': Researching the Senegalese beach-boys 'at my side'. *Anthropology Matters* 11 (1), 1–11.

Visser, G. (2010) White gay women's leisure spaces in Bloemfontein, South Africa. In N. Carr and Y. Poria (eds) *Sex and the Sexual during People's Leisure and Tourism Experiences* (pp. 143–163). Newcastle: Cambridge Scholars Publishing.

Wodon, Q., Montenegro, C., Nguyen, H. and Onagoruwa, A. (2018) *The Cost of not Educating Girls. Missed Opportunities: The High Cost of not Educating Girls*. See https://openknowledge.worldbank.org/bitstream/handle/10986/29956/HighCostOfNot EducatingGirls.pdf?sequence=6&isAllowed=y (accessed August 2020).

Women First (2010) *The Case for Change: Women Working in Hospitality, Leisure, Travel and Tourism*. See www.people1st.co.uk/webfiles/Business%20and%20Training%20 Support/Women%201st/ (accessed February 2019).

World Bank (2018) *World Development Report 2018: The Cost of not Educating Girls*. Washington, DC: The World Bank.

11 Examining Awareness, Knowledge and Perceptions of Tourism and its Links to HIV/AIDS in Maun, Botswana

Naomi Moswete

Introduction

HIV/AIDS is still a major threat to development, economic growth and poverty in Africa and most parts of the poorer nations worldwide (Dixon *et al.*, 2002; Whiteside, 2002). Tourism, commercial sex or prostitution and HIV and AIDS are intertwined as 'no person is an island' because there is a high level of human interaction when people are on holiday. Travel and tourism has now become a major international industry and it is a big business with significant socioeconomic impacts (Goeldner & Ritchie, 2012; Mbaiwa, 2005; UNWTO, 2018). The industry is renowned for its ability to generate foreign exchange, create employment opportunities, even in remote parts of both the developed and developing world, and to improve relations (e.g. peace) between countries (Archer & Fletcher, 1996; WTTC, 2016). It is because of the nature of the tourism business that opportunities for holidays, recreation and leisure in other countries are plentiful and countries with sustainable tourism and open tourism tend to be more peaceful (UNWTO, 2018; WTTC, 2015, 2016). Yet research has also revealed that tourism and HIV/AIDS are interlinked (Hamlyn *et al.*, 2007; Herold and van Kerkwijk, 1992). One of the major ways through which HIV/AIDS is transmitted is by involvement in sexual-related activity with an infected person without protection, especially when away from home or on holiday (Bene & Darkoh, 2012; Easterbrook, 2007). The travel and tourism industry is the second largest generator of foreign exchange, while HIV and AIDS is a challenge to the continued growth of the tourism sector in the world.

Tourism in Botswana has shown signs of continuous increase in international tourist (visitor) numbers and related employment creation (Mbaiwa, 2005; Moswete *et al.*, 2009; WTTC, 2017). Accordingly, the tourism sector has created about 23,226 direct and 58,783 jobs countrywide (WTTC, 2013). Although Botswana has been classified as a middle-class country, it still experiences challenges associated with human immunodeficiency virus (HIV/AIDS) (Upton, 2002; Upton & Dolan, 2011) that have, so far, negatively affected the general economy. Notwithstanding that the HIV/AIDS epidemic poses one of the biggest problems worldwide, with developing countries being the most affected (Cohen, 2001; Lacey, 2012; Omondi & Ryan, 2017), research has shown that HIV/AIDS prevalence is one of the major challenging developmental issues for Botswana. This relates to the potential for working age and skilled people to contract the disease and the continued lack of a cure (Allen & Heald, 2004; Carter, 1998; Dixon *et al.*, 2002; Stephens *et al.*, 2012; Toska *et al.*, 2017). Other studies have discovered that in sub-Saharan Africa, Botswana included, the agricultural sector has been hard hit by HIV/AIDS, with many old people left to work on the farms to produce food to feed themselves, the sick and AIDS orphans (Bene & Darkoh, 2012; Rajaraman *et al.*, 2006). HIV/AIDS rates have been rapidly increasing in Botswana (Upton, 2002; Upton & Dolan, 2011; World Bank, 2005), and both rural and urban area dwellers have been negatively affected (Bene & Darkoh, 2012; Ketshabile, 2011; Stephens *et al.*, 2012; World Bank, 2005). Subsequently, most of the skilled and productive workforce in the country, including those working in the leisure and tourism sectors, has been impacted (BIDPA, 2000; Dixon *et al.*, 2002; Ketshabile, 2011; Kgathi & Motsholapheko, 2011).

According to Ngwenya *et al.* (2007) and Upton (2002), HIV/AIDS in Maun village, Botswana, is increasing among the local people (Ketshabile, 2011; Upton, 2002). Other researchers have found that the disease is one of the three key shocks in the country's tourism hotspots and the biodiversity rich region in the Ngamiland district (Kgathi *et al.*, 2011; Kgathi & Motsholapheko, 2011). Furthermore, the adverse impacts of HIV/AIDS on livelihood activities have marginalised and impoverished some community members in the northern tip of the country, including Shorobe, Gudigwa and Seronga villages (Kgathi *et al.*, 2011). Successfully combating the rising incidence of HIV/AIDS in the nation, particularly among the economically active segment of the population, continues to be one of the government's major challenges (Kgathi & Motsholapheko, 2011; Government of Botswana (GoB), 2016).

Observations and research have discovered that HIV/AIDS affects young and economically active people and, as such, it can have devastating effects on the ailing economies of most developing countries (Bollinger & Stover, 1999; Brayley *et al.*, 1990; Lacey, 2012; Miller *et al.*, 2011; Rajaraman *et al.*, 2006).

Figure 11.1 HIV and AIDS awareness information in Maun

In the case of Botswana, the government has had several strategies and programmes in place aimed at reducing the spread of the disease, as well as improving the living standards of the people. Some of the programmes include television and radio drama and frequent documentaries on HIV/AIDS scenarios that target all citizens, with more focus on the youth and others who fall into the sexually active band, including holidaymakers at popular destinations (Figure 11.1).

In the case of the households in the Ngamiland region of northern Botswana (Maun, Okavango), families have started to use social capital as a strategy to ameliorate adverse effects of shocks, including HIV/AIDS and poverty (Kgathi *et al.*, 2011). With specific reference to the social capital theory (see Portes, 1998), community members from different wards in these villages (clusters of households) have formed community based organisations (CBOs) (Ngwenya *et al.*, 2007) where they form groups (informal social clubs) to share experiences and skills, and learn from one another about health and social issues affecting them, such as HIV/AIDS (see Kang'ethe, 2014).

Commercial sex encounters, HIV/AIDS and the travel industry

Sex tourism is defined as tourism in which the main motivation, or at least one of its aims, is to engage in commercial sexual activity (Hope, 2013) while other motivations may include romance (Bauer & McKercher, 2003; Herold *et al.*, 2001; Jeffreys, 2003). In a study in Kenya, Kibicho (2016) defines sex tourism as the form of tourism where a foreigner or a citizen travels to a destination of choice with an intention to engage in sexual activity with prostitutes as the main reason or as one of the aims of the trip. From these definitions, a prostitute is someone, commonly a female, who allows somebody, usually a male, to have sexual activity with them in exchange for money (Bender & Furman, 2004; Omondi & Ryan, 2017; Oppermann, 1999). A male who makes his body available for sexual activity for the purpose of financial exchange is also regarded as a prostitute (Bender & Furman, 2004; Hope, 2013). According to Herold *et al.* (2001) and Oppermann (1999), female sex tourists engage in sexual affairs or romantic activities with male prostitutes, usually young men at the sex tourism destination, in exchange for money or goods (Jeffreys, 2003; Herold & Van Kerkwijk, 1992; Herold *et al.*, 2001; Oppermann, 1999; Taylor, 2001). However, male prostitutes are not common as the job has been/is associated with females (Bender & Furman, 2004; Mmeso, 2015; Taylor, 2001). It is important to note that not all sexual encounters between tourists and local people are commercial, as individuals on holiday can choose to engage in casual, free sexual activities. Based on the manner in which sexually transmitted infections (STI) spread, it should be noted that non-commercial sex interactions can also be responsible for transmitting infections (Bender & Furman, 2004; Botswana IAMAT, 2020).

Research has shown a substantial increase in travel and tourism across the world (UNWTO, 2018), with more people searching for adventure and novel places, and this is especially common among younger generations and retirees (Carter, 1998). There was an increase of about 7% in the total number of international tourist arrivals across the world in 2017, which was noted as the highest increase since the 2009 global economic crisis (UNWTO, 2018). In the same period (2017), international tourist arrivals in Africa were estimated to have increased by 9% (UNWTO, 2018). Tourists choose different countries and regions of the world for holidays based on their motivations. Included among travel motivations, sex and romance adventures drive some individuals to tourist destinations (see Herold *et al.*, 2001; Hope, 2013; Kayawe, 2017). Sex encounters during holidays have become adventurous for some, and sex work provides substantial local economic and social benefits to others (Bisika, 2009; Kibicho, 2016). Following on from the recognition of sex and romance as holiday motivations, research is beginning to show interlinkages between sex tourism and incidences of STIs and HIV/AIDS (Bisika, 2009; Herold & Van Kerkwijk, 1992). Thus, the growth of sex tourism and its associated problems have become a major challenge within countries and globally (Bender & Furman, 2004; Brayley *et al.*, 1990; Herold & Van Kerkwijk, 1992; Whiteside, 2002). When people are away from where they live and work, are involved in leisure travel and tourism and have free time and disposable income, they are often more likely to participate in activities from which they can derive fun, relaxation, sexual gratification and quality vacation time (Bender

& Furman, 2004; Carter, 1998; Hope, 2013). Other researchers have identified how the leisure travel/tourism industry is intertwined with sexual adventures and sex work (Bender & Furman, 2004; Bisika, 2009; Herold *et al.*, 2001). However, HIV/AIDS, which has become a major health problem and a great challenge to the economies of poorer nations and some parts of the developed world, is associated with leisure and tourism pursuits in various ways (BIDPA, 2000; Bisika, 2009; Herold & van Kerkwijk, 1992; Ketshabile, 2011; Whiteside, 2002).

According to Upton (2002), HIV/AIDS represents a major threat to the lives of the communities of Maun, Botswana. It is noteworthy that Maun and Gaborone (the capital city of Botswana) are major urban centres where tourism traffic and development are relatively high (Mbaiwa *et al.*, 2007; Moswete *et al.*, 2009). In Botswana, the tourism sector is relatively new and tourism as business does not exist in some communities or rural towns in the country (Moswete & Mavondo, 2003). Although the government has identified tourism as the second most important economic sector after diamond mining, there is a paucity of research on sex and tourism in Botswana. There is also limited research on the relationships between tourism development, commercial sex and HIV/AIDS, notably at main tourism centres in Botswana, including the case study village of Maun. Lack of data and further information about sex tourists and sex workers leaves a vacuum about the impact of tourism on the health of citizens and tourists. It is against this backdrop that the study examined awareness and understanding of the relationships between tourism, destination communities and HIV/AIDS in Maun. The chapter presents the results of the study that was conducted to determine these relationships between tourism and HIV/AIDS and tourism development in Maun. The research objectives were to: (a) examine perceptions of the effects of tourism development on the local community in Maun; (b) assess the level of knowledge of the relationship between tourism and HIV/AIDS among community members in Maun; (c) examine whether residents are aware that tourism development in their community could increase the spread of HIV/AIDS and (d) assess the level of awareness of the relationship between tourism and HIV/AIDS across demographic variables (age, sex).

Study Area

Maun village, a popular tourist township, is situated in the Ngamiland district in the northwestern part of Botswana (Figure 11.2). Maun is one of the fastest growing villages in the country. Between 1971 and 1981, Maun's population grew from 13,637 to 14,925. This entailed a growth rate of a mere 0.9% per annum. In the period between 1991 and 2001, the population growth rate of Maun increased to 5.1%, resulting in the settlement having 43,776 inhabitants by 2001 (GoB, 2001).

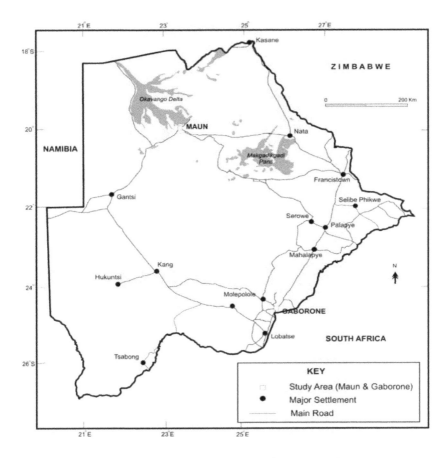

Figure 11.2 Maun village location map – Botswana (G. Koorutwe)

According to the last Botswana population census in 2011, the total populace of Maun was approximately 60,263 (CSO,[1] 2011). For Maun and the associated localities, 90,333 people were recorded. Maun has been designated and assigned equivalent status of an urban centre in the Botswana National Settlement Policy (NSP) hierarchy (GoB, 1998).

Maun is renowned as a major administrative centre for the northwestern district, and a headquarters for the Department of Wildlife and National Parks (GoB, 2001). In the context of tourism, Maun is popularly known as the gateway to the tourist hotspots of the Okavango Delta region (Figure 11.3), incorporating the Chobe sub-district, Chobe National Park, Moremi Game Reserve, Kasane Forest Reserve and other protected areas in northern Botswana.

The main touristic attractions in Maun include the historic Thamalakane River (Figure 11.4) and the wetland of the Okavango region. The Maun tourist 'township' offers a variety of services to different

Figure 11.3 Signage in Maun village

Figure 11.4 Thamakalane River by the crocodile campsite in Maun

holidaymakers that include the business market, honeymooners, romance tourists, safari school groups, long haul and domestic tourists. It is a busy township that offers safari and air-charter operations (Mbaiwa *et al.*, 2007). Three principal market segments for Maun have been identified as lodge clients, incorporating mainly affluent international tourists who fly directly to Maun and then out to the Okavango Delta, self-drive holidaymakers and overlanders[2] (Mbaiwa, 2005).

Methods

This chapter is based on a mixture of qualitative and quantitative data. Secondary data sources such as books, journal articles, government reports, policy documents, online material and grey literature were used. In addition, primary data were collected via a pre-coded semi-structured survey, which incorporated closed and open-ended questions.

The questionnaire was translated from English to the local language (Setswana – which is spoken by almost all citizens and is taught in schools) by a University lecturer from the Faculty of Humanities in order to reduce misinterpretation. This was to ensure consistency so as to reduce the chances of any language barrier clouding the results of the study. A total of 500 heads of households were contacted and requested to participate in the survey. All the 500 households completed the survey. Whenever the head of household was not present or at home, the eldest person who was 18 years or older, related to the household and had lived in the home for a period of 12 months was requested to complete the survey. In instances where one house/yard/compound was home to more than one household (as is the cultural tradition of rural Botswana), the head of each household was asked to do the survey. In some instances, individual questionnaires were administered face to face in the local language to those who could not read and write. A systematic sampling method was used to select households for the survey. Two research assistants with project experience and a college (university) degree were trained and involved in conducting the survey.

In addition, key informant interviews were undertaken with government personnel such as government extension workers, headmen, social workers, district officers, politicians, vocational school instructors, college lecturers and researchers. A total of 11 key informants were interviewed. Each interview lasted for about 45–60 minutes. In-depth, face-to-face informal interviews with key informants were conducted mainly to support and authenticate the quantitative data obtained from the household survey (Creswell & Clark, 2011; Veal, 2006). Both purposive and snowball sampling were used to select the participants for interview. The interviews were conducted by the same research assistants who conducted the survey.

The survey data were analysed using the Statistical Package for Social Sciences (SPSS) software. In line with the exploratory nature of the study, the analysis was mostly descriptive, and frequency and pivot tables were used in presentation of the results. Where appropriate, bivariate, non-parametric tests were also employed. Interview and/or qualitative data analysis was carried out through open, axial and selective coding (Creswell & Clark, 2011; Hatch, 2002; Rossman & Rallis, 2017). These coding methods enabled the researcher to arrange and organise information in different meaningful classes.

Results and Discussion

Socio-demographic characteristics of the respondents

The respondents ranged from 16 to 75 years of age. The majority (61%) of the respondents were 40 years and below. Among respondents in Maun, 37% were in the 31–40 age range, followed by 24% in the 16–30 age range, 22% in the 41–50 age range and 17.2% in the 51–75 age range. Also, 45% of the respondents were males and 55% were females.

Of the total sample, 54.6% indicated they were in formal employment in Maun, 12.4% were self-employed and 32.2% reported they were unemployed. Although a high proportion of residents did not disclose (i.e. refused to disclose) their monthly income (54%), there was a sizeable proportion of people who earned an income that was less than P500 (U$83.00) a month. Most people had an income of between P1001and P2000 (U$167.00 – U$333.00) a month.

Benefits of tourism (importance of tourism) to Maun

When the respondents were asked if tourism was an important industry to Maun and whether it should be encouraged, a sizable majority of the respondents (84.4%) said that tourism was very important to Maun and that tourism related businesses and individuals derive benefits from it (Moswete *et al.*, 2009; Ndubano, 2000). For instance, 13% of the respondents said tourism has opened employment opportunities, with approximately 5% of respondents indicating that they owned land that was used purposely for tourism. Some of the benefits of tourism alluded to by the respondents were job creation, business opportunities such as roadside stalls for the sale of souvenirs (Figure 11.5), infrastructure development (improved internal roads, shopping complex) and increased visibility for local crafts.

Figure 11.5 Local people's roadside display of souvenirs for tourists in Maun

Knowledge of HIV/AIDS and Tourism

When asked if they had ever heard about tourism in their community, about 95% of survey respondents and all the key informants indicated they had and knew of tourism as business. Additionally, the survey respondents were asked, 'Is there a relationship between the development of tourism and the increasing HIV/AIDS in Maun?' As shown in Table 11.1, 46.2% of respondents were aware of the relationship between tourism and HIV/AIDS. Of those who indicated that they knew or were aware of the relationship, 26% were females and 20.2% were males. There were slightly more females (16.6%) than males (13.2%) who said there was no relationship or link between tourism and HIV/AIDS. Almost the same percentage of males (11.6%) and females (12.4%) answered that they did not know if there was an association between the two (Table 11.1).

As can be seen in Table 11.1, the respondents were also asked, 'Do you think travel and tourism can increase the spread of HIV/AIDS in your town (Maun)?' The second question on HIV/AIDS was asked in order to establish whether the respondents were knowledgeable about the idea that travel and tourism can increase the spread of the disease. Overall, respondents did not demonstrate a high awareness of the relationship. Over 50% responded that they did not know that travel and tourism could enhance the spread of the HIV/AIDS. Furthermore, cross-tabulation was undertaken to examine HIV/AIDS awareness based on the gender of the respondents (see Table 11.1). The data reveal that 28.6% of females and 24% of males did not know that tourism has the potential to increase the spread of the disease; a large and worrisome proportion

Table 11.1 Relationship between tourism and HIV/AIDS by respondents (gender)

Questions/Statements	Response	Maun (n = 500)	Gender (n = 500): M (Male n = 225); F (Female n = 275)
Is there a relationship between growth of tourism and incidences of HIV/AIDS?	Yes	231 (46.2%)	101 (20.2%) M 130 (26%) F
	No	149 (29.8%)	66 (13.2%) M 83 (16.6%) F
	Don't Know	120 (24.0%)	58 (11.6%) M; 62 (12.4%) F
	Total	500	500 (100%)
Do you think travel and tourism can increase the spread of HIV/AIDS in your town (Maun)?	Yes	137 (27.4%)	59 (11.8%) M; 78 (15.6%) F
	No	100 (20.0%)	46 (9.2%) M; 54 (10.8%) F
	Don't Know	263 (52.6%)	120 (24%) M; 143 (28.6%) F
	Total	500	500 (100%)

(52.6%) of the respondents (see Bene & Darkoh, 2012). The results of a Chi square test show no statistically significant difference between the men and women in terms of their awareness of the relationship between tourism and the spread of HIV/AIDS. The percentages of men (9.2%) and women (10.8%) from the study site who claimed that they did not know or were not aware that travel and tourism could increase the spread of HIV/AIDS were similar, as shown in Table 11.1.

In terms of age, the data show that 27.2% of those aged 16–40 and 16.4% of the 41–75 olds were aware of the relationship between tourism and HIV/AIDS. However, 28.8% of the 16–40 age group and 23.6% of the 41–75 age group said they did not know if there was a link between the development of tourism in their area and the increasing prevalence of HIV/AIDS. Additional statistical analysis shows a significant difference between the age groups ($\chi^2 = 37.388$, $p < 0.021$) in terms of knowledge or awareness that the development of tourism has the potential to increase the spread of HIV/AIDS in Maun. Above all, the data indicate that residents (72.6%[3]) were likely to say they did not know about or that there is no relationship between tourism growth and the increased spread of HIV/AIDS.

The second part of the analysis is based on material from key informant interviews. Of the 11 key informants, 7 were males and 4 were females. They were between 30 and 65 years old. The interview guide had open and closed questions. All of the interviews were conducted in English. All participants had high school certificates, vocational diplomas, college degrees or doctorates. In the interviews, they were asked if there is sex tourism in Maun. Some of them alluded to prostitution, especially female prostitutes engaged in heterosexual sex. For purposes of confidentiality, each individual key informant was assigned a pseudonym. Below are some of the direct quotes from the interviews with informants.

Ai-6-MD noted:

> Maun is known to be a transit for many international tourists going into the Okavango Delta, the Chobe National Park and a transfer hub linking major tourist centres such as Victoria Falls and Windhoek. Therefore, in my view I would like to believe that there is sex tourism in Maun so as to cater for sex tourists. In addition to that, there are some confirmations[sic] made by some of the Maun residents that sex tourism exists in Maun. The confirmations[sic] note that there is a certain place affectionately called 'Harare'[a city in Zimbabwe] identified for prostitution practices. Although that is the case, I have not made any observations regarding that. It is worth noting that I usually read about sex tourism in the form of prostitution in the newspapers and the internet. In a nutshell, if sex tourism really exists in Maun it is still a hidden practice.

Bae-15 K said:

I also learn there are some ladies who loiter around Maun lodge in the evenings. They offer service to visitors at Maun lodge. This one I have not seen but I have heard it is something that is going on.

All the key informants observed that there was a relationship between tourism development and incidences of HIV/AIDS and that tourism has the potential to contribute to the growth of HIV/AIDS in Maun. For example, there is high prevalence of HIV/AIDS in Maun (see Upton & Dolan, 2011).

Cai-3 stated:

In my view I believe that there is a relationship between HIV/AIDS and sex tourism. The relationship between HIV/AIDS and sex tourism is that there are risks involved in the sexual service transactions. For instance, sex workers engaging in commercial sex are vulnerable to HIV and also sexually transmitted diseases (STDs) due to having multiple sex partners. Also, the sex workers may have unprotected sex with a HIV positive client which ultimately puts their lives in danger as they are likely to get infected as well. This usually happens because some customers may demand not to use condoms indicating that using condoms reduces the sense of sexual pleasure. In essence, the relationship between HIV/AIDS and sex tourism exists.

Nyi-1M said:

... I think the question on the relationship between prostitution and HIV/AIDS is a tricky one. From a layman's perspective I think there is. So long as we know that the most commonly cited mode through which HIV spreads is sex, I would imagine prostitution provides a convenient ground for this spread; not least because sex providers can easily be compromised given their inferior economic status relative to that of their clients.

As stated by the above informants, there is indeed a link between tourism, prostitution and the transmission and spread of HIV/AIDS. This is because many times sex workers find themselves in compromising situations regardless of whether they are HIV/AIDS positive or negative.

Cai-3-L argues:

Prostitutes are a high-risk population for sexually transmitted diseases because many of their customers do not want to use condoms, and some of these could be carriers of STDs in general and the HIV virus in particular.

Bae- 15 K asserts:

I once visited one old man in my *ward* [residential block] here in Maun, who I always meet up with to discuss certain *ward* issues with. He stays at Boyei ward [name of the residential block in vernacular language] in Maun. I was to brief him about our meetings as I am the secretary, and he is the chairperson. It was in the evening. When I entered the yard, I saw three ladies. One of the ladies rushed to me and asked me 'do you want it?' I innocently asked her 'I want what?' She pointed to an area between her thighs. She was putting on a very low-cut skirt and evocative clothes. I quickly realised what she meant. I told her I was looking for an old man who lived in the area ... She showed me the house in which the old man lives. ... The lady I was speaking to was with three other ladies. All of ... origin [Foreigners] from the accent/tone and spoke non-local language. ... Later on I learnt the street where the yard is located is called 'Harare'. Ladies, especially of Zimbabwean origin, (plus some Batswana) ply the street in the evenings. The dark spot 'Harare' is now popular and some men go there 'to buy sex'. I am told the ladies are public as they offer their phone numbers. Once connected with a client they offer kickbacks [sexual service]. They service anybody who calls them or visits them. I am not sure if travellers go there. But I would like to believe if given contacts they would go there.

Almost all the interviewees demonstrated a high level of knowledge about sex work and/or commercial sex in Maun, but felt that it takes place in the dark. Despite this, the sex work clients and the spots they frequent are known.

Moi-11-R states:

... as sex and tourism is related to prostitution, I can say that sex tourism can be a vehicle for spreading HIV/AIDS especially through unprotected sex.

As you may be aware, prostitutes service many clients with different health status. Prostitutes have a higher chance of contracting STIs. Therefore, prostitutes have higher chances of infecting their clients [including] tourists with HIV and AIDS or re-infecting their client; tourists who get re-infections make it difficult to treat their HIV condition; prostitutes who are HIV negative may get infected by HIV positive tourists [or any of their clients]. Prostitutes who are already HIV positive may have re-infections providing an uphill battle against combating HIV/AIDS infections. – I say tourism has the potential for spreading and increasing HIV and AIDS at well-defined tourist destinations, as alluded to in Butler's (1980) destination lifecycle development stage.

Additionally, the informants demonstrated familiarity with the idea that tourism can exacerbate the spread of HIV/AIDS.

Upton (2002) concluded that there was a high level of awareness of HIV/AIDS in Maun in particular and Botswana in general. In contrast, in this study a large number of the household heads (respondents of the survey) in Maun had no knowledge of the disease. Furthermore, Upton (2002) states that the National AIDS Control Programme was established in 1989 and that there were billboards along major routes which helped to publicise information about the disease to the people (Figure 11.1). This current study, however, suggests the need to educate the residents of Maun about HIV/AIDS, sex and tourism. They need to be educated to know that what is done in the dark comes to light when an individual finds themselves with sexually transmitted diseases such as HIV/AIDS, or on the wrong side of the law since commercial sex, sex tourism and prostitution are illegal in Botswana.

The strategy for disseminating information needs to be varied and placed at strategic locations. The people should have access to electronic media since it has the potential to visually attract the attention of many people compared to leaflets and other print media. The use of electronic media is practical in Botswana, especially in urban centres and major villages. Also, a handful of rural villages are electrified, and have access to cellular phone towers and antennae. Consequently, even in these places some individuals would have access to cell phones, Botswana television (Btv) and radio stations. Facebook and WhatsApp remain the most popular social media in the urban areas of Botswana (Centre for Investigative Journalism, 2020). Social media, including Facebook and Twitter, is becoming more prevalent in Africa (Jotia, 2018), and 'in Botswana social media is being used and accessed without state of restrictions' (Jotia, 2018: 275). Radio is the main and relatively cheap information dissemination tool in rural and remote parts of the country. Also, the government provides radios and often times television sets in schools, regardless of geographic location. Ideally, more HIV/AIDS programmes should be aired to increase awareness. As it is, there are billboards along major roads, internal Maun roads (Figure 11.1) and public spaces or buildings with HIV/AIDS awareness messages. For example, 'why give it a blind eye when HIV/AIDS is so serious' or 'Aids can be stopped by: Abstaining; Condomising; No to premarital sex'.

In this study, the researcher observed that most of the written messages on billboards were in English and Setswana. The limiting factor in this case was that not all residents, especially the older ones, the commercial sex workers, prostitutes and the tourists have English or Setswana as their first language. This means that getting the message on HIV/AIDS across to everyone may not work.

Overall, the chapter argues that there is an inadequate knowledge about the relationship between tourism, travel and HIV/AIDS among the residents of Maun. This result was not expected as Upton (2002), and Upton and Dolan (2011) found evidence of HIV/AIDS education and prevention programmes in Botswana and Maun (Figure 11.1). The basic level of understanding/awareness of the relationship between tourism and HIV/AIDS and the possible increased spread of HIV/AIDS through travel and tourism can be linked to the HIV/AIDS study carried out in the Ngamiland district in 2006–2007. This study discovered that residents of the five villages within the Community Based Natural Resources Management Tourism Trust (or community tourism projects) had a greater awareness (or understanding) of the relationship between tourism and HIV/AIDS than those communities without a tourism industry (see Ngwenya *et al.*, 2007).

However, in the case of Maun the residents appear to comprehend the socio-economic benefits of tourism (Table 11.1), but tend to fail to fully appreciate the potential negative repercussions of association with the tourism industry. To maximise understanding of the positive and negative impacts of the link between sex and tourism, residents must be included in the planning and development of tourism projects, particularly in the early stages of projects (Butler, 1980). Effective educational programmes that engage with local people are also needed to boost their understanding of the relationships between sex, tourism and HIV/AIDS.

With reference to the literature, prostitution, same-sex work, female sex workers and sex tourism are illegal in Botswana (Lekorwe & Moseki, 2014; NACA,[4] 2009), but they happen anyway. They do not just happen in key tourism destinations such as Maun or the Okavango Delta region, but throughout Botswana. As a result of them being illegal, they take place in the dark or secretly. Around the world, Botswana is the country with the highest population living with HIV/AIDS (Bene & Darkoh, 2012; GoB, 2001; Ketshabile, 2011; Lekorwe & Moseki, 2014). Against this backdrop, we find some citizens who abhor prostitution and commercial sex (Bareki, 2019) and do not support it being legalised (Lesole, 2007). As observed:

> ... they imagine prostitutes as other people's sisters; other people's aunts, other people's mothers and other people's daughters – not relating to them directly. They dehumanise women they wish for prostitution. They reduce them from being intelligent beings to the level of wild beasts and then move swiftly to commodify them. After emptying such women of every imaginable humanity, they flip the argument and paint such women as lucky and fortunate to be making a bit of profit by selling themselves! What disgust!

> Over the past 10 years, we have seen a steady increase in Botswana's tourism that has gone far to diversify our national economy. To suggest that such tourism should be extended to the sale of female sex is insulting, piteous and the greatest expression of human debauchery. (Lesole, 2007: 1)

This kind of view is not, of course, unique to Botswana. Instead, it can be found in a wide range (geographically and economically) of countries. Some countries have not legalised prostitution and/or sex tourism and therefore operate with restrictive policies that have been formulated to guard against the growth of such activities.

In contrast, within Botswana there are those that argue for sex work or prostitution to be legalised (see Bauer & McKercher, 2003; Bell, 2009; Kayawe, 2017; Letshabo, 2001; Taylor, 2001; Ward-Pelar, 2010). There is lots of debate around sex work and sex and tourism globally. Referring to their edited book, *Sex and the Sexual during People's Leisure and Tourism Experiences,* Carr and Poria (2010: 181) recognised that through debates about sex and tourism it is possible to bring issues of sex that are often hidden in the dark into the light of public debate. Indeed, they stated that their book 'seeks to begin to rectify this situation by bringing the position and nature of sex and the sexual into the light of academic debate'. Amongst such debates are various arguments. For instance, there are those who support sex work due to the economic benefits for those involved despite the problems of HIV/AIDS (Hanson, 1997; Overall, 1992; Toska *et al.*, 2017; Ward-Pelar, 2009). In contrast, there those who are against sex work and abhor it as a result of the health related challenges of sex work and prostitution, and its impact on cultural traditions (Bauer & McKercher, 2003; Bareki, 2019; Bisika, 2009; Carter, 1998; Easterbrook, 2007; Hamlyn *et al.*, 2007; Kibicho, 2016; Lekorwe & Moseki, 2014; Lesole, 2007; Omondi & Ryan, 2017). In the case of Botswana, a country known to have the highest HIV/AIDS in the world, Letshabo argues:

> ... The fact that sex work is illegal and the homophobia attached to it drives the industry underground. It is high time our society starts doing something about commercial sex work. By stigmatising sex works we are allowing the abuse and exploitation of those who benefit from it. We ignore the fact that sex work is a collective strategy to meet certain needs in society ... Our country faces the problem of high HIV/AIDS prevalence. By accepting sex work as a normal part of our society we are actually inviting the sex workers to come out and help us in this struggle against AIDS. (Letshabo, 2001: 28)

Consequently, we can see arguments that negatively portray Botswana's policies that do not support sex work. At the same time, HIV/AIDS is ever increasing among the 15 to 24 age group in Botswana (NACA, 2009). This situation is also a challenge for other parts of the world, including, Kenya (Kibicho, 2016), Vietnam (Prideaux & Agrua, 2002) and Malawi (Bisika, 2009).

Conclusion

The study found that the proportion of respondents in Maun who did not have knowledge about the relationship between HIV/AIDS and tourism was high. This is a warning sign of looming problems in the country with the highest proportion of people living with HIV and where the tourism industry is continuing to expand. There seems to be an inadequate knowledge of the link between HIV/AIDS and tourism within the community. Hence, the residents of Maun should be educated both formally and informally in order to understand the relationship and how they can avoid situations that could put them at risk of infection. Several government programmes are in place, yet awareness is still very low. Assessment of the awareness of the relationship between HIV/AIDS and tourism can be measured by understanding the host community's perception of the nature of the positive and negative impacts of tourism. Based on the previous findings by Botswana Review (2003, 2005), BTDP (1998), Ngwenya *et al.* (2007), Mbaiwa, (2005), Moswete *et al.* (2009), Ketshabile (2011), Lesole (2007) and WTTC (2013), it can be concluded that tourism is important for Botswana, especially as it generates jobs and income for rural dwellers, such as in Maun. However, Botswana also needs to pay attention to the negative global image of the country borne by HIV/AIDS and its potential effects on growth of the tourism industry (WTTC, 2017) and health of both local people and tourists (see GoB, 2016).

Information dissemination about the relationship between HIV/AIDS and tourism can occur through the traditional public assembly (Kgotla[5]). The Kgotla is the intuition through which there is facilitation of participatory governance (UNDP, 2002). This entity offers a potential route through which to educate the local population about sex work, prostitution and the tourism industry. In addition, Village Development Committees (VDCs) are village level institutions that should offer a link between people in the villages and government institutions and Non-Governmental Organisations (NGOs) that assist with HIV/AIDS to initiate awareness programmes. In doing so, they can further help to educate people about the links between HIV/AIDS and tourism and how to ensure that associated negative implications of tourism are minimised.

The government should also examine other communication channels to educate people about the linkage between travel, tourism and the transmission of HIV/AIDS. Although social media use (especially WhatsApp, Facebook) is practical in the country, it is fairly new and does not reach all the vulnerable communities in rural and the most remote parts of the country. However, radio is the main and reasonably cheap information dissemination tool in rural Botswana. Although the government provides radios and often times television sets in schools, the scope for coverage remains a challenge. Despite this, increased use and accessibility of these communication and information distribution tools could help towards understanding of the relationship between sex tourism and the spread and transmission of HIV/AIDS in Botswana. Such tools could also be of use elsewhere in the world.

Finally, it is important that further research is undertaken throughout Botswana, and other countries, especially those with high rates of HIV/AIDS, on the links between this disease and tourism. This is vital in the face of the growing scale and importance (to individuals' livelihood and the health of national economies) of tourism. Through research, we can help to combat ignorance, positively influence public opinion, increase individual welfare and protect the tourism industry from the negative imagery associated with HIV/AIDS.

Acknowledgements

The author gratefully acknowledge all survey respondents whose participation made this study possible. In particular, I would like to thank Gotsileone Mosimanegape, Goitseone Begani, Johnny Marudu and Kenosi Nkape for assisting in the data collection and Mr Goitsemodimo Koorutwe for making the site map. In particular, this research has been made possible by the provision of financial support by the University of Botswana, Research and Development Unit.

Notes

(1) CSO: Central Statistics Office.
(2) Tourists and holidaymakers who travel across the land by car, off-road vehicles or horse safaris but not by sea or airplanes across countries to destinations.
(3) A total of 72.6% of No and Don't know responses combined (see Table 11.1).
(4) NACA: Botswana National AIDS Coordinating Agency.
(5) A formal meeting place or assembly associated with the institution of traditional leadership (Mgadla & Campbell, 1989).

References

Allen, T. and Heald, S. (2004) HIV/AIDS policy in Africa: What has worked in Uganda and what has failed in Botswana. *Journal of International Development* 16, 1141–1154.

Archer, B. and Fletcher, E. (1996) The economic impact of tourism in the Seychelles. *Annals of Tourism Research* 23 (1), 32–47.

Bareki, K.A. (2019) Sex and Intimacy 101: Sex Tourism has become fashionable. *Midweek Sun*. See http://www.themidweeksun.co.bw.p.13 (accessed February 2020).

Bauer, T. and McKercher, B. (eds) (2003) *Sex and Tourism Journeys of Romance, Love and Lust*. New York: Haworth Hospitality Press.

Bell, K.J. (2009) A feminist's argument on how sex work can benefit women. *Inquiries Journal/Student Pulse* 1 (11). See http://www.inquiriesjournal.com/a?id=28 (accessed February 2020).

Bender, K. and Furman, R. (2004) The implications of sex tourism on men's social, psychological, and physical health. *The Qualitative Report* 9 (2), 176–191.

Bene, M. and Darkoh, M.K. (2012) Trends and perceived determinants of HIV/AIDS in Rural Areas: The case of Thamaga and surrounding villages, Botswana. *Eastern Africa Social Science Research Review* 28 (2), 2–26.

Bisika, T. (2009) Sexual and reproductive health and HIV/AIDS risk perception in the Malawi tourism industry. *Malawi Medical Journal* 21 (2), 75–80.

Bollinger, L. and Stover, J. (1999) *The Economic Impact of AIDS in Botswana*. The Policy Project: The Futures Group International in collaboration with Research Triangle Institute (RTI) and the Centre for Development and Population Activities (CEDPA). See http://www.policyproject.com/pubs/SEimpact/botswana.pdf (accessed August 2018).

Botswana IAMAT (2020) *Botswana General Health Risks: Sexually Transmitted Infections*. See www.iaamat.org/country/Botswana/risk/sexually-transmitted–infections (accessed January 2020).

Botswana Institute Development for Policy Analysis (BIDPA) (2000) *Macroeconomic Impacts of the HIV/AIDS Epidemic in Botswana. Final Report*. Gaborone.

Botswana Review (2003) *Botswana Review* (22nd edn). Botswana Export Development & Investment Authority. Gaborone. Botswana.

Botswana Review (2005) *Botswana Review* (25th edn). Botswana Export Development & Investment Authority. Gaborone. Botswana.

Botswana Tourism Development Program (BTDP) (1998) *Visitor Survey*. Ministry of Commerce and Industry. Gaborone. Botswana.

Brayley R., Sheldon, P. and Var, T. (1990) Perceived influence of tourism on social issues. *Annals of Tourism Research* 17, 285–289.

Butler, R.W. (1980) The concept of a tourism area cycle of evolution: Implications for management of resources. *Canadian Geographer* 24 (1), 5–12.

Carr, N. and Poria, Y. (eds) (2010) *Sex and the Sexual during People's Leisure and Tourism Experiences*. Newcastle: Cambridge Scholars Publishing.

Carter, S. (1998) Tourists' and travelers' social construction of Africa and Asia as risky locations. *Tourism Management* 19 (4), 349–358.

Centre for Investigative Journalism (2020) Facebook remains the most popularly used social media platform in Botswana. See https://inkjournalism.org/1571/ (accessed February 2020).

Central Statistic Office (CSO) (2011) *2011 Botswana Population and Housing Census*. See http://www.gov.bw/en/citizens/topics/statistics/ (accessed September 2019).

Cohen, D. (2001) Joint epidemics: Poverty and AIDS in sub-Saharan Africa. *Harvard International Review* 23, 54–59.

Creswell, J.W. and Clark, V.L.P. (2011) *Designing and Conducting Mixed Methods Research* (2nd edn). Los Angeles: Sage.

Dixon, S., McDonald, S. and Roberts, J. (2002) The Impact of HIV and AIDS on Africa's economic development. *British Medical Journal* 324, 232–234.

Easterbrook, P. (2007) Sexual health: Overview. *Occupational Medicine* 57, 311–212.

Goeldner, C.R. and Ritchie, J.R.B. (2012) *Tourism: Principles, Practices, Philosophies* (12th edn). Hoboken, NY: John Wiley and Sons.

Government of Botswana [GoB] (1998) *Botswana National Settlement Policy*. Government Paper No. 2 of 1998. Gaborone: Government Printer.

Government of Botswana [GoB]. (2001) *Botswana National Atlas*. Department of Surveys & Mapping, Botswana.

Government of Botswana [GoB] (2016) *Vision 2036: Achieving Prosperity for All*. Prepared by the vision 2036 presidential Task Force, July 2016. Lentswe La Lesedi PTY, LTD. Gaborone, Botswana.

Hamlyn, E., Peer, A. and Easterbrook, P. (2007) Sexual health and HIV in travelers and expatriates. *Occupational Medicine* 57, 313–321.

Hanson, J. (1997) Sex tourism as work in New Zealand: A discussion with Kiwi prostitutes. In M. Oppermann (ed.) *Pacific Rim Tourism* (pp. 196–205). Wallingford: CABI.

Hatch, J.A. (2002) *Doing Qualitative Research in Education Settings*. Albany, NY: State University of New York Press.

Herold, E.S. and Van Kerkwijk, C. (1992) Aids and sex tourism. *Aids Society* 4 (1), 1–8.

Herold, E., Garcia, R. and Demoya, T. (2001) Female tourists and beach boys: Romance or sex tourism? *Annals of Tourism Research* 28 (4), 978–997.

Hope, K.R. (2013) Sex tourism in Kenya: An analytical review. *Tourism Analysis* 18, 533–542.

Jeffreys, S. (2003) Sex tourism: Do women do it too? *Leisure Studies* 22, 22238

Jotia, A. L. (2018) The role of social media in freeing Botswana from state control of the media. *Journal of Contemporary African Studies* 36 (2), 264-278.

Kang'ethe, S.M. (2014) Social capital from informal networks can be a fertile niche to mitigate HIV/AIDS and poverty: Examples from South Africa and Botswana. *Journal of Human Ecology* 47 (2), 185–192.

Kayawe, B. (2017) *Revealed: The Dark World of Male, Female Sex Work.* See https://www.mmegi.bw/index.php?aid=71405&dir=2017/september/01 (accessed May 2019).

Kgathi, D.L. and Motsholapheko, M.R. (2011) Livelihood activities and income portfolios in rural areas of the Okavango Delta, Botswana. In D.L. Kgathi, B.N. Ngwenya and M.B.K. Darkoh (eds) *Rural Livelihoods, Risk and Political Economy of Access to Natural Resources in the Okavango Delta, Botswana* (pp. 35–54). New York: Nova Science Publishers.

Kgathi, D.L., Ngwenya, B.N., and Darkoh, M.B.K. (eds) (2011) *Rural Livelihoods, Risk and Political Economy of Access to Natural Resources in the Okavango Delta, Botswana.* New York: Nova Science publishers.

Ketshabile, L. (2011) Utilising tourism potential in combating the spread of HIV/AIDS through poverty alleviation in rural areas of Botswana. *Journal of Business Management and Economics* 2 (1), 1–11.

Kibicho, W. (2016) *Sex Tourism in Africa: Kenya's Booming Industry.* London: Routledge.

Lacey, G. (2012) A review of sex tourism in Africa: Kenya's booming industry. *Tourism Geographies* 14 (3), 528–531.

Lekorwe, M. and Moseki, K. (2014) Afrobarometer Dispatch No 8. Batswana Affirm Their Personal Freedoms but Disapprove of Same-sex Relationships. See http:// www.afrobarometer.org/sites/default/files/publications/ Dispatch/ab_r6_dispatchno8.pdf.

Lesole, I. (2007) Sex tourism is an insult. See http://www.sundaystandard.info/sex-tourisminsult (accessed May 2019).

Letshabo, M.L. (2001) The noticeboard: Where views are aired and issues discussed. In M. Segwabe and V. Chipfakacha (eds) *AIDucation Brochure: The AIDS Information Booklets.* Gaborone, Botswana.

Mbaiwa, J. (2005) Enclave tourism and its socio-economic impacts in the Okavango Delta, Botswana. *Tourism Management* 26, 157–172

Mbaiwa, J., Toteng, E. and Moswete, N. (2007) Problems and prospects for the development of urban tourism in Gaborone and Maun, Botswana. *Development Southern Africa* 24 (5), 725–739.

Mgadla, P.T. and Campbell, A.C. (1989) Dikgotla, dikgosi and the protectorate administration. In J.D. Holm and P. Molutsi (eds) *Democracy in Botswana* (pp. 48–57). Athens, OH: Ohio University Press.

Miller, C.L., Bangsberg, D.R., Tuller, D.M., Senkungu, A., Kwawuma, A., Frongillo, E.A. and Weiser, S.D. (2011) Food insecurity and sexual risk in an HIV endemic community in Uganda. *AIDS Behaviour* 15 (7), 1512–1519.

Mmeso, P. (2015) Male prostitution growing in Botswana, The Patriot Newspaper. See http:// www.thepatriot.co.bw/lifestyle/item/846-male-prostitution-growing-inbotswana.html (accessed May 2019).

Moswete, N. and Mavondo, F. (2003) Problems facing the tourism industry of Botswana. *Botswana Notes and Records* 35, 69–78.

Moswete, N., Toteng, E.N. and Mbaiwa, J. (2009) Resident involvement and participation in urban tourism development: A comparative Study in Maun and Gaborone, Botswana. *Urban Forum* 20 (5), 381–394.

[NACA] Botswana National AIDS Coordinating Agency (2009) *The Second Botswana National Strategic Framework for HIV and AIDS – 2010-2016.* Gaborone: Botswana National AIDS Coordinating Agency. See https://www.healthpolicyproject.com/ pubs/462_HPPBotswanaBriefMarchFINAL.PDF (accessed February 2020).

Ndubano, E. (2000) The Economic Impacts of Tourism on the Local People: The case of Maun in the Ngamiland-Sub District. Unpublished Thesis. University of Botswana.

Ngwenya, B.N., Potts, F.C. and Thakadu, O.T. (2007) *The Impact of HIV/AIDS on CBNRM in Botswana: The case study of Ngamiland*. IUCN, CBNRM Support Programme. Occasional Paper N0. 16. Gaborone.

Omondi, R.K. and Ryan, C. (2017) Sex tourism, romantic safaris, prayers and witchcraft at the Kenyan Coast. *Tourism Management* 58, 217–227.

Oppermann, M. (1999) Sex tourism. *Annals of Tourism Research* 26 (2), 251–266.

Overall, C. (1992) What's wrong with prostitution? Evaluating sex work. *Signs: Journal of Women in Culture and Society* 17 (4), 705–724.

Portes, A. (1998) Social capital: Its origins and application in modern sociology. *Annual Review in Sociology* 24, 14.

Prideaux, B.R. and Agrua, J. (2002) Tourism and the threat of HIV/AIDS in Vietnam. Asia Pacific *Journal of Tourism Research* 7 (1), 1–10.

Rajaraman, D., Russell, S. and Heymann, J. (2006) HIV/AIDS, income loss and economic survival in Botswana. *AIDS CARE* 18 (7), 656–662.

Rossman, G.B and Rallis, S.F. (2017) *An Introduction to Qualitative Research: Learning in the Field* (4th edn). Singapore: Sage.

Stephens, L.L., Bachhhuber, M.A., Seloilwe, E., Gungqisa, N., Mmelesi, M., Bussmann, H. Marlinkm, R.G. and Western, C.W. (2012) HIV-Knowledge, attitudes and practice among educated young adults in Botswana. *Journal of AIDS and HIV Research* 4 (6), 159–164.

Taylor, J.S. (2001) Dollars are a girl's best friend? Female tourists' sexual behaviour in the Caribbean. *Sociology* 35 (3), 749–764.

Toska, E., Pantelic, M., Meinck, F., Keck, K., Haghighat, R. and Cluver, L. (2017) Sex in the shadow of HIV: A systematic review of prevalence, risk factors and interventions to reduce sexual risk taking among HIV-positive adolescents and youth in sub-Saharan Africa. *PloS One* 12 (6), e0178106 Epub.

United Nations Development Programme [UNDP] (2002) *Human Development Report*. New York: Oxford University Press.

United Nations World Tourism Organisation [UNWTO] (2018) *World Tourism Organisation Tourism Highlights 2018*. See https://www.e-unwto.org/doi/pdf/10.18111/9789284419876 (accessed February 2020).

Upton, R.L. (2002) Perceptions of and attitudes towards male infertility in Northern Botswana: Some implications for family planning and Aids Prevention Policies. *African Journal of Reproductive Health* 6 (3), 103–111.

Upton, R.L. and Dolan, E.M. (2011) Sterility and stigma in an Era of HIV and AIDS: Narratives of risk assessment among men and women in Northern Botswana. *African Journal of Reproduction Health* 15 (1), 95–102.

Veal, A.J. (2006) *Research Methods for Leisure and Tourism: A Practical Guide* (3rd edn). Essex, UK: Pearson Education.

Ward-Pelar, J.M. (2010) Rationalizing sexual tourism: How some countries benefit from selling sex. *Inquiries Journal/Student Pulse* 2(04). See http://www.inquiriesjournal.com/a?id=235 (accessed February 2020).

Whiteside, A. (2002) Poverty and HIV in Africa. *Third World Quarterly* 23 (2), 313–332.

World Bank (2005) *World Development Report*. Oxford: Oxford University Press.

World Travel and Tourism Council (WTTC) (2013) *Botswana: The Impact of Travel and Tourism on Jobs and the Economy*. London: World Travel and Tourism Council.

World Travel and Tourism Council (WTTC) (2015) *Jamaica: The Impact of Travel and Tourism on Jobs and the Economy*. London: World Travel and Tourism Council.

World Travel and Tourism Council (WTTC) (2016) *Tourism as a Driver of Peace: Quantitative Analysis on the Link between Peace and Tourism*. London: World Travel and Tourism Council.

World Travel and Tourism Council (WTTC) (2017) *Botswana: The Impact of Travel and Tourism on Jobs and the Economy*. London: World Travel and Tourism Council.

Part 3: The Dark Side of Sex and Tourism: Child Sex Tourism and Sexual Harassment

12 Sexual Harassment in the Hotel Housekeeping Department

Irina Oliveira and Vitor Ambrósio

Introduction

The housekeeping profession is a historically devalued, invisible kind of work, where employees face various forms of abuse and exploitation, with research indicating that risk of sexual harassment is very high (Gilbert *et al.*, 1998). Hotel employees may be more susceptible to these abuses, given employees work unusual hours in an environment of much social interaction. In addition, there is an inherent sexual implication to the concept of hospitality service, wherein a hotel's management is eager to please wealthy clients, even if that means turning a blind eye to the complaints of their staff (Guerrier & Adib, 2000; Harris *et al.*, 2011). These women (because housekeeping is a profession dominated by women) work in isolated halls, without security or the means of calling for help.

With this chapter we ask: What is the extent of sexual harassment involving housemaids in Portuguese hotels? And what are the sexual harassment issues housemaids deal with in Portuguese hotels? This is an unashamedly exploratory chapter, one that delves into a dark side of the tourism industry where few industry operators or tourism researchers have shone a light.

Theoretical Framework

Farley (1978) coined the phrase 'sexual harassment' and introduced it to the public's attention. She claimed that sexual harassment was the result of the union of capitalism and patriarchy mutually reinforcing women's inferior position in the labour force.

Much of the literature on sexual harassment has lacked a universal definition of the problem. Sexual harassment can be perceived differently depending on contextual and legal perspectives. Sexual harassment in one third of the countries in the world is defined by labour law as violating the citizen's rights to equal employment opportunities. These laws and rules were established in terms of education and housing, and especially presenting sexual harassment in work environments (Wang, 2006).

The European Commission report *Sexual Harassment at the Workplace in the European Union* (1999) defines sexual harassment as an unwanted conduct of a sexual nature, or other conduct based on sex affecting the dignity of women and men at work, such as unwelcome physical, verbal or non-verbal conduct. The International Labor Organization (2019) defines sexual harassment as acts, innuendo, forced physical contact and/or irrelevant invitations provided that they have one of the following characteristics: (a) be a clear condition for maintaining employment; (b) change in career promotions; (c) harm the professional performance, humiliate, insult or intimidate the victim.

In Portugal, Article 29 of the Labour Code defines sexual and moral harassment as unwanted behaviour based on discrimination, practiced upon those who desire access to employment, self-employment, work or training, with the purpose or effect of disrupting or embarrassing the person, affecting the dignity of the person or creating an intimidating, hostile, humiliating or offensive environment (Portuguese Labor Code, 2018). According to the Comissão para a Igualdade e para os Direitos das Mulheres – Portuguese Commission for Equality and Women's Rights, sexual harassment is a form of violence that particularly affects women, and that occurs because some men perceive women as an inferior species, especially in the working world. It reduces female individuality to women's physical and body image and is the result of men treating women as sexual objects (Comissão para a Igualdade e para os Direitos das Mulheres, 2003).

The effects of harassment on the workforce translate into decreased productivity and severe economic losses for the organisation (Sandroff, 1992). Research shows that sexual harassment in the hotel industry has perverse negative effects on the organisation's workforce, including increased absenteeism and turnover, decreased motivation and loyalty and broader psycho-social consequences for the victim of harassment (Filby, 1992; Gilbert *et al.*, 1998; Gutek, 1985).

Williams *et al.* (1999) state that in some cases, reporting sexually unpleasant behaviour to the manager does not result in a complaint of sexual harassment, and it may often result in the loss of employment for the person who reported the case. Similarly, Folgero and Fjeldstad (1995) concluded that those who complained frequently of sexual harassment were reprimanded by their co-workers and encouraged to either take it or leave.

Hotels may be more susceptible to these abuses, given employees work unusual hours in an environment of much social interaction. In addition, there is an inherent sexual implication to the concept of hospitality service, wherein a hotel's management is eager to please wealthy clients – even if that means turning a blind eye to the complaints of one of their staff (Guerrier & Adib, 2000; Harris *et al.*, 2011). The everyday insecurities in this industry regarding sexual harassment in the workplace has been called a pandemic problem illustrated by decreased productivity, increased absenteeism, lowered morale, high employee turnover and sometimes resulting in costly legal suits (Gilbert *et al.*, 1998).

A very familiar case in tourism is the difference of status and economic means between tourists and employees in the tourism industry. The situation is often further complicated by the presence of cultural and racial/ethnic differences between hosts and guests.

Within this context there are several questions that need to be raised about sexual harassment: Can it happen only to women? Must it occur more than once? Must it be deliberate? Is it tied to the factors of a job? Can it only happen in situations of uneven power? Can sexual harassment include comments, touching, cornering, joking, posters, leering and obscene gestures?

Purpose of the Study

While the literature cited above demonstrates the risk, prevalence and impact of sexual harassment on the hotel workforce, it is still arguably an under-researched issue given its importance and the size of the global hotel industry. In addition, there is a scarcity of research on Portuguese hotel and service organisations regarding sexual harassment. This is compounded by the fact that employment in the Portuguese tourism sector has reached record numbers and in 2018 represented 6.7% of the national economy (Turismo de Portugal, 2019).

The purpose of the study on which this chapter is based was to: (1) Identify the themes related to the experience of sexual harassment for hotel housekeepers; and (2) Measure the prevalence of reports of sexual harassment in the sample.

Methodology

We adopted a qualitative interview approach to understand the experience of the participants with sexual harassment. Quantitative data were also collected via a survey, in order to measure the frequency of reports of sexual harassment, as well as the prevalence of situational variables.

For this study, we investigated housekeeping employees' experiences of sexual harassment in five hotels; four hotels that belong to a national hotel chain (that is, a Portuguese hotel brand) and one that belongs to an international hotel chain in Lisbon (that is, a foreign hotel brand). The hotels agreed to participate while being assured of their anonymity. All hotels were located in the greater Lisbon area.

Qualitative interviews

The data were collected by semi-structured interviews that lasted between 15 and 30 minutes. It is important to mention that our initial objective was to include more hotels in the sample, but unfortunately that was not possible due to the fact that the majority of the hotels contacted did not wish to take part in the study. We take a qualitative, exploratory and generative approach to analyse the experiences of the hotel housekeepers concerning the issue of sexual harassment in the workplace. The goal of this analysis is to examine the impact of sexual harassment and generate new research perspectives. Kvale (1996) defines qualitative research interviews as an 'attempt to comprehend the world from the subject's point of view, to clarify the meaning of people's experiences (...)'. We used qualitative interviewing for two reasons. Firstly, this method gives the participants the opportunity to provide the researcher with a full description of their experiences and with it a wider understanding. Secondly, through qualitative research directions for future research can be derived from the data (Eyisi, 2016).

When we think about research into sexual harassment, quantitative research methods have been adopted in most cases. For a better, more nuanced understanding of the sexual harassment experiences of housekeepers it is crucial to undertake a qualitative study. Social differences and cultures are sometimes neglected in the research findings of work on sexual harassment (Welsh, 1999). Qualitative research methods can reveal sexual harassment seen and experienced in the daily work environment (Folgero & Fjeldstad, 1995) and the coping strategies developed by women (Hughes & Tadic, 1998).

Quantitative survey

In addition to interviews, we explored the extent of reports of sexual harassment issues in the sampled hotels through the use of survey results. The goal was to understand common patterns in the behaviour of sexual harassment, identifying four key issues: gender difference in reactions to sexual behaviours in the hotel industry; initiators of sexual behaviours in the hotel workplace; hotel employee's knowledge of the existence of policies and procedures about sexual harassment in the hotel; and how the policies of the hotel moderate sexual harassment.

Participants

Sixty participants, 58 females and only two males took part in the study. The participants were between 21 and 64 years of age. Concerning the academic qualifications of the sample, 25% have 4th grade, 48.3%

have 9th grade, 20% have 12th grade qualifications and 6.7% have a bachelor degree. We can conclude that the majority of the participants have between 4th grade (four school years) and 9th grade (nine school years) qualifications. Concerning the time working in the organisation, the participants replied as follows: 10% had been working for less than 6 months in the organisation; 8.3% between 6 months and 1 year; 21.7% between 1 and 5 years; 28.3% between 5 and 10 years; 16.7% between 10 and 20 years; and 15% for more than 20 years.

The interviews took place in the guest rooms, without the use of audio-recording devices. The guest rooms were chosen as the location of the interviews in order to assure the privacy of the respondents. The first hotel where the interviews were conducted was a four star hotel with more than 500 rooms, which belongs to an international chain. These interviews occurred in April of 2012. A total of 25 employees were interviewed. The second hotel is a five star hotel with more than 140 rooms, where 13 housekeepers were interviewed in July of 2012. The third is a four star hotel that is composed of more than 150 rooms, where 10 housekeepers were interviewed in July of 2012. The fourth hotel is a four star one that is composed of 24 apartments and belongs to a national hotel chain. Three housekeepers were interviewed at this hotel in July of 2012. The fifth hotel has 124 rooms and belongs to a national hotel chain. Nine housekeepers from this hotel were interviewed in July of 2012. All of the participants were asked to fill out the survey before the start of the interview.

Findings

The respondents described various experiences related to sexual harassment organised around the themes of security, isolation and fear of the consequences. One housekeeper of African heritage described an incident that occurred while she was cleaning a room and the guest entered. She thought it was odd when he locked the door as he entered. While she was cleaning she bent down, at which point the guest grabbed her. She ran away from him around the room and then ran over the bed, opened the door and exited the room. She complained to the manager who wanted to press charges but she declined. She stated that she was too afraid of the consequences for her reputation, for her husband and children, and that people would not believe her story. This case illustrates the problem of isolation and lack of security, as well as the fear of confronting the perpetrator, in this case even with management support.

The problem of isolation and lack of security comes up frequently, usually with stories of abusive guests. One participant from Brazil said that a foreign guest, who did not speak Portuguese, saw her cleaning the hallways and motioned for her to enter his room. When she entered, he put on a pornographic movie, which made her feel very uncomfortable, causing her to leave. A similar story was told by a Portuguese housekeeper who was 50 years of age. She described an incident where a guest saw her cleaning the hallways at a late hour and signalled for her to enter his room. When she entered, she saw various sex toys around the room. The guest asked her to spend the night with him, which caused her to feel anxious and leave.

The respondents often described stories of abusive guests who saw the isolation of the housekeeper as an opportunity for sexual behaviour. One Portuguese woman described a recurring guest who was known for walking naked in the halls. One day, she was cleaning his room and bent down, at which point he grabbed her, causing her to panic. She ran outside the room and he followed her, naked. She reached the elevator and got away, and asked for help from a security guard. The security guard went to the guest's bedroom, but at this stage he was dressed, and no action was taken. A similar story was told by a woman of African descent. She spoke of a recurring guest who would often talk to her, always being very polite. He asked her for her telephone number and she declined to give it. After leaving and returning to the hotel once again, he asked her to have dinner with him. She declined once again, but this time he became aggressive and grabbed her arm roughly. She pushed him away and screamed. She ran and escaped to the elevator, finding a security guard to ask for help. The guard spoke to the guest, warning him that his behaviour was not acceptable.

The problem of abusive guests may present itself as stories of aggressors, but sometimes the stories describe men who do not understand the limits of the housekeeping service. One woman of Eastern European descent described a man who grabbed her in his room. She pushed him away and left the room, but he asked her to return, offering her one euro to have sexual relations with him (in fact, only one euro). Another housekeeper, a middle-aged Portuguese woman, spoke about a Middle-Eastern man who offered her money to have sexual relations with him. She declined and he did not insist.

These cases illustrate the themes of lack of security, isolation, abusive guests and fear of confrontation. Understanding the most important issues that housekeepers deal with concerning the problem of sexual harassment is a crucial step in developing a research agenda and defining policy recommendations.

Survey Analysis

In this section we use descriptive statistics to analyse the responses to the survey, with the goal of measuring the extent of reports of sexual harassment related issues in the sample. We begin with a global analysis of the sample and then proceed to describe the significant differences in answers between the different categories of hotel chains; namely we compare the national hotel with the international hotel chains.

In reply to the question, 'What do you understand by sexual harassment in the working relationship?' 28.3% of the respondents replied that sexual harassment in the working environment to them is physical (i.e. touching, kissing, rape and physical assault). Twenty percent of the respondents replied that sexual harassment in the working relationship to them is an unwelcome sexual advance. Thirty percent of the respondents replied that sexual harassment in the working relationship to them is verbal; in other words, it is inappropriate remarks about clothes, sexual remarks and/or comments on how they look. Eighteen percent of the respondents answered that sexual harassment in the working relationship is requests for sexual favours.

When asked, 'Have you ever been sexually harassed?', 58.3% of participants replied 'yes'. When asked, 'What kinds of harassment have you suffered?', 30% of the participants replied that they had been harassed physically, 50% of the participants replied that they had been harassed verbally.

When asked, 'In your opinion, what are the causes of sexual harassment in the hotel?', 66.7% of the participants answered that the cause of sexual harassment in the hotel is 'an abuse of power and hostility'. When asked, 1.7% of the respondents stated that the sexualisation of women is the cause of sexual harassment in the hotel. 13.3% of participants replied it was linked to spending long hours with guests. 16.7% of respondents answered it was due to the intimacy, non-sexual, shared by guests and employees.

To determine hotel employee's knowledge of the existence of policies and procedures on sexual harassment in the hotel property they were asked, 'Have you ever complained to your superior of being sexually harassed?' Only 35% of the respondents replied with 'yes'. In reply to the question 'In the hotel where you work, are the staff and directors given guidelines for dealing with sexual harassment?', 80% of the participants replied with yes, with the remaining 20% stating that the hotel they work in has no guidelines.

As part of the survey, respondents were asked about their views regarding the impact of sexual harassment policies in the workplace. In response to the question, 'Can the work environment influence the occurrence of sexual harassment in the workplace?', 60% of the participants replied with 'yes'.

Comparison of National Hotel Chain with International Hotel Chain

When asked, 'Have you ever had training about sexual harassment in the hotel where you work?', all 25 respondents of the international hotel replied 'yes' to having had training. On the contrary, all the participants of the national hotel chain answered 'no' to ever having training about sexual harassment in the hotel where they work.

Conclusion and Recommendations

In this exploratory study, more than half of the participants (58.3%) reported having been sexually harassed. At the same time, the results show that only 35% of the sample said they had actually complained. The results suggest that discussing sexual harassment is still a 'taboo' and because of that most women choose to remain silent. We can compare these results with Gutek's study (1985), where 35% of the female and 37% of the male respondents reported experiencing some form of harassment. In this study the results showed that even with the existence of clear guidelines for staff and management, the employees do not complain to their superiors.

Our results also show that only one of the hotels in our sample offered training about sexual harassment to its housekeepers, specifically the international hotel. This suggests that employees do not have balanced information about this issue, making them even more vulnerable. Future research should investigate the reasons why some hotels choose to invest in sexual harassment training while others do not, and how this affects the employees.

The results of this research show that sexual harassment is a very real problem for housekeeping staff working in Portugal. With the interviews conducted, we demonstrated that the participants suffered various types of sexual harassment: physical, verbal, inappropriate requests for massages, unwelcome sexual advances and requests for sexual favours.

Upon review of notable examples of policy guidelines, namely the European Commission *Sexual Harassment at the Workplace in the European Union* (1999), the Australian Human Rights Commission *Code of Practice for Employers* (2008), and the Comissão para a Igualdade e para os Direitos das Mulheres – Portuguese Commission for Equality and Women's Rights (2003), we conclude that the employer has the ethical responsibility of reducing, avoiding and/or preventing sexual harassment or discrimination. The hotel employer should take reasonable steps to prevent sexual harassment. For it to be possible to prevent sexual harassment from occurring, it is crucial for an employer to have a sexual harassment policy and try to implement it as fully as possible and monitor its effectiveness.

We suggest that the hospitality industry use some of the following steps in order to prevent sexual harassment: get high-level management support for implementing a comprehensive strategy to address sexual harassment, write and implement a sexual harassment policy, develop a written handbook which prohibits sexual harassment and ensure the policy can be consulted on the organisations' intranet. When new staff start working in the hotel, it is important to provide them with the policy and other relevant information on sexual harassment. In the case of housekeeping, since a majority of housekeepers do not have much academic background it is crucial to translate the policy into relevant community languages where required so it is accessible to staff from linguistically and culturally diverse backgrounds. Since sexual harassment is such a sensitive topic, it is important to conduct training to augment knowledge and understanding of specific behaviours and attitudes that may amount to sexual harassment under the sex discrimination act.

It is crucial to provide employees with advice on what to do if sexually harassed, with a strong focus on confidentiality and the assurance that even if they complain they will not be victimised or ridiculed. It is important that staff are given information on how to deal with sexual harassment themselves and they should not be pressured into confronting their harasser unless they are confident enough to do so. All complaints should be treated in a fair, sensitive and confidential manner. Encouraging the reporting of behaviour which violates the sexual harassment policy could promote appropriate standards of conduct at all times.

When selecting management positions, we should ensure that one of the requirements for these positions is an understanding of and ability to deal with sexual harassment issues as part of the overall responsibility for human resources. Finally, there should be a periodical review of the policy to ensure its effectiveness and update the information.

Much of the research to date in this field has focused on the sexualisation of employees in the hospitality industry and the role of the clients as instigators (Gilbert et al., 1998; Guerrier & Adib, 2000). Future research should explore the role of managers and peers in the phenomenon of sexual harassment. This could be done by measuring the attitudes and beliefs of potential instigators regarding sexual harassment behaviour. In addition, future research should explore the differences between guidelines aimed at reporting harassment by guests and employees. There is also clearly a need to expand the results highlighted in this chapter to explore the situation in other countries and different segments of the tourism and hospitality industries. This should include, but not be limited to, the airline industry, restaurant sector and cruise industry. In all cases there is a need to explore sexual harassment by guests and employees. There is also a need to explore in detail why some employers train staff about sexual harassment and others do not. This will help inform the development and uptake of tools and systems to protect employees from such harassment. In other words, there is a lot to be done in this sub-field of sex in tourism. Doing so not only has the potential to push knowledge forward but for researchers to make important contributions to the wellbeing of tourism and hospitality employees. This links to the increasing calls for researchers to ensure the impact of their work is activated, to be activists rather than merely witnesses (refer to the final chapter of this book).

References

Australian Human Rights Commission (2008) *Effectively Preventing and Responding to Sexual Harassment: A Code of Practice for Employers*. Sydney: Australian Human Rights Commission.

Comissão para a Igualdade e para os Direitos das Mulheres (2003) *II Plano Nacional para a Igualdade*. See https://dre.pt/home/-/dre/437013/details/maximized (accessed February 2020).

European Commission (1999) *Sexual Harassment at the Workplace in the European Union*. See https://publications.europa.eu/en/publication-detail/-/publication/9c49e8af-2350-46dc-9f4b-cc2571581072 (accessed February 2020).

Eyisi, D. (2016) The usefulness of qualitative and quantitative approaches and methods in researching problem-solving ability in science education curriculum. *Journal of Education and Practice* 7 (15), 91–100.

Farley, L. (1978) *Sexual Shakedown: The Sexual Harassment of Women on the Job*. New York: McGraw-Hill.

Filby, M. (1992) The figures, the personality and the bums' service work and sexuality. *Work, Employment and Society* 6 (1), 23–42.

Folgero, I. and Fjeldstad, I. (1995) On duty – off guard: Cultural norms and sexual harassment in service organizations. *Organization Studies* 16 (2), 299–314.

Gilbert, D., Guerrier, Y. and Guy, J. (1998) Sexual harassment issues in the hospitality industry. *International Journal of Contemporary Hospitality Management* 10 (2), 48–53.

Guerrier Y. and Adib, S. (2000) 'No we don't provide that service': The harassment of hotel employees by customers. *Work, Employment and Society* 14 (4), 689–705.

Gutek, B. (1985) *Sex and the Workplace: The Impact of Sexual Behavior and Harassment on Women, Men, and Organizations*. San Francisco: Jossey-Bass Publishers.

Harris, C., Tregidga, H. and Williamson D. (2011) Cinderella in Babylon: The representation of housekeeping and housekeepers in the UK television series Hotel Babylon. *Hospitality and Society* 1 (1), 47–66.

Hughes, K. and Tadic, V. (1998) Something to deal with: Customer sexual harassment and women's retail service work in Canada. *Gender, Work & Organization* 5 (4), 207–219.

International Labor Organization (2019) *New International Labour Standard to Combat Violence, Harassment, At Work Agreed*. See https://www.ilo.org/ilc/ILCSessions/108/media-centre/news/WCMS_711321/lang--en/index.htm (accessed February 2020).

Kvale, S. (1996) *InterViews: An Introduction to Qualitative Research Interviewing*. Thousand Oaks, CA: Sage.

Portuguese Labor Code (2018) *Article XXIX*. See http://cite.gov.pt/pt/legis/CodTrab_indice.html (accessed February 2020).

Sandroff, R. (1992) Sexual harassment – the inside story. *Working Woman* June, 47–51.

Turismo de Portugal (2019) See http://www.turismodeportugal.pt/pt/Turismo_Portugal/visao_geral/Paginas/default.aspx (accessed February 2020).

Wang, F. (2006) *Few people aware of sexual harassment regulations. Taipei Times*. See http://www.taipeitimes.com/News/taiwan/archives/2006/06/19/2003314406 (accessed February 2020).

Welsh, S. (1999) Gender and sexual harassment. *Annual Review of Sociology* 25, 169–90.

Williams, C., Giuffre, P.A. and Dellinger, K. (1999) Sexuality in the workplace: Organizational control, sexual harassment, and the pursuit of pleasure. *Annual Review of Sociology* 25, 73–93.

13 The Distorted Reach to Local Stakeholders in the Global Fight Against Child Sex Tourism: The Case of Thailand, the Dominican Republic and The Gambia

Frans de Man and Arnoud Lagendijk

Setting/Organising the Ambition

The post-war period has witnessed a growing problem of child sex tourism (CST).[1] With tourism networks expanding globally, CST has been facilitated by access to areas where inequality and anonymity create safe havens for predators to prey on vulnerable children. Internationally, CST is seen as a serious crime. Yet, even though many national governments have taken harsh measures to tackle it, the fight against CST warranted international support through civil society organisations, partnerships and networks. A major result from such an NGO-initiated partnership has been the 'Tourism Child Protection Code' (TCPC), a sixfold 'Code of Conduct' intended to 'clean up' the tourist value chain from the top (major tour operators and hotel chains) to the bottom (onsite hotels and resorts). The TCPC is considered an example of good practice in participation and partnership as it has taken centre stage in the Sustainable Development Goals in literature on deliberative and participatory governance (Arts & Lagendijk, 2009; Dodds, 2019) and has been addressed in case studies in tourism literature (Hall *et al.*, 2015; Jamal & Getz, 1999, 1995; Scheyvens & Biddulph, 2018). However, the impact of the TCPC has been limited. After 20 years of action and in spite of international recognition through (business) awards, less than

400 businesses have signed up, out of at least 187,000 hotels worldwide, according to STR Global estimates (Roper, 2017).[2]

This chapter seeks to explain the limited reach and impact of this institutionalised, global campaign against CST. It revolves around two core concepts: 'multi-stakeholder responsibility', and 'effective and affective reach'. Because of its global scope and complexity, no single partner can solve the problem of CST on its own, warranting the organisation of responsibility in a multi-stakeholder setting. This responsibility subsequently needs to be translated into action and commitment reaching out to the 'sites of crime', requiring both protocols (effective reach) and affinity (affective reach). Only once these are realised can the fight against CST be fully effective throughout the global tourism chain. Our core argument is that TCPC's limited impact can be attributed to what Allen (2016) describes as the 'distortion' of reach, effectively but notably affectively. To illustrate this distortion, we zoom in onto three cases: Thailand, the Dominican Republic and The Gambia.

Taking responsibility

There is a global call for accountable and inclusive societies that are open to more participation of civil society. This results in shifting decision-making processes from government, to civil society and industry, calling for stronger collaborations and partnerships. This takes place in a setting where government is accountable to all stakeholders for the common good while the private sector and NGOs have delineated responsibilities concerning specific public interests, confined by their roles and accountability to their shareholders, target groups and/or constituents. Governments are supposed to persuade these stakeholders to participate and take responsibility not only for their own interests but for the 'social good', and to create institutional orders offering a level playing field (notably market regulation) and collaboration frameworks (such as Public Private Partnerships, PPPs) (Bäckstrand, 2006).

For the private sector, taking and organising responsibility for pressing societal issues (such as tackling CST) heavily depends on Corporate Social Responsibility (CSR). Businesses are encouraged, although not obliged, to employ CSR by the UN *Global Compact* and the UN *Guiding Principles on Business and Human Rights,* a key expectation being that companies will take responsibility not only for their short-term profits but also for social goals. Consequently, they 'must operate responsibly in alignment with universal principles and take actions that support the society around them. Then, to push sustainability deep into the corporate DNA, companies must commit at the highest level, report annually on their efforts, and engage locally where they have a presence' (UN, 2014: 77). These CSR practices prescribe how to select relevant issues and stakeholders for collaboration, resulting in patterns of agenda setting, and inclusion and exclusion. These partnerships and their inclusion of stakeholders have been addressed in tourism literature, mainly focused on local initiatives and best practices (Graci, 2013; Simpson, 2008; Waligo *et al.*, 2013). In this chapter, we will look at a global collaborative CSR instrument, the Tourism Child Protection Code (de Man & Bah, 2014; George & Smith, 2013).

The responsibilities of NGOs are organised and shaped by the advancing neoliberal discourse which has moved beyond the liberal idea of autonomous, entrepreneurial agents (consumers and businesses) making their 'own' responsible decisions with some constraints set by a regulating state. Rather, it promotes the idea that agents need to be moulded and framed so as to behave both rationally and responsibly in market-based settings, fostering both collaboration and competition (Arts & Lagendijk, 2009). Anderson (2016) describes this adherence to and belief in orchestrated markets as the 'neoliberal affect'. An important manifestation of this affect is the discourse on multi-stakeholder cooperation in pursuing societal aims. In return for having a share in Public Private Partnerships and funding for their projects NGOs were expected to work in line with CSR activities of the private sector. Therefore, they needed to adjust to market-oriented standards, cooperate with industry and organise their work on a more commercial basis. To boost competition, lump sum funding was replaced by project funding, forcing NGOs to become performance-based organisations with market-led projects, often accompanied by an overall reduction of available state subsidies. This move to a more 'entrepreneurial' setting was further orchestrated by the introduction of concepts such as 'Theory of Change' or 'LogFrames', the need to formulate projects as a 'business case' and internal and external evaluation procedures in close cooperation with the private sector[3] (Oxman & Fretheim, 2009).

In the following account of the TCPC, we examine the role of a partnership supporting CSR in tourism, focusing on social aspects of sustainability. We will address the way the 'neoliberal affect' has impinged upon the functioning of NGOs (internally and externally) as representatives of Civil Society in their interaction with industry, state and community stakeholders. To do so, we use the analytical concept of 'reach'.

Reach

Tourism presents a complex network. Its stakeholders collaborate in various space and time dimensions, both as a process (tourism development) and as a product (tourist services) throughout the lifecycles of tourism. Besides the collaboration between numerous private sector stakeholders in the tourism value chains, a long history of multi-stakeholder cooperation exists between industry, government and civil society. This has been reinvigorated by the shifts in governance described above. A specific development has been the instituting of collaboration into partnerships formalised through scripts and equipped with goals, targets, means and procedures. Our topic, the TCPC, presents such a partnership originating from an international NGO campaign to stop child sex tourism carried out through national actions in destinations, all with different needs and varying implementation programmes.

A key challenge for each international partnership operating in a neoliberal, market-oriented setting is to gain 'reach' (Allen, 2016). That is, to truly and widely arrive and make an impact at the sites of relevance (in our case, the sites of crime). Reach comes into play when actors cannot just 'push the button' and directly implement policies or regulations nor expect practices to change accordingly. Rather, reach involves what Allen describes as the use of subtler, less overt, more impalpable registers of power, with the help of means of 'presence' and persuasion (Allen, 2016: 22). Rather than exercising hierarchical power and pulling strings ('power over'), reach occurs through bringing to presence new ideas and codings, and reframing the way local agents think and act ('power to'). While this may occur in the 'shadow of hierarchy', reach cannot be achieved on the basis of 'hard power', which would automatically induce full compliance. In the case of the TCPC, for instance, the international headquarters of the campaign in Bangkok cannot demand compliance in local destinations in Latin America. Other, softer registers of power are needed, through which aims, targets and conventions are relayed and perform locally over several layers of collaboration. Such registers entail codifications, scripts and engagements, enabling communication and persuasion. In the case of the TCPC, this consists of the charter of six guidelines of the Code of Conduct to which partners can sign up.

Allen (2016) draws attention to a dimension that is important for reach but often overlooked in organisational and institutional perspectives, that of the 'affective'. Through emphasising 'presence' rather than coordination at a distance, individuals and organisations must find a certain 'click', a nexus combining emotional and directional affinity. This is especially true in multi-stakeholder settings with people from different backgrounds and cultures and with different interests and power structures, as in the fight against CST. Click is based on feelings of communality as well as a shared sense of purpose and it requires a certain level of trust (Ebbekink & Lagendijk, 2013). When equality between unequal partners is scripted into a multi-stakeholder setting, affective conditions are critical in order to prevent distortion of reach. As Allen claims: 'authority has to be conceded before it is complied with' (Allen, 2016: 69).

Because of the criticality of affective conditions, reach is vulnerable. In Allen's words, reach is easily 'distorted'. One prominent distortion of reach is when 'power over' emerges out its shadow and thwarts the 'soft' consensus and click. Jamal and Getz (1999) describe how in Canada the government (and its appointees) use their power to set the rules and use mechanisms of in- and exclusion in creating tourism partnerships. Reach can also be distorted by the power that financial donors of NGOs and partnerships exercise, thwarting collaboration. Another distortion emerges when effective top-down doctrines, such as the neoliberal imposition of competition, limit the scope for collaboration. At the end of the day the powerful always have the option to walk out or bring their power to effect in other ways outside the partnership.

Furthermore, establishing reach proves much more elusive and deceptive than suggested by conventional accounts of globalisation, communication and even actor-network thinking. According to Allen, 'the apparent neatness of many an institutional arrangement often belies the more mutable nature of power relationships when situations change and open up in unpredictable ways' (Allen, 2016: 61). This fragility has both effective and affective roots. Effective work warrants a continual application of expediency and strategic intelligence, which is often in short supply. Changes in affective conditions may remove the 'presence' warranted for persuasion and commitment: 'what can be drawn into reach can also be placed beyond or out of reach' (Allen, 2016: 53). Certainly, this is likely to be the case in the long, fragmented and complex value chains of tourism.

There are also some important 'external' hallmarks that determine the power of reach, such as the moments in which persuasive stories and images go 'viral', as in the case of Marc Dutroux in 1996. His arrest in 1996 for the abduction and sexual abuse of six girls, of whom only two survived, led to massive public outcry, which translated into multilateral support for child rights organisations. Governments (and journalists for that matter) who had initially turned down invitations to take part in the First World Congress on Commercial Sexual Exploitation of Children in Stockholm, now got in line to participate. The Dutroux case shocked Europe and the power of affective reach resulted in expanded effective reach through a plethora of new legislation and scripts like the TCPC (which was conceived at the Stockholm Congress) (Alexander *et al.*, 2000).

These distortions of reach pose a challenge for NGOs. In a globalising, market-dominated world, the coining and elaboration of the concepts of participation, and stakeholder and multi-stakeholder collaboration created the global stage through which the reach of the TCPC could be expanded. The NGOs involved in the TCPC engage with tactical and strategic manoeuvring on effective and affective terrain, to enrol industry and government, garner wider support and mobilise other resources. However, hovering between affective and effective work, these NGOs struggle continuously to cope with distortions in achieving and sustaining reach. What deserves our close attention, accordingly, is the interweaving of affective and effective dimensions, and how attempts for reach cope with distortions. Let us now explore TCPC's reach.

The Tourism Child Protection Code

The initiative for the TCPC stems from ECPAT,[4] a global network of NGOs combating commercial sexual exploitation of children. In the 1990s, ECPAT Sweden reached out to the tourism industry with a CSR script to combat CST. Through multi-stakeholder negotiations, the script evolved into a formal Code of Conduct, helping businesses to embed child protection in their CSR ambitions. The TCPC entails six mandatory guidelines:

(1) To establish a policy and procedures against sexual exploitation of children.
(2) Train employees in children's rights, the prevention of sexual exploitation and how to report suspected cases.
(3) Include a clause in contracts with suppliers stating a common repudiation and zero tolerance policy of sexual exploitation of children.
(4) Provide information to travellers on children's rights, the prevention of sexual exploitation of children and how to report suspected cases.
(5) Support, collaborate and engage stakeholders in the prevention of sexual exploitation of children.
(6) Report annually on the implementation of the TCPC.[5]

Drawing on global and national conventions on CSR and the rights of children, the TCPC organises reach with technical-procedural means (more present in Guidelines 1, 3 and 6) and means of persuasion (2, 4, 5). Echoing the market orientation of current times, and building on CSR commitment, it helps NGOs to connect to industry and facilitates multi-stakeholder cooperation for 'good causes'. Building on 'affect', the TCPC represents a method to channel a deep-seated human urge to protect children from sexual abuse into a more programmed ambition. Reach is sought by targeting the entire tourism value chain, from the CEOs of multinational organisations to the communities at risk. The TCPC is scripted to support reach into networks vertically through the value chain and horizontally through institutionalising collaboration between stakeholders.

While the Code was initiated by ECPAT, after a decade its ownership was handed over to the industry, symbolised by handing over control of the TCPC Board, with five out of nine members being industrial representatives. This Board oversees the local advocacy networks rolling out TCPC scripts and practices in tourism destinations. Recently, however, after a controversial evaluation by the main funder, SECO, in 2016 (Bureau Wyser, 2016), ECPAT has taken back control. Where formerly the key term used was 'industry driven', this drive has now been toned down to the less obliging 'under leadership of professionals from the industry'.[6] At national levels, NGO control has always remained. The TCPC is locally represented through Local Code Representatives (LCR), almost all of which have been run by local ECPAT groups from the start.[7] Contracted through an agreement with the international board (vertically), LCRs reach out to stakeholders at the national level (horizontally) and to stakeholders in the targeted tourism regions (vertically). The latter increasingly entail tourism areas developed around new regional airports, serving all-inclusive resorts, often far away from the national capitals where the NGOs have their base. As we will discuss in more detail below, tourism companies tended not to meet the expectations raised, which complicated the sharing of responsibilities between stakeholders.

Zooming in to our three case studies, we will address the following questions:

- Does the TCPC reach fully and effectively throughout the global tourism chain into the destinations?
- What are the roles of the different stakeholders in multi-stakeholder cooperation in different settings?
- Which factors distort TCPC's reach?
- Can the regulation of sexual abuse in tourism be left to voluntary CSR initiatives?

The case study research is based on the active participation of the first author in drafting and negotiating the TCPC with the industry, and in its implementation and evaluation in a wide variety of destinations. The main method, accordingly, is action research, carried out between 1990 and 2016. We will also refer to other evaluations and research carried out over the past decade.

Thailand: The Role of CSR

Fighting CST in Thailand

CST is widely associated with Thailand. Sex tourism in Thailand originated with American soldiers seeking relaxation during the Vietnam War, after which the sex industry found new clientele in the growing foreign tourism market. Yearly, an estimated 300,000 children are being trafficked in Thailand, of whom 60,000 end up in prostitution in tourism

(Glover, 2006). In Pattaya, famous for its open brothels, young, often poor, girls and boys are exploited by *preferential offenders* (paedophiles who prey on the youngest children operating in criminal networks) and *situational offenders* (without a specific plan or preference for exploiting children) (Davis, 2013; de Man, 2013; ECPAT, 2013). Most perpetrators belong to the latter group (The Protection Project, 2007).

As early as the 1980s, sex tourism evoked protest in Thai civil society. An NGO initiated by Australian clergy (ECPAT) reached out to European NGOs to raise awareness among tourists. Under the aegis of European ECPAT groups, the TCPC was born. Its secretariat moved to Bangkok, hosted by ECPAT International headquarters. The TCPC international secretariat is also responsible for implementation of the TCPC in Thailand.

Distortions of reach

Over time, various NGOs on children's rights have been fighting against CST in Thailand (e.g. World Vision, Friends International, Child Safe and Safe Child). Most seem to have been able to establish an affective base in Thailand better than the TCPC secretariat or ECPAT headquarters. When the TCPC reached out to them, the national tourism associations in Thailand and some relevant institutions within the Department of Tourism remained disengaged since they had *'been pressured to help World Vision's Project Childhood against child sex tourism due to ties with the Australian government'* (de Man, 2013: 5). Accordingly, in spite of the fact that Thailand is a renowned CST hotspot, the number of Thai signatories to the TCPC is embarrassingly low, recently not more than eight.[8]

However, to help transnational tourism companies take their responsibility worldwide, especially in those destinations where good governance is lacking, the TCPC has been scripted to deal with cases where local support for child protection is missing. Guideline 3 (sourcing contracts) stipulates that a company should compel its suppliers to adhere to the Code, based on the core assets of corporate social responsibility, value chain management and sourcing policies. However, an evaluation of the relevant value chains (ECPAT, 2013) showed this had not materialised. In the CST hotspot of Pattaya, 23 hotels were inspected which supplied three major TCPC affiliated tour operators (TUI, Thomas Cook and Kuoni) and/or belonged to the ACCOR hotel chain (a TCPC board member). Remarkably, only the three ACCOR-affiliated hotels complied satisfactorily. None of the other 20 hotels, no matter if they worked with one, two or all three tour operators, had implemented any of the TCPC guidelines nor had they been made aware by the tour operators of the TCPC. Most hotels had accepted the fact that guests bring prostitutes to the hotel and required a 'joiner' fee of around US$20, thus actually making money out of sex tourism. Although all hotels claimed not to admit children without a guardian, many would allow tourists to take under-aged girls to their rooms. A telling example is a hotel handing out a card to guests stipulating that children can only be brought along with *prior notification* (ECPAT, 2013). The local hotels seemed not to have been provided with the right information to define the issue clearly and acknowledge their responsibilities in an unequivocal manner.

An interesting difference was found between tour operators and hotel chains in how they implement Guideline 3. The obligation for a tour operator is to persuade every link in its supply chain to comply in a failsafe manner through its sourcing process and sales conditions, while if the CEO of a hotel chain[9] signs the TCPC, every hotel using the brand is obliged to enforce Code implementation. Furthermore, implementation and repudiation depend on corporate perspectives and cultures and here size matters. Companies with CSR and legal departments tend to be better able to implement Code procedures than smaller businesses, which are often part of the informal economy and operate without contracts.

Initially, NGOs had formulated Guideline 3 in much stronger terms to make the value chain 'cleanse itself'. The first drafts demanded legal action by companies against their suppliers when caught facilitating CST.[10] The industry refused to go that far and finally only accepted a watered-down version of the clause merely 'requiring common repudiation' and 'zero tolerance'. This is a rather weak statement, considering that CST is generally considered a serious crime with even the possibility of capital punishment (in India, the Philippines and Thailand, for example). However, even the 'common repudiation' turned out to be too demanding. Most hotels that were visited in Pattaya could not give examples of how this repudiation is expressed and many ascribed their failure to do so to the complexity of getting everyone on the same page, from legal staff, product developers, marketing, PR, CSR department to CEO.

Impact on Code implementation

It is remarkable that in a country manifesting a serious history of child sex tourism, and home to the initiator and owner of the TCPC, the Code's reach is so paltry. This distortion stems from a combination of a failure of the industry to enforce the TCPC through the traditional value chain and the lack of a Code representative with affective reach. Nobody has assumed the responsibility to promote, coordinate or monitor Code implementation. It is quite worrying that in the international cradle of CST, Pattaya, the (then) three biggest tour-operators of the world, all related to the Code board, had not been able, or willing, to persuade their providing hotels to adhere to the Code.

The Dominican Republic: The Role of NGOs

Fighting CST in the Dominican Republic

According to the UN, the Dominican Republic is a child sex tourism hotspot (Moloney, 2017) with around 25,000 children being commercially sexually exploited (ECPAT, 2006). In places like Sosua, in the northern province of Puerto Plata and Boca Chica near the capital Santo Domingo, tourists sexually exploit vulnerable girls and boys, often of Haitian decent, refugees from the 2010 earthquake. Perpetrators are often situational offenders, not specifically targeting younger girls, but simply not bothered to check their age. Most girls know that minors are not allowed to work in the sex industry and that they will be expelled from the bars so they do their best to look older. Even if a tourist asked for an ID, forged 'cedulas' (IDs) with a fake age are available in the local supermarkets. On top of being sexually exploited, these children run the risk of being extorted by the local police. One girl who had been observed by a policeman while being interviewed by the project researcher had to pay the officer a 'commission' for having been with 'a client'.[11]

In 2000, ECPAT Sweden helped its local partner, MAIS (ECPAT-DR), a small NGO working with deprived schoolchildren in the city of Puerto Plata, to introduce the TCPC in the Dominican Republic. Since then MAIS has been funded for implementing the TCPC by many groups such as ECPAT Netherlands (since 2010), UNICEF (training on a project basis) and PLAN (since 2016), as well as tour operators (German in 2006–2007, Swiss in 2008 and 2011 and Canadian in 2009), and in cooperation with ACCOR (2012), and TUI and RIU hotels (since 2016). With the publicity this generated, MAIS became known as a best practise for the TCPC and was subject to a number of evaluations (de Man, 2010, 2012, 2015)

Distortion of reach

As a grassroots children's rights organisation, MAIS had always been very critical of government and industry, which they viewed as responsible for ignoring children's rights and protection.[12] It was, therefore, challenging for MAIS to reach out to their 'natural opponents' and enter into partnerships with them. Fortunately, the regional tourism association, ASOHANORTE, chaired by a president running a hotel belonging to the Wyndham chain, a signatory to the TCPC, helped bringing MAIS and the industry together. By linking the business association's membership with that of the TCPC, more hotels were expected to sign up. ASONAHORTE also introduced MAIS in Punta Cana (an important upcoming destination), attracting new Code members.

MAIS had managed to reach out successfully in their home province of Puerto Plata, where many people know its two managers for their bottom up approach: teaching deprived children skills, helping them pursuing careers, notably in hospitality, and organising displays on the beach informing tourists about the dangers of CST. Cooperation with ASONAHORTE and Kuoni introduced MAIS into the hotels. However, they needed assistance from Dutch NGOs to expand, since reaching out to regions where it did not have an affective base posed challenges. For instance, the corporate all-inclusive hotels in Punta Cana initially put up bureaucratic hurdles varying from denying them entrance to asking them to negotiate with, consecutively, the HR, PR, CSR and marketing managers, the General Manager and sometimes even the international chain.

The success of the campaign brought pressure to expand and raise demands for quality of services and transparency. In an attempt to help them professionalise and extend their reach, MAIS was pressured to accept the formal position of LCR, lending them more effective power over the TCPC. Initially they had rejected this, as it would interfere with their core activities and their critical standpoint. There was not just fear of being compromised but also that the agreements with the international Code board contained tasks that might be incompatible with each other (e.g. providing training and consequently monitoring whether the training was up to standard). However, eventually MAIS yielded to the soft power exercised by the Code and ECPAT International, which then both benefited from MAIS' status as 'best practice' and a funding magnet.[13] Accordingly, MAIS became responsible for TCPC promotion, monitoring and evaluation, and collecting of membership fees (all far beyond their capacity as a grassroots children's rights organisation).

Meanwhile UNICEF tried to boost the reach of both the Code and their own CSR fundraising programme 'Huesped de Corazon'[14] by requiring participating hotels to sign the TCPC. By doing so, these hotels expected related Code training. Yet, while the money (and goodwill) raised went to UNICEF, MAIS, as LCR, was held responsible for delivering this service. Although UNICEF paid them for some of the training, MAIS saw this as an injustice. The entangling of two different CSR scripts led to a lack of clarity and conflict, decreasing MAIS' trust in governments. This was exacerbated when UNICEF asked the Dominican branch of the multinational NGO PLAN to intervene in MAIS' work. At the same time, the Dutch group ECPAT-NL, long-time funder of MAIS, was obliged by their government to partner with PLAN-NL (the Dutch PLAN branch) as a condition to be eligible for Dutch ministry funds. Where MAIS already viewed the involvement of PLAN-DR as unfair competition, now their Dutch funding partners required them to liaise with that organisation. It was especially concerning to MAIS that in return for funding they now not only had to maintain close ties with government and industry but also with their competitors. On top of that MAIS had observed and reported that the private sector, while adopting a more demanding attitude as a client of MAIS' services, had not been engaging sufficiently in the TCPC and that tourism business associations had shown a lack of coherence by not enforcing their condition for membership of joining the Code.

To make things worse, most businesses preferred to work with what in their eyes were more professional organisations (e.g. PLAN-DR and UNICEF). This came, however, with two interesting exceptions. One was the RIU hotel in Punta Cana which had built a good working relation with MAIS and saw itself as a best practice in CSR and child protection. However, the TUI Care Foundation (the charity of TUI, corporate owner of the RIU chain) worked closely with the Dutch PLAN and ECPAT programme and wanted to put its own stamp on the TCPC when they got involved in the Dominican Republic. The RIU hotel saw this as an unfair intrusion in their affairs and this led to tensions between these two branches of the same corporation.[15] The other exception was Palladium hotels which, due to changing market conditions and value chains, took Code related initiatives themselves and obliged their industry partners (like tour-operator TUI) to engage with Palladium's preferred partner MAIS, thus challenging the top down value chain structure of the Code.

The difference in approach between MAIS and its sponsoring partners was illustrated in the production of information leaflets, revealing a gap between effective and affective forms of reach. MAIS had used funds to produce a number of different brochures. Applying the information and education standards of Dutch government funding, most of these products would not have qualified for approval as effective information materials. Nevertheless, they were a big success locally, ending up in homes, supermarkets and churches, contributing invaluably to local awareness about CST. This required some creativity in reporting results (de Man, 2012) and education materials made for on-the-job training were listed as public information campaign materials, because otherwise they would not have met the funders' script for training requirements.

Attempts at reconciliation aside, from 2014 to 2015 tensions grew and surfaced in meetings of MAIS with the NGO parties. In the meetings, the Dutch NGO consultants exposed the local groups to hours of detailed PowerPoints and spreadsheets on standard methodological scripts like the 'Theory of Change', Public Private Partnerships and 'business cases', which are a far cry from MAIS' affective and anti-establishment community engagement. Whatever affective base remained was lost in those hours of training in English, a language which most of the NGO representatives did not command. The result was a breach of trust and eventually mutual accusations of abuse of power and fraud. Consequently, UNICEF, the Dominican Government and the tourism industry created their own 'tripartite' body to govern implementation of child protection in tourism and wanted to take responsibility for the TCPC (de Man, 2012; ECPAT, 2013). ECPAT-NL and PLAN-DR intervened and tried to persuade MAIS to comply with the help of 'soft' mediation. When that failed, they resorted to the 'hard' means of financial repercussions. However, MAIS struck back in equal measure, by claiming effective ownership and monopoly over the TCPC as the officially accredited LCR. MAIS maintained its position and the funding NGOs had to concede, although for some territories outside of MAIS' 'home' base responsibilities were transferred to other NGOs (de Man, 2016).

Impact on Code implementation

Despite the hundreds of thousands of Euros funnelled into the Dominican TCPC, not more than 25 Dominican enterprises have signed the Code.[16] Some notorious CST areas, such as Boca Chica, are not covered at all. Although successes could be claimed, for instance in the number of trained staff and the local awareness of the problem, chain performance has been disappointing. Between 2010 and 2015, assessments of TCPC implementation by partners in the TUI value chain (from agents in Holland via international air transport to hotels in Cabarete) showed a marked lack of positive results.[17] Some crucial elements of the TCPC that are not part of MAIS core business, such as Guidelines 4 (informing tourists) and 6 (monitoring/reporting), lacked attention. This was compounded by a lack of communication and coordination along the private sector value chain.

Besides limited local reach, the tensions between NGOs revealed another, more global consequence. Pushed to the limits in its fight for ownership of the Code, MAIS claimed monopoly over Code implementation, excluding other partners from rendering services such as membership approval, and training for and monitoring of signatories. From a perspective of transparency and accountability, however, combining these responsibilities in one hand is not desirable and might even be prohibited in some countries.[18]

The Gambia: The State

Fighting CST in The Gambia

The Gambia is globally known as a sex tourism destination (ECPAT, 2009; Unicef, 2003; US Department of Labor, 2009). A lack of effective governance and enforcement made it a popular destination when Asian countries cracked down on CST in the late 1990s. Known for both male and female sex tourism, CST is still primarily a male tourist affair in The Gambia. Minor victims are aged between 14 and 17 years and although they are mainly girls the number of young boys exploited is on the rise. Perpetrators target vulnerable children from poor families, building relationships by providing sponsorship and support (de Man & Bah, 2014).

In 2004, ECPAT-CPA (Child Protection Alliance) The Gambia introduced the TCPC, which was immediately adopted by the Gambian Tourism Authority (GTA now GTBoard). Rather than relying on CSR or NGOs, the Gambian government regarded CST as too serious to leave to private and civil-society initiatives. It created an obligatory governmental Gambian 'Code of Conduct for the Protection of Children from Sexual Exploitation in Tourism', switching from the soft means of persuasion typical for the TCPC to the hard measure of formal obligation. If they did not sign the Gambian Code, a company would be denied a license to operate. A multi-sectorial taskforce was installed to adapt the international Code to The Gambia and monitor it. Up until now, the Gambian Code is state enforced and since it is obligatory all important tourism players in the country adhere to it (de Man & Bah, 2014).

Distortion of reach

Relying on mandatory compliance, The Gambian Code could, in principle, present an effective script for child protection. What the Gambian case shows, however, is the difficulties associated with achieving genuine institutional and social reach and adoption. Where businesses are forced to concede, they might not become truly committed and engaged. One overall observation was that 'because it is state regulated, the business sector does not feel it as its own initiative and is rather passive in the implementation, waiting for the government to initiate action' (de Man & Bah, 2014: 41). Lacking ambition and complying only minimally, the industry expected the government to act and set an example. The only presence of the Code in the hotels visited (in 2014) was an obligatory Code poster. This actually matched findings in other areas in which the TCPC had been enforced by the government, where hotel inspectors encountered nothing more than a poster (e.g. in the state of Pernambuco, Brazil).[19] Complicating factors were that international tour-operators had not required commitment to the Code from their supplying hotels and that large international hotel chains like ACCOR, who are successful in Code implementation, have not been allowed into The Gambia.

The distortion of reach had various manifestations. Government agencies showed incoherent behaviour and lack of action. The reporting hotline was often not accessible and the police complained that reports of incidents could not always be addressed due to lack of money to buy petrol for their cars. A hotel manager reported: *'I had a case involving a French man ... with boys as young as 12 years ... I called the police ... and he was arrested and taken to the police station. Later in that evening, I was shocked to see the man return to the hotel without any escort and checked out of his room. ... the offender bribed the police with D60,000 and the case was aborted with no charges sent to the court'* (de Man & Bah, 2014: 25). To make things worse there was often no care for victims rescued from sexual exploitation. These conditions led to a lack of trust and even more passiveness from the private sector. As a result, lacking an affective basis, 'hard' government enforcement might even seem to work counterproductively.

Although the local ECPAT partner, CPA has been involved in some trainings, they have been lacking the position and local power to claim ownership and enhance the Code's reach and implementation. They have attempted to address the issue and create a sense of urgency and motivation amongst the tourism industry via baseline research and the organisation of some meetings. In one of these meetings, meant to build trust between stakeholders, the minister of tourism showed up and took the lead. He used the data from the research to accuse the industry and threaten to revoke their licenses, thus disrupting the affective reach CPA had hoped to create. Although badly needed, not many NGOs jumped in to assist CPA, in contrast to what happened in the Dominican Republic. This has been complicated by the fact that, for a long time, the TCPC did not acknowledge the Gambian Code as part of their industry driven programme.

Impact on the Code implementation

At the time of the research, there was no national NGO representing the TCPC in The Gambia. The state-based taskforce, on the other hand, did not function as an institutional actor as it only convened when specific issues emerged (de Man & Bah, 2014). It should be noted, though, that when the Minister of Tourism invited stakeholders to present the results of the baseline study, all relevant stakeholders showed up. Furthermore, when he ordered them to validate the conclusions and promise improvements, they all did. Unfortunately, for reasons mentioned above, the encounter did not induce more compliance, better state support, or a stronger business commitment and reach along the value chain. Suppliers to hotels (taxi drivers, tour guides and watchmen) could thus remain active as middlemen between sex tourists and children without disturbance (de Man & Bah, 2014). TUI's Gambia 2013 country guide even advertised a notorious 'pick-up' bar known to allow Gambian under-aged sex workers.[20] In the meantime, the TCPC

ECPAT/CPA has been allowed to become the official Gambian TCPC Local Representative. However, until June 2019 only one Gambian Code signatory had been registered.[21]

Obviously, because of its specific institutional context, The Gambia presents a rather unique case of Code reach and adoption. In practical terms, it illustrates the pervasive impact of a lack of good governance and local representation, and hence the need for support from other NGOs and involvement by the TCPC secretariat. We can conclude that in the Gambian case, the use of hard power as intended by the government did not have better results than CSR or NGO drives.

Conclusion

Despite widespread public revulsion and strong legal action, child sex tourism has proven to be very hard to fight against. In a globalised, neoliberal setting, the combat against CST, we argue here, warrants an approach in which global stakeholders reach out to local tourist businesses, and persuade and help them to stop their guests from sexually exploiting minors. The key stakeholders are international and local tour operators, hotels, and NGOs, supported by national and regional state authorities. An important vehicle to bring stakeholders together and to acquire reach has been the 'Tourism Child Protection Code'. The TCPC, established as an industry driven CSR instrument, invites the industry to sign up and 'clean' their premises as well as their value chain. However, after 20 years of operation reach has remained very limited. The TCPC has been signed by only a few hundred tourism accommodation units globally, and of these only a fraction participate in monitoring activities.

This chapter has sought to explain this failure by looking at stakeholder actions and relations in shaping, diffusing and adopting the TCPC throughout the tourism value chain. Using Allen's (2016) approach, we consider reach as a mix of 'effect' and 'affect'. That is, as a combination of formal scripts and commitments on the one hand, and persuasion and motivation on the other. The key argument put forward here is that to gain reach and have impact warrants affective 'click' between stakeholders. We studied three cases, each of which worked from the perspective of one major stakeholder; business (Thailand), NGO (Dominican Republic) and state (The Gambia). We looked at the power of reach through Allen's ideas on emotional and directional affinity, establishing 'click' between stakeholders, and bringing CST concerns and actions to light in tourist destinations. We found that in all three cases, affective conditions were lacking and the click did not materialise, which distorted the power of reach.

In more detail, our findings point towards the following 'distortions' of reach.

Half-hearted commitment of stakeholders

Attuning and aligning the roles and responsibilities of stakeholders in the fight against CST proved difficult. The governments under study in this chapter either provide little support for endorsing and spreading the TCPC (Thailand, Dominican Republic), or prefer to work with a more-or-less 'lame' alternative (The Gambia). A number of corporate and local businesses express interest in and commitment to CSR and even agree that industry should have a leading role in establishing and implementing the TCPC. In practice, however, most firms show only a half-hearted adoption of the TCPC. Our general impression is that shareholders' interests concerning growth and continual expansion largely trump the urge to fight one of the most serious crimes induced by tourism. NGOs manifest some aberrations of their own. To be eligible to receive funds, NGOs have to comply with funding conditions set in neoliberal scripts, formats and performances. Consequently, the 'market' turn of NGOs raised the need for 'business' elements such as management, marketing and PR, while curtailing capacities for pungent, lasting and strenuous local action. They find themselves in a double bind; they need to meet the market-oriented expectations of the state as well as overcome the lack of interest and support from the industry. In the case of the TCPC, this is exacerbated by the lack of experience in collaborating with industry, which requires an unfamiliar commercial instinct. The average NGO also lacks an understanding of how tourism companies should integrate the TCPC into their Corporate Social Responsibility policies.

Failing value chain

The TCPC pursues reach by pushing its scripts through business value chains. TCPC's Guideline 3 is specifically coded in line with international CSR formats, asking companies to bring the issue to the attention of other companies in their supply chain. It gives crucial responsibilities to the Code signatories to source only from providers that also adhere to the Code. Yet, not only did the industry manage to narrow Guideline 3 down to a mere 'common repudiation', its implementation has been rather mixed. Some businesses have shown devotion to the 'self-cleansing' of the industry, notably through corporate hierarchies and networks such as ACCOR (in Thailand) or a strong CSR department such as Kuoni (in the Dominican Republic)[22] However, in most cases – as exemplified here by Thailand and The Gambia – the biggest issue has been the half-hearted way corporate business (e.g. tour-operators and hotel chains) have included the TCPC in their value chain through supplier contracts. It is important to highlight the industry's oft-heard excuse for thwarting implementation of the Code, namely the difficulties they face in aligning and focusing the different interests between their various internal business departments (marketing, PR, CSR, CEO, procurement).

Blurry institutionalisation

TCPC's reach is not only established through the value chain but also through top-down multi-stakeholder advocacy networks reaching out via the Local Code Representatives. The evaluations carried out between 2008 and 2016 found the LCR to be the Achilles heel of the Code. In countries where the NGO sector is strong, most LCRs seem to fulfil their purpose. In contrast, in those countries with weaker governance structures, the goal of empowering NGOs through an LCR contract with 'scripted' powers is rarely achieved. In Thailand there is no LCR, the Gambian LCR is an NGO unrelated to the (government driven) Code, and in the Dominican Republic turf fights between NGOs broke the network apart, with MAIS using the powers assigned to them through the LCR agreement to claim the monopoly in the fight against CST. The LCR contract, institutionalising the relation between international board and local representative, contains tasks and functions that are not compatible with each other and does not constitute a business case, generating tensions between stakeholders.

Power and equality

The powers available to each of the three stakeholders are drivers. The state has the democratically legitimised 'hard' power to enforce government decisions and to demand compliance. Equally, business corporations exert 'hard' power through their access to capital and the power of the purse in their value chains. NGOs, however, rely largely on 'soft' powers like persuasion. Their 'hardest' form of power is indirect, through urging their constituencies to elect politicians or to 'vote with their feet' by purchasing or boycotting certain products and services. Although scripts like the TCPC attempt to generate new types of leverage emulating hard power for NGOs within multi-stakeholder partnerships, the powers at work remain mostly 'soft', persuasive, affective and committing. Their effectiveness is threatened by the need to span many borders (both territorial and conceptual) and deal with the complexity of the CST problem. In all three cases, the lack of trust is a fundamental factor complicating bridging power issues. However, for many NGOs their raison d'être is to be an (often distrusted) watchdog of government and industry.

For effective multi-stakeholder partnerships, it is important that the operative scripts do not just meet the agendas of the powerful. Scripting should contribute to a level playing field based on (perceived) equality between partners, generating softer registers of power to meet shared interests. However, the script of the TCPC has not been able to stem the impact of hard power, which is always present in the background, like a gun in a pocket. On top of that, equality within a partnership cannot be isolated from power relations around it; the powerful can always walk out and/or bring power to effect outside the reach of the partnership. In the TCPC, the lack of equality is further visible in practical operations, when NGOs are expected to convince business. In general, the business sector does not easily concede to NGOs, and in developing countries this is even harder since the private sector hardly recognises the role of NGOs.

Ownership and drive

While equality is a basic condition for a partnership, there is also a need for a primus-inter-pares, a partner who feels they are the owner of the cause and will take responsibility and drive action. Our case studies show that state, industry and NGOs each have their own way to distort reach when they take the lead. We saw that in the competitive conditions of the neo-liberal era, instead of taking ownership in the sense of feeling responsible for the cause, stakeholders are primarily interested in taking ownership in the sense of 'issue capture', monopolising the cause for their own benefit. An interesting case is the Dominican Republic, where this not only distorted cooperation between different stakeholders but also drove a wedge between stakeholders of the same sector, both for NGOs (between MAIS and PLAN) and for industry (between RUI and TUI). On a positive note, the Dominican case also showed that when industry, like KUONI, pro-actively takes ownership and assists NGOs in introducing the Code to business partners, local companies will be persuaded to comply. It is, however, significant that the TCPC has been struggling with ownership and drive since its inception, having changed from an NGO-driven via an industry-owned and later industry-driven instrument, back to currently striving to be an NGO under the aegis of another NGO, ECPAT.

Neoliberal affect

The affective dimension of reach embraces more than mutual understanding and alignment of action between stakeholders. Affect is also about how the deeper drives and motives draw stakeholders together. In a fundamental way, these drives and motives stem from the way stakeholders emerge as subjects in an evolving, wider political-economic playing field. That is, how they are formed and become under the actual 'Zeitgeist', current discourses, and dominant political-economic relations. Therefore, we addressed the significance of, to use Anderson's (2016) term, the 'neoliberal affect', and how this has impinged upon NGOs as the key advocates and linchpins in the fight against CST.

In our view, the 'neoliberal affect' is a major factor in the distortion of reach. The neoliberal mantra that competition will drive innovation and performance, not only in the business sector but also in society at large, has had major implications for how NGOs work. One of the main implications has been the rise of funding practises not based on institutional funding but on short-term projects based on competitive bidding, accompanied by overall budget cuts. This has pitted NGOs against each other. The resulting 'war of position' pushed NGOs to extend their reach vertically and horizontally, not for advocacy but for visibility and accountability. We noticed how NGOs compete in Thailand, with the Australian government lobbying for their own groups, and how MAIS felt threatened by competition from other NGOs.

This turn has radically changed the meaning of collaboration. Rather than fundamental, collaboration has become instrumental, responding to the donors' interests in larger projects and cooperation with larger consortiums. The Dominican case showed how Dutch NGOs, pressured by state funding conditions, imposed their practices of coordination, outreach and accountability, echoing the workings and tactics of transnational corporations. Stemming from countries where funds are generated, this 'forced' collaboration was exported to the tourism destinations, with disruptive effects on the affective power of reach. Especially in developing countries, reach depends on a sensitive balance and click between businesses, NGOs, authorities, and law-enforcement, which cannot be easily moulded into the Eurocentric multi-stakeholder cooperation models which presuppose equity, respect and good governance.

Established NGOs, accordingly, increasingly show a preference for projects with higher earning potential. The TCPC, because of its moral appeal, fuelled by global disgust about CST, presented a 'donor darling' for funding agencies and a 'cash cow' for NGOs. For some children's rights NGOs, assisting the private sector in improving their CSR performance through TCPC implementation poses attractive opportunities to improve their own visibility and fundability. For smaller 'grassroots' NGOs, the patent need for wider exposure makes it more difficult to prioritise their less visible core tasks of protecting community interests. This was manifested in the case of MAIS, which also revealed how visible success in TCPC implementation attracted competing foreign NGOs wanting to join in the 'success'. However, the same NGOs showed less interest in taking up challenges in areas with less visibility and opportunities for success. In The Gambia, for instance, with its more difficult circumstances and lack of immediate results, the local TCPC-related NGO, CPA/ECPAT, was left struggling and isolated. Not only did the need for visibility and fundability induce spatial selectivity, it also prompted NGOs to try to claim individual responsibility for success even in collective projects. The need for visibility also prompted hotels to try to link signing the TCPC to exclusive use of the Code logo in their region. In our view, this 'issue capture' has been a pervasive, devious result of the spreading neoliberal affect.

Outlook: Can the regulation of sexual abuse in tourism be left to voluntary CSR initiatives supported by NGOs?

The intention of scripts like the Code, aiming to assist NGOs in adapting to neoliberalism and de-regulation seems straightforward. The move from parliamentary to deliberative and participative forms of governance delegates power to civil society organisations through institutions and Public Private Partnerships like the Code. However, these attempts at civil society involvement cannot camouflage the fact that when it comes down to it, NGOs do not possess the same type of hard power that governments and industry do.

The TCPC relies on power of the value chain. Tourism, however, is a complex sector with many different stakeholders and a complex value network. Power relations in the global value chains have already moved with the exponential growth of tourism and the rise of neoliberalism, trickling down into destinations. Currently we see a change from neo-liberalism to more protectionism and escalating financial capitalism, probably making it more difficult for global social 'scripts' such as the TCPC to reach into destinations. At the same time, power shifts are taking place in destinations where interests are becoming more articulated, creating challenges but also some opportunities. These developments might leave the TCPC behind as an outdated instrument. Guideline 3 of the Code, aimed at driving the fight against CST through the value chain by sharing a 'common repudiation' is already a very narrow reflection of what is meant by CSR. The changes in value networks in the post neo-liberal era call for a serious reformulation of this crucial guideline.

In conclusion, the case of the TCPC shows that regulating sexual abuse in tourism cannot be left to voluntary CSR initiatives implemented by NGOs. Where business carries the primary blame for the lack of implementation of the Code, NGOs also need to reflect on their role. Unfortunately, NGOs in general, and the NGOs involved in the TCPC in particular, have not been able to overcome the constraints imposed upon them by a neoliberal regime that results in pursuing aims through competition. Current moves to a more protective and restrictive capitalism do not seem to offer an improvement for NGOs. The sexual exploitation of children in tourism is too serious a crime and the intentions and positions of the stakeholders too weak to leave solutions up to voluntary multi-stakeholder initiatives. Although the state cannot do it alone, as shown in The Gambia, the state's hard power will be necessary to root out commercial sexual exploitation of children from tourism destinations.

Notes

(1) There is some contention regarding the use of this term, as discussed in Chapter 1, but the authors feel it is the correct one to use as it clearly refers to the objective of such tourists.
(2) http://www.thecode.org/who-have-signed/members/ checked 10-10-2018.
(3) In order for project proposals to be accepted by the funders of TCPC (amongst others, the EU, GTZ, SECO and the Dutch ministry of Foreign Affairs) they have to be structured in preconceived formats. These are based on methodologies which happen to reflect the spirit of the time. During the 1990s and the early 2000s the so-called Logical Framework (LogFrame) dominated the scene but then it was largely replaced by the 'Theory of Change'.
(4) ECPAT originally was an acronym for End Child Prostitution in Asian Tourism. For a number of reasons, partly dealt with in this chapter, activities expanded to other areas and the full name was adapted accordingly to End Child Prostitution, Pornography and Trafficking. When the institution grew and got more known the acronym itself became the 'brand' and did not need further explanation.
(5) www.thecode.org checked 17-10-2018.
(6) http://www.thecode.org/about/organizational-structure/ checked 10-11-2018.
(7) All local LCRs are ECPAT groups or other NGOs with a few exceptions: South Africa, Mauritius and Belize, http://www.thecode.org/who-have-signed/local-code-representatives/ checked 14-10-2018.
(8) http://www.thecode.org/who-have-signed/members/ checked 10-10-2018
(9) There are different types of hotel chains with contracts varying from direct ownership to franchise agreements.
(10) Debates in the 1990s between ECPAT groups and industry associations.
(11) Personal conversation between the researcher and the girl.
(12) Even when the Dominican tourism industry association (ASONAHORES) had been one of the first to sign the TCPC globally.
(13) Discussions with stakeholders for the preparation of de Man (2016).
(14) Basically, a UNICEF box for donations on the front desk.
(15) Conversations of frans de Man with PLAN and TUI responsibles in 2016.
(16) http://www.thecode.org/who-have-signed/members/ for the Dominican Republic, checked 14-10-2018.
(17) The baseline for this assessment was created in de Man (2010) and re-assessment took place in 2011, 2012, 2013, 2015 and 2016.
(18) Conversation with ECPAT France in December 2015 for the evaluation of their European project: 'Don't look away'.
(19) Personal conversation with CSR manager of Golden Tulip hotel in Recife 2015.
(20) Personal conversation with TUI representative in The Gambia, 2014.
(21) http://www.thecode.org/who-have-signed/members/ for The Gambia checked 21-06-2019.
(22) Kuoni was at the time of research one of the largest tour operators in the world. In the following years it dissolved and broke up into three parts.

References

Alexander, S., Meuwese, S. and Wolthuis, A. (2000) Policies and developments relating to the sexual exploitation of children: The legacy of the Stockholm conference. *European Journal on Criminal Policy and Research* 8 (4), 479–501.

Allen, J. (2016) *Topologies of Power: Beyond Territory and Networks*. London: Routledge.

Anderson, B. (2016) Neoliberal affects. *Progress in Human Geography* 40 (6), 734–753.

Arts, B. and Lagendijk, A. (2009) The Disoriented State. In B. Arts, A. Lagendijk and H. Van Houtum (eds) *The Disoriented State. Shifts in Governmentality, Territoriality and Governance* (pp. 231–247). Vienna: Springer.

Bäckstrand, K.J.E.E. (2006) Multi-stakeholder partnerships for sustainable development: Rethinking legitimacy, accountability and effectiveness. *European Environment* 16 (5), 290–306.

Bureau Wyser (2016) *Institutionalizing the Code? Evaluation of: Protection of Children in Tourism, Phase II*. Nijmegen Bureau Wyser.

Davis, M. (2013) Differentiating child sexual abusers. *InPsych: The Bulletin of the Australian Psychological Society Ltd* 35 (5), 14.

de Man, F. (2010) Promotion of the Protection of Children against Sexual Exploitation in Tourism 2009-2010. Monitoring Mission. Nijmegen: Retour Foundation. Unpublished.

de Man, F. (2012) Combating Child Sex Tourism in the Dominican Republic, Report of the midterm monitoring visit. Nijmegen: Retour Foundation. Unpublished.

de Man, F. (2013) *Case Thailand*. Preparatory report for ECPAT 2013 Protection of children against sexual exploitation in tourism. Capacity building and awareness raising activities in Thailand, Cambodia, Philippines, Gambia and Dominican Republic. Unpublished.

de Man, F. (2015) *Creating a common understanding and an action plan for the project 'Reducing sexual violence against children, with special attention for sexual exploitation of children in travel and tourism' in the Dominican Republic. Report of activities and results*. Leiden: ECPAT-The Netherlands.

de Man, F. (2016) *Elaboración de Términos de Referencia del Órgano de Representación Local Tripartito. Report of the process towards a Multi-Stakeholder LCR in the Dominican Republic*. Nijmegen: Retour Foundation. Unpublished.

de Man, F. and Bah, A. (2014) DON'T LOOK AWAY! Be aware and report the sexual exploitation of children in travel and tourism, Assessment on sexual exploitation of children related to tourism and reporting mechanisms in Gambia. Leiden: ECPAT the Netherlands. See https://www.defenceforchildren.nl/media/2483/3979.pdf (accessed December 2019).

Dodds, F. (2019) *Stakeholder Democracy: Represented Democracy in a Time of Fear*. London: Routledge.

Ebbekink, M. and Lagendijk, A. (2013) What's next in researching cluster policy: Place-based governance for effective cluster policy. *European Planning Studies* 21 (5), 735–753.

ECPAT (2006) *Global de las acciones en contra de la explotación sexual comercial de niños, niñas y adolescentes. República Dominicana*. Bangkok: ECPAT Internatational.

ECPAT (2009) *Child Sex Tourism Fact Sheet. Child Protection Alliance. Gambia*. Bangkok: ECPAT International.

ECPAT (2013) *Protection of Children against Sexual Exploitation in Tourism. Capacity Building and Awareness Raising Activities in Thailand, Cambodia, Philippines, Gambia and Dominican Republic*. Leiden: ECPAT Netherlands.

George, E.R. and Smith, S.R. (2013) In good company: How corporate social responsibility can protect rights and aid efforts to end child sex trafficking and modern slavery. *New York University Journal of International Law and Politics* 46 (1), 55–114.

Glover, K. (2006) Human trafficking and the sex tourism industry. *Crime and Justice International* 22 (92), 4.

Graci, S. (2013) Collaboration and partnership development for sustainable tourism. *Tourism Geographies* 15 (1), 25–42.

Hall, C.M., Gössling, S. and Scott, D. (2015) Tourism and sustainability: An introduction. In C.M. Hall, S. Gössling and D. Scott (eds) *The Routledge Handbook of Tourism and Sustainability* (pp. 1–11). Abingdon: Routledge.

Interagency Working Group (2016) *Terminology Guidelines for the Protecton of Children from Sexual Exploitaton and Sexual Abuse*. Luxembourg: ECPAT.

Jamal, T. and Getz, D. (1999) Community roundtables for tourism-related conflicts: The dialectics of consensus and process structures. *Journal of Sustainable Tourism* 7 (3–4), 290–313.

Jamal, T.B. and Getz, D. (1995) Collaboration theory and community tourism planning. *Annals of Tourism Research* 22 (1), 186–204.

Moloney, A. (2017) Child sex tourists do 'dirty business' with impunity in Dominican Republic. *Reuters*. See https://www.reuters.com/article/us-dominican-sexcrimes/child-sex-tourists-do-dirty-business-with-impunity-in-dominican-republic-idUSKBN19727B (accessed September 2018).

Oxman, A.D. and Fretheim, A. (2009) Can paying for results help to achieve the Millennium Development Goals? Overview of the effectiveness of results-based financing. *Journal of Evidence-Based Medicine* 2 (2), 70–83.

Roper, A. (2017) *Vertical Disintegration in the Corporate Hotel Industry: The End of Business as Usual*. New York: Routledge.

Scheyvens, R. and Biddulph, R. (2018) Inclusive tourism development. *Tourism Geographies* 20 (4), 589–609.

Simpson, M.C. (2008) Community benefit tourism initiatives – A conceptual oxymoron? *Tourism Management* 29 (1), 1–18.

The Protection Project (2007) *International Child Sex Tourism. Scope of the Problem and comparative Case Studies 158*. Baltimore: John Hopkins University.

UN (2014) *UN Global Compact, Guide to Corporate Sustainability*. New York: United Nations.

Unicef (2003) *Study on the Sexual Abuse and Exploitation of Children in The Gambia*. New York: United Nations.

US Department of Labor (2009) *Country Profiles. The Gambia*. Washington: US Department of Labor.

Waligo, V.M., Clarke, J. and Hawkins, R. (2013) Implementing sustainable tourism: A multi-stakeholder involvement management framework. *Tourism Management* 36, 342–353.

14 Child Sex Tourism and the Role of Local Communities

Athina Papageorgiou

Introduction

The United Nations World Tourism Organization defines sex tourism as '*an organized trip in the tourism industry, or outside of it but with the use of structures of the tourism industry, with the primary objective to facilitate a commercial sexual relationship between the tourist and residents of the destination*' (UNWTO, 1995). This definition refers to the use of both legal and illegal structures and also legally and illegally prostituted individuals of all ages, often forced to prostitution against their will. Sex tourism is known to contribute significantly to human trafficking and child prostitution, as well as forced prostitution by poor families living within certain destinations. However, several local communities and local authorities show a peculiar tolerance for it (and also drunkenness, vandalism and drug trafficking), due to the considerable economic benefits the surrounding area enjoys from the presence of tourists (UNODC, 2018; UNWTO, 2016; U.S. Department of State, 2019).

The United Nations are opposed to sex tourism and promote its health, social and cultural impacts (OSAGI, United Nations, 1995; UN Department of Public Information, 2000) and also its devastating effect on human trafficking and child prostitution (Guzder, 2009). The European Commission estimates that half a million children are trafficked each year in Western Europe to be used as beggars or prostitutes (UNODC, 2012). Human trafficking is the third most profitable illegal business in the world, following drugs and arms, with profits estimated to be 12 billion US dollars annually (UNODC, 2012). It is worrying that child victims of human trafficking increased from 23% in 2006 to 30% in 2016 (UNODC, 2018) while East Asian victims were found in 64 countries around the world (UNODC, 2012).

Despite common perceptions, child sexual exploitation and trafficking are only occasionally related or coinciding, despite the fact that in most cases they have a similar impact on victims. Among trafficking victims, 59% are trafficked for sexual exploitation, of which 68% are women, 26% are girls and 3% are boys (UNODC, 2018). These figures suggest that the large number of boys and girls involved in child prostitution in most destinations come from local communities. Therefore, strategies to address and prevent both child sexual exploitation and trafficking for sexual exploitation must focus on a variety of causes, including poverty, victim vulnerability, increased demand, recognition of paedophiles and other individuals practicing child sex, knowledge of the characteristics of perpetrators, exposure of illegal enterprises, transformation of local community attitudes and assistance and rehabilitation of young victims (ECPAT, 2008a, 2019; Koops *et al.*, 2017; UNODC, 2018).

The aim of this chapter is twofold. First, to explore the attitudes of local communities in paedo-sexual destinations and second to record current strategies and identify new methods that could help combat child sex tourism.

The Magnitude of the Problem

Child exploitation is an unethical and illegal practice that occurs in many countries worldwide regardless of the state of their economy. As a term it encompasses, but is not restricted to, sexual abuse and slavery. Sexual abuse is sub-divided into forced prostitution, sexual slavery, child pornography and commercial sex tourism (Whitley (2013) cited in Mekinc & Music, 2015). Slavery describes conditions where children are forced to beg on the streets and work in factories, hotels, restaurants and hospitals, often without pay (ILO, 2014; Seager, 2009).

According to the UN, 1 million children every year are sold in Asia to be forced into prostitution. In addition, the number of individuals who travel as tourists to practice child sex is estimated to be 1% of the total number of travellers to a child sex destination (UNODC, 2012). The most popular countries for child sex tourism are Cambodia, Thailand and Malaysia, and the most popular cities are Bangkok, Phuket and Pattaya. Mexico, Brazil, Cuba, Costa Rica and the Dominican Republic are the most popular destinations in Latin America, as are Tanzania and Kenya in Africa, while many European countries show an increasing trend in sex tourism (ECPAT, 2014; Maeseele, 2007; UN, 2003a). Individuals travelling to practice child sex tourism at these destinations come mostly from the United States, Australia, Japan, Germany, England and Canada. Of these tourists, 57% are between 40 and 60 years of age. Travel agencies that organise these trips attract customers by promising high quality experiences and continuous rotation of children during their stay (ECPAT, 2008b; ECPAT International, 2008; Hanel, 2017; Mekinc & Music, 2015).

It is estimated that 25% of all sex tourists worldwide are Americans, while in specific areas such as Costa Rica and Cambodia Americans represent almost 80% and 38% of all sex tourists, respectively (Silberman, 2013). These individuals tend to buy commercial travel packages as normal tourists, thus remaining unnoticed both in their destination and at home. There is no reliable data about the number of travellers practicing child sex tourism worldwide because scientific research on this subject is extremely difficult to undertake (Mano, 2017; UNWTO, 2016).

It has to be noted that there is a serious misconception regarding the profile of these travellers. Firstly, it is true that many people travel to child sex destinations due to motivations that align with the push-pull model described by Dann (1977). According to this model, 'push' factors are intrinsic motivations. In this context, sex tourists' holidays are linked to a desire to 'escape', stop hiding their true identity, act freely and fulfil their 'needs' in anonymity, with limited danger in an adventurous environment. These are precisely the *anomie* and *ego-enhancement* factors that Dann described as the principal travel motives (Dann, 1977). They refer mainly, but not exclusively, to paedophiles. Similarly, regarding 'pull' factors for this population one must consider the ease of access to their objects of 'desire' and the ability to explore their fantasies safely. Destinations that fulfil these requirements are obviously the destinations of choice (Anderson, 2011; Anderson & O'Connell Davidson, 2003; Martin & Woodside, 2012). On the other hand, not all travellers practicing child sex at a destination seem to have travelled for this purpose, although it is largely assumed that most of them are indeed child sexual abusers (Seabrock, 2000). Research has revealed two distinct groups (ECPAT, 2016; ECPAT International, 2008; Seabrock, 2000): individuals who travel to a certain destination where they incidentally have the opportunity to have child sex and others who travel to a certain destination aiming exclusively to practice child sex. However, it is not clear if the preferential group consists only of paedophiles, as many of these individuals also have sex with adults, while paedophiles do not (Earp, 2017; Turner *et al.*, 2014). Following these findings, we think that child sex tourists could be divided into situational and preferential abusers, with the latter sub-divided into child sex seekers (or child sexual abusers) and paedophiles. This categorisation might be helpful in recognising these people in destinations and/or when they return home. Our view is supported by the findings of the ECPAT global study which revealed that there is no typical offender (ECPAT, 2016; UNWTO, 2016). Indeed, sexual exploitation of children in travel and tourism involves international and domestic tourists, business travellers, and migrant and transient workers. There is also no profile stereotype, despite the one often portrayed in the media (i.e. white, western, middle-aged wealthy men). Rather, offenders are mostly situational, can come from any background and can be foreigners or locals and even women or children. The only common feature among child sex tourists seems to be the practice of child sex in a corrupted environment where identification and punishment is rare (ECPAT, 2016).

Factors Affecting Child Sex Tourism Development

There are several factors that have helped to facilitate the expansion of child sex tourism in recent years from the demand side. These include affordable travel, internet accessibility and use, extreme poverty, corruption and community tolerance (Ekberg, 2005; O'Connell Davidson, 2004; UNWTO, 2016; Zahid Shahab, 2005). Globalisation has contributed to child sex tourism development, as nowadays travel has become widely affordable and many people are able to visit distant destinations (Seabrook, 2000). This means that a paedophile or a child sex seeker can easily mix with other tourists who travel in groups or individually to a popular destination that is also a child sex location. Globalisation has been aided by the internet, which is a unique tool for people searching for child sex opportunities in various destinations, as well as child pornography and information exchange. Moreover, the internet has enabled child sex providers to easily reach paedophiles and child abusers via specific sites, particularly, though not exclusively, on the dark web. In this way they are able to arrange travel itineraries and meetings with young prostitutes, as many of them run (or work with) a legal travel agency. In both cases, travel is organised as a regular tourism package for business or leisure, making the identification of these people almost impossible (Hughes, 2000; UNWTO, 2016).

Corruption is also thought to be a key factor associated with the growth of child prostitution. For family-pushed child prostitution (see below) the police, social workers and the local community simply accept this phenomenon either as a result of bribery or as an indirect economic 'support' to the families and the community, thinking that by silencing this situation they help poor individuals and families obtain the means to survive (Maeseele, 2007; UNWTO, 2016; U.S. Department of State, 2019). However, most trafficking-forced child prostitution would fail without the support of corrupt public and sometimes private sector officials who allow or even facilitate human trafficking for a certain price. Corruption ranges from active involvement to passive negligence, leading to easy victim selection, and uneventful transportation and retention of children against their will (UN.GIFT, 2008).

One would think that Caucasian males in Far East countries or Asian males in western countries seeking child sex should be easily spotted in most areas where child sex tourism thrives. Similarly child prostitution enterprises (operating everywhere, from five star hotels to brothels) ought to be easily revealed by the authorities. However, this is not the case, as corrupt police officers, local government and city officials and hotel managers assist in covering up this profitable business. Money provides a strong motivation for the protection of illegally operating enterprises, as child sex tourism has become one of the most profitable segments of the tourism industry in recent years. It is estimated that child sex tourism may be worth 20 billion USD per year (ECPAT, 2014), while it has also been reported that one third of the 800,000 prostitutes in Cambodia are minors (Hansen, 2005). This results in two behavioral patterns as far as the local community is concerned: tolerance and cover-up (ILO, 2001; UNWTO, 2016).

However, as stated earlier, not all children are forced into prostitution as a result of trafficking or kidnapping (Giese, 2005; Poulin, 2003; Roby, 2005), as in some cases children or their families living in extreme poverty may choose prostitution in order to survive (Farley *et al.*, 2004; ILO, 2001; Landgren, 2005; Maeseele, 2008; Servin *et al.*, 2015). Theoretically and morally this is still a case of forced prostitution but reasons differ, as certain conditions may, in our opinion, affect this attitude. These reasons include extreme poverty, social inequality, natural disasters and armed conflict. Research revealed that family dysfunction (domestic violence, drug use and neglect) leading to children running away from home, physical and sexual abuse, teen pregnancy and limited education are factors perpetuating vulnerability for the underage, forcing them into prostitution (Farley *et al.*, 2003; ILO, 2001; Servin *et al.*, 2015).

All of these issues make people vulnerable and also destroy family support structures, community bonds and self-protection mechanisms that might otherwise act as a buffer against child exploitation. These disenfranchised communities often lack social cohesion and consist of individuals experiencing social exclusion and an inability to access basic education, welfare and rehabilitation services and decent work opportunities. All these conditions may lead them to choose prostitution as a life-saving necessity (Andrews, 2004; EC, 2015; ILO, 2001; O'Connell Davidson, 2004; Servin *et al.*, 2015; UN.GIFT 2008). Finally, sexual exploitation of children may result from people acting, on the surface, as 'good Samaritans'. Indeed, according to ECPAT (2008b) some tourists support poor families with children, aiming to gain their trust before exploiting the children, thus succeeding in having child sex and ensuring the silence of their victims' family.

All these conditions give individuals seeking child sex a number of 'moral' excuses. For instance, they argue that in some cultures child sex is accepted and sexual relations with children are somehow legal. This view is reinforced by the fact that marriage in several countries is allowed at a very young age for the girls, with minimum legal ages at marriage varying across states/provinces, ethnic groups, religious groups and forms of marriage (UN, 2003b). These people also use scientific research to justify their behavior, as it has been revealed that in certain Asian countries a prostitute can financially support up to five people (Andrews, 2004) while the desire of the parents' for extra income and luxury items leads parents or legal guardians to sell children to traffickers or force minors into prostitution (Bales, 2004; Maeseele, 2008).

However, the sexual exploitation of children is not physically and emotionally harmless. Rather, it results in a range of physical, psychological and social consequences that can be both long-lasting and life-threatening (Oram *et al.*, 2012; UN.GIFT 2008). The main health problems are pregnancy, sexually transmitted infections, drug addiction and genitalia trauma injuries resulting from forced, multiple and violent intercourses. Sex slaves also experience imprisonment, beating and rape, all of which are used to keep victims obedient to clients. These children also experience psychological and emotional trauma, as they suffer from depression, develop constant guilt, have low self-respect and occasionally attempt suicide. They also remain stigmatised by the community and excluded from proper education, leading to further psychological trauma. As adults, these children may practice commercial sex and remain socially excluded for life. Finally, as far as AIDS is concerned, research has shown that sexually exploited children are more susceptible to HIV infection, as no protective measures are taken during intercourse (ECPAT, 1996; Nair, 2007; Silverman *et al.*, 2007).

The Roles of Local Communities

The victims of child sex tourism come from various environments. Disenfranchised socioeconomic areas with poverty and extreme crime, struggling families, orphanages, ethnic minorities and refugee camps are the most common places where traffickers buy or kidnap children for sexual exploitation (Mekinc & Music, 2015). These victims are uneducated boys and girls, many of whom have previously been sexually abused by strangers or members of their family. Homeless or orphan children are sold by the managers or the members of staff of orphanages and camps (Mekinc & Music, 2015; Turner *et al.*, 2014) as there is limited supervision or control of these establishments by the police or local authorities. Corruption at both the individual and societal level leads to tolerance and cover-up as governments and local authorities deliberately ignore and/or hide the problem in the back streets, away from public areas and tourist attractions. In doing so, they try not to disturb or turn away tourists and jeopardise tourism development (Mekinc & Music, 2015; UNWTO, 2016).

There has been a dearth of analysis of child sex tourism related corruption, which may not be surprising given how difficult and dangerous it is to reach the individuals involved (UNWTO, 2016). Therefore, most available data come from studies on the corruption levels of countries that also have high levels of child sex tourism. These results, even coming from such limited research, are not irrelevant as corruption remains one of the main causes of extreme poverty in a number of undeveloped countries (Transparency International, 2015).

Mekinc and Music (2015) analysed the findings of three major studies conducted by Transparency International (2013), NUMBEO (2014) and the World Economic Forum (2013). The first study was based on expert opinions, the second on a questionnaire posted to several websites and the third focused on police forces' effectiveness data, public opinion data, survey data of the Executive Board of the World Economic Forum and quantitative data obtained from publications of a number of expert sources, such as IATA, UNWTO and UNESCO. The authors applied all available data to compare the top 25 child sex tourism countries according to ECPAT (2008a, 2008b). The results of this analysis show that corruption runs in both the private and public sector and is related to low levels of democracy or high levels of autocracy in the countries in question, a finding previously reported by Dobovcek (2008, cited in Mekinc & Music, 2015). The levels of corruption, crime rates and the police's lack of reliability correlate with the presence of child sex tourism in countries such as Kenya, Honduras, South Africa and Russia. However, corruption levels, organised crime and inability to enforce the law are not the only factors related to child sex tourism. For instance, countries such as Malaysia and Costa Rica are assessed as having low levels of corruption but remain within the top 25 countries related to child sex tourism, while in other countries, such as Argentina, police enforcement levels are highly ranked but child sex tourism is still widespread (Mekinc & Music, 2015). This may suggest that the roles of the local communities in aiding child sex tourism may be more important than previously understood.

Tourism development has various negative impacts on tourism destinations, both developed and undeveloped (Telfer & Sharpley, 2008). These impacts have been extensively studied in relation to crime increase (Belisle & Hoy, 1980), drug use and alcohol consumption (Pizam, 1978) and cultural degradation (Stronza, 2001). Prostitution has profound economic, social, cultural and health impacts that affect local communities (Belisle & Hoy, 1980; Haralambopoulos & Pizam, 1996; Monterrubio & Bello, 2010; Teye et al., 2002). Wall and Mathieson (2006) state that tourism has created locations that attract prostitutes and clients and Liu and Var (1986) report that most responders (64%) in their study agreed that tourism increased prostitution in Hawaii. In contrast, Haralambopoulos and Pizam (1996) did not find any correlation between tourism and prostitution in Samos Island, Greece. These contradicting findings may be explained by the findings of Ryan (2003) who concluded that tourism possibly confirms patterns of prostitution that already exist within destinations.

In a very interesting study conducted in Mexico City, a place that has been identified as an emerging child sex tourism destination, residents stated that tourists mainly visit the city for its attractions and only 9% agreed that tourists visit the city to practice commercial sex (Monterrubio & Bello, 2010). However, this finding was in contrast to the respondents' views on other questions regarding the reasons for tourist engagement in commercial sex, as 70% of them stated that this was due to the sex opportunities given to tourists and 71% believed that tourism offers work opportunities through prostitution (Monterrubio & Bello, 2010). This is a common attitude against tourism side effects in many destinations, as locals choose to simply ignore the problem in order to protect their 'tourism product' and income (Yan *et al.*, 2018). Indeed, bad publicity may affect mainstream tourist's decision to travel and therefore reduce tourism income for the community, but this has yet to be studied.

Why do tourists seek commercial sex? Research has identified that both opportunity and anonymity are factors behind this behaviour. Oppermann (1998) stated that many tourists practice commercial sex either because they have an opportunity to do so or because they merge with other people who think as they do at a destination. Other scholars think that anonymity in a tolerant environment encourages tourists' delinquent behaviour, including the procurement of commercial sex (McKercher & Bauer, 2003).

However, opportunity is also supported by local attitudes. Residents understand that tourism creates certain financial and employment benefits and tend to see criminal behaviour, including prostitution, as only an unfortunate side effect (Monterrubio & Bello, 2010). This is a rather peculiar attitude towards prostitution and especially child prostitution as it mostly develops in countries with strong religious bonds within the society that are avowedly against all forms of prostitution. Poverty, therefore, seems to be a much stronger motive to bear this 'sin' than it is to oppose to it (Jenness, 1990; Monterrubio & Bello, 2010). It is obvious that we need to understand the attitudes (cognitive, affective and behavioural) of the locals, as acts to tackle criminal behaviour and combat sexual exploitation and child sex tourism must strongly involve a committed local community in order to succeed.

It is also important that this community engagement is in place before taking any punitive measures to develop policies and strategies that can act as barriers and protective factors against sexual exploitation of children in general and especially child sex tourism. These actions should involve the police, state officials (both local and government authorities), the media and various organisations and professionals within the private sector; namely tour operators, hotel managers and employers, local tourism organisations and professionals of the tourism industry, such as taxi drivers, club owners and tourist guides. There are reports that in certain countries, such as Peru, corrupt police officers practically guard brothels and help traffickers in recruiting children for sexual exploitation (U.S. Department of Justice, 2014), while child sexual exploitation has also been reported to be related to unaccompanied minor refugees in European countries (Maeseele, 2007). There are also reports of weak responses by certain countries, such as Cambodia and Nigeria, to the recommendations made by major international organisations to reduce child exploitation (U.S. Department of State, 2019). However, it is encouraging that, at present, 32 nations have adopted acts allowing the prosecution of their nationals accused of child sexual exploitation committed abroad (U.S. Department of State, 2013, 2019) and also that many destination countries are developing strategies to tackle child sex tourism. For instance, the government of Brazil has initiated a large-scale national and international campaign to combat sexual exploitation of children in tourism. Furthermore, Ghana has formed local watchdog groups and encourages community members to provide follow-on support and reintegration services to the survivors of child sex exploitation. In comparison, Benin has led a public awareness campaign that incorporated an inspection programme conducted at the markets and along roads connecting major cities. Similarly, Moldova has designed a community-based approach to enhance law enforcement efforts and coordinate victim identification and assistance. Cambodia, one of the most affected countries, has established a special police unit to combat child sex tourism, although with limited results so far (Mekinc & Music, 2015; U.S. Department of State, 2019). Imprisonment and public castigation seem to be the strongest disincentives for most individuals.

Current Actions and Further Suggestions

The UN General Assembly in 1989 adopted the Rights of the Child code (UN, 1989). It declared that the child, for the full and harmonious development of his or her personality, must grow up in a family environment and also in an atmosphere of happiness, love and understanding. Children living in exceptionally difficult conditions need special consideration and governments must take all appropriate legislative, administrative, social and educational measures to protect them from all forms of physical or mental violence, injury or abuse, neglect or negligent treatment, and maltreatment or exploitation, including sexual abuse. Such protective measures include effective procedures for the establishment of social programmes to provide necessary support for the child and also for the prevention and identification, reporting, referral, investigation, treatment, follow-up and, if possible, judicial involvement of instances of child maltreatment.

Following the UN, the United Nations World Tourism Organization (UNWTO) adopted the *Text of Principles* for the prevention of organised sex tourism in 1995 and, in 1999, established the *Global Code of Ethics for Tourism*, in which the tourism industry was called upon to address the issue of children's exposure to sex tourism (UNWTO, 1999). The UN General Assembly states that the exploitation of human beings in any form, particularly sexual, especially when applied to children, conflicts with the fundamental aims of tourism. As such, in accordance with international law, it should be energetically combated with the cooperation of all the States concerned and penalised without concession by the national legislation of both the countries visited and the countries of the perpetrators of these acts, even when they are carried out abroad (UNWTO 1999, Article 2.3).

The UNWTO and the European Union joined forces in 2000 to tackle child sex tourism. However, results have been heavily criticised (Maeseele, 2007), mainly because the proposed measures did not seem to be efficient in improving the poor social, economic and political conditions that contribute to the generation of child sex tourism. The EU has developed further actions, like the *Protocol to Prevent, Suppress and Punish Trafficking in Persons, Especially Women and Children*, supplementing the United Nations *Convention against Transnational Organized Crime* (UNODC, 2004). It has conducted several conventions on the protection of children against sexual exploitation and abuse and also issued the Directive 2011/93/EU of the European Parliament and Council that harmonised criminal offences relating to sexual abuse committed against children, the sexual exploitation of children and child pornography throughout the EU (Maeseele, 2007).

The tourism sector has taken independent measures to combat and reduce child sex tourism and the sexual exploitation of children since the middle of the 1990s. In particular, the International Air Transport Association (IATA) adopted, in 1995, a *Final Resolution Condemning Commercial Sexual Exploitation of Children* (UNWTO, 1995). The European Travel Agents' and Tour Operators' Association (ECTAA) also adopted, in 1996, a *Declaration against Child Sex Tourism within EU* (ECTAA (1996) cited in Mekinc & Music, 2015) and the Federation of International Youth Travel Organizations (FIYTO) adopted, in 1997, a *Resolution to Combat Child Sex Tourism* (Mekinc & Music, 2015).

One of the most important codes so far that enrols the local communities in the battle against child sex tourism was produced in 2004 by the End Child Prostitution in Asian Tourism (ECPAT) organisation. The *Code of Conduct to Protect Children from Sexual Exploitation in Travel and Tourism* proposed the collaboration of local communities with victims and at-risk individuals as a principal act to combat child sex tourism through knowledge, policing and legal shielding. Communities were also urged to provide appropriate education for all children and anti-poverty programmes for families and children at risk. Furthermore, communities were asked to monitor tourists (to reveal paedophile behaviour), develop programmes to keep children in safe accommodation (by administering medical and psychological treatment and non-discriminating isolation), train locals to accept and reintegrate victims of child sex tourism into the community, create information networks, and strengthen existing laws against the trafficking of boys and girls (ECPAT, 2004). It is encouraging that many countries have today criminalised sex tourism not only in their territory but also beyond their borders, an act designed to reduce the facilitation of the demand for child sex tourism. We think that the supportive and protective roles of local communities, as well as the severe punishment of the 'customer', are probably the most effective measures to help the fight against child sex tourism.

At present, important recommendations have been made by major international organisations, addressed to governments and aimed at preventing child sexual exploitation. These include measures against trafficking and the social inequality that is linked to an inability to access basic education, health and work opportunities. In our view, however, what is needed the most in this field are more preventive measures. Prevention should include a wide range of measures to address all factors that contribute to the vulnerability of children (mainly social, economic and structural factors) and lead to child exploitation and abuse. Extended international research, as presented above, has in our view revealed a number of actions that need to be undertaken.

Communities should be reinforced and empowered by governments as full partners in the fight against child sex tourism. If well informed, the public can be the eyes and ears of their communities and put pressure on law enforcement and all stakeholders to make this fight a priority.

Governments and local authorities should provide financial support for poor areas where child sexual exploitation is proliferating. State financed job offerings could provide a good start, offering a sustainable livelihood in a safe and regulated environment. A wide range of small affordable urban houses or low-rent apartments in well-policed areas could also be offered. This welfare policy should be monitored by the state while the money needed could come from international donors and wealthy nations. Local authorities should also create strategies to eliminate criminalisation of victims and promote the coordinated cooperation of all stakeholders, local and international, private and public.

Authorities should make school attendance mandatory, at least for the elementary level. Non-cooperating families might be persuaded to do so if warned that they will be excluded from social welfare programmes for not responding.

State-funded and confidential consultations with psychologists and social workers should be offered to all victims of child sex tourism to limit the psychological burden on these children. Authorities should also provide children with information on exploitation risks and ways to report threatening situations. To this end, local authorities should use properly trained personnel. Using young popular artists committed to the cause is a potential way of ensuring that children will engage with this information.

Countries that have become child sex tourism destinations should require the global travel industry to develop preventive activities. All personnel should undergo training on children's rights and ways to identify suspicious travellers. Companies should adopt measures to prevent sexual exploitation and understand methods for reporting suspects to the relevant authorities. The travel industry should also provide information to customers and support all key stakeholders (non-governmental organisations, law enforcement bodies, etc.) in the prevention of the sexual exploitation of children.

Local and regional authorities should also collaborate with the media to reveal and not cover-up the problem. Training and awareness raising among journalists is needed, as they must not be afraid to reveal child sex tourism and do so in a way that does not further traumatise the victims of child prostitution. State officials should also urge media and local communities to sensitise the public to the realities of child sex tourism. These children are not 'happy hookers' but unfortunate, poor, scared, uneducated and possibly tortured human beings.

States and international organisations should encourage and finance scholars to further research human behaviour on the subject in order to provide authorities with all the information needed to confront all forms (current and emergent) of sexual exploitation of children adopted by paedophiles, child sex tourists, promoters and traffickers. They should also instruct police authorities to develop novel strategies and internal processes to remove corruption within organisations related to child sex tourism. The development of uniform international procedures for the identification and protection of children in danger is also required. There is also a need to enact laws to acknowledge children as victims of the crime of sexual exploitation, protect them from secondary victimisation by law enforcement and the criminal justice system, and raise penalties for all individuals involved in child sex tourism, both at home and abroad. These penalties need to be applied to everyone involved in child sex tourism, including parents/legal guardians, traffickers, hotel owners, travel agency's managers, police officers, social workers, website administrators and, of course, customers/perpetrators.

It is apparent that communities need to become more responsible for and committed to the fight against child sex exploitation. They should also be made more aware of how to identify vulnerable families and children and create a safety net for these individuals within the community. It may be a sad reality that not all the suggested measures are feasible, can be enacted immediately or have an immediate impact. However, adopting preventive measures, as well as creating protective strategies, empowering law enforcement agencies and seeking the strong commitment of all stakeholders, are in our view the basic acts needed to tackle this ongoing crime.

Acknowledgements

The author would like to thank Professor Marios Sotiriadis for his remarks and dedicate this chapter to the loving memory of Professor Pericles Lytras.

References

Anderson, B. (2011) Moving children? Child trafficking, child migration and child rights. *Critical Social Policy* 31 (3), 454–477.

Anderson, B. and O'Connell Davidson, J. (2003) Is Trafficking in Human Beings Demand Driven? A Multi-Country Pilot Study. *IOM Migration Research Series*, No. 15. Geneva: IOM (International Organization for Migration). See https://publications.iom.int/system/files/pdf/mrs_15_2003.pdf (accessed July 2020).

Andrews, S.K. (2004) U.S. Domestic prosecution of the American international sex tourist: Efforts to protect children from sexual exploitation. *The Journal of Criminal Law and Criminology* 8 (4), 415–454.

Bales, K. (2004) *Disposable People: New Slavery in the Global Economy*. Berkeley: University of California Press.

Belisle, F. and Hoy, D. (1980) The perceived impact of tourism by residents: A case study in Santa Marta, Colombia. *Annals of Tourism Research* 7 (1), 83–101.

Dann, G. (1977) Anomie, ego-enhancement and tourism. *Annals of Tourism Research* 4 (4), 184–194.

Earp, B.D. (2017) *Pedophilia and Child Sexual Abuse are Two Different Things – Confusing them is Harmful to Children*. See https://blogs.bmj.com/medical-ethics/2017/11/11/pedophilia-and-child-sexual-abuse-are-two-different-things-confusing-them-is-harmful-to-children/ (accessed July 2020).

EC-European Community (2015) *Study on High-Risk Groups for Trafficking in Human Beings*. See https://ec.europa.eu/anti-trafficking/sites/ antitrafficking/files/study_on_children_as_high_risk_groups_of_trafficking_in_human_beings_0.pdf (accessed July 2020).

ECPAT (1996) *Commercial Sexual Exploitation of Children, Report of the First Year Following the Congress Against the Commercial Sexual Exploitation of Children*. See https://www.ecpat.se/uploads/2.PDF/Rapporter/ECPAT-Sweden-OP-May-2011.pdf (accessed July 2020).

ECPAT (2004) *Code of Conduct to Protect Children from Sexual Exploitation in Travel and Tourism*. See https://www.ecpat.org/wp-content/uploads/2016/04/Code_of_Conduct_ENG.pdf (accessed August 2020).

ECPAT (2008a) *Against the Sexual Exploitation of Children and Adolescents*. See https://www.ecpat.org/wp- content/uploads/legacy/Thematic_Paper_Prostitution_ENG.pdf (accessed July 2020).

ECPAT (2008b) Young person's guide to combating child-sex tourism. See http://www.ecpat.org/wp-content/uploads/legacy/Young%20person%27s%20 Guide%20to%20CST_ENG.pdf (accessed July 2020).

ECPAT (2014) *The Commercial Sexual Exploitation of Children in Europe*. See https://www.ecpat.org/wp-content/uploads/legacy/ Regional%20CSEC%20Overview_Europe.pdf (accessed July 2020).

ECPAT (2016) *Global Study on Sexual Exploitation of Children in Travel and Tourism.* See https://www.humandignity.foundation/wp-content/uploads/2018/11/Global-Report-Offenders-on-the-move.pdf (accessed July 2020).

ECPAT (2019) *Perceptions of Frontline Welfare Workers on the Sexual Exploitation of Children in the Pacific.* See https://www.ecpat.org/wp-content/uploads/2019/06/Perceptions-of-Frontline-Welfare-Workers-on-the-Sexual-Exploitation-of-Children-in-the-Pacific-ECPAT-research-June-2019.pdf (accessed July 2020).

ECPAT International (2008) *Combating Child and Sex Tourism: Questions and Answers.* Saladaeng Printing Co. Ltd. Bangkok. See http://www.ecpat.org/wp-content/uploads/legacy/cst_faq_eng.pdf (accessed July 2020).

Ekberg, G. (2005) *The Swedish Law That Prohibits the Purchase of Sexual Services: Best Practices for Prevention of Prostitution and Trafficking in Human Beings* (updated version). See http://www.prostitutionresearch.com/ pdf/EkbergVAW.pdf (accessed July 2020).

Farley, M., Cotton, A., Lynne, J., Zumbeck, S., Spiwak, F., Reyes, M., Alvarez, D. and Sezgin, U. (2004) Prostitution and trafficking in nine countries: An update on violence and posttraumatic stress disorder. *Journal of Trauma Practice* 2 (3/4), 33–74.

Giese, K.L. (2005) Where have all the women gone: trafficking in women, a global problem. *Journal of Undergraduate Research* 5, 1–14.

Guzder, D. (2009) *The Economics of Commercial Sexual Exploitation.* Accessed 31 July 2020 http://pulitzercenter.org/blog/untold-stories/economics-commercial-sexual-exploitation.

Hanel, J. (2017) Child Exploitation and Tourism at the Example of Orphanage Tourism: A Situation Analysis on the Current Situation of Orphanage Tourism in Myanmar Including a Comparison of Myanmar and Cambodia. Master Thesis. Eberswalde University for Sustainable Development. See https://www.tourism-watch.de/system/files/migrated/ hanel_julia_master_thesis.pdf (accessed July 2020).

Hansen, C. (2005) Children for Sale: Dateline goes undercover with a human rights group to expose sex trafficking in Cambodia. *NBC News.* See http://www.nbcnews.com/id/4038249/ns/dateline_nbc/t/children-sale/#.XyNKSeFR3IU (accessed July 2020).

Haralambopoulos, N. and Pizam, A. (1996) Perceived impacts of tourism: The case of Samos. *Annals of Tourism Research* 23 (3), 503–526.

Hughes, D.M. (2000) The internet and sex industries. *IEEE Technology and Society Magazine* 19 (1), 35–42.

ILO-International Labor Office (2001) *The Filippino Children in Prostitution.* See https://www.ilo.org/wcmsp5/groups/public/---asia/---ro-bangkok/---ilo-manila/documents/publication/wcms_437078.pdf (accessed July 2020).

ILO-International Labor Office (2014) Commercial Sexual Exploitation of Children. See http://www.ilo.org/ipec/areas/CSEC/lang--en/index.htm (accessed July 2020).

Jenness, V. (1990) From sex as sin to sex as work: COYOTE and the reorganization of prostitution as a social problem. *Social Problems* 37 (3), 403–420.

Koops, T., Turner, D., Neutze J. and Briken, P. (2017) Child sex tourism – prevalence of and risk factors for its use in a German community sample. *BMC Public Health* 17, 344. See https://www.ncbi.nlm.nih.gov/pmc/articles/ PMC5397735/ (accessed July 2020).

Landgren, K. (2005) The protective environment: Development support for child protection. *Human Rights Quarterly* 27, 214–248.

Liu, J.C. and Var, T. (1986) Resident attitudes toward tourism impacts in Hawaii. *Annals of Tourism Research* 13 (2), 193–214.

Maeseele, T. (2007) Towards a European Policy concerning Child Sex Tourism: Reality or Rhetoric? Master Thesis. Ghent University. See https://pdfs. semanticscholar.org/ 4c74/b0a50247b8b8683cc06ac90b4888ed3211ba.pdf (accessed July 2020).

Mano, A.P. (2017) An innovative approach to sex trafficking research: The methodological advancement of attride-stirling's thematic network analysis. *International Annals of Criminology* 55 (1), 40–59.

Martin, D. and Woodside, A.G. (2012) Structure and process modeling of seemingly unstructured leisure-travel decisions and behavior. *International Journal of Contemporary Hospitality Management* 24 (6), 855–872.

McKercher, B. and Bauer, T. (2003) Conceptual framework of the nexus between tourism, romance, and sex. In T. Bauer and B. McKercher (eds) *Sex and Tourism: Journeys of Romance, Love and Lust* (pp. 3–17). New York: The Haworth Hospitality Press.

Mekinc, J. and Music, K. (2015) Sexual exploitation of children in tourism. *Innovative Issues and Approaches in Social Sciences* 8 (2), 64–85.

Nair, P.M. (2007) Trafficking women and children for sexual exploitation. *Handbook for Law Enforcement Agencies in India*. New Delhi: UNODC. See https://www.un.org/ruleoflaw/files/Handbook_for_Law_Enforcement_Agencies_in_India[1].pdf (accessed July 2020).

Monterrubio, J.C. and Bello, A. (2010) Local community attitudes towards the impact of tourism on prostitution. *Journal of Tourism – Studies and Research in Tourism*. See https://www.researchgate.net/publication/227576617 Local_community_attitudes_towards_the_impact_of_tourism_on_prostitution (accessed July 2020).

NUMBEO (2014) Crime Index for Country 2014 [online]. See http://www.numbeo.com/crime/rankings_by_country.jsp (accessed July 2020).

O'Connell Davidson, J. (2004) Child sex tourism: An anomalous form of movement? *Journal of Contemporary European Studies* 12 (1), 31–46.

Oppermann, M. (1998) Introduction. In M. Oppermann (ed.) *Sex Tourism and Prostitution: Aspects of Leisure, Work and Recreation* (pp. 1–19). New York: Cognizant Communication Corporation.

Oram, S., Stöckl, H., Busza, J., Howard, L.M. and Zimmerman, C. (2012) Prevalence and risk of violence and the physical, mental, and sexual health problems associated with human trafficking: Systematic review. *PLoS Med* 9 (5). See https://www.ncbi.nlm.nih.gov/pmc/articles/PMC3362635 / (accessed July 2020).

OSAGI, United Nations (1995) *Gender Mainstreaming Mandates: Beijing Platform for Action*. See http://www.un.org/womenwatch/osagi/gmcrimeprev.htm (accessed July 2020).

Pizam, A. (1978) Tourism's impacts: The social costs to the destination community as perceived by its residents. *Journal of Travel Research* 16 (4), 8–12.

Poulin, R. (2003) Globalization and the sex trade: trafficking and the commodification of women and children. *Canadian Women Studies/Les cahiers de la femme* 22 (3–4), 38–43.

Roby, J.L. (2005) Women and children in the global sex trade. *International Journal of Social Work* 48 (2), 136–147.

Ryan, C. (2003) *Recreational Tourism: Demands and Impacts*. Clevedon: Channel View Publications.

Seager, J. (2009) *The Penguin Atlas of Women in the World* (4th edn). New York: Penguin Books.

Seabrook, J. (2000) *No Hiding Place: Child Sex Tourism and the Role of Extraterritorial Legislation*. London: Zed Books, ECPAT Europe Law Enforcement Group.

Servin, A.E., Brower, K.C., Gordon, L., Rocha-Jimenez, T., Staines, H., Vera-Monroy, R., Strathdee, S. and Silverman, J. (2015) Vulnerability factors and pathways leading to underage entry into sex work in two Mexican-US border cities. *Journal of Applied Research on Children: Informing Policy for Children at Risk* (1), 3. See https://www.ncbi.nlm.nih.gov/pmc/articles/PMC4412591/ (accessed July 2020).

Silberman, J. (2013) *How to Stop Global Child Trafficking. The Christian Science Monitor*. See http://www.csmonitor.com/World/Making-a-difference/Change-Agent/2013/0816/How-to-stop-global-child-trafficking (accessed July 2020).

Silverman, J.G., Decker, M.R., Gupta, J., Maheshwari, A., Willis, B.M. and Raj, A. (2007) HIV prevalence and predictors of infection in sex-trafficked Nepalese girls and women. *JAMA* 298 (5), 536–542.

Stronza, A. (2001) Anthropology of tourism: Forging new ground for ecotourism and other alternatives. *Annual Review of Anthropology* 30, 261–283.

Teye, V., Sönmez, S.F. and Sirakaya, E. (2002) Residents' attitudes toward tourism development. *Annals of Tourism Research* 29 (3), 668-688.

Telfer, D.J. and Sharpley, R. (2008) *Tourism and Development in the Developing World*. London: Routledge.

Transparency International (2013) *Corruption Perceptions Index 2013*. See http://www. transparency.org/cpi2013/results (accessed July 2020).

Transparency International (2015) *Corruption perceptions Index 2015*. See https://www. transparency.org/en/cpi/2015# (accessed July 2020).

Turner, D., Rettenberger, M., Lohmann, L., Eher, R. and Briken, P. (2014) Pedophilic sexual interests and psychopathy in child sexual abusers working with children. *Child Abuse & Neglect* (2), 326–35.

UN (1989) *Convention on the Rights of the Child*. See http://www.un.org/documents/ ga/ res/44/a44r025.htm (accessed July 2020).

UN (2003a) *Report of the Special Rapporteur on the Sale of Children, Child Prostitution and Child Pornography*. See https://www.ohchr.org/EN/HRBodies/HRC/RegularSessions/ Session25/Documents/A-HRC-25-48_en.doc (accessed July 2020).

UN (2003b) *Legal Age of Marriage*. See http://data.un.org/DocumentData.aspx?id=336 (accessed July 2020).

UN Department of Public Information (2000) New Global Treaty to combat sex slavery of women and girls. *10th United Nations Congress on the Prevention of Crime and the Treatment of Offenders*. See https://digitallibrary.un.org/record/411556 (accessed July 2020).

UN.GIFT – United Nations Global Initiative to Fight Human Trafficking (2008) *The Vienna Forum Report: A Way Forward to Combat Human Trafficking*. See http:// www.un.org/ga/president/62/ThematicDebates/humantrafficking/ebook.pdf (accessed July 2020).

UNODC (2004) United Nations convention against transnational organized crime and the protocols thereto. See https://www.unodc.org/documents/ middleeastandnorth africa/organised-crime/UNITED_NATIONS_ CONVENTION_AGAINST_TRANS-NATIONAL_ORGANIZED_CRIME_AND_THE_PROTOCOLS_THERETO.pdf (accessed July 2020).

UNODC (2012) *Global Report on Trafficking in Persons*. See https://www.unodc.org/ documents/data-and-analysis/glotip/ Trafficking_in_Persons_2012_web.pdf (accessed July 2020).

UNODC (2018) *Global Report on Trafficking in Persons 2018*. See http://www. unodc. org/documents/data-and-analysis/glotip/2018/GLOTiP_2018_ BOOK_web_small.pdf (accessed July 2020).

UNWTO (2016) *Report of the 31st meeting of the World Tourism Network on Child Protection*. ITB Berlin, Germany. See http://cf.cdn.unwto.org/ sites/all/files/pdf/report_ of_the_31st_meeting_of_the_ world_ tourism_network_on_child_protection_2_2.pdf (accessed July 2020).

UNWTO (1999) *Global Code of Ethics for Tourism*. Accessed 31 July 2020 http://ethics. unwto.org/ content/full-text-global-code-ethics-tourism.

UNWTO (1995) *Statement on the Prevention of Organized Sex Tourism*. See https://web. archive.org/web/20030814172032/http://www.world-tourism.org/protect_children/ statements/wto_a.htm (accessed July 2020).

U.S. Department of Justice (2014) *The Child Exploitation and Obscenity Section*. See http://www.justice.gov/criminal/ceos/subjectareas/ (accessed July 2020).

U.S. Department of State (2019) Trafficking in persons report. See https://www.state.gov/ reports/2019-trafficking-in-persons-report/ (accessed July 2020).

U.S. Department of State (2013) *The Facts about Child Sex Tourism*. See http://crime. about.com/od/sex/a/cst1.htm (accessed July 2020).

Wall, G. and Mathieson, A. (2006) *Tourism: Change, Impacts and Opportunities*. London: Pearson Education Ltd.

World Economic Forum (2013) *The Travel & Tourism Competitiveness Report 2013*. See http://www3.weforum.org/docs/WEF_TT_Competitiveness_Report_ 2013.pdf (accessed July 2020).

Yan, L., Xu, J. and Zhou, Y. (2018) Residents' attitudes toward prostitution in Macau. *Journal of Sustainable Tourism* 26 (2), 205–220.

Zahid Shahab, A. (2005) *Poverty, Globalization, Social Customs & South Asian Children in Prostitution*. See http://www.humiliationstudies.org/ documents/Ahmed AsianChildrenProstitution.pdf (accessed July 2020).

15 Delving into the Uncharted Terrains of Sex in Tourism: Conclusions and Ways Forward

Neil Carr and Liza Berdychevsky

Introduction

This chapter focuses on how we can build on what we know, from the works presented in this book and elsewhere, about sex in tourism in all its light and dark shades. In order to do this, we need to look carefully and critically at what we think we already know and to creatively speculate on what we still do not know. Once we have identified what else we need to know in order to develop a holistic knowledge of the field of sex in tourism, it is important to consider, as this chapter does, how to gather and analyse the data necessary to fill the gaps in our current knowledge and critically question existing knowledge. As part of this process, careful consideration needs to be given to why sex in tourism is still such an under-researched field. This requires us to think about why so few academics are working in the field and what barriers exist that inhibit others from doing so. This is not only about looking at barriers to entering the field as a whole, but also to the specific topics within it.

This book has advocated for academics not merely to collect and analyse data and present their findings to the academic community. Instead, it has been filled with numerous calls for and examples of academics seeking to help individuals and communities within the context of sex in tourism. As such, this chapter critically examines the call for academics to become activists rather than dispassionate adjudicators or merely collectors and disseminators of *knowledge*. This fits into wider calls about the relevancy of academic studies and the need for researchers to engage with the wider community.

Before beginning the chapter, it is necessary to step back for a little while, to enable the authors of the chapter and editors of the book to reflect on the production of the book. It is safe to say that this has been the most difficult book either of the editors have worked on. Neil was initially approached by the publisher to think about producing a book on sex in tourism. In those early discussions no decision was made about whether it was to be a monograph, textbook, edited book, or some form of hybrid. Neil was, it is fair to say, a little wary of taking on another project at that time. Life was, he reasoned, busy enough. However, the idea gnawed away at the back of his brain, encouraged periodically by Sarah Williams at Channel View. So eventually, interest got the better of sanity and Neil approached Liza, as, Neil would argue, the leading light in the field to come on board as a co-editor for what turned into this book. Experience to that point in time suggested edited books were relatively painless to produce, in addition to being a nice way to reach out to new people working in the field. They are also a great way to push forward knowledge on a subject (e.g. sex in tourism) that has for too long hidden in, or been forced into, the shadows of academic and social debate.

Everything went well to begin with. The range of abstracts submitted, and subsequently accepted, was inspiring. A surprisingly large number of authors were clearly working in the field, looking at a range of issues in new and innovative ways. Then the problems began. Later in this chapter, we will discuss specific barriers to conducting sensitive research on sex in tourism, which inevitably haunted and complicated this project. Even simple tasks like sending an email between authors or editors became challenging because the universities' spam filters obliterated or quarantined any correspondence including the word *sex*. However, the hurdles went far beyond those barriers, with authors having to drop out, not for the usual reasons of being overworked, but for harrowing and deeply personal reasons. It was so sad to see those chapters fall by the wayside but even sadder to see the suffering of people dealing with the fragility of life. It was a sobering reminder of the temporary nature of life and what is really important. However, it is our hope that the ideas these people brought to the book are not lost because they were (and are) important to helping to develop the holistic understanding of the links between sex and tourism that this book tries to drive forward.

Unfortunately, the hurdles in the way of the completion of this book did not stop there. Neil (and he apologies once again here to Liza) faced an ever increasing mountain of work in his last 18 months as Head of the Department of Tourism at the University of Otago. This is not a unique burden, but it certainly inhibited the amount of time and energy Neil was able to devote to the book. As a result, progress crawled by, the process at times becoming painful rather than joyful and rewarding.

Then, just when we would have thought things could not have got any worse, the COVID-19 pandemic hit the globe. Everyone's lives were turned upside down and the time and energy available to write and edit was severely constrained. Yet throughout it all, the authors have been patient and understanding and the co-editors have managed to resist the temptation to scream (at least Neil never heard Liza scream even if she did, fairly, get exasperated with him at times).

So what lessons can we take away from this experience? That human life is fragile and fleeting, and that enjoying it while we have it is infinitely more important than anything else. This is not a call to abandon the academic work for a fun-filled, hedonistic life. Instead, it is a recognition that we should not allow work to take over our lives. For many academics, this is a difficult task. It may be said to be, at least partially, because of the pressures our institutions are increasingly under that in turn pressure individual academics to do more in less time and with less resources. Yet, this is to miss the point that we are often our own worst enemies. Academics tend to love their work, have a deep passion for all aspects of what they do, and this can drive them to easily blur the divides between work and leisure. The result can be that academics find themselves working significantly more than forty hours per week. This is not a healthy or sustainable situation, as has been widely reported elsewhere (Blake & Gallimore, 2018; Currie, 1996; Jacobs & Winslow, 2004). Therefore, a lesson learned is to remember to take time off, to do something occasionally that is different from the academic work we love. If that means not everything gets done, then fine, the world will keep on turning. Yet, universities have a responsibility not to take advantage of the love of their work and commitment to it that so many academics demonstrate. High quality work is only achievable over the long term in a sustainable work environment and it is beholden on universities, for both moral and productivity reasons, to ensure that environment is created and maintained.

What We Think We Know and What Is Still Missing?

A fundamental concern is that we cannot know everything that is missing from the bank of knowledge exactly because it is missing. This may seem to be so obvious a statement that there should be no need to say it, but a look at the conclusions at the ends of the innumerable published book chapters and journal articles that indicate where future research is needed suggest this is not the case. These statements about future research directions are almost uniformly painted with certainty, based on the expertise of the authors, as just demonstrated by the preceding content of their article/chapter. There is no uncertainty here. Rather, we see the expert staring into a future they are fully cognisant and the master of. Some academics certainly may think this, safe in their self-perception of their expertise. Others, perhaps the majority, are simply writing in the conventional style, charting a future of certainty while assailed by self-doubt. So, despite having written numerous articles on the topics of sex in tourism, and sex as/in leisure, in addition to having completed a book (Carr & Poria, 2010) and a special issue of *Leisure Sciences* (Berdychevsky & Carr, 2020) on the topics, we admit that the future of research in the field that we chart in this section is limited by what we have studied and read, how we think, and our imaginations. The result will doubtlessly be that some important topics to be worked on are identified while others are missed. Those that are missed are just as important as those noted here. These issues, both missed and noted, cover the range from the light to the dark and everything in between.

We (in the collective, global sense) can begin to think about what we know and what we do not have sufficient knowledge about by examining what is currently available within the literature and what is under-represented within it. For all the diversity that exists under the term *sex*, as noted in the first chapter of this book and elsewhere (Carr, 2016), the majority of the work published to date on sex in tourism tends to revolve, either directly or indirectly, around the physical act of sex. In contrast, there is a relative dearth of analysis of the sexual and sensuality, of the potential promise of sex without the actuality of it. The use of sex in the marketing of tourism is a partial exception, though more work is needed on this huge and diverse topic. As part of this, but not restricted to it, there is a need for further exploration of the displaying of the body and how it is not always, or even often, about sex. This speaks to issues of ownership and appropriation of the body and encompasses various discourses of embodiment, surveillance, sexual double standards, and empowerment in tourism (Berdychevsky *et al.*, 2015; Pritchard *et al.*, 2007; Small, 2007). While often associated with women's bodies, these issues apply to men's as well (Ateljevic & Hall, 2007). Alongside this, there is further work to be done on the sensuality of spaces and experiences in tourism, including hotel bedrooms and food, amongst much else. Previous research on sex, and the sexual and sensual characteristics of tourism spaces (Berdychevsky *et al.*, 2013a; Pritchard & Morgan, 2006) and experiences (Berdychevsky *et al.*, 2013b) unveiled a rich complexity and diversity that should be further studied to aid the understanding of sex in tourism and leveraged for offering insights regarding effective marketing and management for the tourism industry.

Thinking geographically (with all the associated sociocultural issues), work on sex in relation to tourism continues to be western dominated, in terms of who it is undertaken by and conceptualisations of who sex tourists are. While there are exceptions (e.g. Mendoza, 2013; Ying & Wen, 2019; Yokota, 2006; Chapter 10 in this book, by Ariya

& Nyamasyo; Chapter 11 in this book, by Moswete), the majority of researchers working on sex in tourism have been located in western universities. Collectively, these exceptions hint at the potential for the development of non-western-centric views and conceptualisations of sex in tourism. The other notable component of geography related to sex in tourism is the focus to date on the supposed sex tourism capitals of the world. As far as western researchers are concerned, these spaces can be identified as the exotic *other*, for both the western tourists and the researchers. In contrast, there has been a dearth of research looking at sex in domestic tourism. This may reflect a focus on conceptualisations of sex tourism as occurring between tourists and hosts where power differentials are significant. Here is the idea that hosts are economically and socially vulnerable to exploitation by wealthy western visitors. While undoubtedly true, as the work in Chapter 10 by Ariya and Nyamasyo, and Chapter 11 by Moswete, as well as elsewhere (Jeffreys, 1999; Scheyvens, 2012), shows, this is an overly simplistic rendering of a complex reality. If it encourages researchers to focus on the exotic and international tourism, this conceptualisation also does a disservice to the field and those involved in sex in tourism. The majority of tourism, even before the COVID-19 pandemic, occurs at the domestic level and it is erroneous to think that this type of tourism is not associated with sex in myriad ways. It is also pertinent to ask whether the exotic other is actually an attraction to researchers that lures them away from studying more mundane but equally important realities. In relation to animals, both inside and beyond a tourism focus, it has been argued that researchers have been guilty of focusing on the exotic, ignoring more mundane animals in the process (Carr, 2014). Are researchers in the field of sex in tourism guilty of the same, searching out instances of sex in tourism in exotic destinations while ignoring what is happening in their own backyard? Within this context, could COVID-19 result in an unexpected benefit, forcing those academics no longer able to travel the world due to border closures and/or financial restrictions to look at what is happening closer to home?

The focus of western, or western-based, academics on sex in tourism outside of the west may be viewed, in a negative light, as a form of colonialism. On the flipside, it may be constructed as an attempt by researchers to bring to light the colonial-style domination of the Global South by privileged western visitors. The battle between these two views has been highlighted in Chapter 13 by de Man and Lagendijk, which displays the concerns associated with the imposition of western views through NGO's and other bodies concerned with preventing the exploitation of people in the Global South for the sexual gratification of western visitors. This is an evolving issue that everyone involved needs to resolve to ensure that well-intentioned research and related work is not misunderstood and, therefore, rejected.

Traditionally, there has been a focus on heterosexuality within the sex in tourism literature, something that reflects wider dominant social values. Yet, attention on gay sex in tourism is increasing (cf. Vo, 2020; Vorobjovas-Pinta & Dalla-Fontana, 2019) as, to a lesser extent, is work on lesbian sex (Poria, 2006). However, all of this work still does a poor job of representing the diversity of sex and sexualities. Where, for example, is the work on trans-sex, beyond passing comments on trans-sex workers? Likewise, there is, to date, a dearth of published work on the position of animals as objects of human sex, both in and outside of the tourism experience. Moving beyond this, there is also a lack of research on the position of sex between (non-human) animals in the tourism experience. Where, for example, is the research looking at human reactions to the reality of sex between animals in zoos in full view of visitors, both adults and children? As noted in Chapter 4, by Carr and Nava, on summer camps, the topic of sex in tourism in relation to children has also, in many ways, been under-studied. Yes, there has been work published, although arguably not enough, on the issue of the exploitation of children by adult tourists for sex (e.g. Beddoe *et al.*, 2001; Frohlick, 2010; Kibicho, 2009; Montgomery, 2001). However, work on sex and the sexual amongst children in the tourism sphere seems to be missing. This, of course, ignores the fact that there is a huge number of *children* who while chronologically and legally defined as such are sexually mature (at least physically, if not emotionally).

If early research on sex in tourism focused on male tourists, it is clear that since then there has been significant work undertaken on female tourists. In this context, as shown in this book (e.g. Chapter 5, by Everingham *et al.*; Chapter 6, by Sacramento), women, through sex in tourism, may gain empowering experiences and further the emasculation of heteronormativity and hegemonic masculinity, or at least resist it and the positions it seeks to pigeonhole women in. This speaks to the recognition of women as sexual creatures in their own right rather than merely as sex objects for the titillation of men. In this context, the research on women in sex in tourism has become nuanced and complex, reflecting the reality of the experienced sex in tourism and its setting within the wider social reality (cf. Berdychevsky, 2016; Berdychevsky *et al.*, 2013b, 2015). It builds on, and stands alongside, the work that has been done on recognising the exploited realities of the lives of many women involved in sex in tourism (Jeffreys, 1999; Scheyvens, 2012). Alongside this, as noted in Chapter 10, by Ariya and Nyamasyo, we also see ongoing discussions about the disempowered/empowered position of women as sex workers. These emotive discussions add to wider debates taking place around the world that reflect concerns regarding the legality/illegality and criminalisation/decriminalisation of prostitution. The contested nature of such debates was recently highlighted in New Zealand, a country where prostitution was decriminalised in 2003.

Kiwibank, which NZ Post has a controlling stake in, announced in 2020 that as part of a responsible banking plan, it would not be working with the adult entertainment industry. Within days of this announcement the bank had, in the face of public criticism, reversed its policy related to brothels and strip clubs, though it still identified them as 'a sensitive sector with high potential for harm' (RNZ, 2020). The head of the New Zealand Prostitutes' Collective, Dame Catherine Healey, spoke out on this issue, stating that 'It's not good to have a policy that draws a line across a class of people who have received certificates from the Ministry of Justice to say that they're fit and proper to operate a brothel' (RNZ, 2020). This speaks to the continued stigmatisation of sex work.

While the work on women in relation to sex in tourism is becoming increasingly nuanced, recognising and reflecting the complex socio-cultural reality, the same cannot necessarily be said for men. It is right that the predatory nature of some males has been highlighted and castigated, though much work is still needed in this field, but to see all males, heterosexual or otherwise, and their sexual desires as such is to miss a more complex reality. Within this context, studies of the position of males as providers and/or emblems of sex in tourism continues to be limited. Yes, work has been done on the males providing sexual experiences in exotic locations to western female visitors (e.g. Chapter 9, by Jenkins et al.; Frohlick, 2013). Similarly, a limited amount of work has been done on males providing for those seeking homosexual encounters (e.g. Cordova Plaza, 2010; Padilla, 2007). However, these works do not reflect the extent of the nuanced realities of either male sex workers or the sexual experiences and desires of men as tourists. Chapter 3, by Berdychevsky, started addressing this gap by focusing on men's and women's sexual perceptions and experiences in tourism and examining gender differences and similarities. Within this context, the liminal space of the tourism experience may be said not just to offer opportunities for women and homosexual men to explore their identity and experiment with their sexualities but also for heterosexual men to do the same. This whole situation is based on the recognition of the need to step away from a simple binary representation of gender.

There is an implicit assumption in the sex in tourism research published to date that it must involve more than one person. This is, of course, erroneous. Likewise, there has been a dearth of research looking at sex involving multiple people at the same time in the tourism space. In contrast, the majority of the work published to date has focused, either explicitly or implicitly, on the idea of sex as occurring between two people. Work is clearly needed that breaks this norm to help us recognise that the number of partners involved in sex acts is variable rather than fixed at two.

So much of what has been published on sex in tourism relates to moralising, either seeking to help maintain the social status quo or to break it in the name of empowerment. In itself this work is not problematic, at least not the work that seeks to break the status quo to prevent the abuse of the disempowered. However, it is problematic in that it seems to have contributed to the dearth of research that has been published on the notion of sex as fun. Too often as academics we have been guilty of stripping the fun from life and failing to recognise that sometimes humans simply engage in experiences, including sex, because it is fun, enjoyable (Berdychevsky & Carr, 2020). This may well link to more socially moralistic arguments regarding empowerment and exploitation but that makes it even more important for us to understand sex as fun rather than shunting it to the side of academic debate and labelling it as simply frivolous. Frivolity is, of course, a label frequently slapped on tourism and leisure, and the study of it.

This book has focused on sex in tourism, but perhaps there is also a need to explore the position of tourism in sex. Here it is suggested that the conceptualisations of tourism as liminal space, journey of enlightenment, search for self, and hedonism, among much else, offer important lenses through which new understandings of sex can be derived.

How to Fill in the Gaps and Breaking Down Barriers

As has been argued elsewhere (Carr, 2016; Hall, 1992), the social moral compass appears to have been a strong driver of research on sex in tourism. In this context, the first obstacle to overcome for anyone wishing to conduct research in this field is the idea that studying sex is unacceptable and that to do so is to be potentially branded as some kind of pervert. Overcoming this barrier only leads to new ones governed by the moral compass. Here lies the question of what is morally acceptable to research in the field of sex in tourism. Empowerment, prevention of abuse, and the search for positive identities of self all fit under the heading of being morally acceptable, yet even here some issues are more acceptable than others. As noted above, working in this context it is acceptable to look at women in relation to sex in tourism. However, looking at children or animals, as anything other than victims, in relation to sex in tourism is still problematic. The moral compass is responsible for judging whether it is acceptable to explore different sexualities in relation to sex in tourism. So, at least in liberal democracies, it is increasingly acceptable to research not just heterosexual, but also gay and lesbian sex in tourism experiences. In comparison, experiences of other sexualities are still left in the dark, remaining misunderstood or ignored.

The moral compass is only a metaphorical compass and as such cannot act alone. The direction the compass points in is influenced by society and governed by the *moral guardians*, often self-appointed, of society. They are the ones who do not just tell us what is acceptable but also police it, imposing fines and sanctions on those who transgress whenever it is necessary to do so. In relation to research on sex in tourism, these guardians are multiple and some of them are very powerful indeed. They include family members, peers, supervisors, heads of department, ethical boards, research funding bodies, the police, journal editors, and publishing companies, as well as religious figures. Many have the potential to sanction or prevent research on sex in tourism. Some may publicly castigate such research. Others may urge researchers down different routes, away from topics dealing with sex, arguing that to pursue such research agendas is to endanger careers (Berdychevsky, in press; Berdychevsky & Carr, 2020).

What we are fundamentally talking about here is the notion of academic freedom and the empowerment of researchers. Academic freedom is a powerful concept, one that is easily open to abuse. It is arguably to safeguard against such abuse that we have seen over recent decades the development of stringent research ethics processes. Yet, increasingly, concerns are being raised that such detailed and demarcated processes are inhibiting research and even censoring it when it comes to sex research (Berdychevsky, in press). This is arguably especially the case for research fields outside of the core focus of academic institutions, including sex in tourism. In this context, a more flexible approach to ethics has been called for that places the responsibility for undertaking ethical research on the researcher. This demands *trust* being placed in the individual researcher. While it is easier to impose rules than to give trust, especially in the face of instances where trust is abused, doing so impinges upon academic freedom. As argued by those seeking to overturn the dominance of procedural ethics, there is a need to educate people about the importance of trust and freedom, and to give it to researchers who, when they receive trust, must act in an appropriate, ethical manner (Gini, 2006; Gray, 2018). As far as sex in tourism is concerned, the giving of trust and freedom as a form of researcher empowerment requires those guardians identified above to aid this process rather than seek to disempower researchers through the imposition of procedural ethics.

While it may still be a struggle for researchers to work in the field of sex in tourism, it is clear that there are those in the world who want to help facilitate this work. The prime example here is, of course, the publisher of this book. Likewise, the willingness of the editors of *Leisure Sciences* to publish a special issue on the innovation and impact of sex as leisure in research and practice (Berdychevsky & Carr, 2020) speaks to how the guardians of academic research are opening up to the idea, importance, and value of research in this field. Yet, more needs to be done to support young academics not just to build research careers in this field but to even consider doing so. Looking beyond the bubble of the liberal democracies of the world, we need to think about how sex in tourism research can be undertaken in more conservative areas of the world where, despite moral guardians wishing the opposite were true, sex in tourism is an important issue that too often currently hides in the dark. It is not just a case of this research being done, but of enabling those living in these countries to undertake and engage with the research.

How, in order to bring it into the light of public debate, do we research issues of sex that are not just socially taboo, but illegal? It is one thing to create an environment in which people feel safe and empowered to undertake research on sex in tourism, but it is something else entirely to get people to openly talk to researchers. Even in liberal democracies where sex is openly displayed through multiple media and sex work is decriminalised and legal, it is still a challenge to get people to willingly talk about sex in an open and unbiased manner. This reflects the point that though we may live in a 'sex-saturated society' (Gini, 2006: 180), we remain reticent to talk about it in all its diversity and complexity.

Questions have long existed about the accuracy of what respondents tell researchers about their sexual desires and behaviours, although careful research has been argued to minimise, if not eradicate, such problems (Schroder *et al.*, 2003a, 2003b). For example, how easy is it to get people to admit to and explain their sexual encounters with animals in the tourism experience or the predators to talk about child sex tourism? Yet, if we cannot gain accurate data on these issues we cannot begin to make meaningful, fully informed contributions to social discussions about these that are designed to prevent abuse. Ethically, we must ask how or even whether we should protect those we find to be abused and potential abusers. Reflexively, we must also question our roles in and impacts on the entire research process and interpretations regarding sex in tourism as well as accept with humility the privileges and responsibilities that come with sharing our research participants' stories (Berdychevsky, in press). More discussion of these issues is provided in the next section when we look at the divide between academics and activists. A flipside of seeking to examine the darkest corners of sex in tourism is a realisation of the need to protect not just participants, but also the mental and physical wellbeing of the researchers. Despite prevalent views, inside academia and beyond, identifying tourism research as flippant, researching deeply disturbing issues like child and animal abuse can take a huge emotional toll as well as even potentially endangering the safety of the researcher in the face of organised crime, for example. Ethics committees have a complex role to play here, ensuring the wellbeing of the researcher while not impinging on the need for the research to be conducted (Berdychevsky, in press).

As the chapters in this book attest, those working in the field of sex in tourism are already utilising a wide variety of data collection tools and techniques. However, as researchers seek to fill the gaps noted above we are going to have to think about ever-more innovative methods to help overcome the dominant social distaste for talking about sex. It is within this context that social media must be viewed as a double-edged sword. On the one hand, it offers the opportunity to dive into people's lived experiences like never before. On the other hand, it can be hard to understand the intentions behind the material presented on social media. This speaks to Goffman's (1959) conceptualisation of front and back-stage, where social media representations may hint at a route to understanding of the latter but can be focused on constructions of the former. Both are, of course, very interesting and important to understand but it is important to distinguish between them, something that is not easy. In this context, Hogan (2010) identifies what we see on social media as an exhibition rather than a performance, an important distinction that reinforces the idea that care must be taken when considering what is viewed on social media and why it is placed there. Alongside social media, Saadat *et al.* (2020) have argued that there is a need for tourism researchers to engage far more with the visual data available through holiday photographs throughout history and this is true for those working on sex in tourism, in particular.

In order to further the work on sex in tourism there is not just a need to utilise appropriate data collection and analysis techniques. Rather, appropriate epistemological and conceptual foundations need to be put in place. One such route is the social-ecological model (Bronfenbrenner, 1979, 1989) discussed in Chapter 1. Yet, it is important to recognise the wide-ranging issues associated with sex in tourism and the related multi-disciplinary interests to ensure that there is space in the field for diverse conceptualisations and epistemological stances. This adds to the fact that both leisure and tourism are best viewed as cross-disciplinary meeting grounds where, in a post-modernistic sense, space must be left for all to flourish in a way that drives the field forward. Despite this, it is hard to see how some epistemologies and conceptual frameworks cannot be part of an ongoing and productive debate about sex in tourism. First amongst these is feminism for its foundational belief in the rights of the oppressed. Related to this, are the more recent masculinities and queer studies, both of which provide much scope to aid understandings of sex in tourism.

The Dispassionate Academic versus the Community Activist

The idea of the dispassionate academic is arguably grounded in positivism, the idea that the scientist can be a neutral adjudicator, capable of measuring and observing without becoming emotionally connected. This isolation of the researcher from the researched is said to be vital for the production of knowledge untainted by personal views and biases. This is the scientific view of research associated with the sterile setting of the laboratory. How well such a worldview works outside of such a setting has been the focus of a long running debate, including within the field of sex-related research. While the laboratory is, as a gold standard of the research environment, a sterile setting where variables are rigorously controlled, the *real* world beyond those four walls is inherently messy. It is this messiness that has led to many calls for social scientists to abandon the desire for the tick of legitimacy associated with the notion of the scientist that is grounded in positivism. Many researchers have heeded this call and pursued a myriad of different epistemological and methodological pathways, all of which share the common belief that research outside of the laboratory setting is and has to be messy because that is the nature of the world.

While academics have long-embraced the idea of the value and legitimacy of research beyond the laboratory and positivist setting, they still often struggle with the idea of stepping over the divide between researcher and activist, to take what they have learned/know and make use of it in a way that benefits others, including in relation to sex in tourism. This is ironic as many of those researchers working in the laboratory, while not labelled as activists, have pursued careers that have often directly resulted in developments that have helped others beyond the academic institution. Think, for example, of all the medical developments that have been driven by academics through their research.

The claim that researchers in universities have not spent sufficient energy on ensuring their research and its implications reach beyond the academic ivory tower to drive policy changes and make a difference in the lives of humans and other animals is, in many ways, not unfair. In this way, an activist can be said to be someone who has engaged with life beyond positivism and seen the value of applying knowledge. Activists can be fuelled by less than comprehensive knowledge of a situation and driven by biased views that ignore rather than set aside opposing views after critically engaging with them. Yet, surely, the role that academics have to play here is ensuring that the gold standard for activists is one that incorporates critical understanding and wrestling with biases while not inhibiting the desire for change that is the hallmark of all activists. In this sense, is there really any difference between the activist and the applied researcher, or at least should there be? Yet, academic snobbery has long encouraged us to look down on activists due to their perceived biases and fragmented knowledge. In failing to engage with them due to this snobbery, is it any surprise when they turn around and say they want nothing to do with academics?

Academic snobbery has also encouraged us to look down on the applied researcher as somehow *less* than a *real* researcher, with the latter being a blue sky researcher focused on basic science (i.e. the creation of knowledge for knowledge's sake). In this context, the applied researcher can sometimes, especially as noted below, be identified as someone who sullies the name of researcher, dirties knowledge by utilising it for a purpose beyond the walls of academia. Yet, such a view is shortsighted and lacking a grip on reality. The oft-cited bulwarks of prestigious academic institutions are their medical and law schools. Yet, the research that goes on in both is almost totally applied. Set alongside this, academics situated in Business Schools and Humanities and Social Sciences faculties are looked down upon, not uncommonly by their own peers, if they dare to focus on applied research. There is a dangerous double standard at play here that not only inhibits applied research but also the academic as activist.

Moving forward, there is a need for academics, including those working in the field of sex in tourism, to embrace the idea of applied research and its associations with activism. It speaks to the need for community engagement that universities and funding bodies are increasingly calling for. From a cynical perspective, this may be seen as just a box ticking exercise, a form of intellectual greenwashing. Yet, it can clearly be much more than that. Undertaken for the right reasons, applied research really can lead to meaningful academic-community engagement. Through this engagement comes the opportunity for activism. This is, therefore, not a call for biased, uncritical activism, but for academics to become involved as activists and to help drive such activism to become what it has always had the potential to be, and in the best cases has already demonstrated it is, a positive force for change to the benefit of individuals and society. Yet, it is not just as simple as this. As the work in Chapter 13, by de Man and Lagendijk, shows, if we adopt the kind of mentality associated with colonialism and fail to actually engage with the *other* as socially active agent, then attempts at applied research and/or activism will rightly fail. It is insufficient to be knowledgeable about a topic. Instead, it is necessary to engage with communities, in all their diversity, to help rather than presume to lead or dominate.

Within the context of sex in tourism, academics as activists have the potential to help society and individuals in a wide range of ways. This incorporates the physical and mental wellbeing of individuals engaged in the diversity of sex in tourism, as participants and victims, both human and non-human. In turn, the accumulative positive effects on individuals' wellbeing have the capacity to challenge the status quo and benefit communities and societies through large-scale transformations in sexual human rights and quality of life. The cross-pollination of these benefits can flow in both grassroots, bottom-up and top-down directions to improve people's lives in general, and sexual lives in particular. The sex in tourism researcher as activist also has the potential to help bring to justice those predators whose sexual abuses currently hide in the dark and to contribute to the local, national, and international policies and laws to prevent sexual abuse and protect vulnerable populations. Finally, they have the potential to help bring together the disparate interest groups linked to sex in tourism, to work towards ensuring the realisation of social and personal benefits through sex in tourism and the eradication of the dangers, to individuals, industries, and societies, that are currently an integral part of sex in tourism.

The dispassionate researcher is told by ethics committees that they are required to take action if/when they encounter behaviours that may endanger the wellbeing of the individual or others during the course of their research. There is also a moral imperative as a person in power to do so anyway. This brings up the issue of when to act and on what grounds. Acting to uphold the status quo of the moral standards of the society is not activism but can nevertheless be important. If we discover instances of child abuse during our research into sex in tourism, for example, there is a clear moral imperative to act to ensure the wellbeing of the child, and to bring the perpetrator to justice. Doing so may override the ethical right of research participants to anonymity, but that is of secondary concern to the rights of the child. In this case, the decision about when to act may be fairly straightforward but, in other instances, it might be more nuanced and ambiguous. In such cases, the imperative is on the researcher, who must rely on their own informed judgement, rather than on standard guidelines set by procedural ethics. This is because guidelines can only ever be *guidelines*, they can never take into account all possible scenarios. Therefore, as argued earlier, there is the need to empower researchers to act ethically beyond the boundaries of procedural ethics.

Deciding whether to act on what we see as we conduct research on sex in tourism and cease to be dispassionate observers of the world can push us into the realm of activism. In such instances, as researchers we must seek to rise above bipartisan views and biased opinions, turning activism into critical activism. The alternative of not acting at all may be easier and more clinical but, in its own way, is morally wrong. The question then becomes how far to go down the activist route, when to step away from the environment/situation in which we, as researchers, find ourselves. Researchers engaging in deep and meaningful communications with their subjects, where trust is developed as part of the process, organically and for the benefit of the quality of the data collected, often grapple with this question. Are they ready to become lifetime activists? There can be no one-size-fits-all answer to this dilemma. Rather, individual researchers must come to their own conclusion, one they are comfortable with. Whatever their decision, if researchers are to truly produce outputs of value and relevance to society, then standing idly by is not an option. Furthermore, engaging with activism, to whatever extent, clearly requires the moral and logistical support of the institutions in which researchers are employed. This is especially challenging as many activists inherently seek to challenge the status quo, something universities are, in many ways, part of.

Activism need not even be restricted to the world beyond the university. Instead, it is clearly beholden on universities and their researchers to inform their students. Research informed teaching is, after all, supposed to be a gold standard of universities. This leads to the question of how to teach about sex in tourism in the classroom. Students at university are, minus a small number, chronologically adults. They will also virtually all be sexually mature, if not sexually active. None of this makes for discussions of sex in tourism comfortable in the classroom setting. Talking about uncomfortable topics is challenging, as is always going to be the case when pushing the boundaries of social morality. The challenge, even in the COVID-19 induced classroom where international student numbers are dramatically down, is enhanced in the 21st century classroom, which is increasingly diverse in terms of culture, religious believes, gender, and sexual identity. The biggest challenge for academics seeking to talk about issues of sex in tourism in the classroom is negative feedback from students. In an era where the student is increasingly viewed as a consumer not to be upset, challenging them to think about uncomfortable, sensitive topics can be dangerous if it leads to negative course or lecturer appraisals. The implications for confirmation of academic positions or promotion applications are clear. Therefore, it is beholden on the academic institutions not just to enable these academics to conduct research on sex in tourism and to protect them while engaged in this, but to help them in the same way when talking about their work to students.

References

Ateljevic, I. and Hall, D. (2007) The embodiment of the macho gaze in South-eastern Europe: Performing femininity and masculinity in Albania and Croatia. In A. Pritchard, N. Morgan, I. Ateljevic and C. Harris (eds) *Tourism and Gender: Embodiment, Sensuality and Experience* (pp. 138–157). Wallingford: CABI.

Beddoe, C., Hall, C.M. and Ryan, C. (2001) *The Incidence of Sexual Exploitation of Children in Tourism*. Madrid: World Tourism Organization.

Berdychevsky, L. (2016) Antecedents of young women's sexual risk taking in tourist experiences. *Journal of Sex Research* 53 (8), 927–941.

Berdychevsky, L. (in press) Reflexivity and ethical considerations in investigating the links between sex and leisure. In C.W. Johnson and D. Parry (eds) *Promiscuous Perspectives: Explorations of Sex and Leisure*. London: Routledge.

Berdychevsky, L. and Carr, N. (2020) Innovation and impact of sex as leisure in research and practice: Introduction to the special issue. *Leisure Sciences* 42 (3–4), 255–274.

Berdychevsky, L., Poria, Y. and Uriely, N. (2013a) Hospitality accommodations and women's consensual sex. *International Journal of Hospitality Management* 34, 169–171.

Berdychevsky, L., Poria, Y. and Uriely, N. (2013b) Sexual behavior in women's tourist experiences: Motivations, behaviors, and meanings. *Tourism Management* 35, 144–155.

Berdychevsky, L., Gibson, H.J. and Poria, Y. (2015) Inversions of sexual roles in women's tourist experiences: Mind, body, and language in sexual behaviour. *Leisure Studies* 34 (5), 513–528.

Blake, M. and Gallimore, V. (2018) Understanding academics: A UX ethnographic research project at the University of York. *New Review of Academic Librarianship* 24 (3–4), 363–375.

Bronfenbrenner, U. (1979) *The Ecology of Human Development: Experiments by Nature and Design*. Cambridge: Harvard University Press.

Bronfenbrenner, U. (1989) Ecological systems theory. In R. Vasta (ed.) *Annals of Child Development* (Vol. 6, pp. 187–249). London: Jessica Kingsley Publishers.

Carr, N. (2014) *Dogs in the Leisure Experience*. Wallingford: CABI.

Carr, N. (2016) Sex in tourism: Reflections from a dark corner of tourism studies. *Tourism Recreation Research* 41 (2), 188–198.

Carr, N. and Poria, Y. (eds) (2010) *Sex and the Sexual during People's Leisure and Tourism Experiences*. Newcastle: Cambridge Scholars Publishing.

Cordova Plaza, R. (2010) Parallel universes: Male sex trade in public spaces of Veracruz, Mexico. In N. Carr and Y. Poria (eds) *Sex and the Sexual during People's Leisure and Tourism Experiences* (pp. 35–55). Newcastle, UK. Cambridge Scholars Publishing.

Currie, J. (1996) The effects of globalisation on 1990s academics in greedy institutions: Overworked, stressed out and demoralised. *Critical Studies in Education* 37 (2), 101–128.

Frohlick, S. (2010) The sex of tourism? Bodies under suspicion in paradise. In J. Scott and T. Selwyn (eds) *Thinking through Tourism* (pp. 51–70). Oxford: Berg.

Frohlick, S. (2013) *Sexuality, Women, and Tourism: Cross-border Desires through Contemporary Travel*. London: Routledge.

Gini, A. (2006) *Why it's Hard to be Good*. New York: Routledge.

Goffman, E. (1959) *The Presentation of Self in Everyday Life*. New York, NY: Anchor Books.

Gray, D. (2018) *Doing Research in the Real World* (4th edn). Los Angeles: Sage.

Hall, C.M. (1992) Sex tourism in South-east Asia. In D. Harrison (ed.) *Tourism & the Less Developed Countries* (pp. 64–74). London: Belhaven Press.

Hogan, B. (2010) The presentation of self in the age of social media: Distinguishing performances and exhibitions online. *Bulletin of Science, Technology & Society* 30 (6), 377–386.

Jacobs, J. and Winslow, S. (2004) Overworked faculty: Job stresses and family demands. *The Annals of the American Academy of Political and Social Science* 596 (1), 104–129.

Jeffreys, S. (1999) Globalizing sexual exploitation: sex tourism and the traffic in women. *Leisure Studies* 18 (3), 179–196.

Kibicho, W. (2009) *Sex Tourism in Africa: Kenya's Booming Industry*. Farnham: Ashgate.

Mendoza, C. (2013) Beyond sex tourism: Gay tourists and male sex workers in Puerto Vallarta (Western Mexico). *International Journal of Tourism Research* 15, 122–137.

Montgomery, H. (2001) *Modern Babylon Prostituting Children in Thailand*. New York: Berghahn Books.

Padilla, M. (2007) 'Western Union Daddies' and their quest for authenticity: An ethnographic study of the Dominican gay sex tourism industry. *Journal of Homosexuality* 53 (1–2), 241–275.

Poria, Y. (2006) Tourism and spaces of anonymity: An Israeli lesbian woman's travel experience. *Tourism* 54 (1), 33–42.

Pritchard, A. and Morgan, N. (2006) Hotel Babylon? Exploring hotels as liminal sites of transition and transgression. *Tourism Management* 27 (5), 762–772.

Pritchard, A., Morgan, N.J., Ateljevic, I. and Harris, I. (2007) Editors' introduction: Tourism, gender, embodiment and experience. In A. Pritchard, N. Morgan, I. Ateljevic and C. Harris (eds) *Tourism and Gender: Embodiment, Sensuality and Experience* (pp. 1–12). Wallingford: CABI.

RNZ (2020) Kiwibank steps back from ban on business with brothels. *NZ Herald*. See https://www.nzherald.co.nz/business/news/article.cfm?c_id=3&objectid=12350335 (accessed July 2020).

Saadat, P., Carr, N. and Walters, T. (2020) Changing representations of fatherhood through the lens of family leisure photographs. *Journal of the Sociology of Leisure* 3 (2), 197–218.

Scheyvens, R. (2012) *Tourism and Poverty*. London: Routledge.

Schroder, K., Carey, M. and Vanable, P. (2003a) Methodological challenges in research on sexual risk behavior: I. Item content, scaling, and data analytical options. *Annals of Behavioral Medicine* 26 (2), 76–103.

Schroder, K., Carey, M. and Vanable, P. (2003b) Methodological challenges in research on sexual risk behavior: II. Accuracy of self-reports. *Annals of Behavioral Medicine* 26 (2), 104 – 123.

Small, J. (2007) The emergence of the body in the holiday accounts of women and girls. In A. Pritchard, N. Morgan, I. Ateljevic and C. Harris (eds) *Tourism and Gender: Embodiment, Sensuality and Experience* (pp. 73–91). Wallingford: CABI.

Vo, T.D. (2020) Rejection and resilience in a 'safe space': Exploratory rapid ethnography of Asian-Canadian and Asian-American men's experiences on a gay cruise. *Leisure Sciences* 42 (3–4), 340–357.

Vorobjovas-Pinta, O. and Dalla-Fontana, I.J. (2019) The strange case of dating apps at a gay resort: Hyper-local and virtual-physical leisure. *Tourism Review* 74 (5), 1070–1080.

Ying, T. and Wen, J. (2019) Exploring the male Chinese tourists' motivation for commercial sex when travelling overseas: Scale construction and validation. *Tourism Management* 70, 479–490.

Yokota, F. (2006) Sex behaviour of male Japanese tourists in Bangkok, Thailand. *Culture, Health & Sexuality* 8 (2), 115–131.

Index

Note: References in *italics* are to figures, those in **bold** to tables; 'n' refers to chapter notes.

CPSIA information can be obtained
at www.ICGtesting.com
Printed in the USA
JSHW051710171121
20543JS00004B/162

9 781845 418588